I was asked to give a speech at my friend's wedding,
so of course I needed to come up with something witty!
At least, that's what I intended, but I couldn't think of anything.
Thankfully I found a transcript of Mr. Torishima's speech
when he spoke at my editor, Uchida's, wedding. So, I
gladly copied—I mean, took inspiration from it.
I'm so sorry...

**—Toyotarou, 2017**

### Toyotarou

Toyotarou created the manga adaptation for the *Dragon Ball Z*
anime's 2015 film, *Dragon Ball Z: Resurrection F*. He is also the
author of the spin-off series *Dragon Ball Heroes: Victory Mission*,
which debuted in *V-Jump* in Japan in November 2012.

### Akira Toriyama

Renowned worldwide for his playful, innovative storytelling and
humorous, distinctive art style, Akira Toriyama burst onto the manga
scene in 1980 with the wildly popular *Dr. Slump*. His hit series *Dragon Ball*
(published in the U.S. as *Dragon Ball* and *Dragon Ball Z*) ran from 1984
to 1995 in Shueisha's *Weekly Shonen Jump* magazine. He is also known
for his design work on video games such as *Dragon Quest*, *Chrono Trigger*,
*Tobal No. 1* and *Blue Dragon*. His recent manga works include *COWA!*, *Kajika*,
*Sand Land*, *Neko Majin*, *Jaco the Galactic Patrolman* and a children's book,
*Toccio the Angel*. He lives with his family in Japan.

**DRAGON BALL SUPER** ③

**SHONEN JUMP** Manga Edition

STORY BY **Akira Toriyama**
ART BY **Toyotarou**

TRANSLATION **Toshikazu Aizawa**
TOUCH-UP ART & LETTERING **Paolo Gattone and Chiara Antonelli**
DESIGN **Shawn Carrico**
EDITOR **Marlene First**

DRAGON BALL SUPER © 2015 BY BIRD STUDIO, Toyotarou
All rights reserved. First published in Japan in 2015 by SHUEISHA Inc., Tokyo.
English translation rights arranged by SHUEISHA Inc.

The stories, characters and incidents mentioned
in this publication are entirely fictional.

Printed in the U.S.A.

Published by VIZ Media, LLC
P.O. Box 77010
San Francisco, CA 94107

10 9 8 7 6 5 4 3 2
First printing, July 2018
Second printing, January 2019

viz.com

shonenjump.com

**PARENTAL ADVISORY**
DRAGON BALL SUPER is rated T for Teen
and is recommended for ages 13 and up.
This volume contains fantasy violence.

SHONENJUMP MANGA

# DRAGON BALL SUPER

## ZERO MORTAL PROJECT!

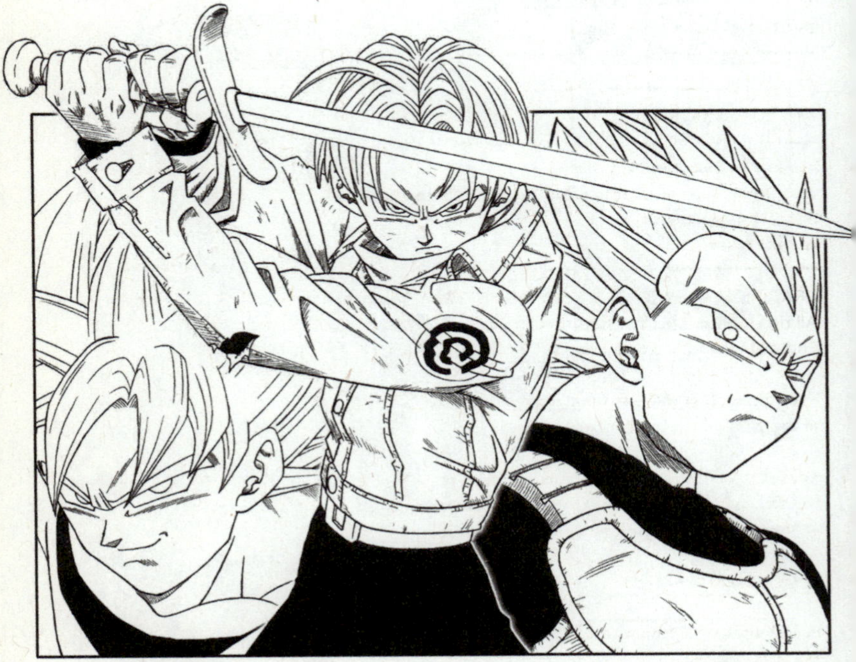

3

STORY BY **Akira Toriyama**
ART BY **Toyotarou**

# CAST OF CHARACTERS

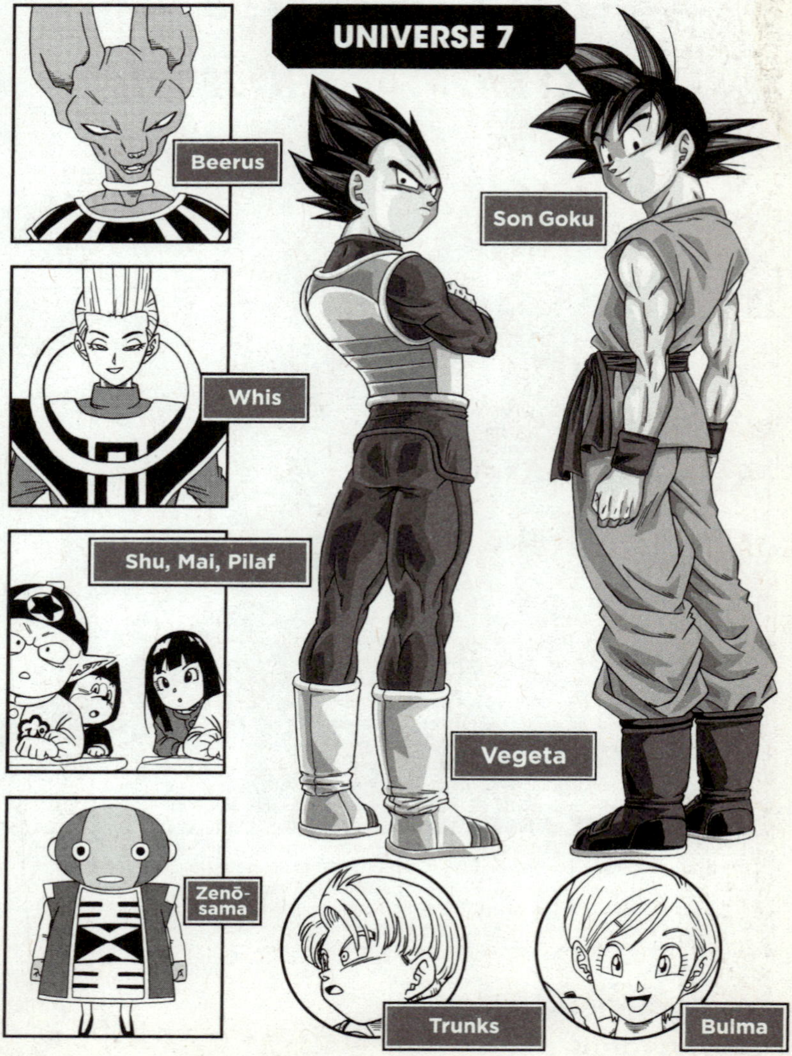
UNIVERSE 7
Beerus
Son Goku
Whis
Shu, Mai, Pilaf
Vegeta
Zenō-sama
Trunks
Bulma

# UNIVERSE 7:
# Future Parallel World

**Trunks (Future)**

**Goku Black**

**Mai (Future)**

**STORY THUS FAR**

A long, long time ago, Son Goku left on a journey in search of the legendary Dragon Balls—a set of seven balls that, when gathered, would summon the dragon Shenlong to grant any wish. After a great adventure, he collects them all. Later, he becomes the apprentice of Kame-Sen'nin, fights a number of vicious enemies, defeats the great Majin Boo and restores peace on Earth. Some time passes, and then Lord Beerus, the God of Destruction, suddenly awakens and sets out in search of the Super Saiyan God. Goku, by becoming the Super Saiyan God, manages to stop Beerus from destroying the Earth and starts training under him with Vegeta. Soon after that, Goku and his allies enter a tournament against warriors from Universe 6 over the Super Dragon Balls. After winning the tournament, Goku makes a promise with Zenō-sama, the Lord of Everything, to hold a tournament across all 12 universes in the future. Suddenly, Future Trunks appears, battered and bruised, looking for Bulma. He tells the gang about a new foe in the future, and this man looks exactly like Goku!

**3**

# DRAGON★BALL SUPER

Contents

CHAPTER 16: FUTURE TRUNKS'S PAST

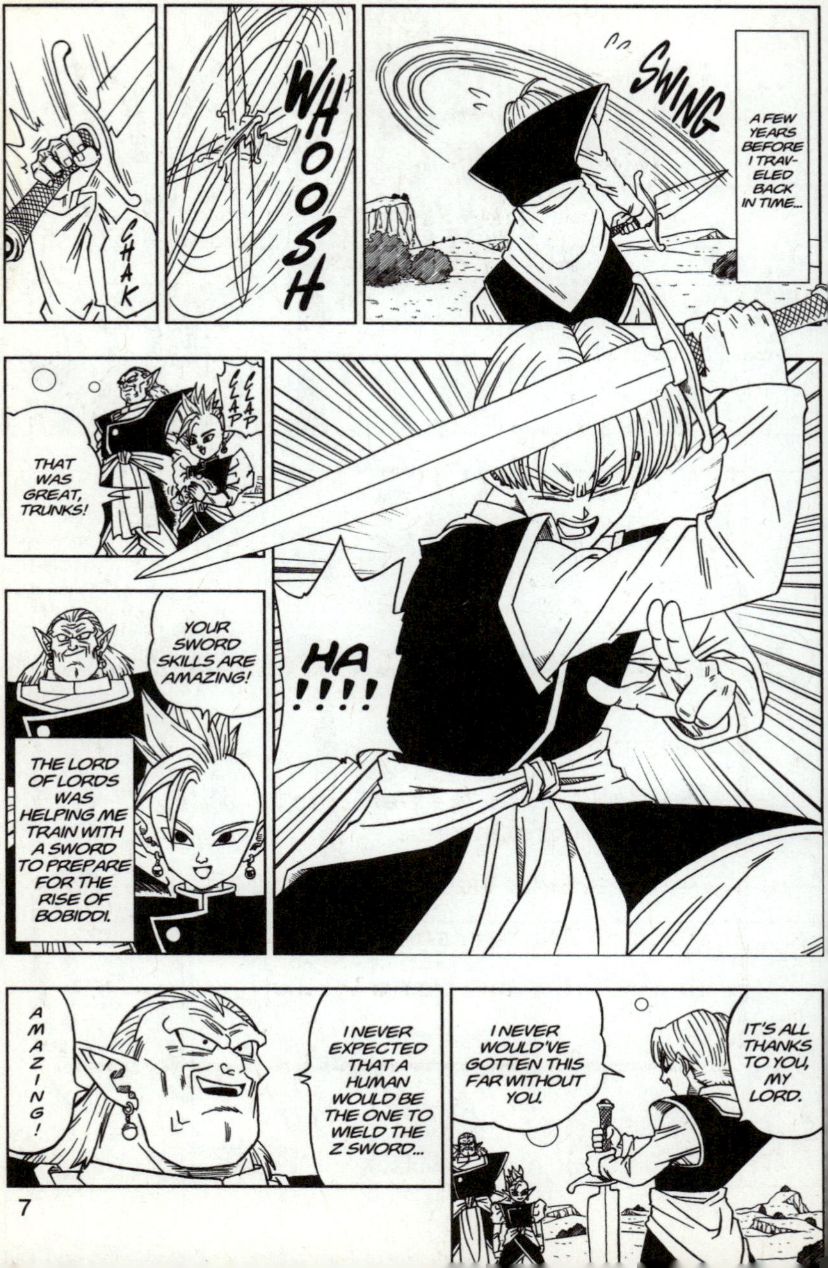
SWING
A FEW YEARS BEFORE I TRAVELED BACK IN TIME...
WHOOOSH
CHAK
HA!!!!
CLAP CLAP
THAT WAS GREAT, TRUNKS!
YOUR SWORD SKILLS ARE AMAZING!
THE LORD OF LORDS WAS HELPING ME TRAIN WITH A SWORD TO PREPARE FOR THE RISE OF BOBIDDI.
IT'S ALL THANKS TO YOU, MY LORD.
I NEVER WOULD'VE GOTTEN THIS FAR WITHOUT YOU.
I NEVER EXPECTED THAT A HUMAN WOULD BE THE ONE TO WIELD THE Z SWORD...
AMAZING!

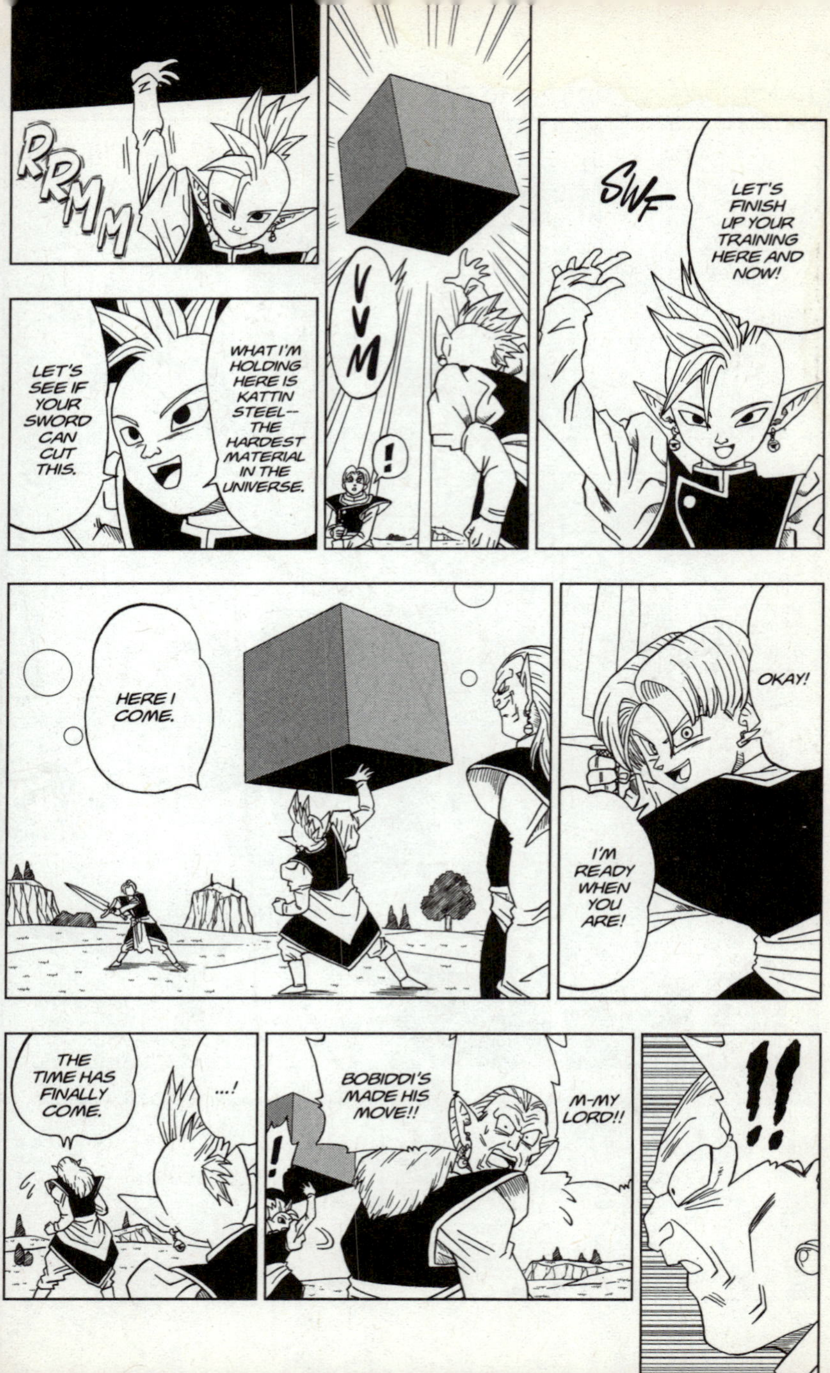
SWF
LET'S FINISH UP YOUR TRAINING HERE AND NOW!
VVM
!
RRMMM
WHAT I'M HOLDING HERE IS KATTIN STEEL-- THE HARDEST MATERIAL IN THE UNIVERSE.
LET'S SEE IF YOUR SWORD CAN CUT THIS.
OKAY!
I'M READY WHEN YOU ARE!
HERE I COME.
!!
M-MY LORD!!
BOBIDDI'S MADE HIS MOVE!!
!
...!
THE TIME HAS FINALLY COME.

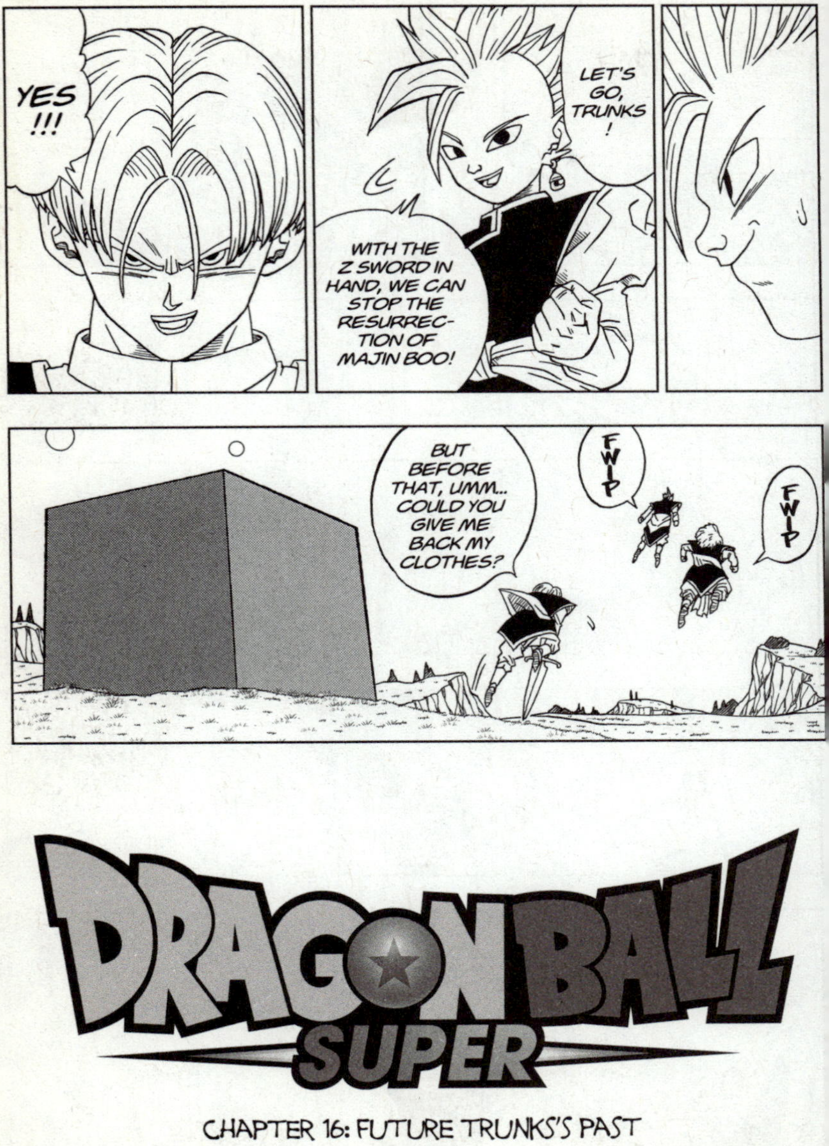
LET'S GO, TRUNKS!
WITH THE Z SWORD IN HAND, WE CAN STOP THE RESURRECTION OF MAJIN BOO!
YES!!!
FWIP
FWIP
BUT BEFORE THAT, UMM... COULD YOU GIVE ME BACK MY CLOTHES?

# DRAGON BALL SUPER

## CHAPTER 16: FUTURE TRUNKS'S PAST

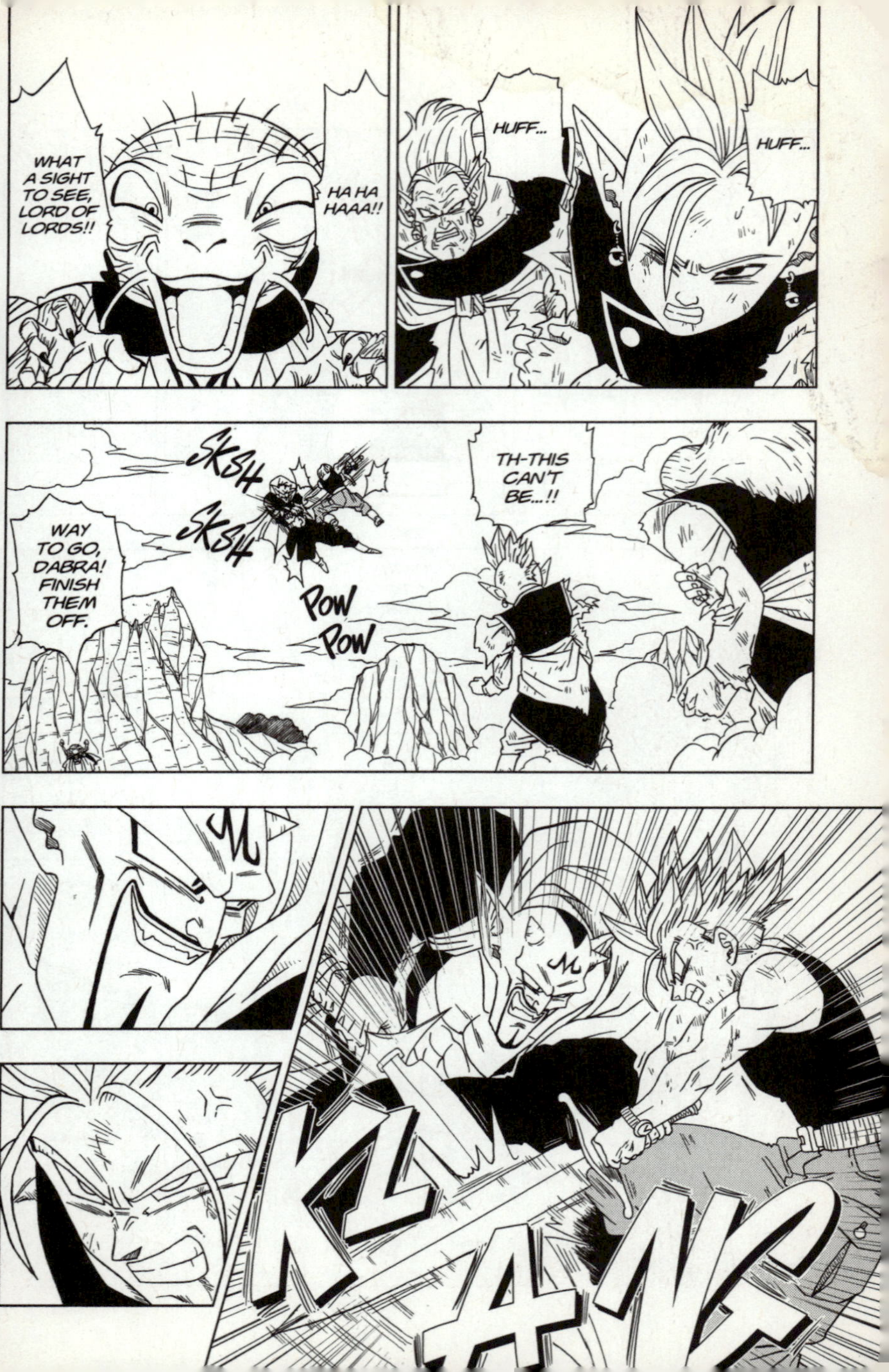
HUFF...
HUFF...
HA HA HAAA!!
WHAT A SIGHT TO SEE, LORD OF LORDS!!
TH-THIS CAN'T BE...!!
SKSH
SKSH
WAY TO GO, DABRA! FINISH THEM OFF.
POW
POW
KLANG

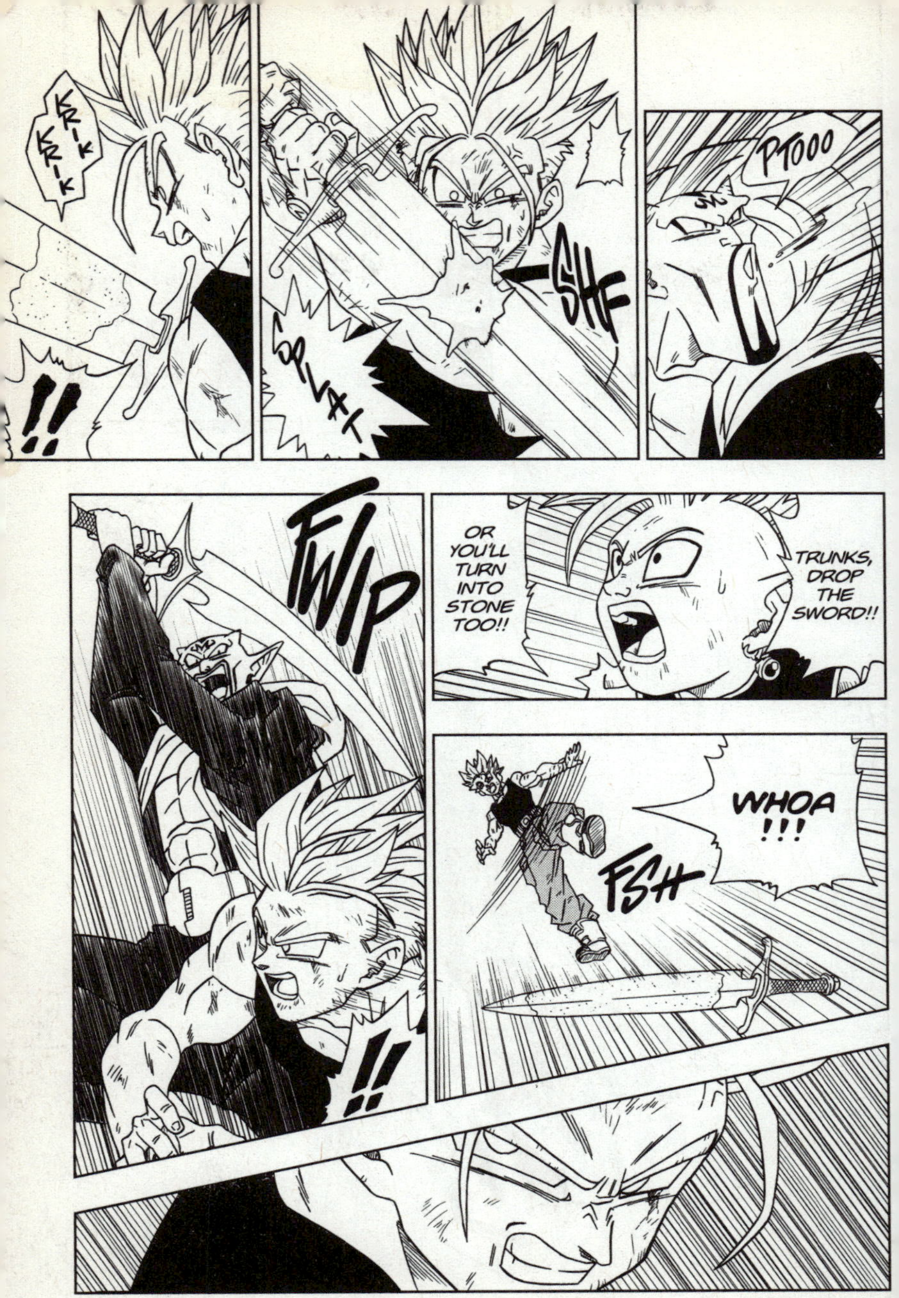
PTOOO
SHF
SPLAT
KRIK KRIK
!!
TRUNKS, DROP THE SWORD!!
OR YOU'LL TURN INTO STONE TOO!!
WHOA!!!
FSH
FWIP
!!

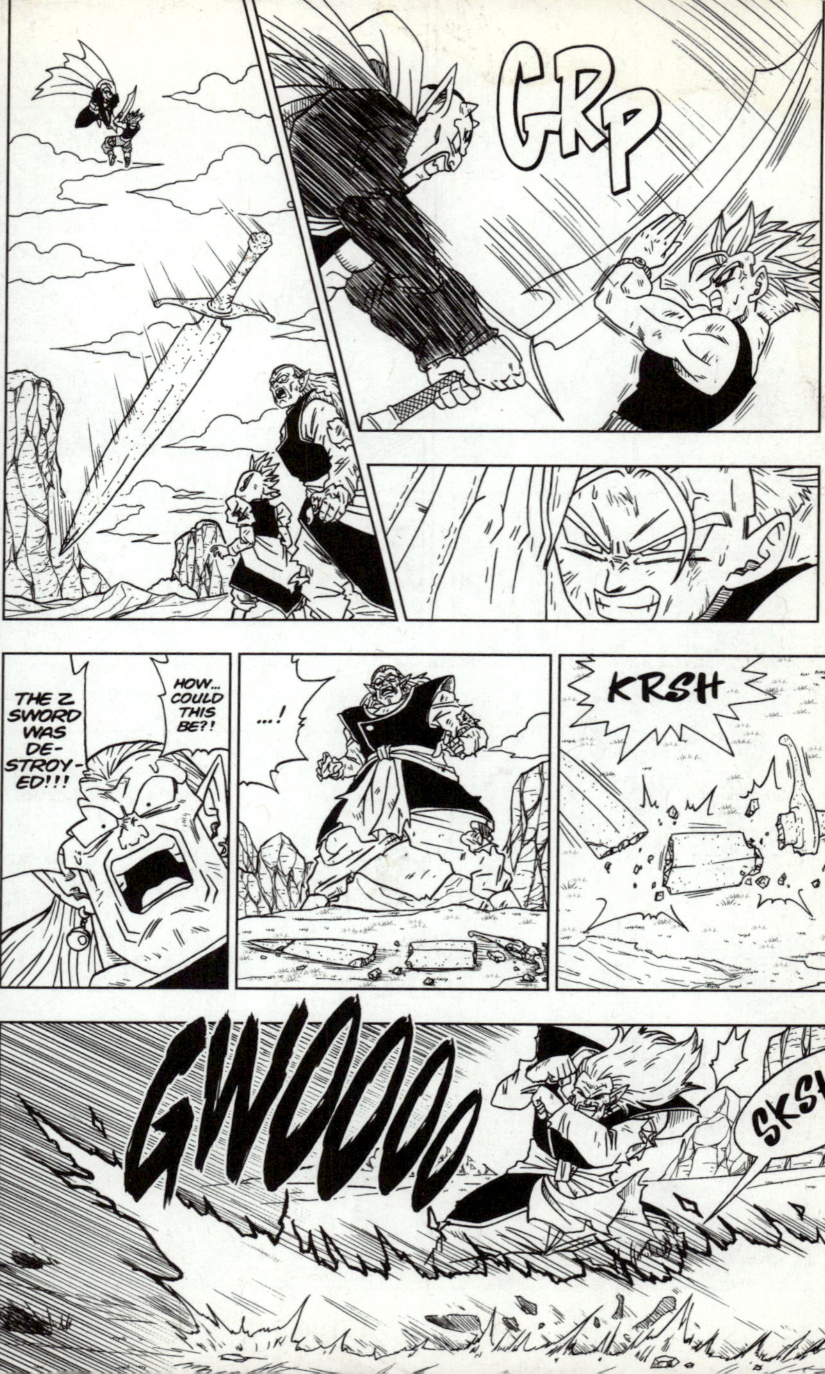
GRP
KRSH
...!
HOW... COULD THIS BE?!
THE Z SWORD WAS DE-STROY-ED!!!
SKSHH
GWOOOOO

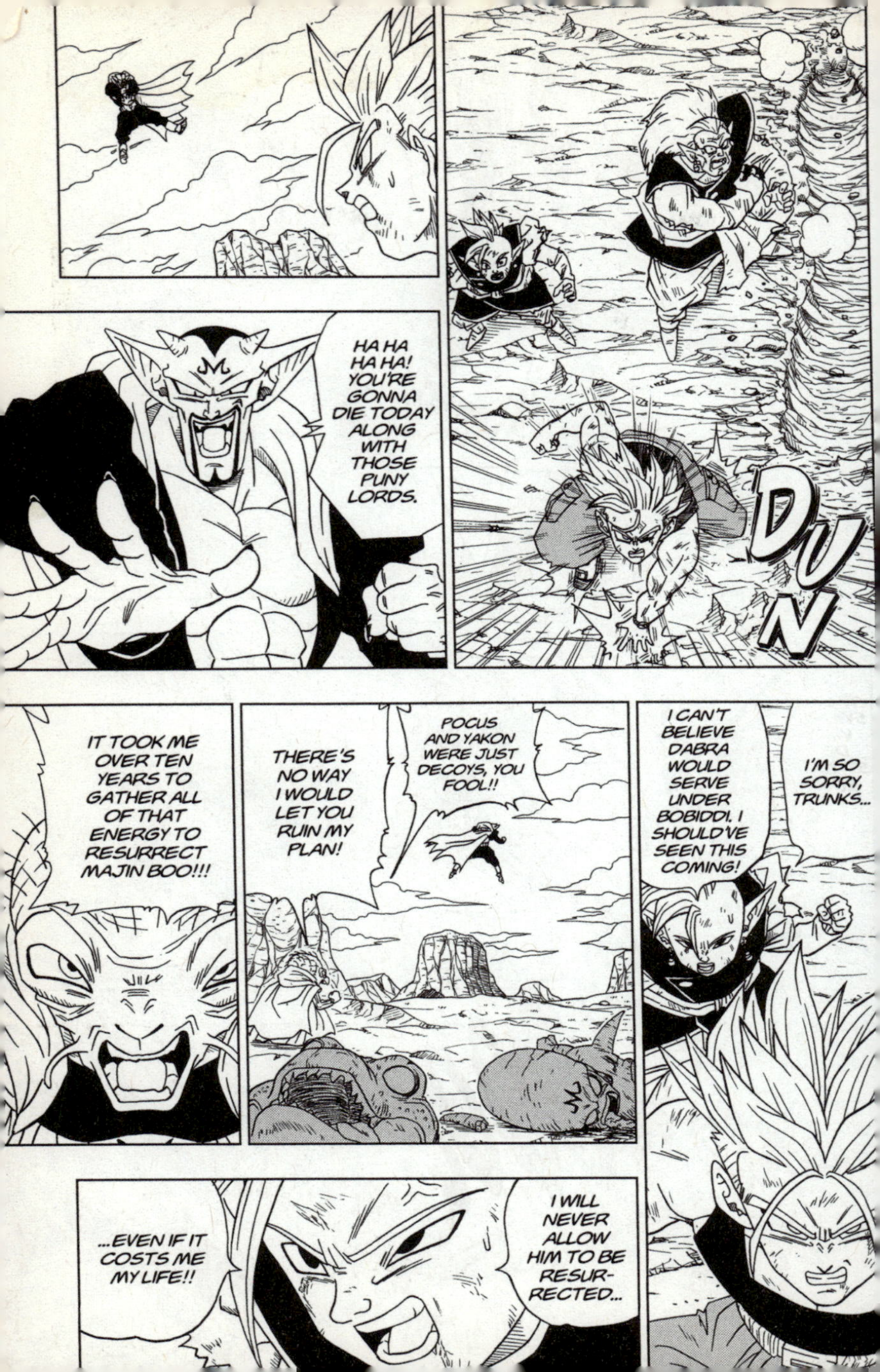
DUN
HA HA HA HA! YOU'RE GONNA DIE TODAY ALONG WITH THOSE PUNY LORDS.
I'M SO SORRY, TRUNKS...
I CAN'T BELIEVE DABRA WOULD SERVE UNDER BOBIDDI. I SHOULD'VE SEEN THIS COMING!
POCUS AND YAKON WERE JUST DECOYS, YOU FOOL!!
THERE'S NO WAY I WOULD LET YOU RUIN MY PLAN!
IT TOOK ME OVER TEN YEARS TO GATHER ALL OF THAT ENERGY TO RESURRECT MAJIN BOO!!!
I WILL NEVER ALLOW HIM TO BE RESUR-RECTED...
...EVEN IF IT COSTS ME MY LIFE!!

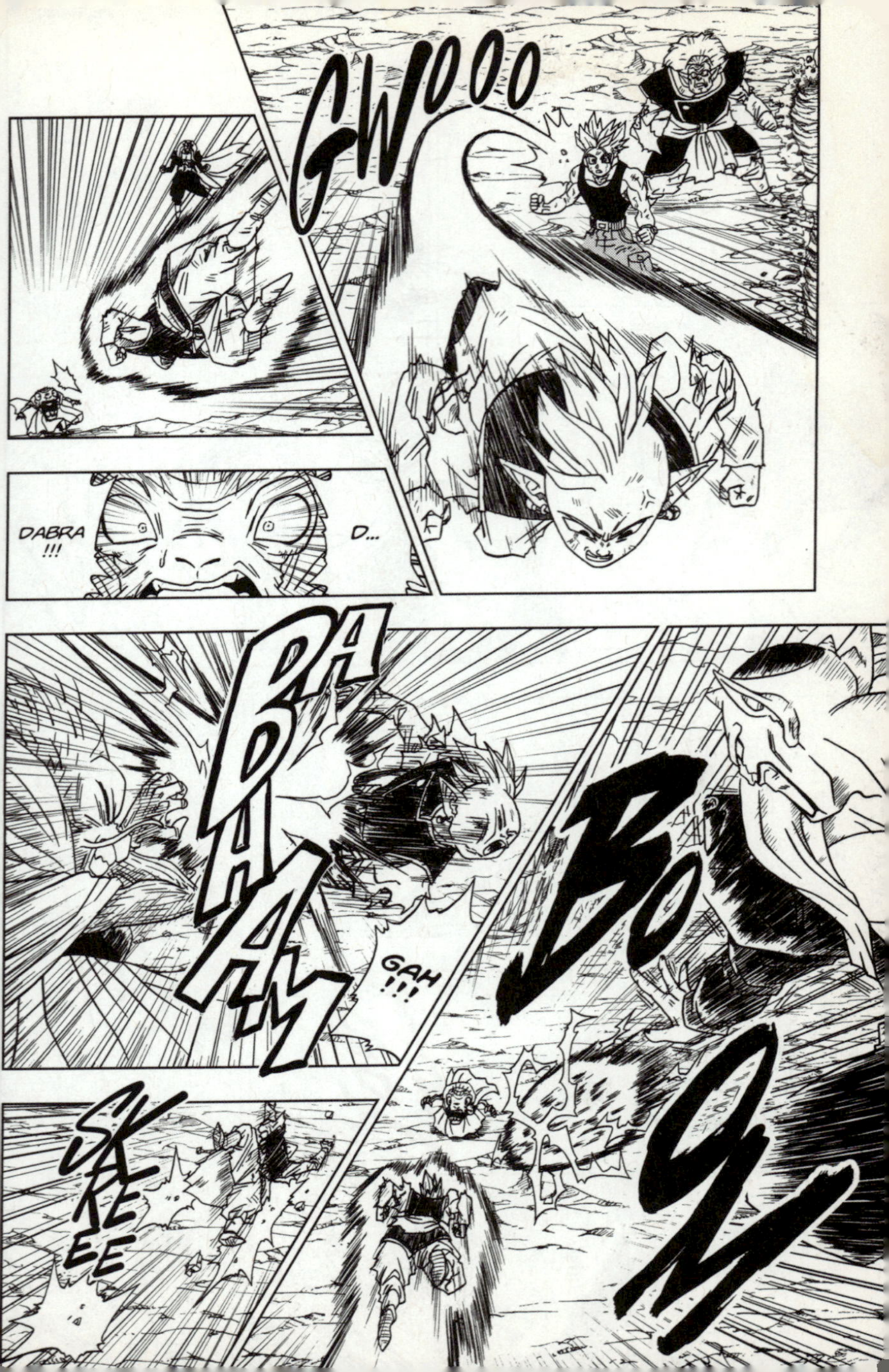

GWOOO
D...
DABRA!!!
BOOM
BADAM
GAH!!!
SKREEE

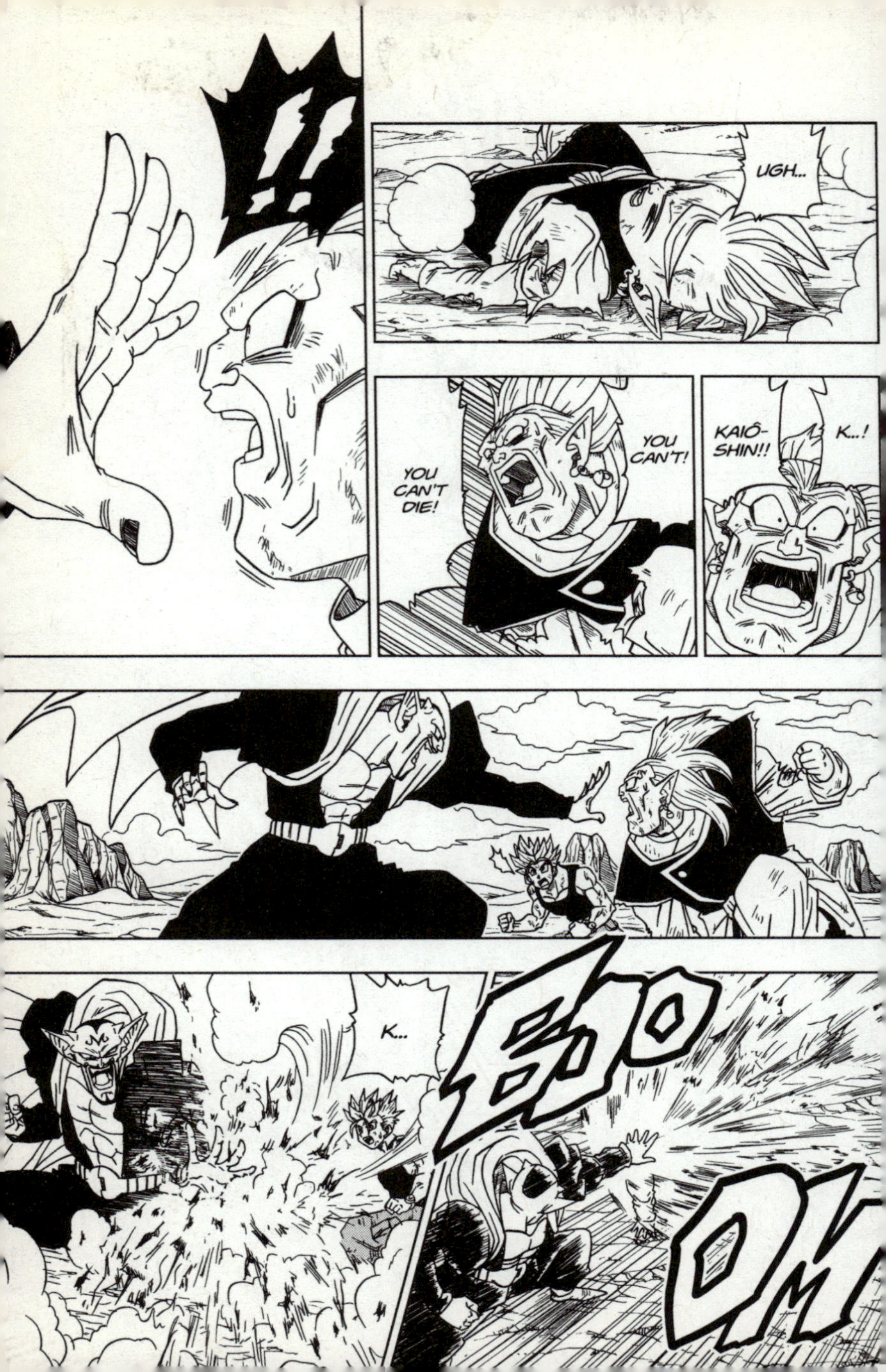

UGH...
K...!
KAIÔ-SHIN!!
YOU CAN'T!
YOU CAN'T DIE!
ZOOM
K...

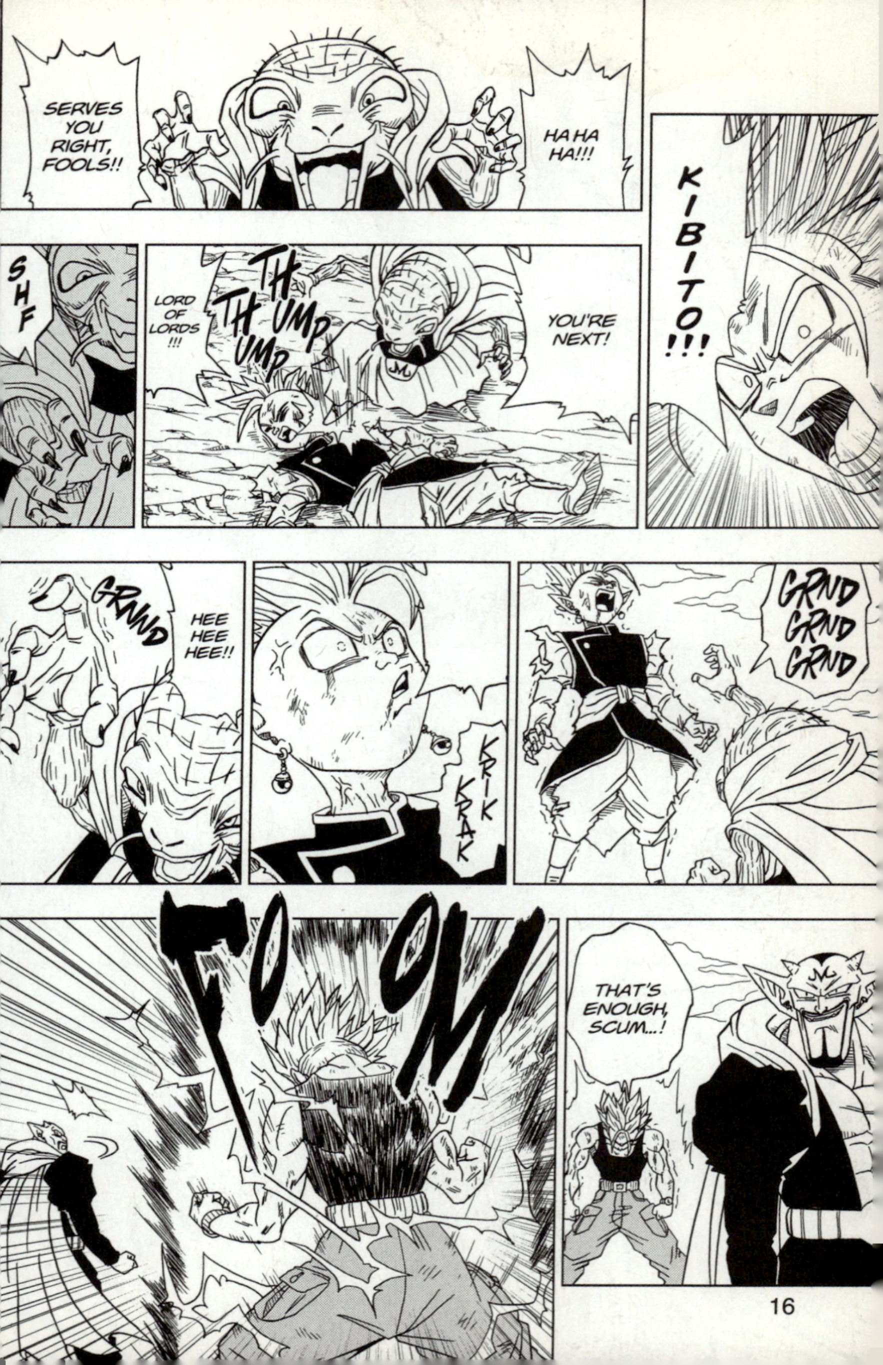
SERVES YOU RIGHT, FOOLS!!
HA HA HA!!!
KIBITO!!!
YOU'RE NEXT!
THUMP THUMP THUMP
LORD OF LORDS!!!
SHF
GRND GRND GRND
KRIK KRAK
HEE HEE HEE!!
GRNND
THAT'S ENOUGH, SCUM...!
FOOM

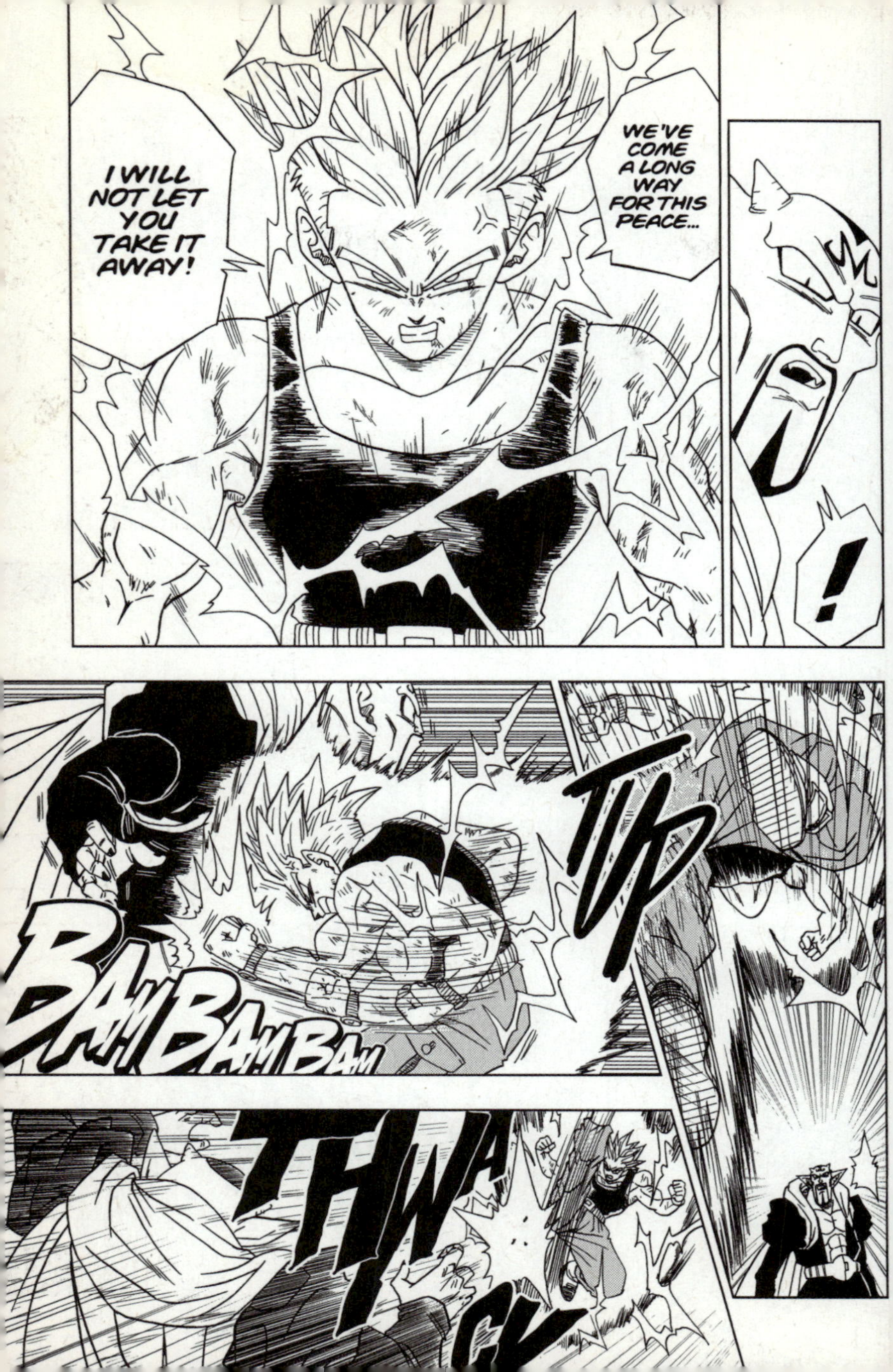
!
WE'VE COME A LONG WAY FOR THIS PEACE...
I WILL NOT LET YOU TAKE IT AWAY!
TAP
BAMBAMBAM
THWACK

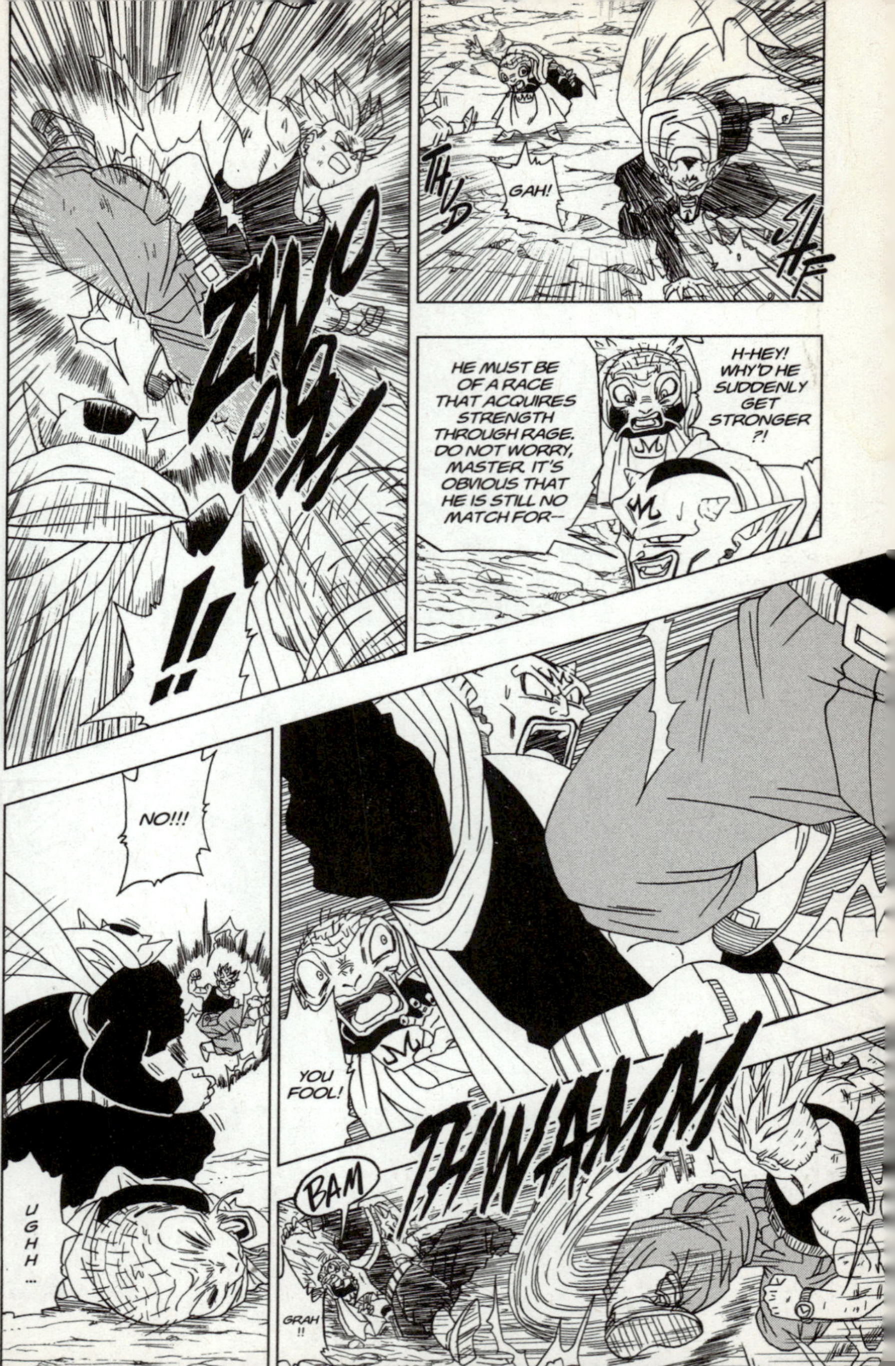

SHF
GAH!
THUD
H-HEY! WHY'D HE SUDDENLY GET STRONGER ?!
HE MUST BE OF A RACE THAT ACQUIRES STRENGTH THROUGH RAGE. DO NOT WORRY, MASTER. IT'S OBVIOUS THAT HE IS STILL NO MATCH FOR--
ZWOOM
!!
YOU FOOL!
THWAMM
BAM
GRAH !!
NO!!!
UGHH ...

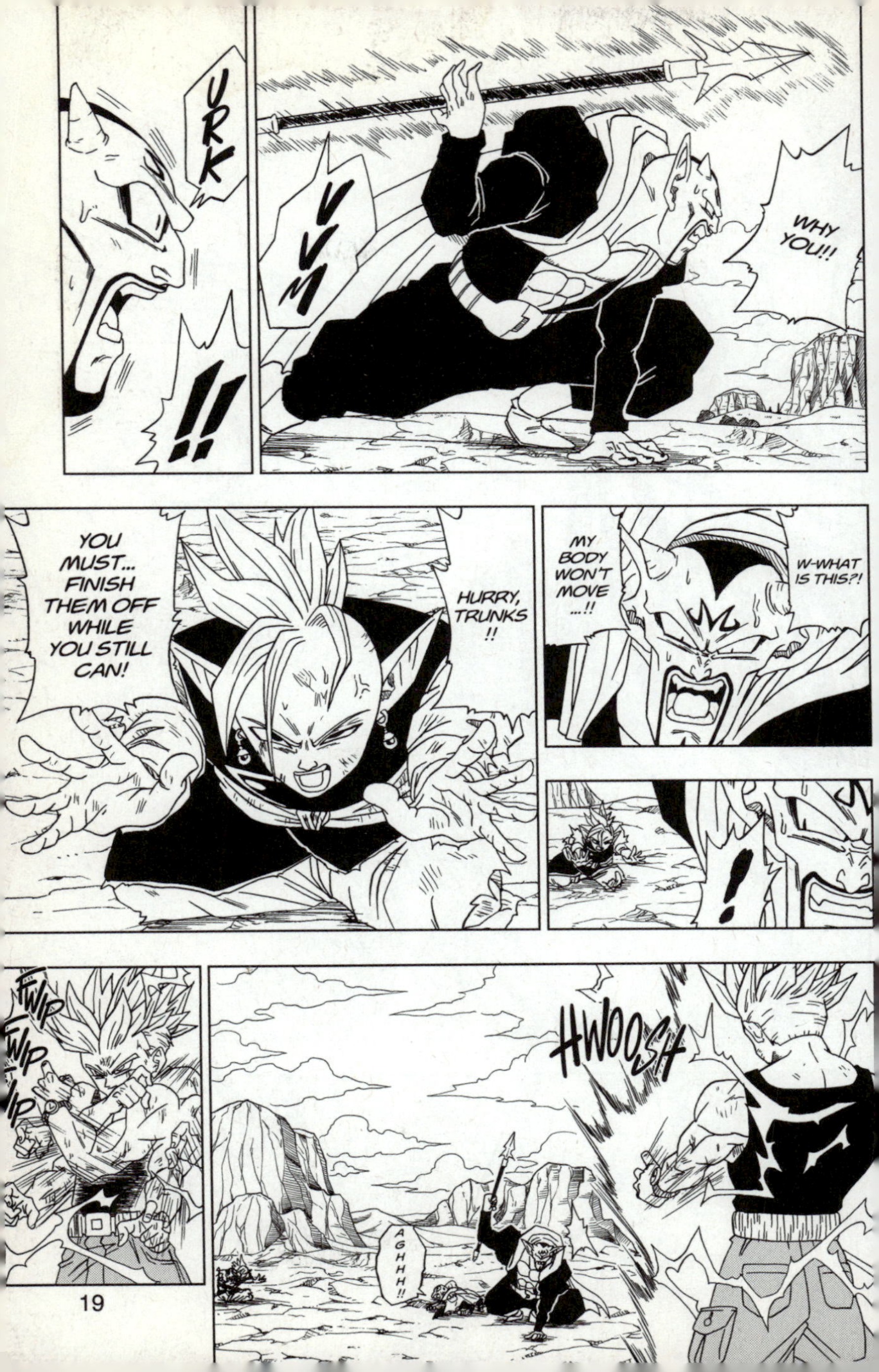
WHY YOU!!
VVMM
URK
!!
W-WHAT IS THIS?!
MY BODY WON'T MOVE ...!!
!
HURRY, TRUNKS!!
YOU MUST... FINISH THEM OFF WHILE YOU STILL CAN!
HWOOSH
AGHHH!!
FWIP FWIP FWIP

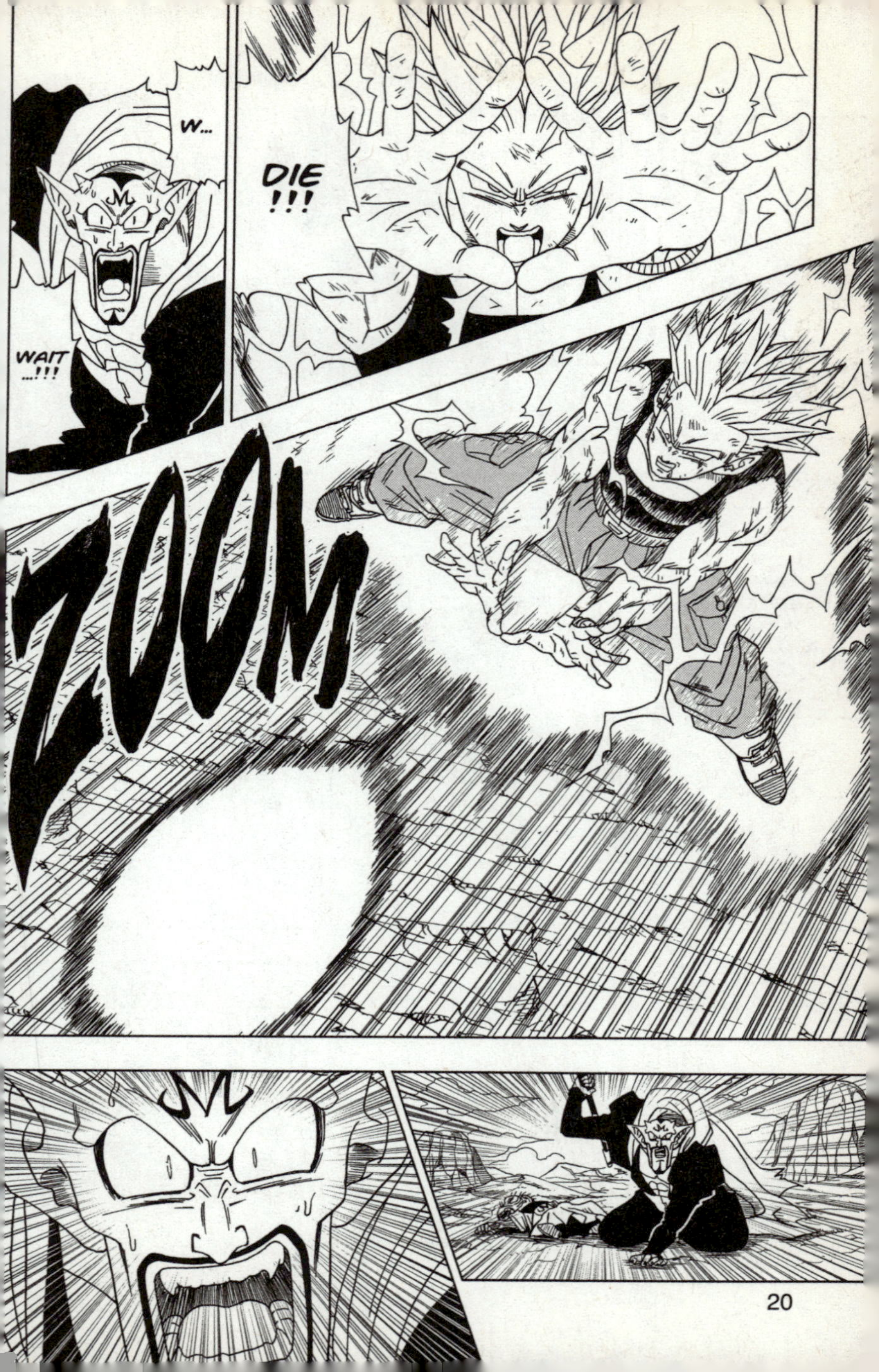
DIE !!!
W...
WAIT ...!!!
ZOOM

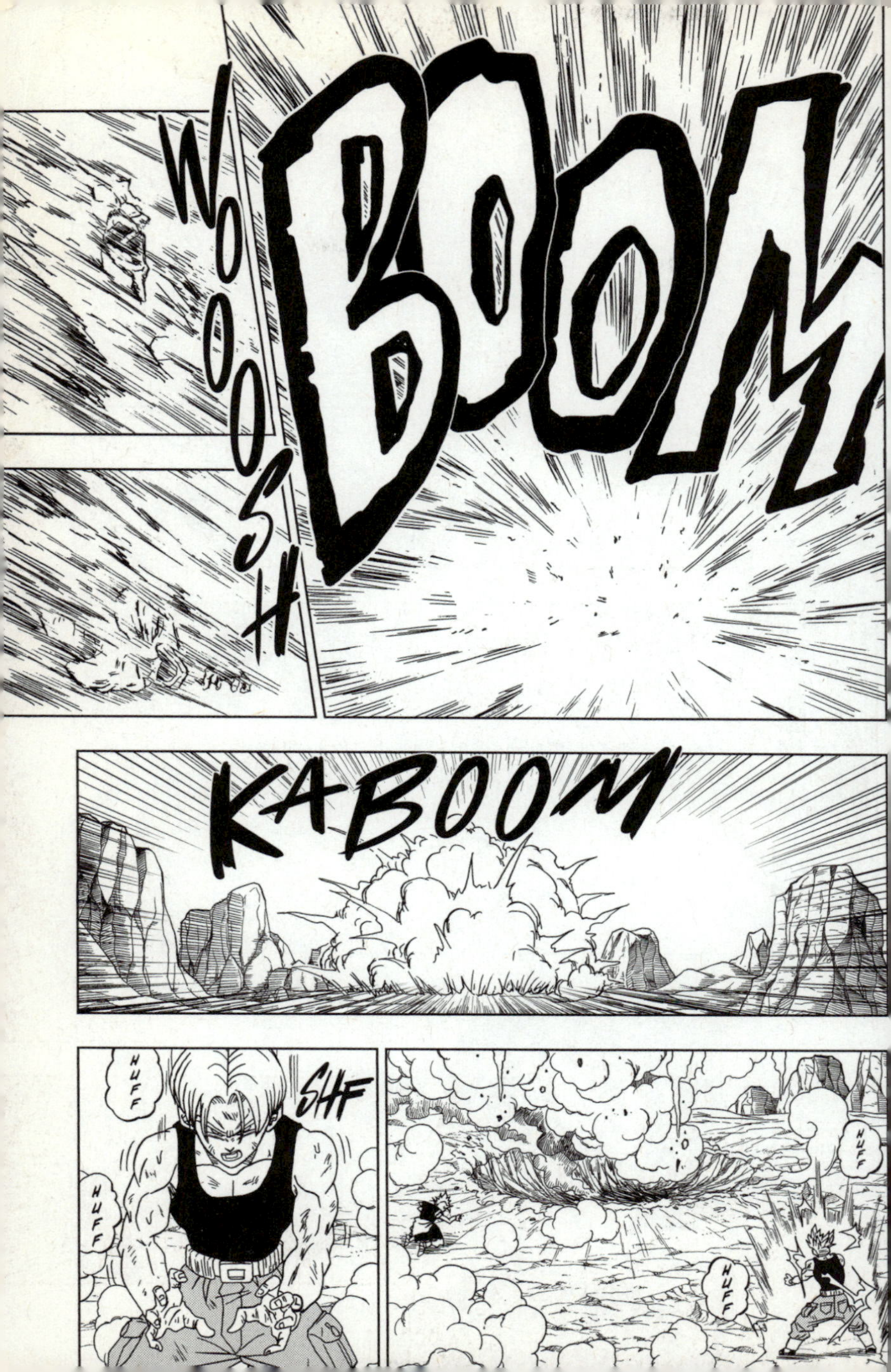
BOOM
WOOOOSH
KABOOM
HUFF
HUFF
SHF
HUFF
HUFF

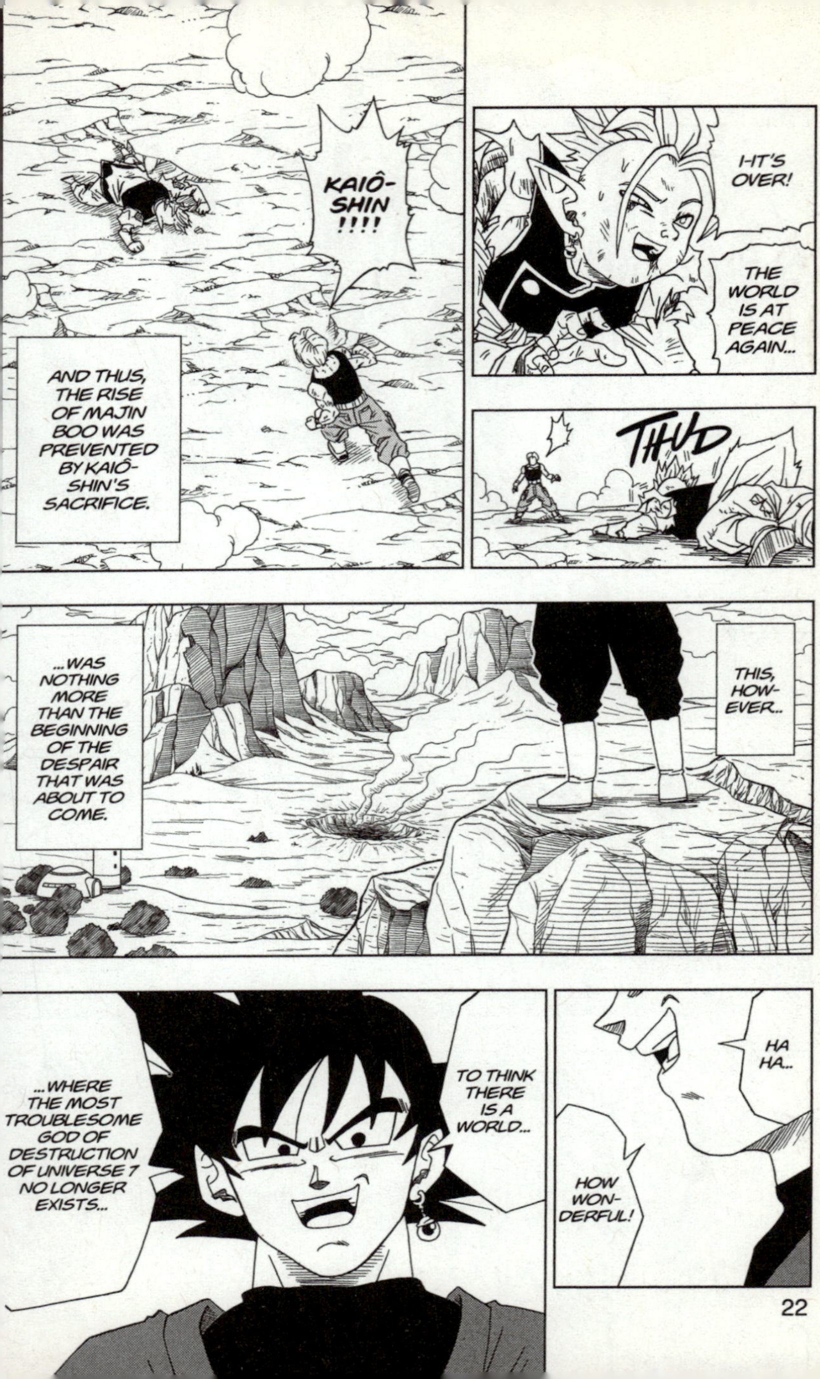
I-IT'S OVER!
THE WORLD IS AT PEACE AGAIN...
THUD
KAIÔ-SHIN!!!!
AND THUS, THE RISE OF MAJIN BOO WAS PREVENTED BY KAIÔ-SHIN'S SACRIFICE.
THIS, HOWEVER...
...WAS NOTHING MORE THAN THE BEGINNING OF THE DESPAIR THAT WAS ABOUT TO COME.
HA HA...
HOW WONDERFUL!
TO THINK THERE IS A WORLD...
...WHERE THE MOST TROUBLESOME GOD OF DESTRUCTION OF UNIVERSE 7 NO LONGER EXISTS...

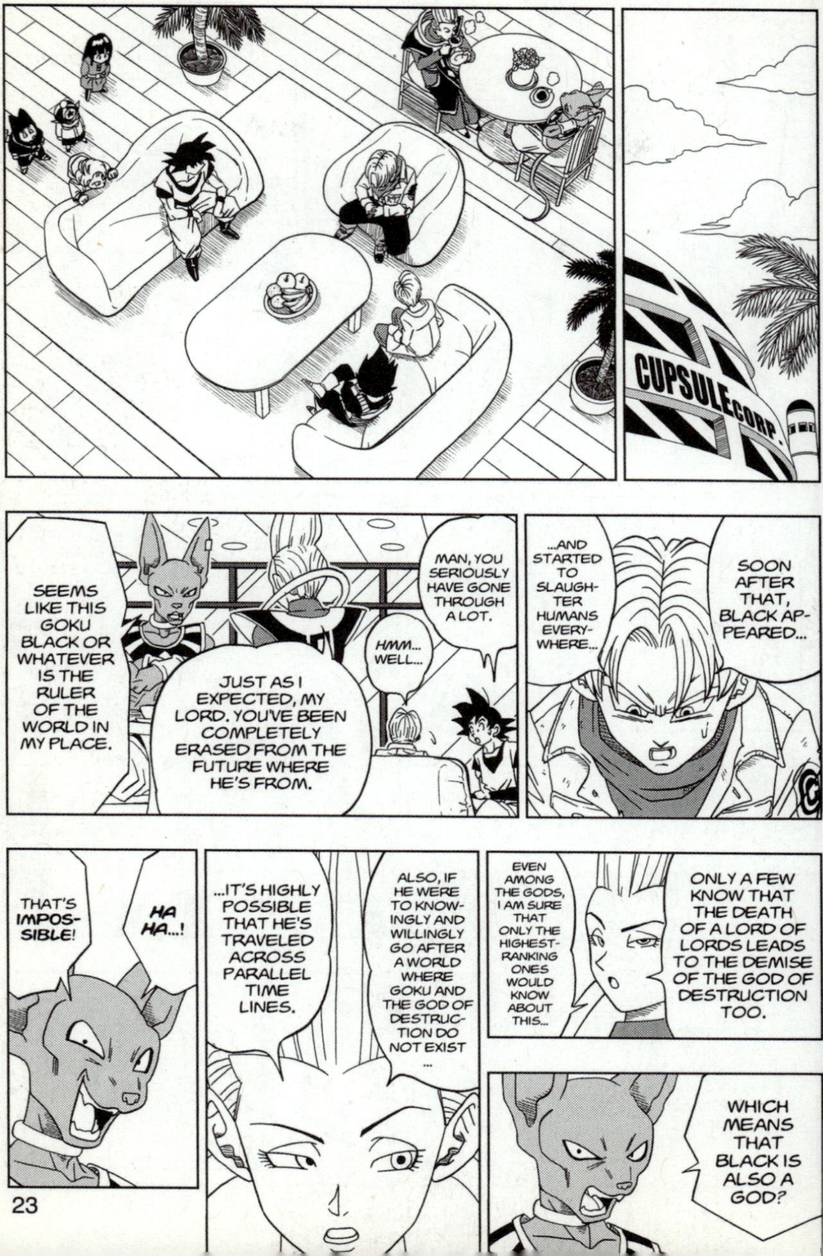
CUPSULE CORP.
SOON AFTER THAT, BLACK APPEARED...
...AND STARTED TO SLAUGHTER HUMANS EVERYWHERE...
MAN, YOU SERIOUSLY HAVE GONE THROUGH A LOT.
HMM... WELL...
SEEMS LIKE THIS GOKU BLACK OR WHATEVER IS THE RULER OF THE WORLD IN MY PLACE.
JUST AS I EXPECTED, MY LORD. YOU'VE BEEN COMPLETELY ERASED FROM THE FUTURE WHERE HE'S FROM.
ONLY A FEW KNOW THAT THE DEATH OF A LORD OF LORDS LEADS TO THE DEMISE OF THE GOD OF DESTRUCTION TOO.
EVEN AMONG THE GODS, I AM SURE THAT ONLY THE HIGHEST-RANKING ONES WOULD KNOW ABOUT THIS...
WHICH MEANS THAT BLACK IS ALSO A GOD?
ALSO, IF HE WERE TO KNOWINGLY AND WILLINGLY GO AFTER A WORLD WHERE GOKU AND THE GOD OF DESTRUCTION DO NOT EXIST ...
...IT'S HIGHLY POSSIBLE THAT HE'S TRAVELED ACROSS PARALLEL TIME LINES.
HA HA...!
THAT'S *IMPOSSIBLE*!

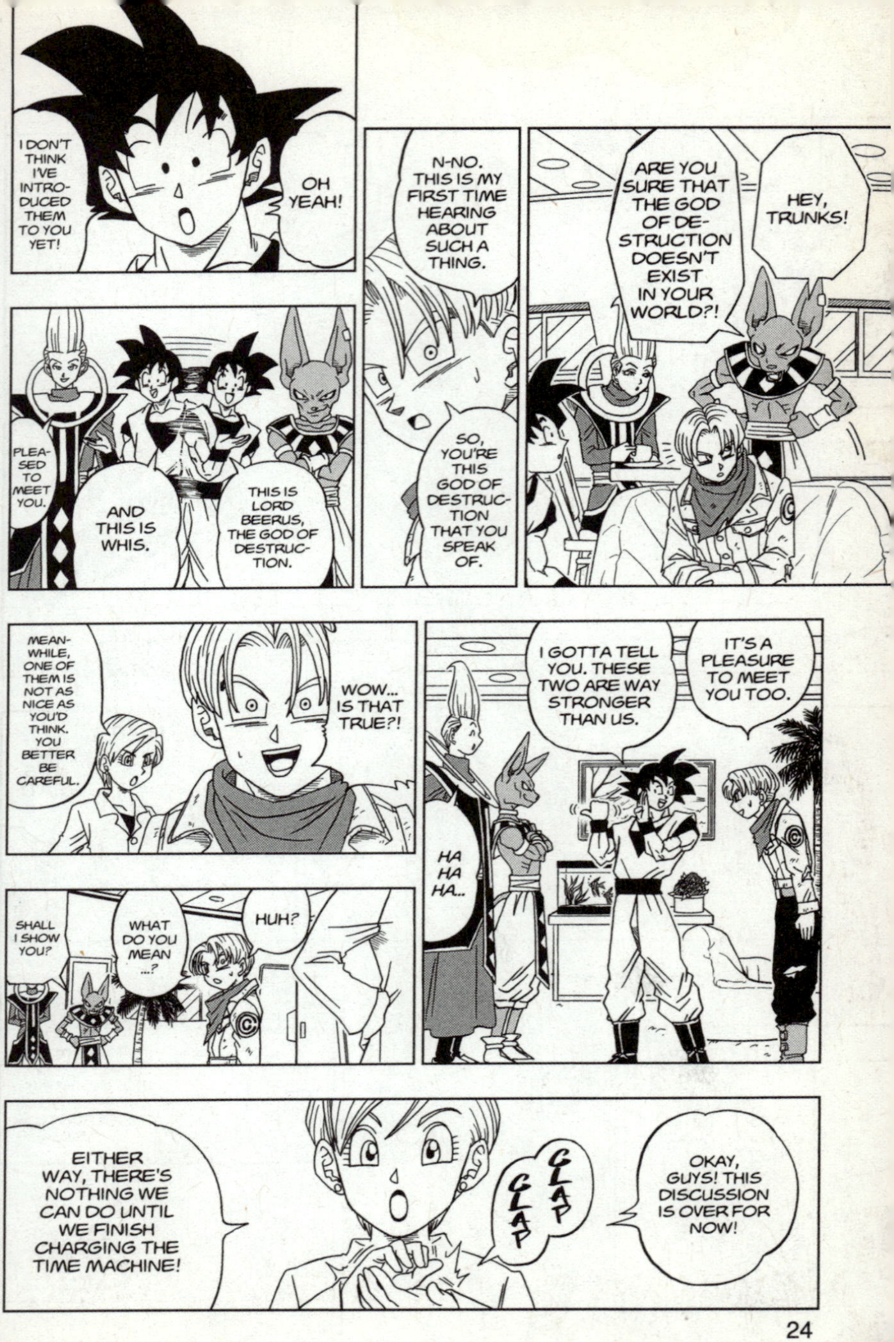
HEY, TRUNKS!
ARE YOU SURE THAT THE GOD OF DE-STRUCTION DOESN'T EXIST IN YOUR WORLD?!
N-NO. THIS IS MY FIRST TIME HEARING ABOUT SUCH A THING.
SO, YOU'RE THIS GOD OF DESTRUC-TION THAT YOU SPEAK OF.
OH YEAH!
I DON'T THINK I'VE INTRO-DUCED THEM TO YOU YET!
THIS IS LORD BEERUS, THE GOD OF DESTRUC-TION.
AND THIS IS WHIS.
PLEA-SED TO MEET YOU.
IT'S A PLEASURE TO MEET YOU TOO.
I GOTTA TELL YOU. THESE TWO ARE WAY STRONGER THAN US.
HA HA HA...
WOW... IS THAT TRUE?!
MEAN-WHILE, ONE OF THEM IS NOT AS NICE AS YOU'D THINK. YOU BETTER BE CAREFUL.
HUH?
WHAT DO YOU MEAN ...?
SHALL I SHOW YOU?
OKAY, GUYS! THIS DISCUSSION IS OVER FOR NOW!
CLAP
CLAP
EITHER WAY, THERE'S NOTHING WE CAN DO UNTIL WE FINISH CHARGING THE TIME MACHINE!

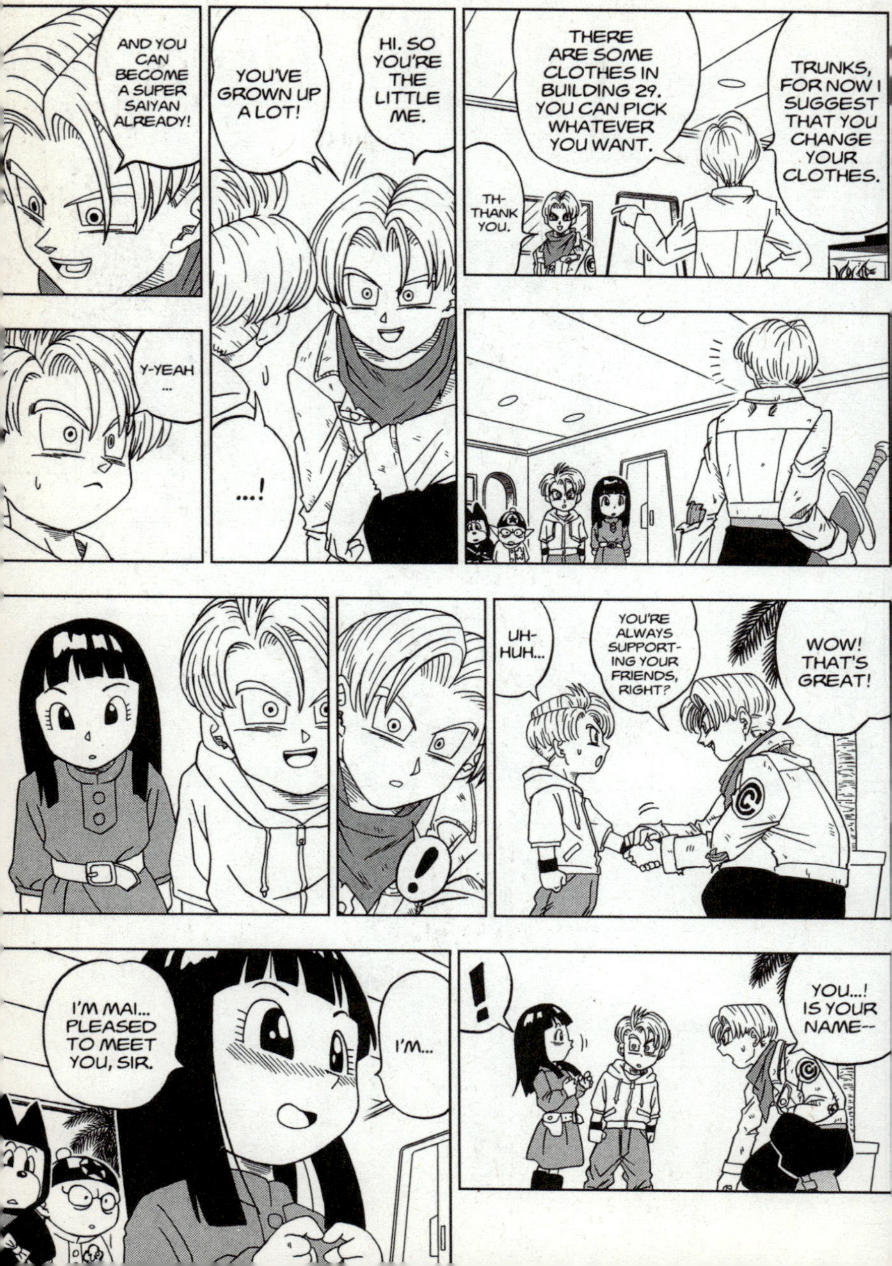
TRUNKS, FOR NOW I SUGGEST THAT YOU CHANGE YOUR CLOTHES.
THERE ARE SOME CLOTHES IN BUILDING 29. YOU CAN PICK WHATEVER YOU WANT.
TH-THANK YOU.
HI. SO YOU'RE THE LITTLE ME.
YOU'VE GROWN UP A LOT!
...!
AND YOU CAN BECOME A SUPER SAIYAN ALREADY!
Y-YEAH...
WOW! THAT'S GREAT!
YOU'RE ALWAYS SUPPORTING YOUR FRIENDS, RIGHT?
UH-HUH...
!
YOU...! IS YOUR NAME--
!
I'M...
I'M MAI... PLEASED TO MEET YOU, SIR.

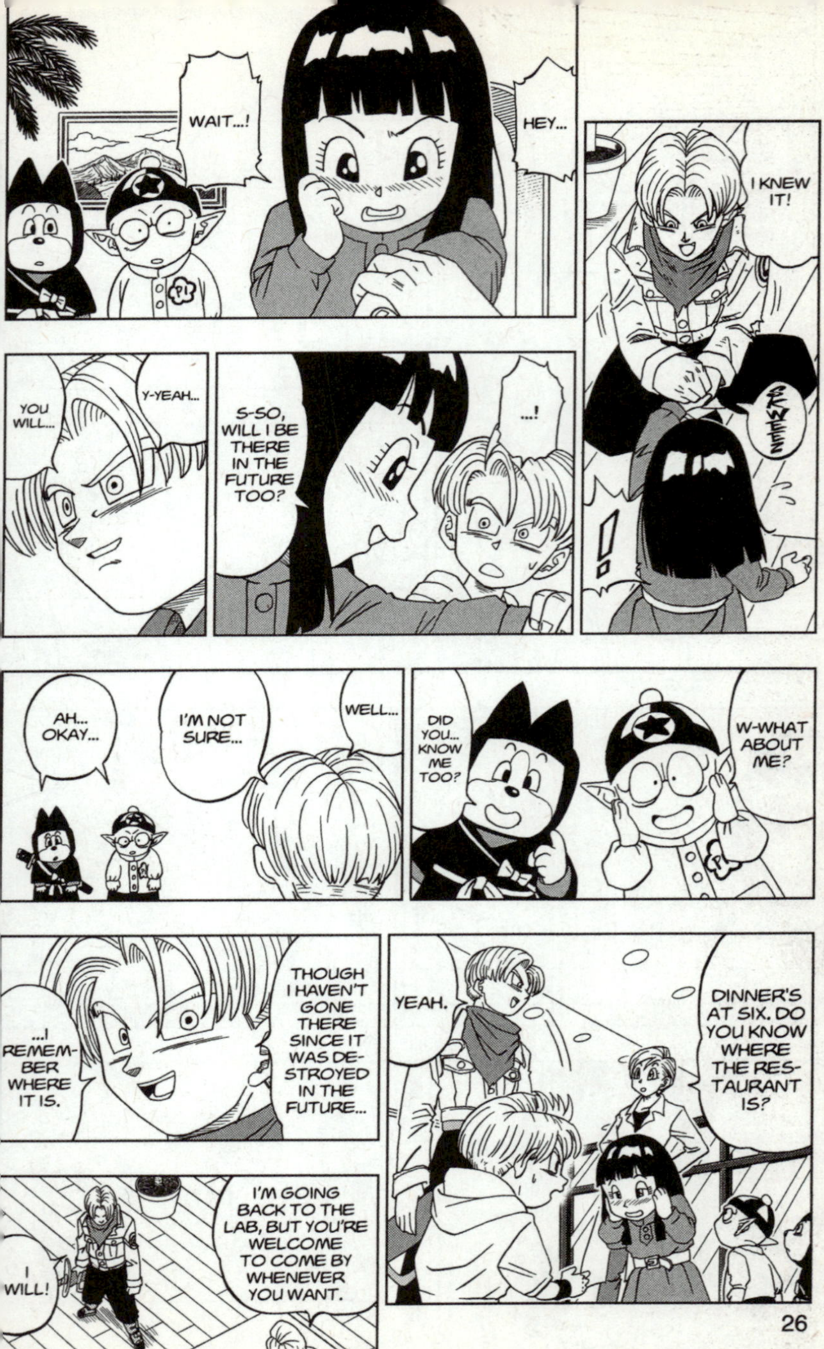
HEY...
WAIT...!
S-SO, WILL I BE THERE IN THE FUTURE TOO?
...!
Y-YEAH...
YOU WILL...
I KNEW IT!
SKWEEN
W-WHAT ABOUT ME?
DID YOU... KNOW ME TOO?
WELL...
I'M NOT SURE...
AH... OKAY...
DINNER'S AT SIX. DO YOU KNOW WHERE THE RESTAURANT IS?
YEAH.
THOUGH I HAVEN'T GONE THERE SINCE IT WAS DESTROYED IN THE FUTURE...
...I REMEMBER WHERE IT IS.
I'M GOING BACK TO THE LAB, BUT YOU'RE WELCOME TO COME BY WHENEVER YOU WANT.
I WILL!

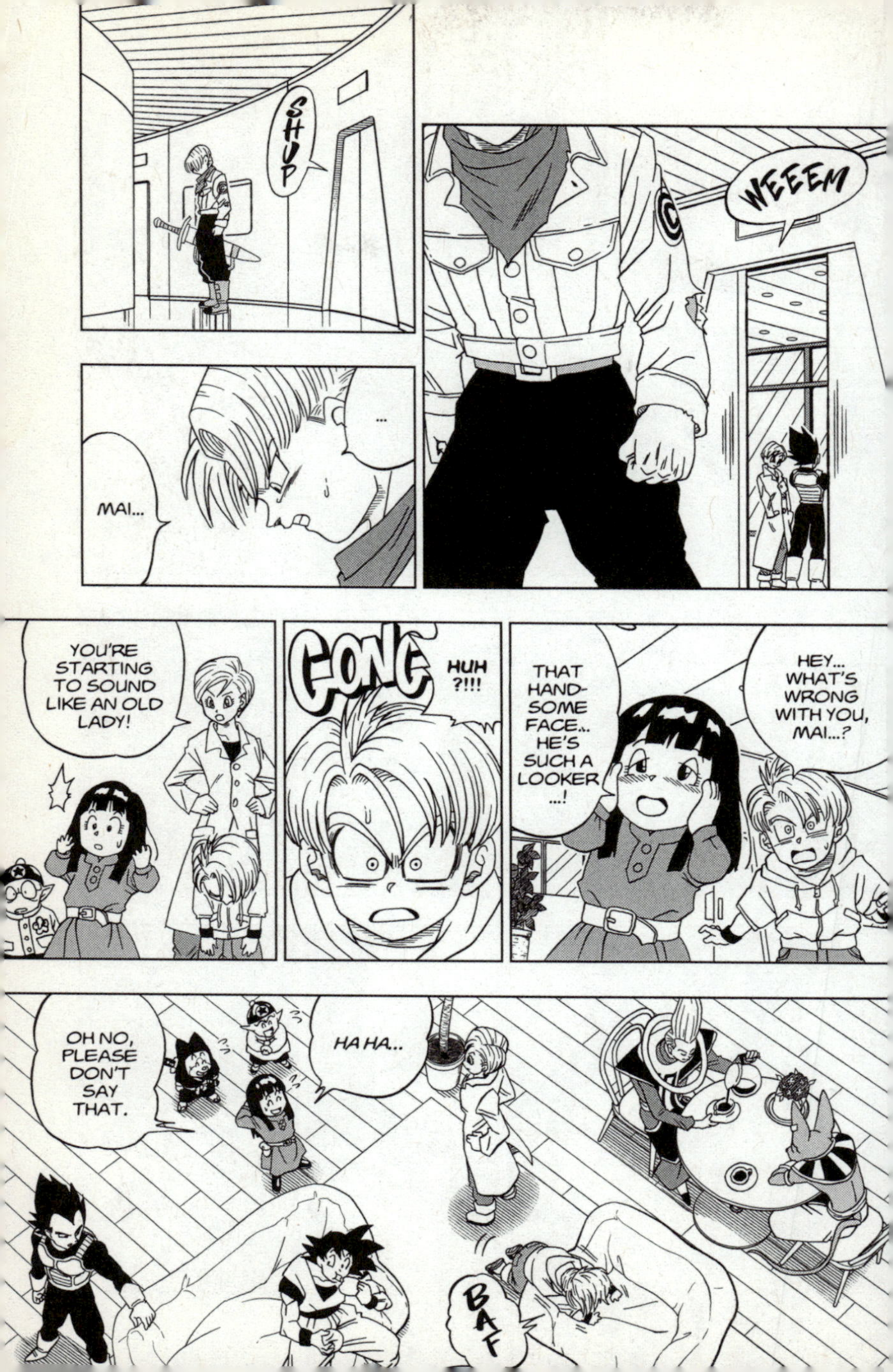
WEEEM
SHUP
...
MAI...
HEY... WHAT'S WRONG WITH YOU, MAI...?
THAT HANDSOME FACE... HE'S SUCH A LOOKER...!
GONG
HUH ?!!!
YOU'RE STARTING TO SOUND LIKE AN OLD LADY!
HA HA...
OH NO, PLEASE DON'T SAY THAT.
BAF

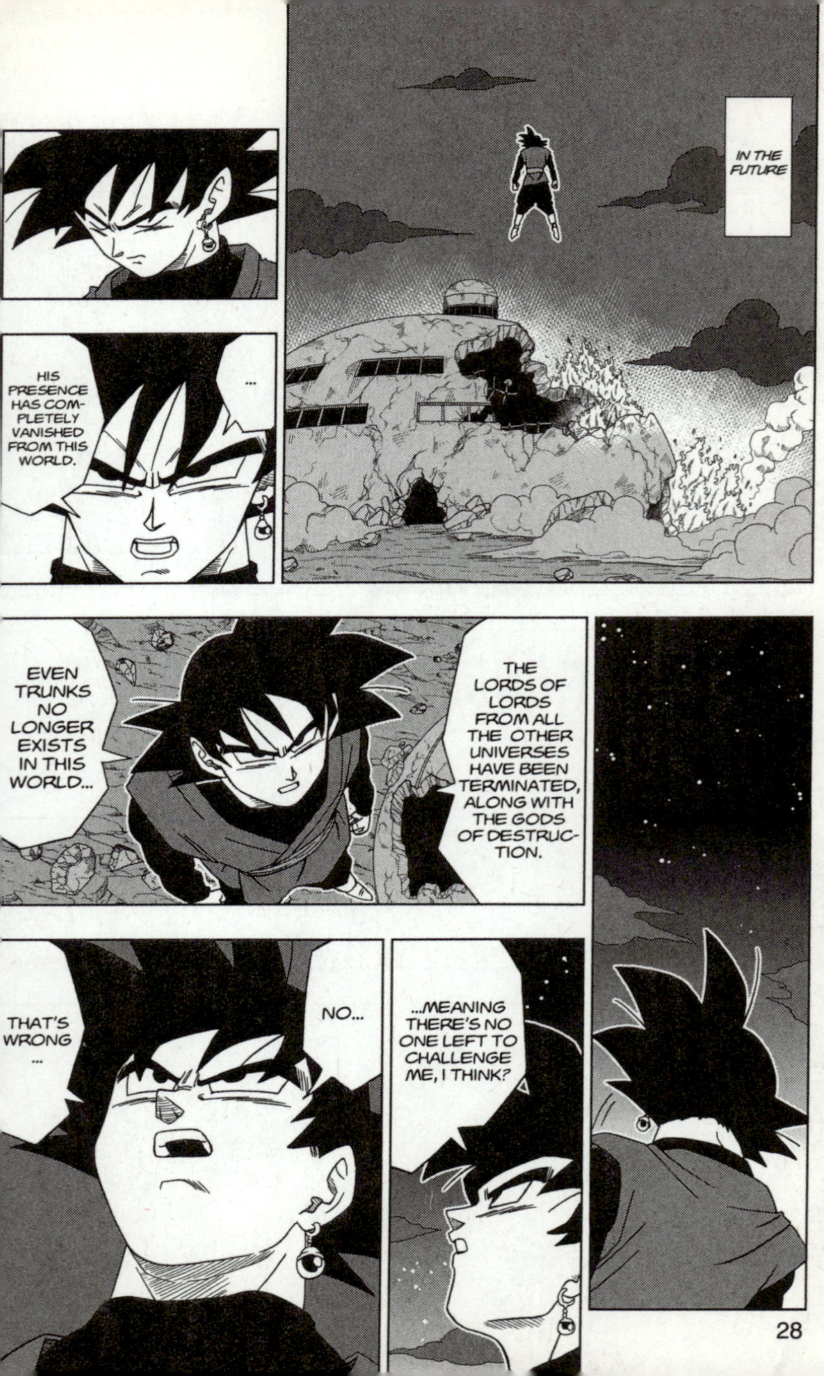
IN THE FUTURE
...
HIS PRESENCE HAS COMPLETELY VANISHED FROM THIS WORLD.
THE LORDS OF LORDS FROM ALL THE OTHER UNIVERSES HAVE BEEN TERMINATED, ALONG WITH THE GODS OF DESTRUCTION.
EVEN TRUNKS NO LONGER EXISTS IN THIS WORLD...
...MEANING THERE'S NO ONE LEFT TO CHALLENGE ME, I THINK?
NO...
THAT'S WRONG ...

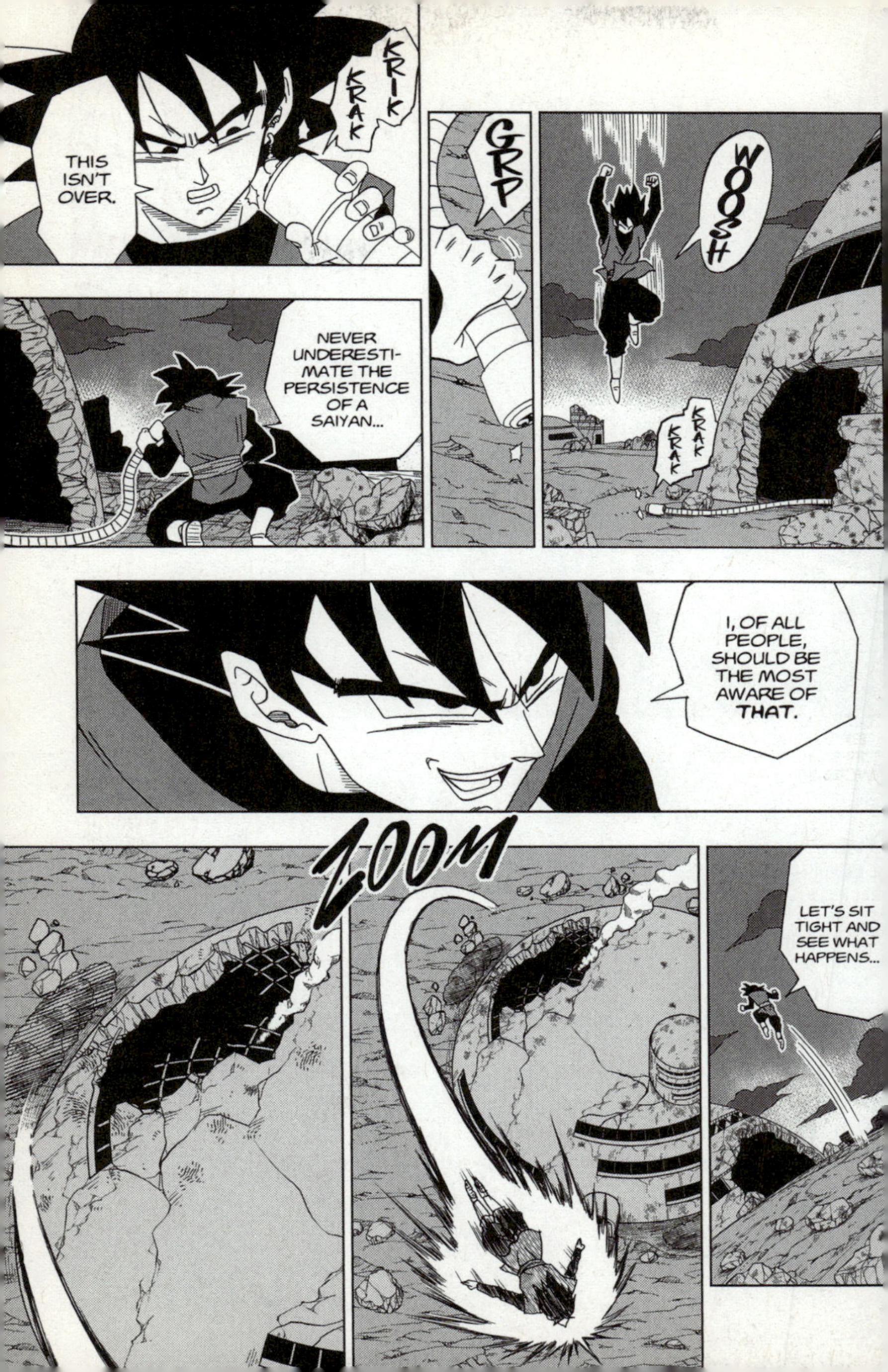
WOOSH
KRAK KRAK
GRP
THIS ISN'T OVER.
KRIK KRAK
NEVER UNDERESTI-MATE THE PERSISTENCE OF A SAIYAN...
I, OF ALL PEOPLE, SHOULD BE THE MOST AWARE OF THAT.
LET'S SIT TIGHT AND SEE WHAT HAPPENS...
ZOOM

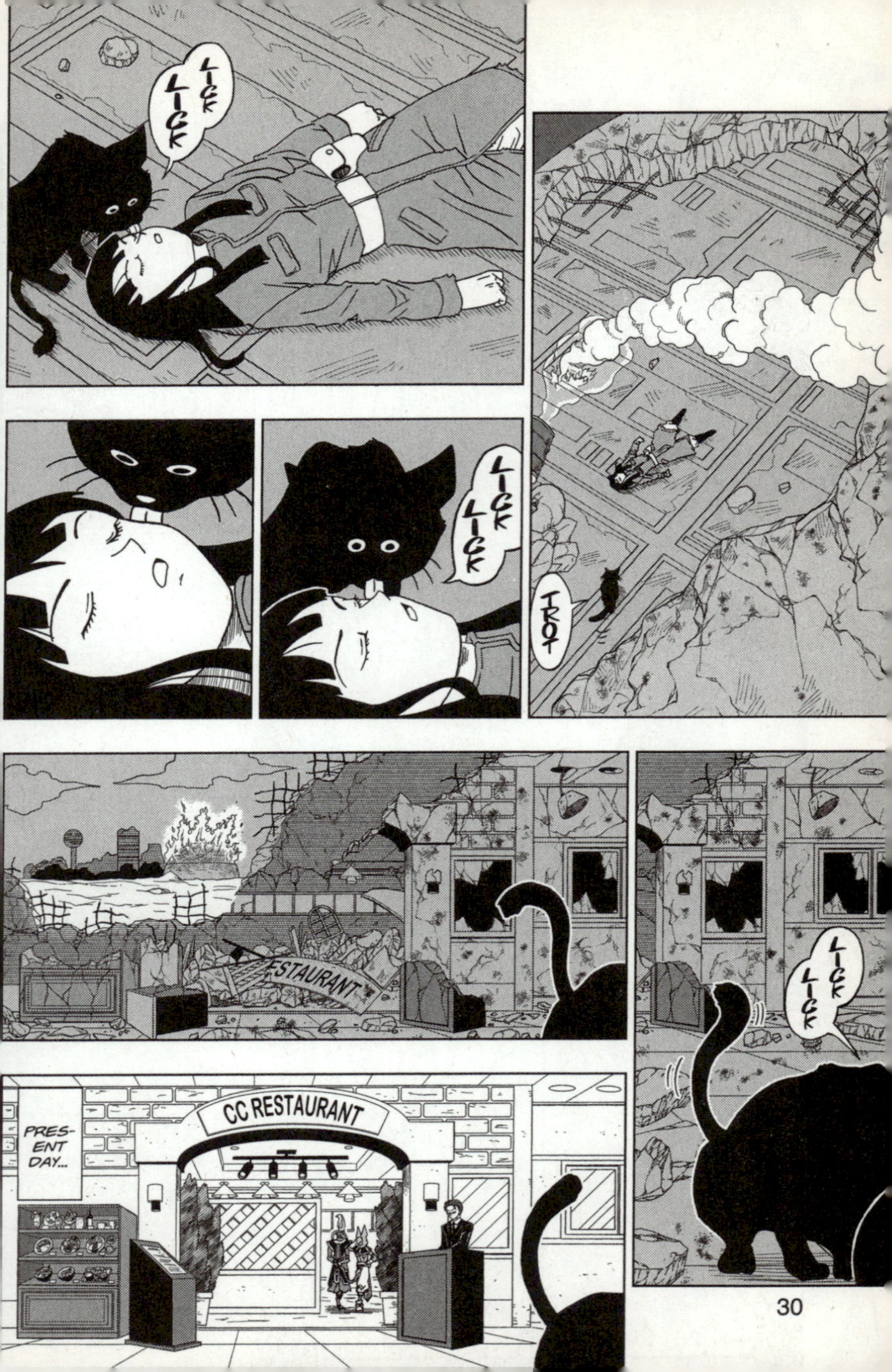
TROT
LICK LICK
LICK LICK
LICK LICK
ESTAURANT
PRES-ENT DAY...
CC RESTAURANT

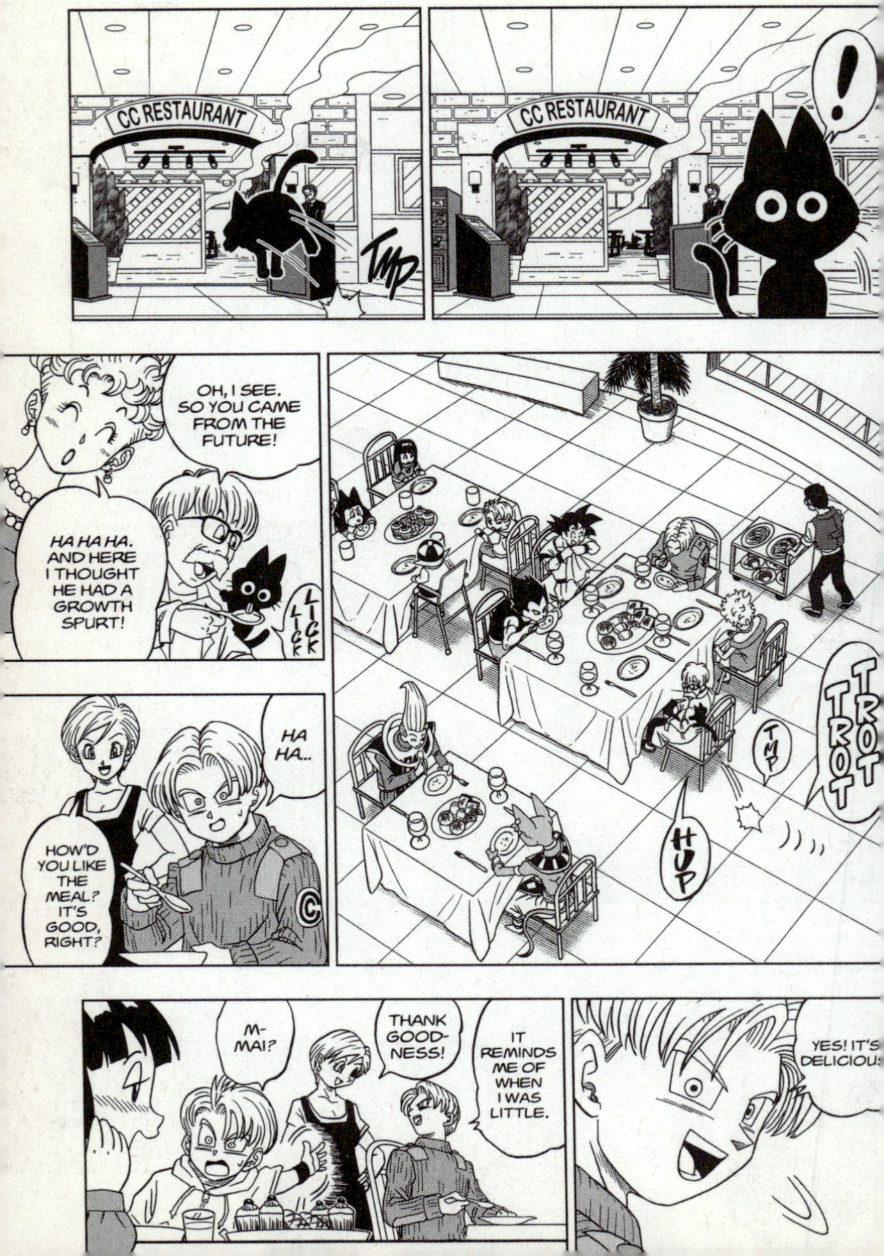
!
TMP
TROT TROT
TMP
HUP
OH, I SEE. SO YOU CAME FROM THE FUTURE!
HA HA HA. AND HERE I THOUGHT HE HAD A GROWTH SPURT!
LICK LICK
HA HA...
HOW'D YOU LIKE THE MEAL? IT'S GOOD, RIGHT?
YES! IT'S DELICIOU
IT REMINDS ME OF WHEN I WAS LITTLE.
THANK GOOD-NESS!
M-MAI?

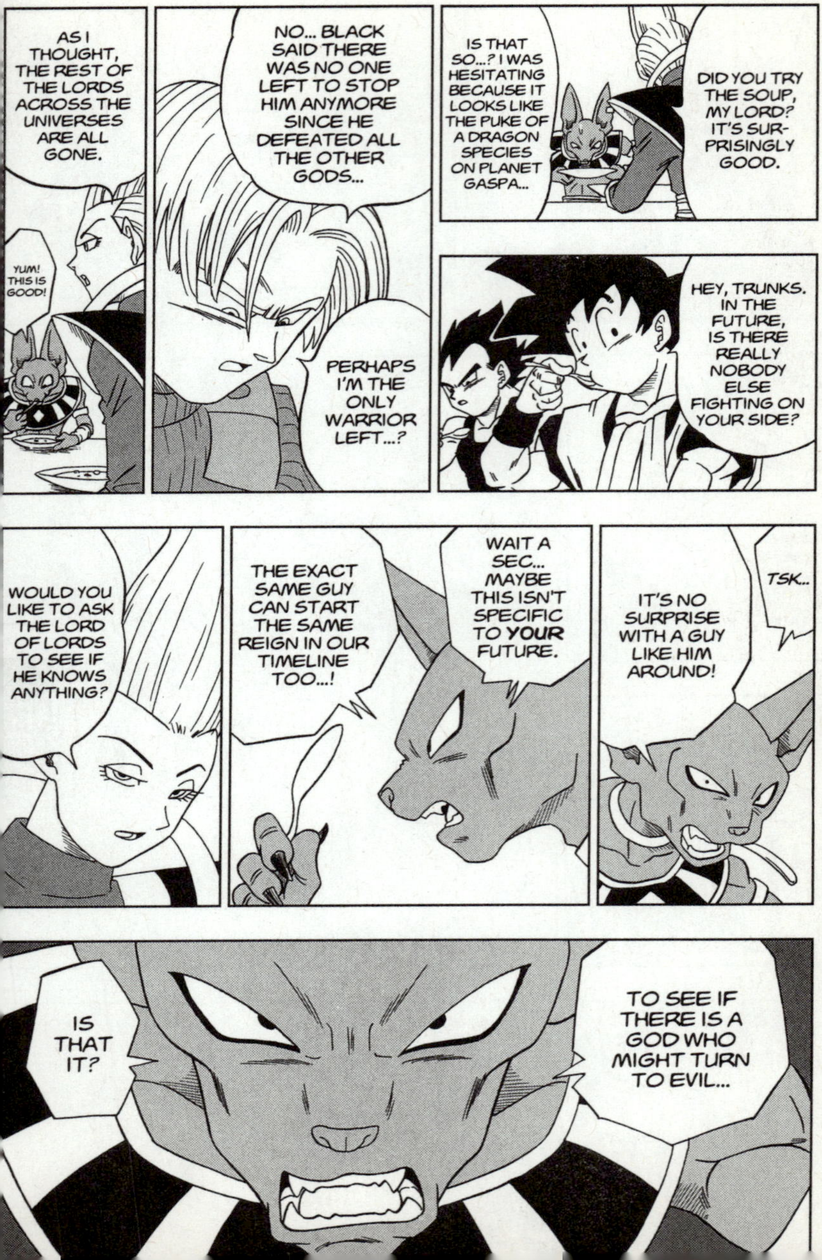
DID YOU TRY THE SOUP, MY LORD? IT'S SURPRISINGLY GOOD.
IS THAT SO...? I WAS HESITATING BECAUSE IT LOOKS LIKE THE PUKE OF A DRAGON SPECIES ON PLANET GASPA...
HEY, TRUNKS. IN THE FUTURE, IS THERE REALLY NOBODY ELSE FIGHTING ON YOUR SIDE?
NO... BLACK SAID THERE WAS NO ONE LEFT TO STOP HIM ANYMORE SINCE HE DEFEATED ALL THE OTHER GODS...
PERHAPS I'M THE ONLY WARRIOR LEFT...?
AS I THOUGHT, THE REST OF THE LORDS ACROSS THE UNIVERSES ARE ALL GONE.
YUM! THIS IS GOOD!
TSK...
IT'S NO SURPRISE WITH A GUY LIKE HIM AROUND!
WAIT A SEC... MAYBE THIS ISN'T SPECIFIC TO **YOUR** FUTURE.
THE EXACT SAME GUY CAN START THE SAME REIGN IN OUR TIMELINE TOO...!
WOULD YOU LIKE TO ASK THE LORD OF LORDS TO SEE IF HE KNOWS ANYTHING?
TO SEE IF THERE IS A GOD WHO MIGHT TURN TO EVIL...
IS THAT IT?

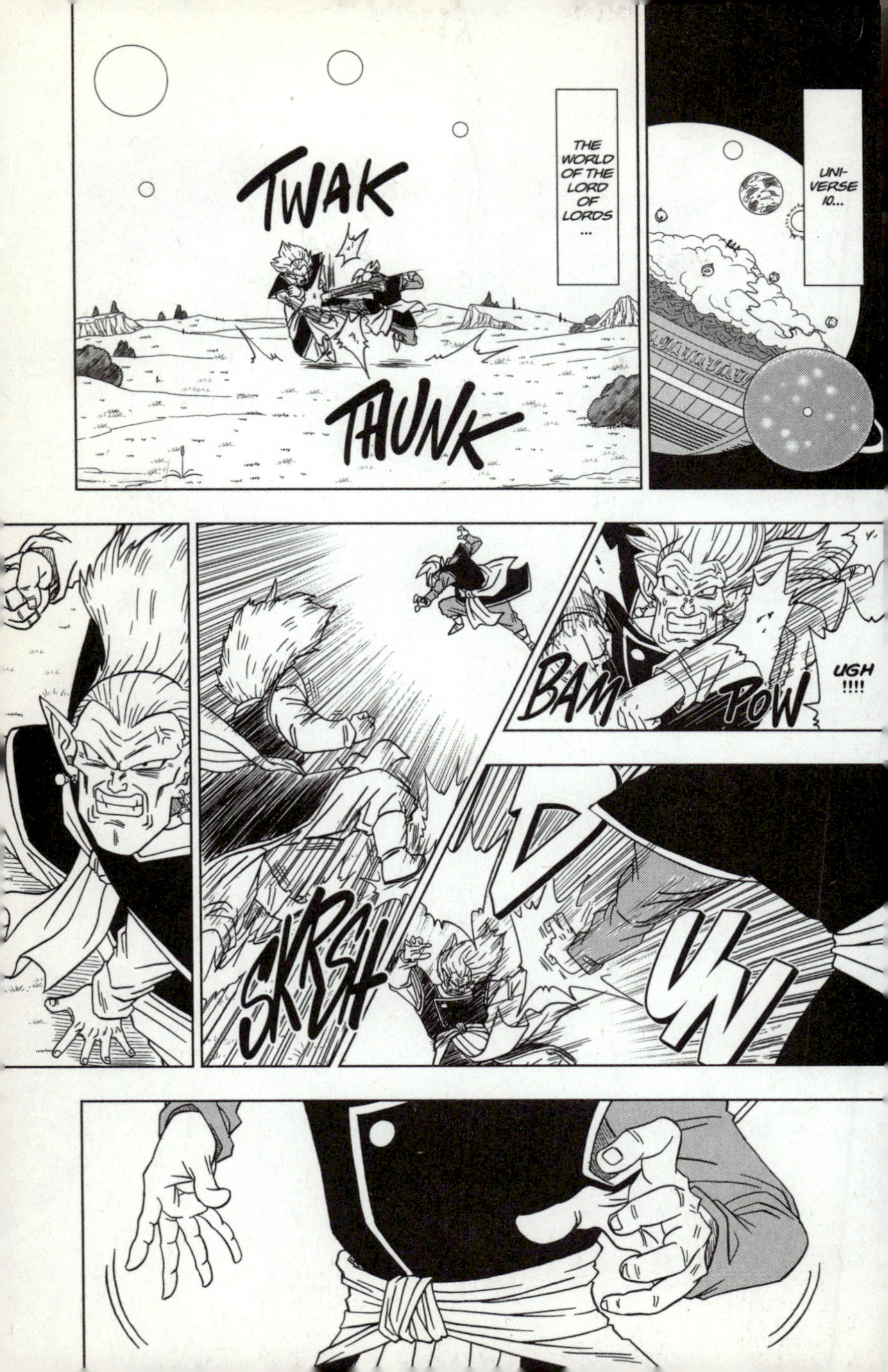
UNIVERSE 10...
THE WORLD OF THE LORD OF LORDS ...
TWAK
THUNK
UGH !!!!
POW
BAM
SKRSH

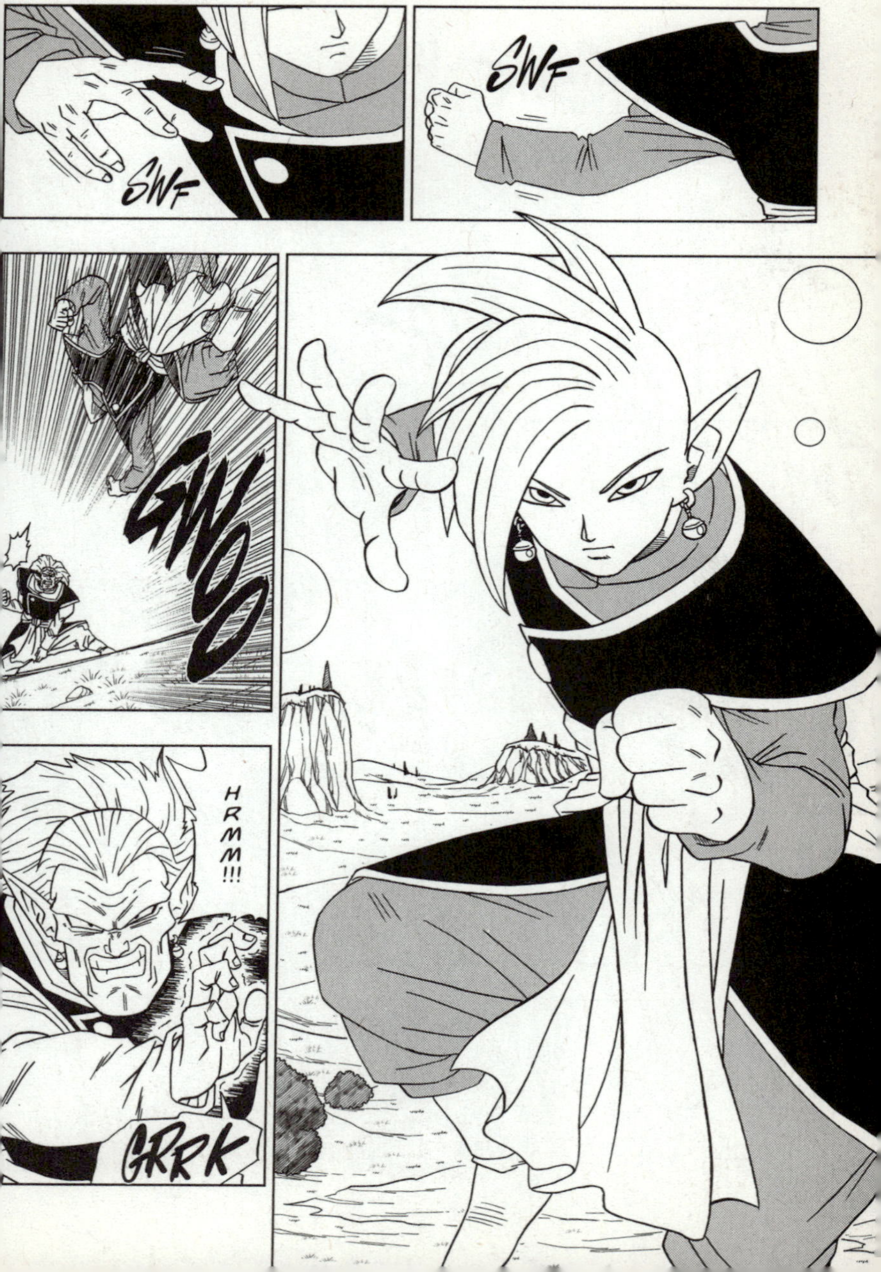
SWF
SWF
GWOO
HRMM!!!
GRRK

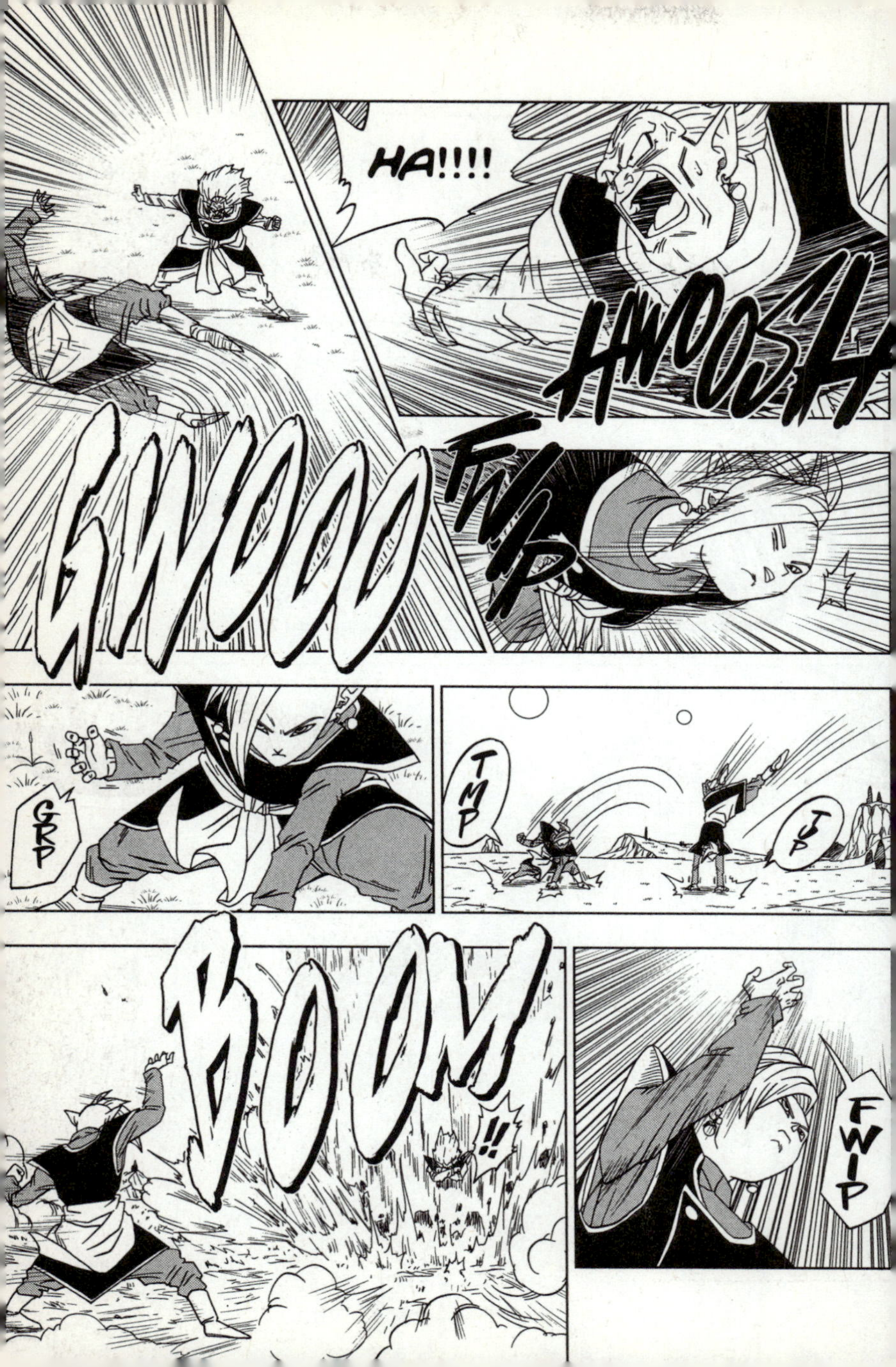
HA!!!!
WHOOSH
FWMP
GWOOO
JUP
TMP
GRP
FWIP
BOOM
!!

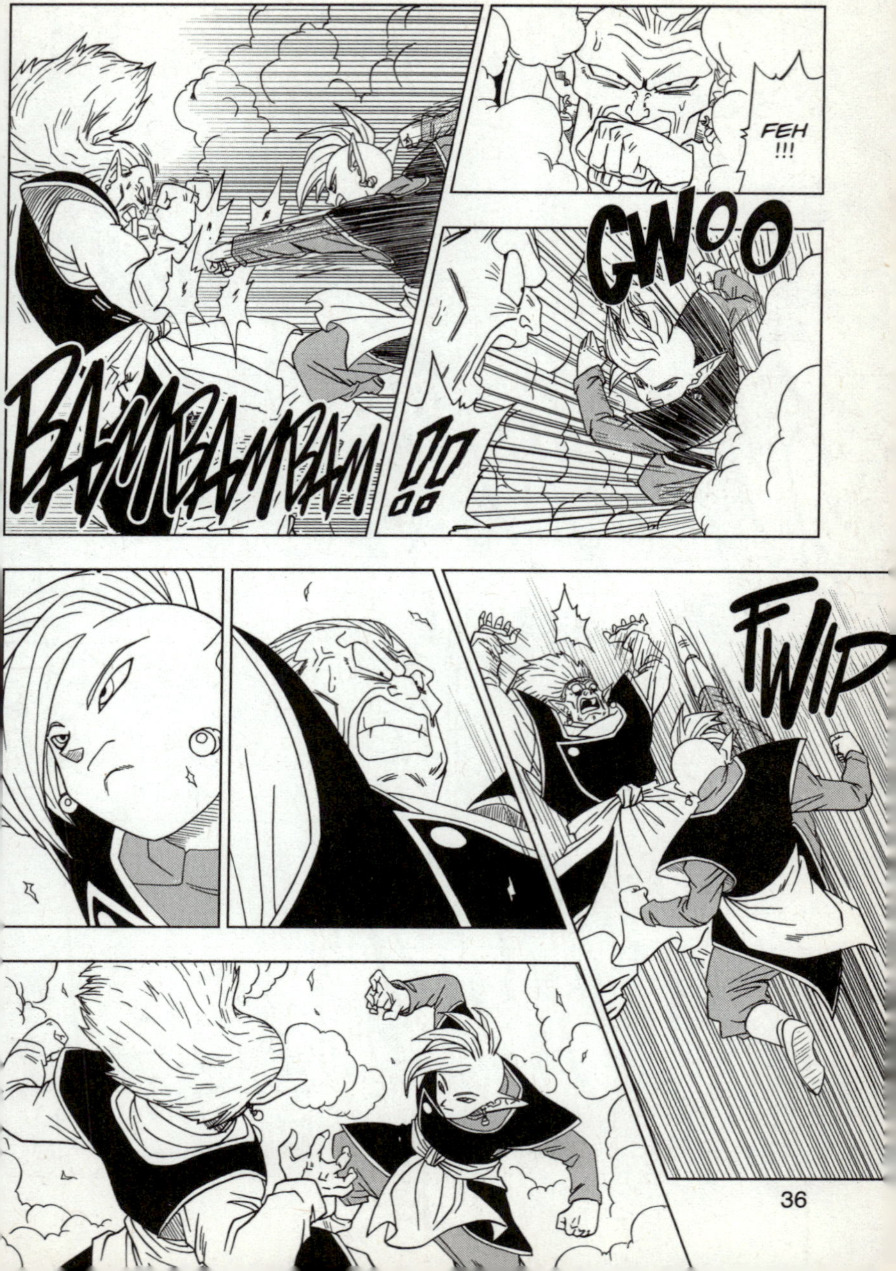

FEH !!!
GWOO
BAMBAMBAM !?
FWIP

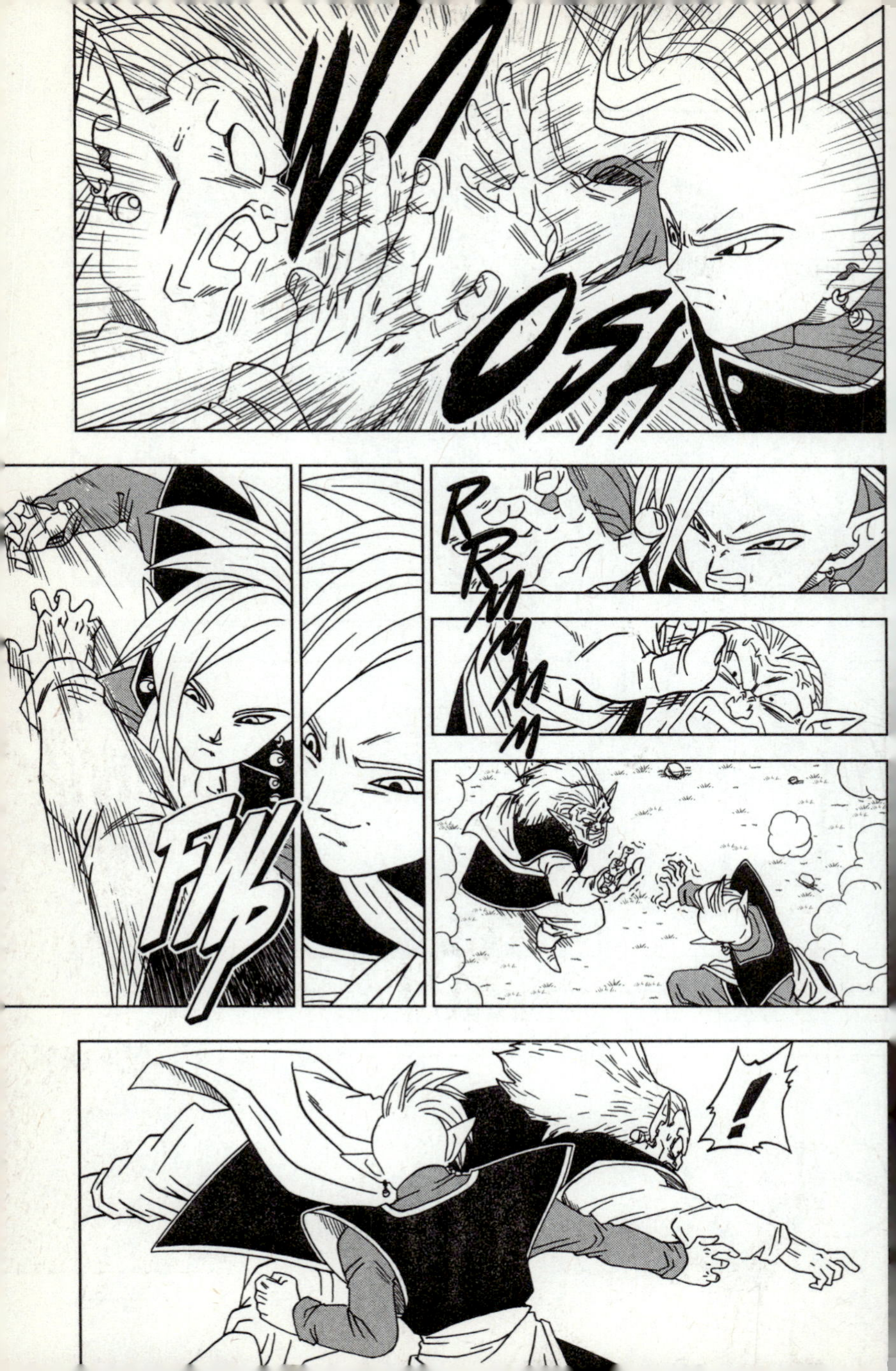
WHOOSH
RRMMMMM
FWP
!

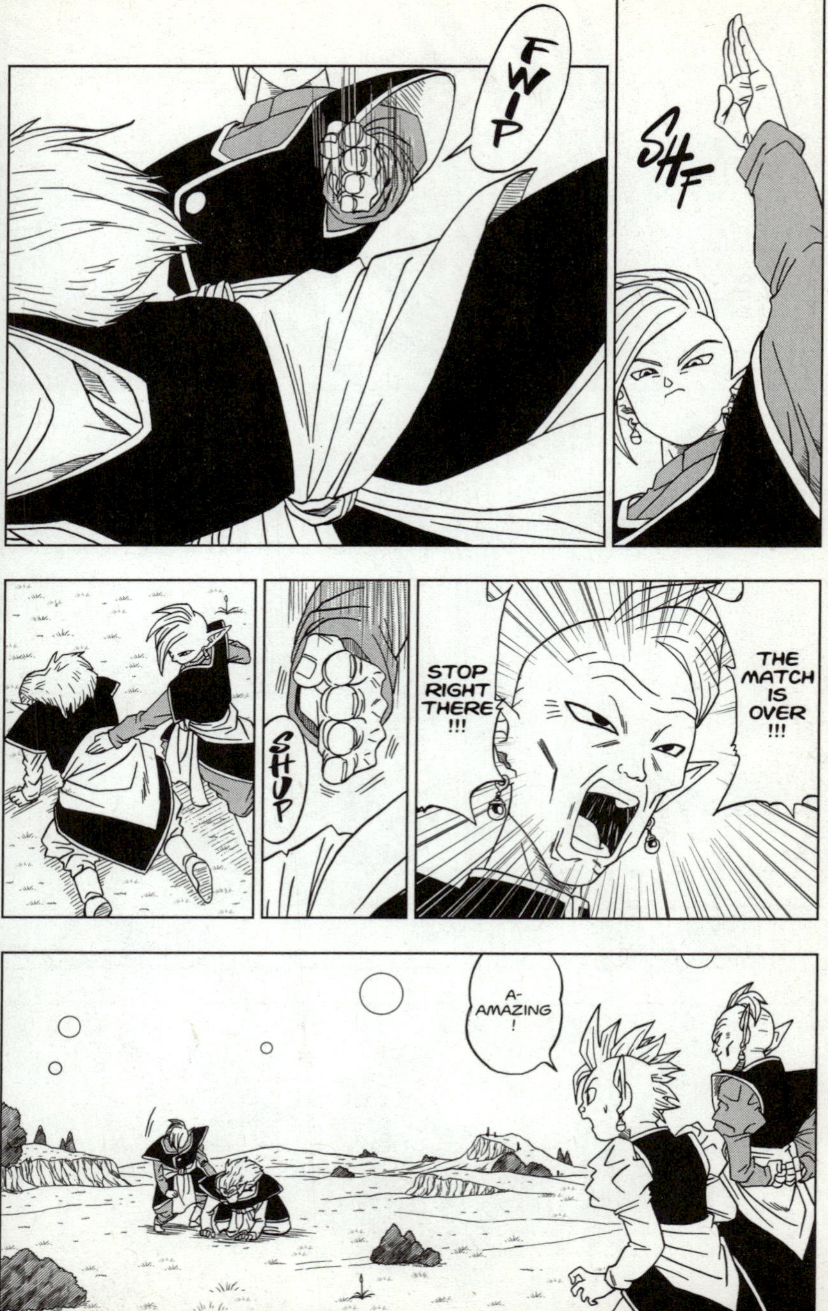
SHF
FWIP
THE MATCH IS OVER!!!
STOP RIGHT THERE!!!
SHUP
A-AMAZING!

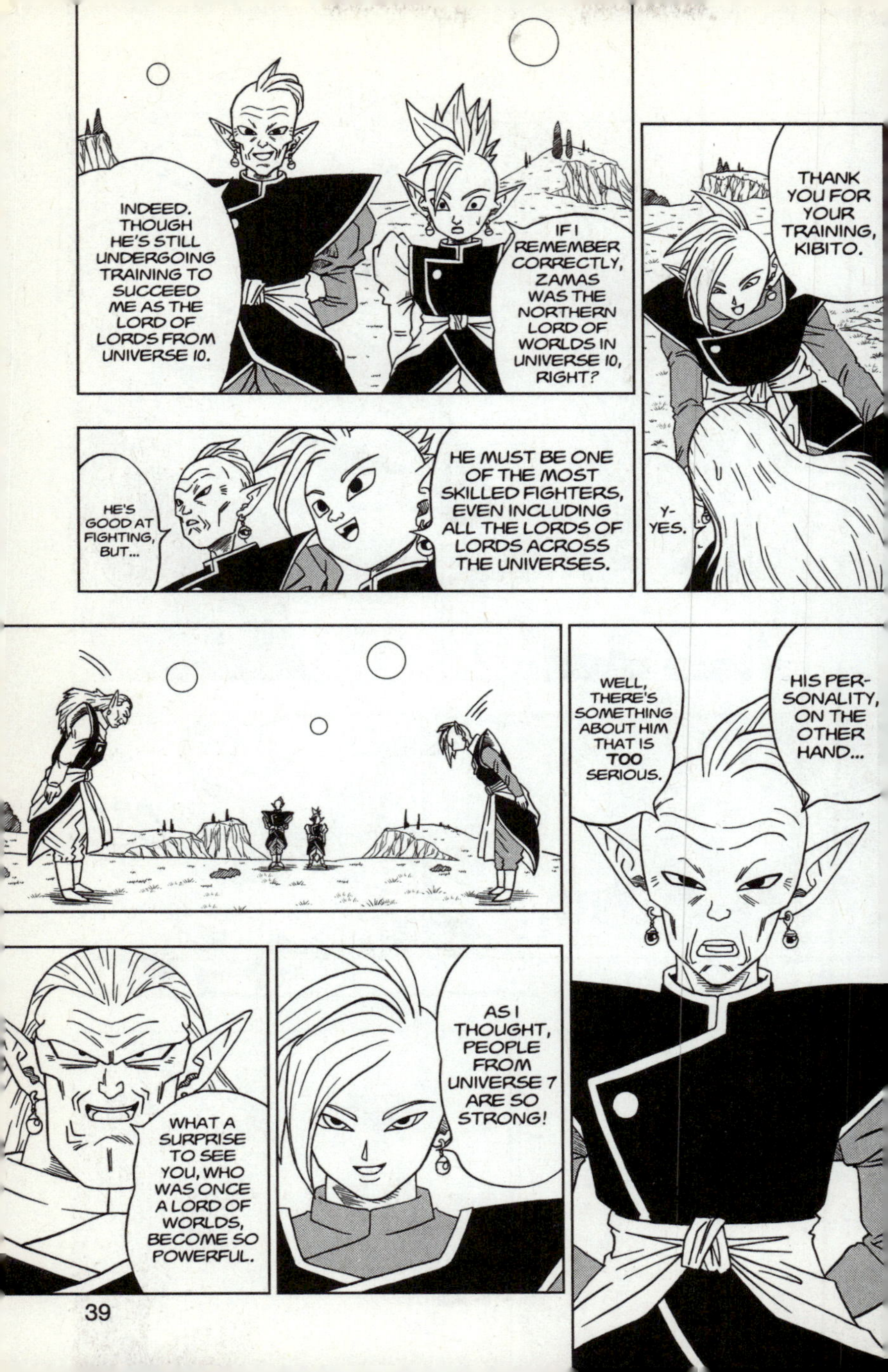
THANK YOU FOR YOUR TRAINING, KIBITO.
Y-YES.
IF I REMEMBER CORRECTLY, ZAMAS WAS THE NORTHERN LORD OF WORLDS IN UNIVERSE 10, RIGHT?
INDEED. THOUGH HE'S STILL UNDERGOING TRAINING TO SUCCEED ME AS THE LORD OF LORDS FROM UNIVERSE 10.
HE MUST BE ONE OF THE MOST SKILLED FIGHTERS, EVEN INCLUDING ALL THE LORDS OF LORDS ACROSS THE UNIVERSES.
HE'S GOOD AT FIGHTING, BUT...
HIS PERSONALITY, ON THE OTHER HAND...
WELL, THERE'S SOMETHING ABOUT HIM THAT IS **TOO** SERIOUS.
AS I THOUGHT, PEOPLE FROM UNIVERSE 7 ARE SO STRONG!
WHAT A SURPRISE TO SEE YOU, WHO WAS ONCE A LORD OF WORLDS, BECOME SO POWERFUL.

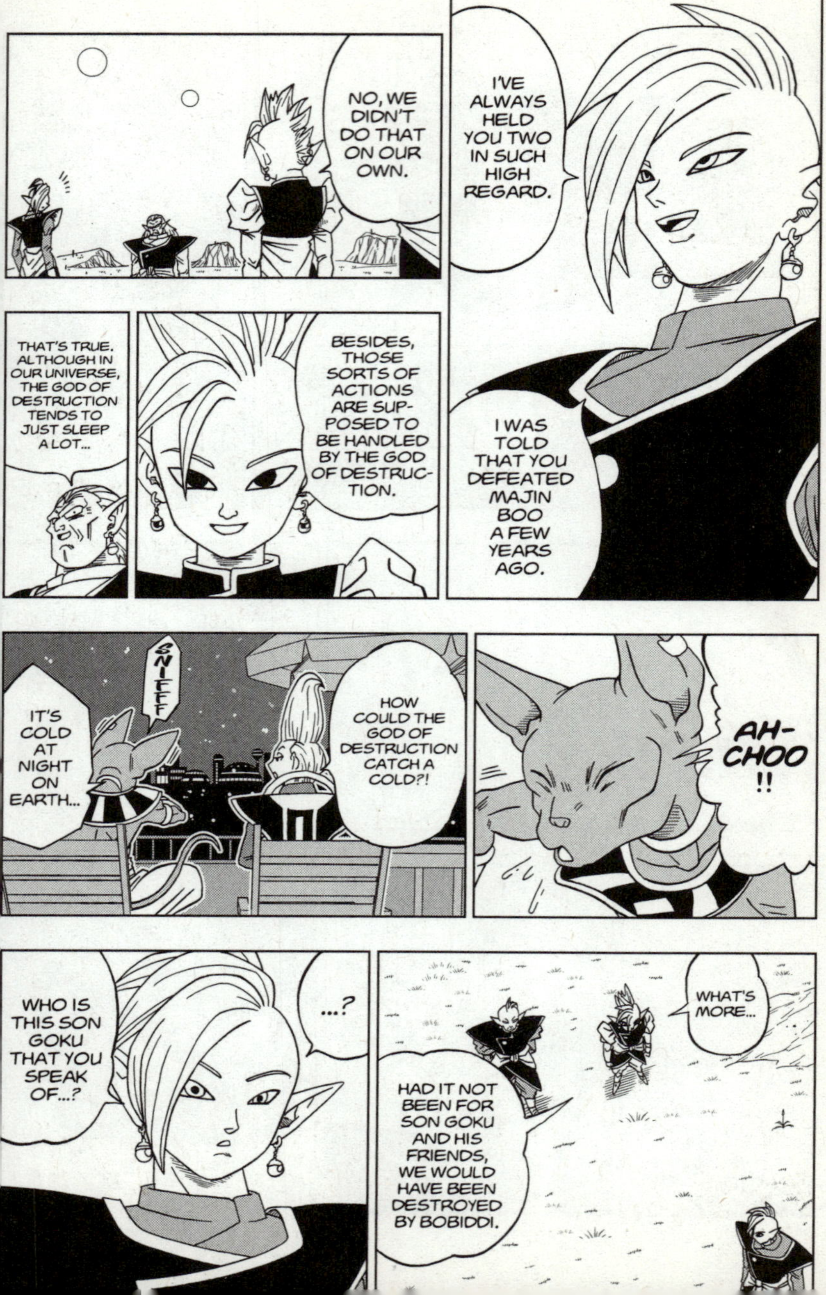
I'VE ALWAYS HELD YOU TWO IN SUCH HIGH REGARD.
I WAS TOLD THAT YOU DEFEATED MAJIN BOO A FEW YEARS AGO.
NO, WE DIDN'T DO THAT ON OUR OWN.
BESIDES, THOSE SORTS OF ACTIONS ARE SUP-POSED TO BE HANDLED BY THE GOD OF DESTRUC-TION.
THAT'S TRUE. ALTHOUGH IN OUR UNIVERSE, THE GOD OF DESTRUCTION TENDS TO JUST SLEEP A LOT...
AH-CHOO!!
HOW COULD THE GOD OF DESTRUCTION CATCH A COLD?!
SNIFFF
IT'S COLD AT NIGHT ON EARTH...
WHAT'S MORE...
HAD IT NOT BEEN FOR SON GOKU AND HIS FRIENDS, WE WOULD HAVE BEEN DESTROYED BY BOBIDDI.
...?
WHO IS THIS SON GOKU THAT YOU SPEAK OF...?

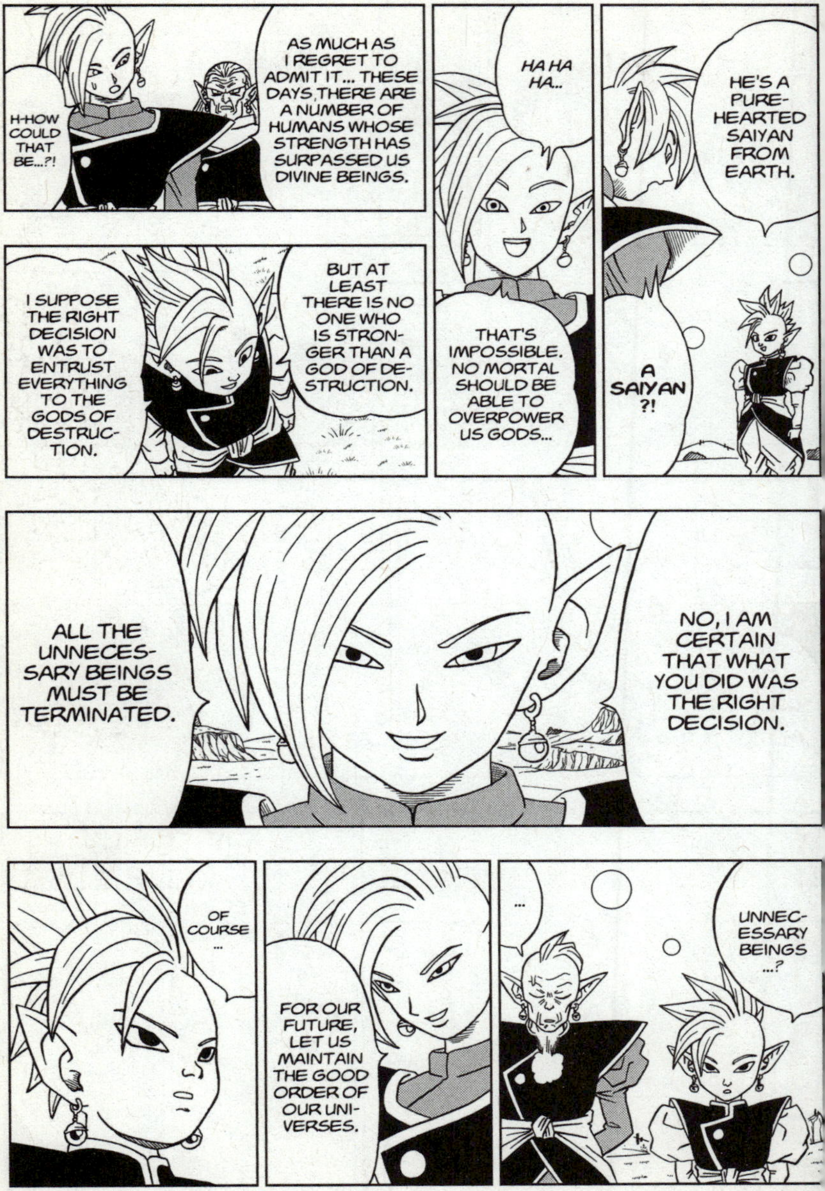
HE'S A PURE-HEARTED SAIYAN FROM EARTH.
A SAIYAN?!
HA HA HA...
THAT'S IMPOSSIBLE. NO MORTAL SHOULD BE ABLE TO OVERPOWER US GODS...
AS MUCH AS I REGRET TO ADMIT IT... THESE DAYS, THERE ARE A NUMBER OF HUMANS WHOSE STRENGTH HAS SURPASSED US DIVINE BEINGS.
H-HOW COULD THAT BE...?!
BUT AT LEAST THERE IS NO ONE WHO IS STRONGER THAN A GOD OF DESTRUCTION.
I SUPPOSE THE RIGHT DECISION WAS TO ENTRUST EVERYTHING TO THE GODS OF DESTRUCTION.
NO, I AM CERTAIN THAT WHAT YOU DID WAS THE RIGHT DECISION.
ALL THE UNNECESSARY BEINGS MUST BE TERMINATED.
UNNECESSARY BEINGS ...?
...
FOR OUR FUTURE, LET US MAINTAIN THE GOOD ORDER OF OUR UNIVERSES.
OF COURSE ...

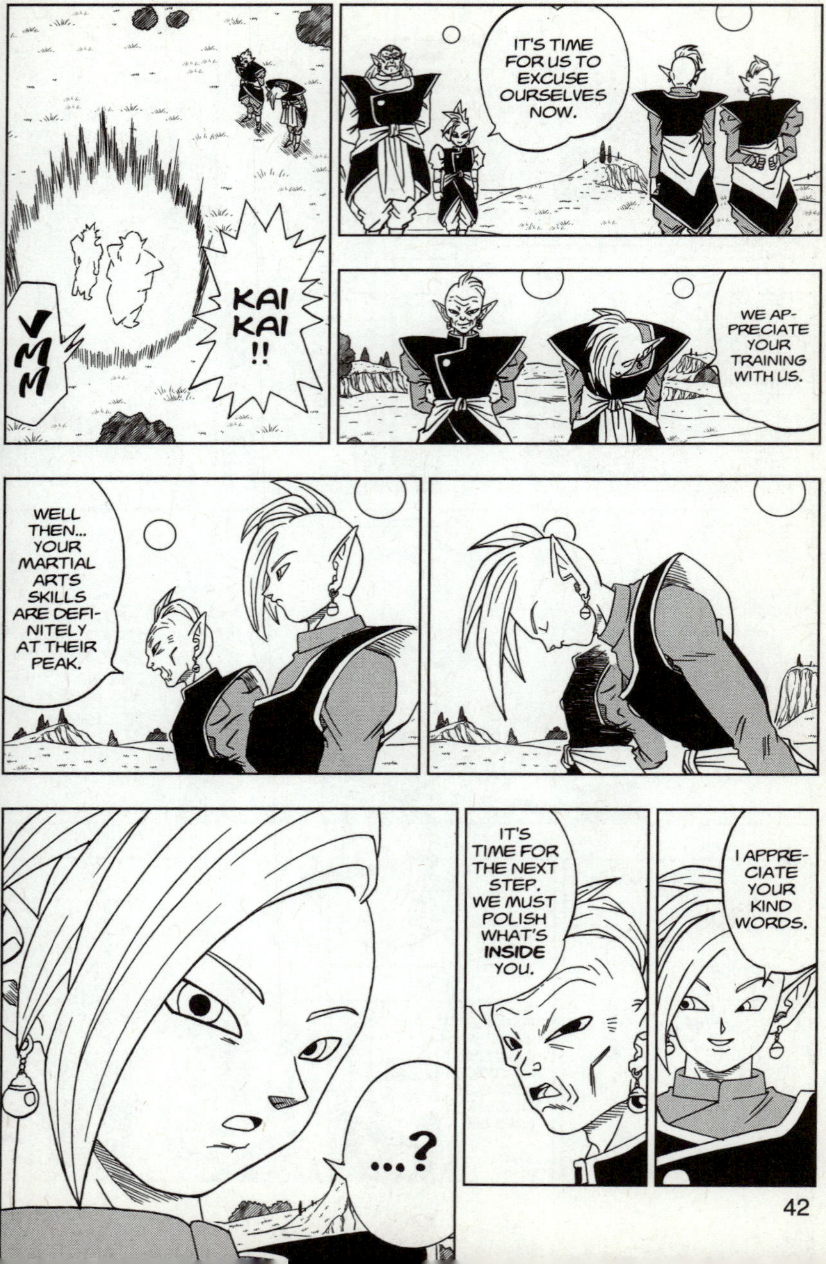
IT'S TIME FOR US TO EXCUSE OURSELVES NOW.
WE AP-PRECIATE YOUR TRAINING WITH US.
KAI KAI !!
VMMM
WELL THEN... YOUR MARTIAL ARTS SKILLS ARE DEFI-NITELY AT THEIR PEAK.
I APPRE-CIATE YOUR KIND WORDS.
IT'S TIME FOR THE NEXT STEP. WE MUST POLISH WHAT'S **INSIDE** YOU.
...?

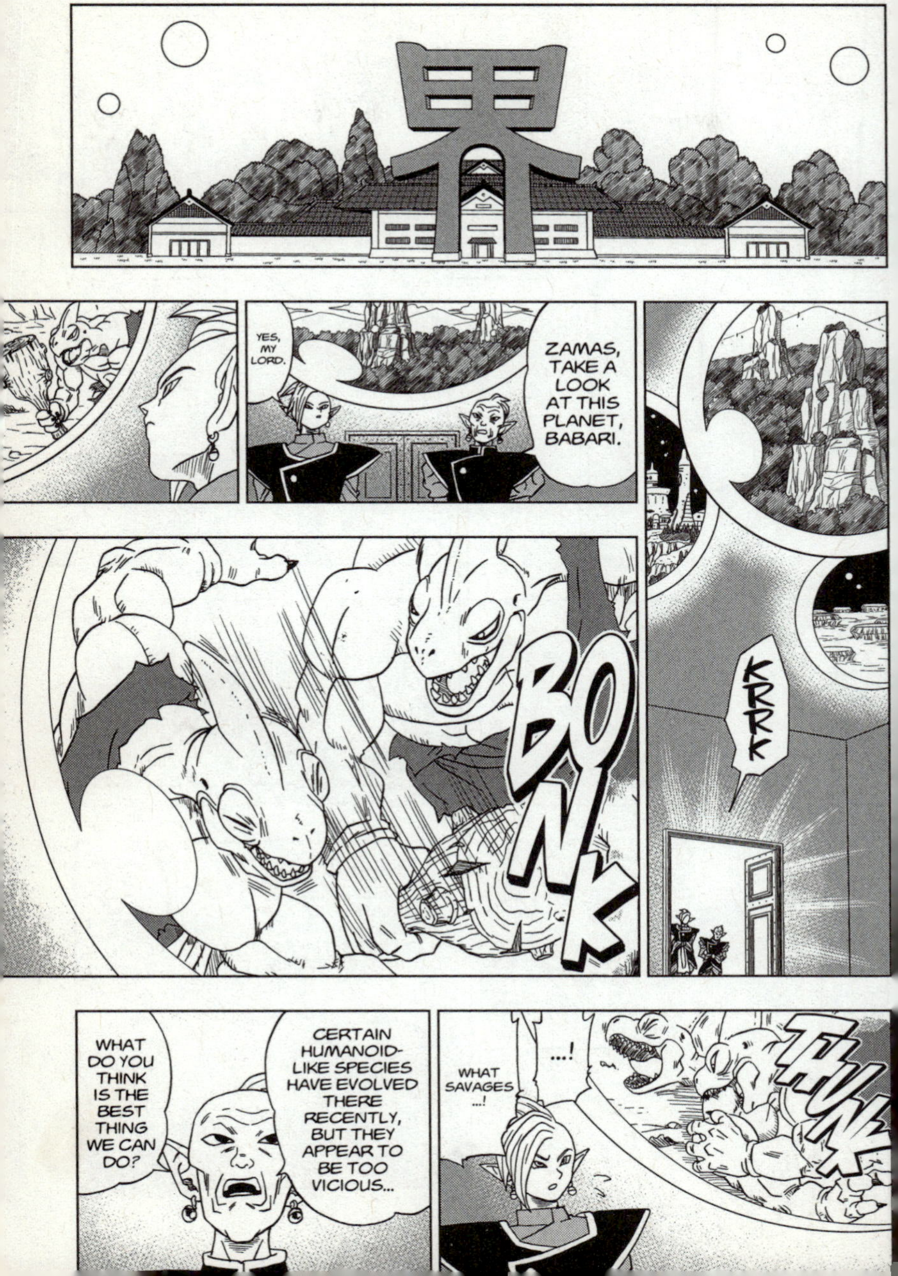
ZAMAS, TAKE A LOOK AT THIS PLANET, BABARI.
YES, MY LORD.
KRRK
BONK
THUNK
....!
WHAT SAVAGES ...!
CERTAIN HUMANOID-LIKE SPECIES HAVE EVOLVED THERE RECENTLY, BUT THEY APPEAR TO BE TOO VICIOUS...
WHAT DO YOU THINK IS THE BEST THING WE CAN DO?

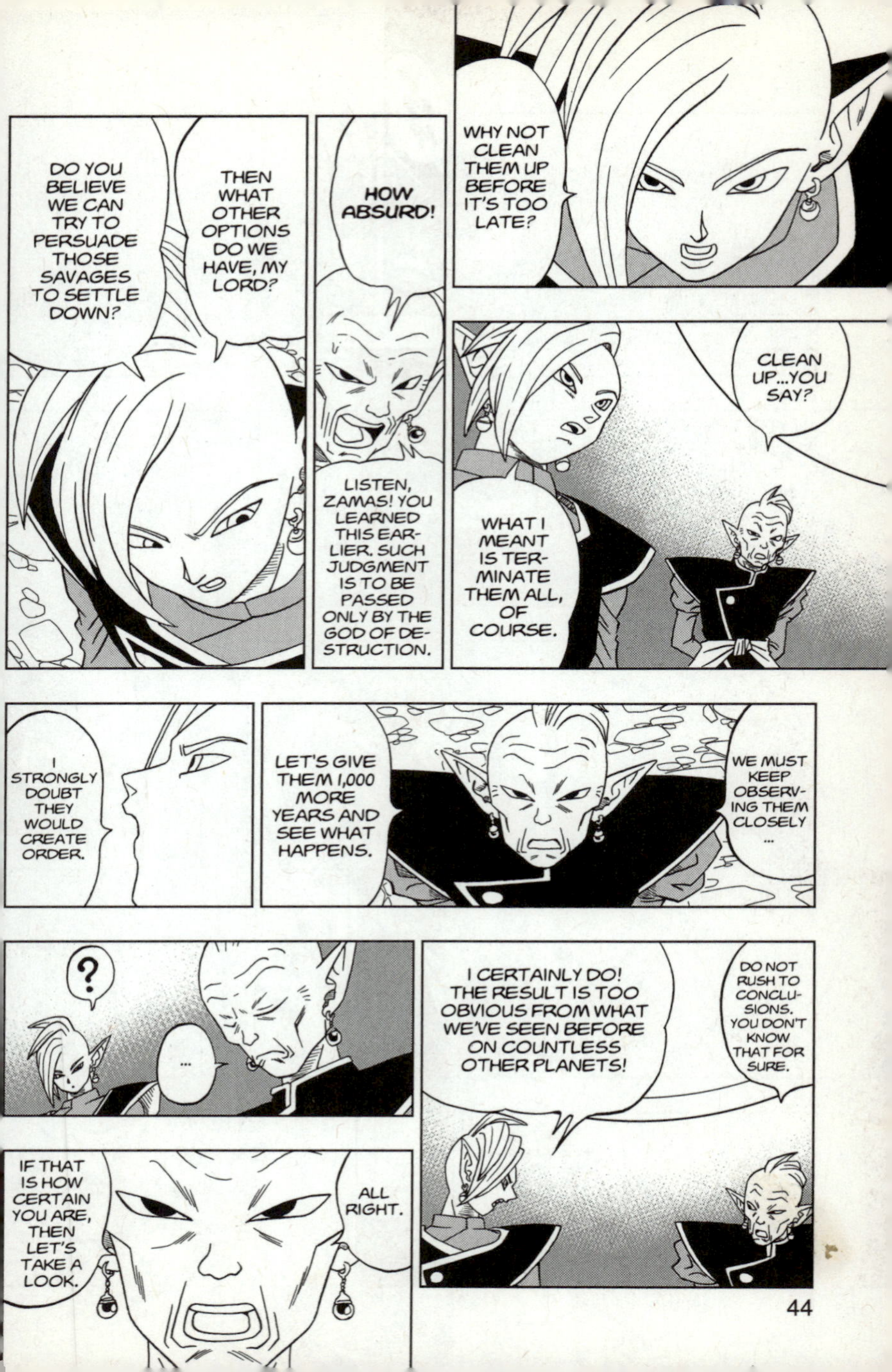
WHY NOT CLEAN THEM UP BEFORE IT'S TOO LATE?
CLEAN UP...YOU SAY?
WHAT I MEANT IS TERMINATE THEM ALL, OF COURSE.
HOW ABSURD!
LISTEN, ZAMAS! YOU LEARNED THIS EARLIER. SUCH JUDGMENT IS TO BE PASSED ONLY BY THE GOD OF DESTRUCTION.
THEN WHAT OTHER OPTIONS DO WE HAVE, MY LORD?
DO YOU BELIEVE WE CAN TRY TO PERSUADE THOSE SAVAGES TO SETTLE DOWN?
WE MUST KEEP OBSERVING THEM CLOSELY...
LET'S GIVE THEM 1,000 MORE YEARS AND SEE WHAT HAPPENS.
I STRONGLY DOUBT THEY WOULD CREATE ORDER.
DO NOT RUSH TO CONCLUSIONS. YOU DON'T KNOW THAT FOR SURE.
I CERTAINLY DO! THE RESULT IS TOO OBVIOUS FROM WHAT WE'VE SEEN BEFORE ON COUNTLESS OTHER PLANETS!
?
...
ALL RIGHT.
IF THAT IS HOW CERTAIN YOU ARE, THEN LET'S TAKE A LOOK.

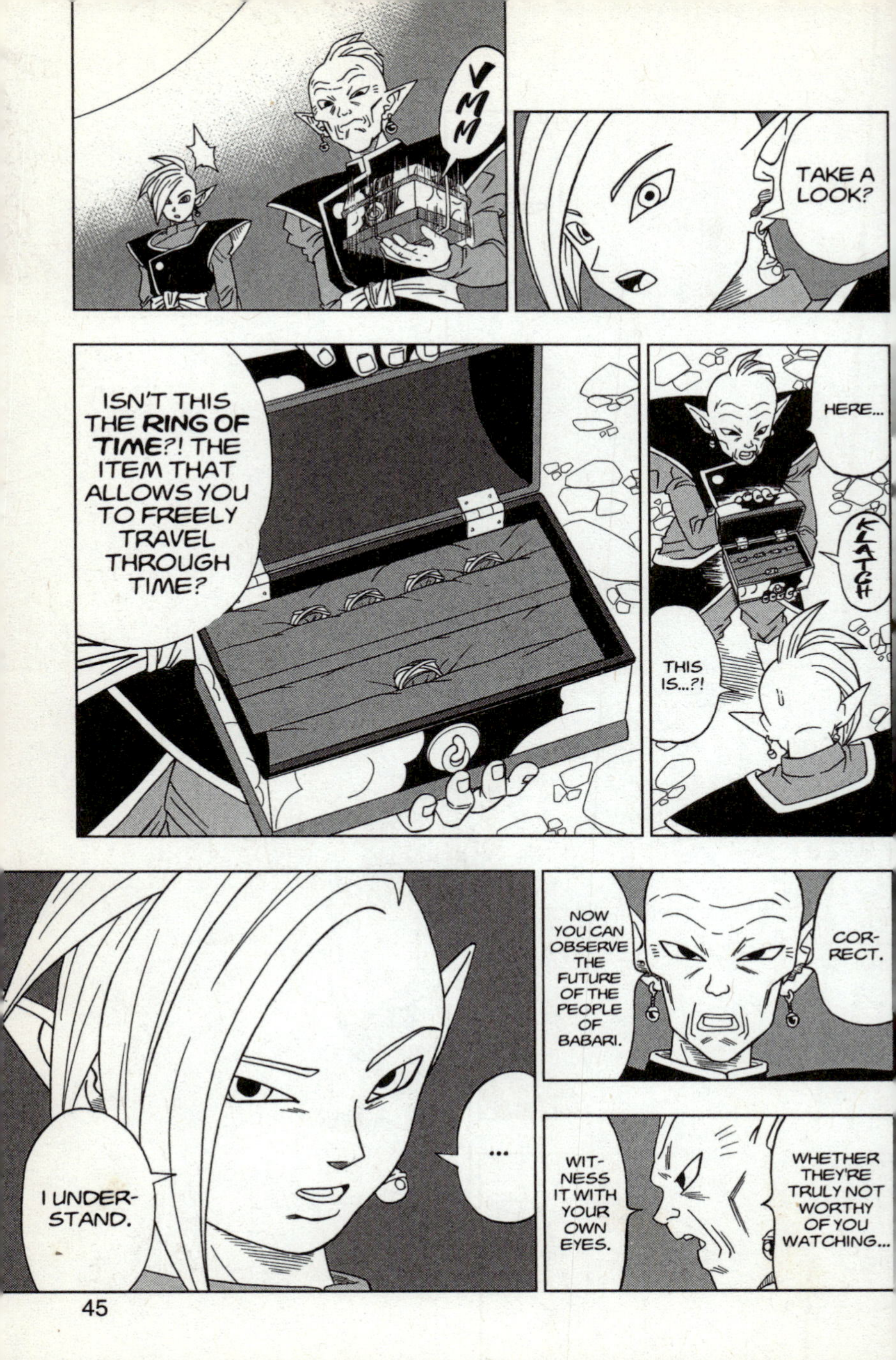
TAKE A LOOK?
VMM
HERE...
KLATCH
THIS IS...?!
ISN'T THIS THE **RING OF TIME**?! THE ITEM THAT ALLOWS YOU TO FREELY TRAVEL THROUGH TIME?
COR-RECT.
NOW YOU CAN OBSERVE THE FUTURE OF THE PEOPLE OF BABARI.
WHETHER THEY'RE TRULY NOT WORTHY OF YOU WATCHING...
WIT-NESS IT WITH YOUR OWN EYES.
...
I UNDER-STAND.

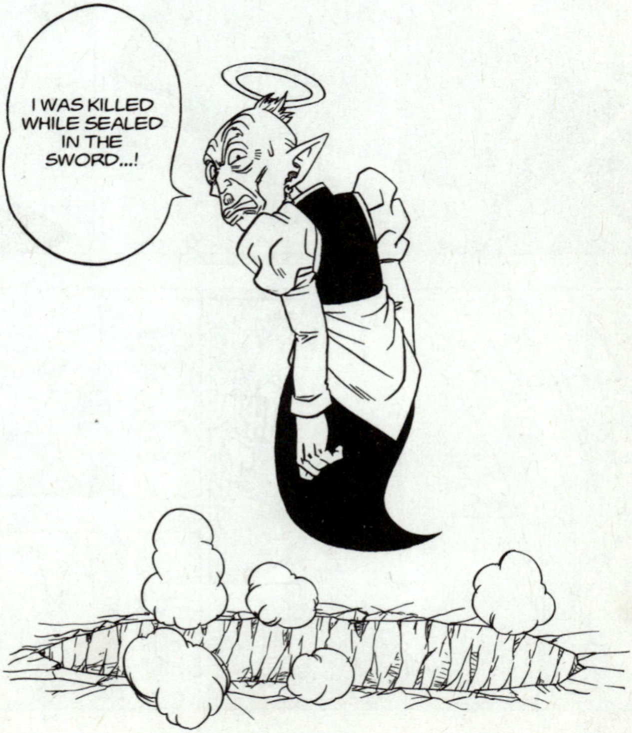
I WAS KILLED WHILE SEALED IN THE SWORD...!

DRAGON BALL SUPER

## CHAPTER 17: ZAMAS: THE NEXT LORD OF LORDS FROM UNIVERSE 10

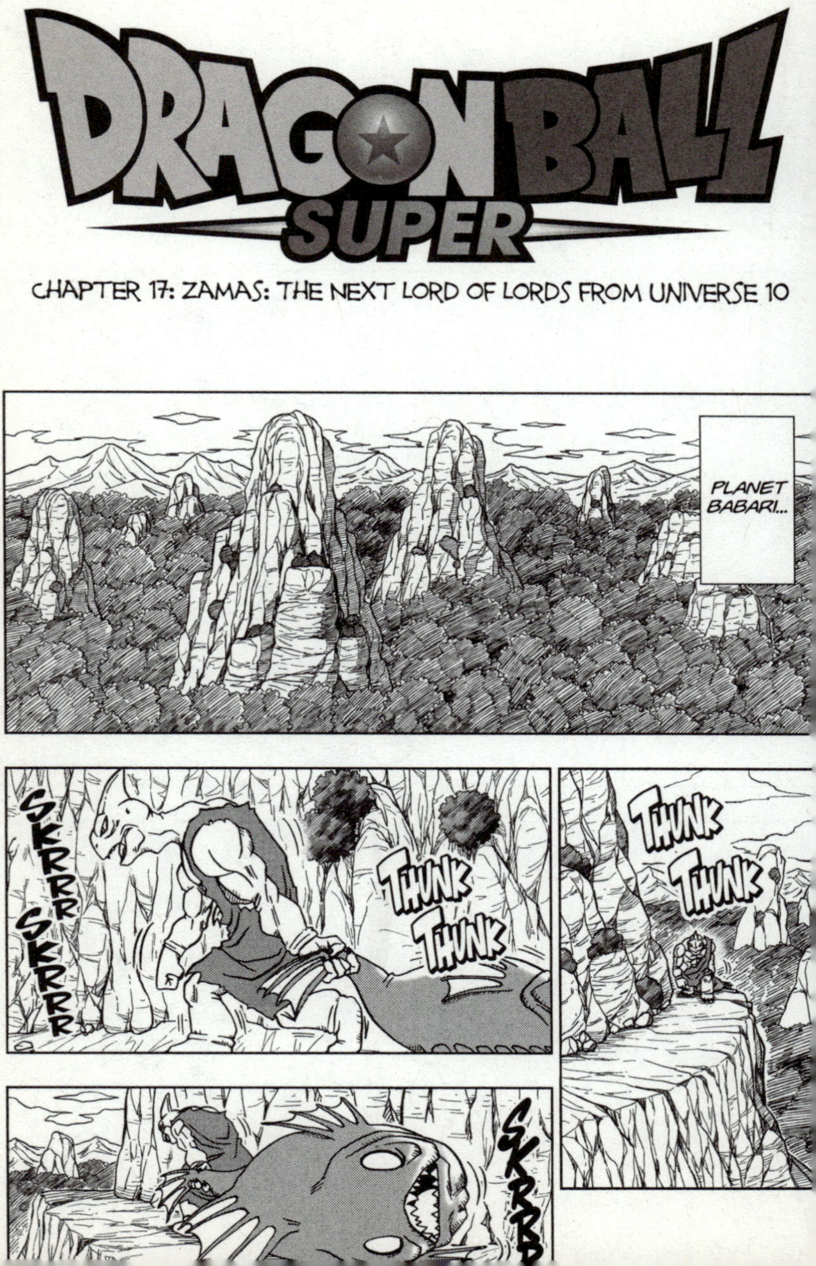
PLANET BABARI...
THUNK THUNK
THUNK THUNK
SKRRR SKRRR
SKRRR

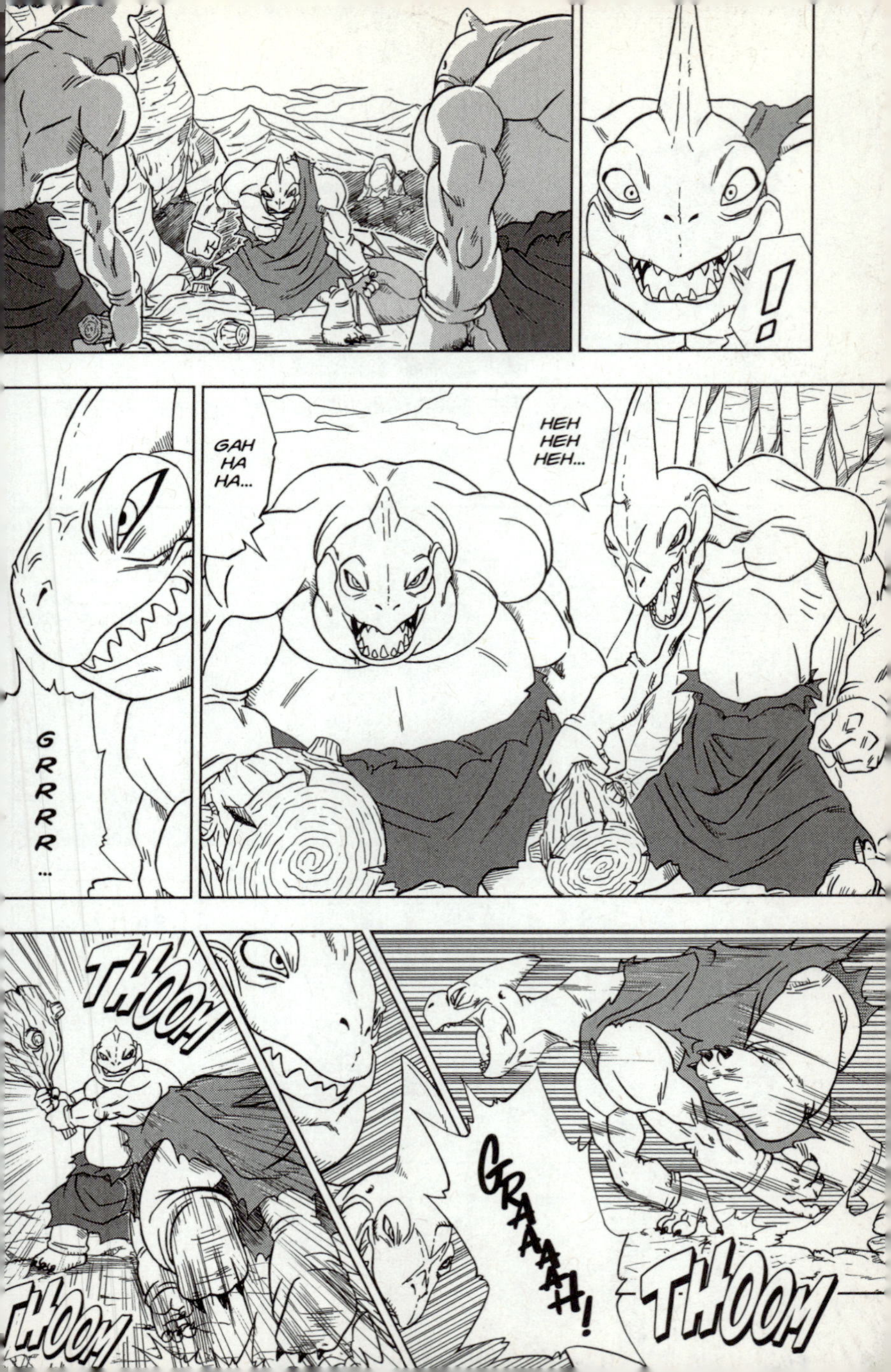
!
HEH HEH HEH...
GAH HA HA...
GRRRR...
THOOM
GRAAAAH!
THOOM
THOOM

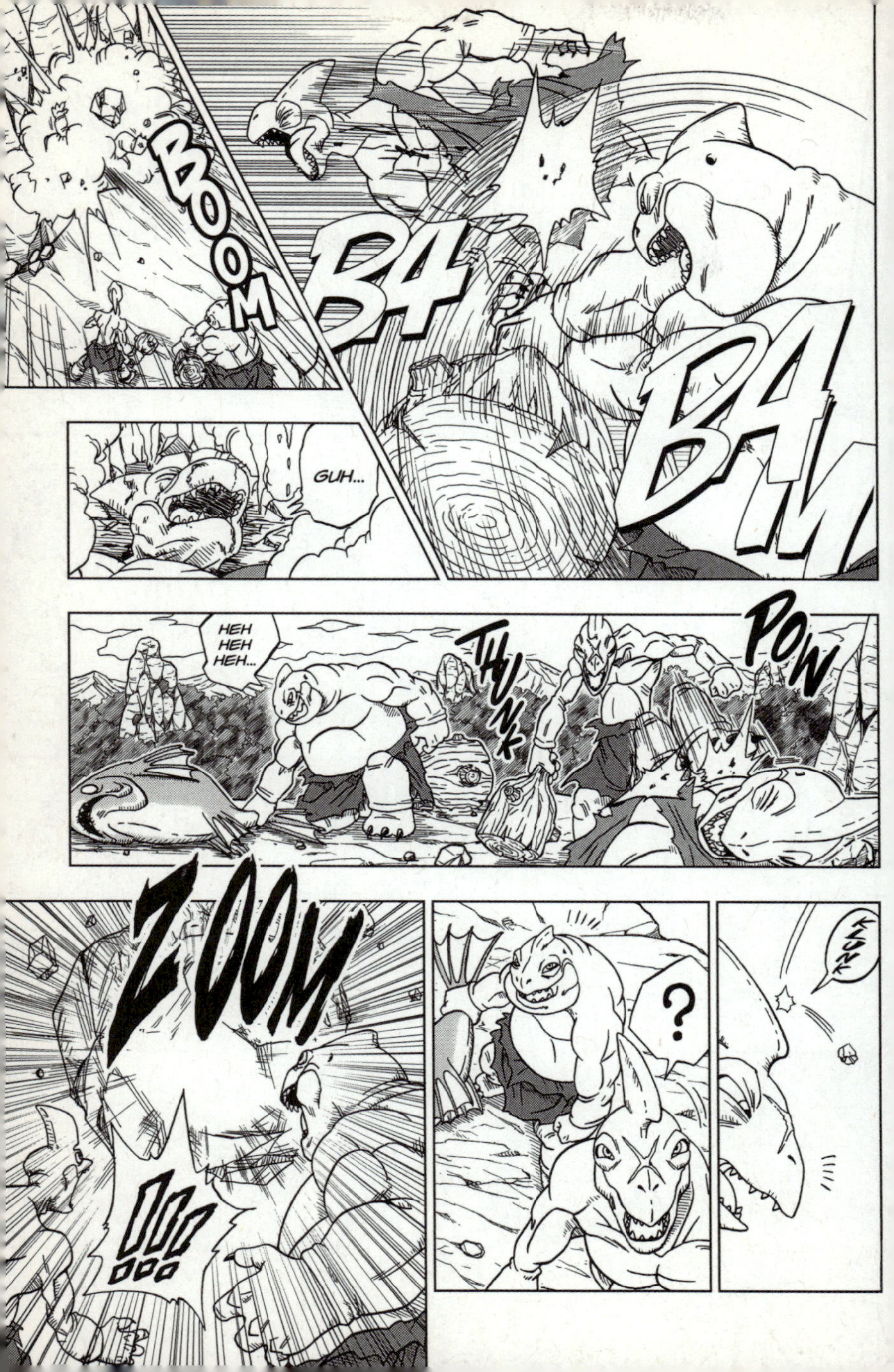
BA
BAM
BOOM
GUH...
POW
THUNK
HEH HEH HEH...
KCHUNK
?
ZOOM

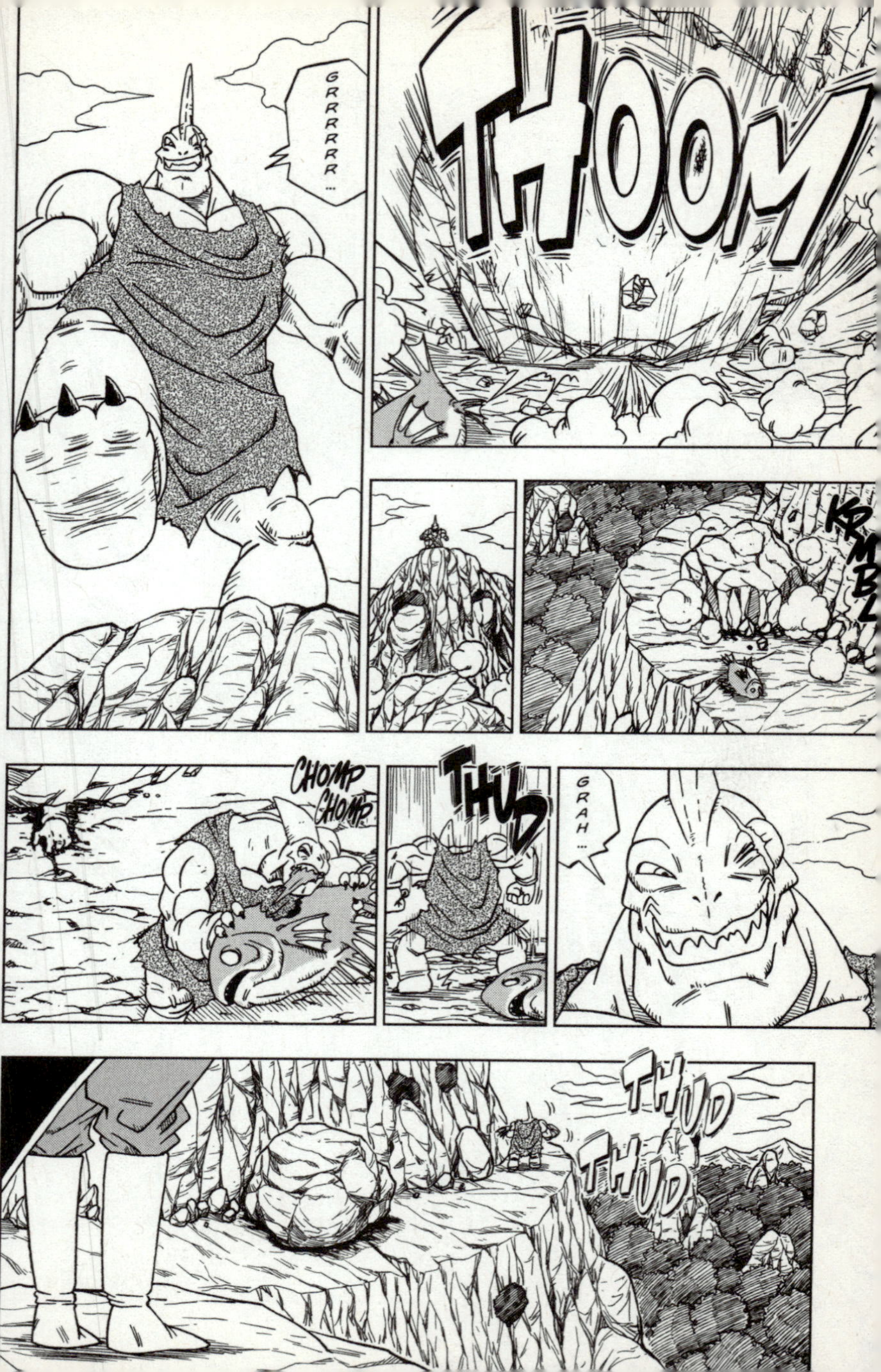
THOOM
KRMBL
GRRRRRRR...
GRAH...
THUD
CHOMP CHOMP
THUD THUD

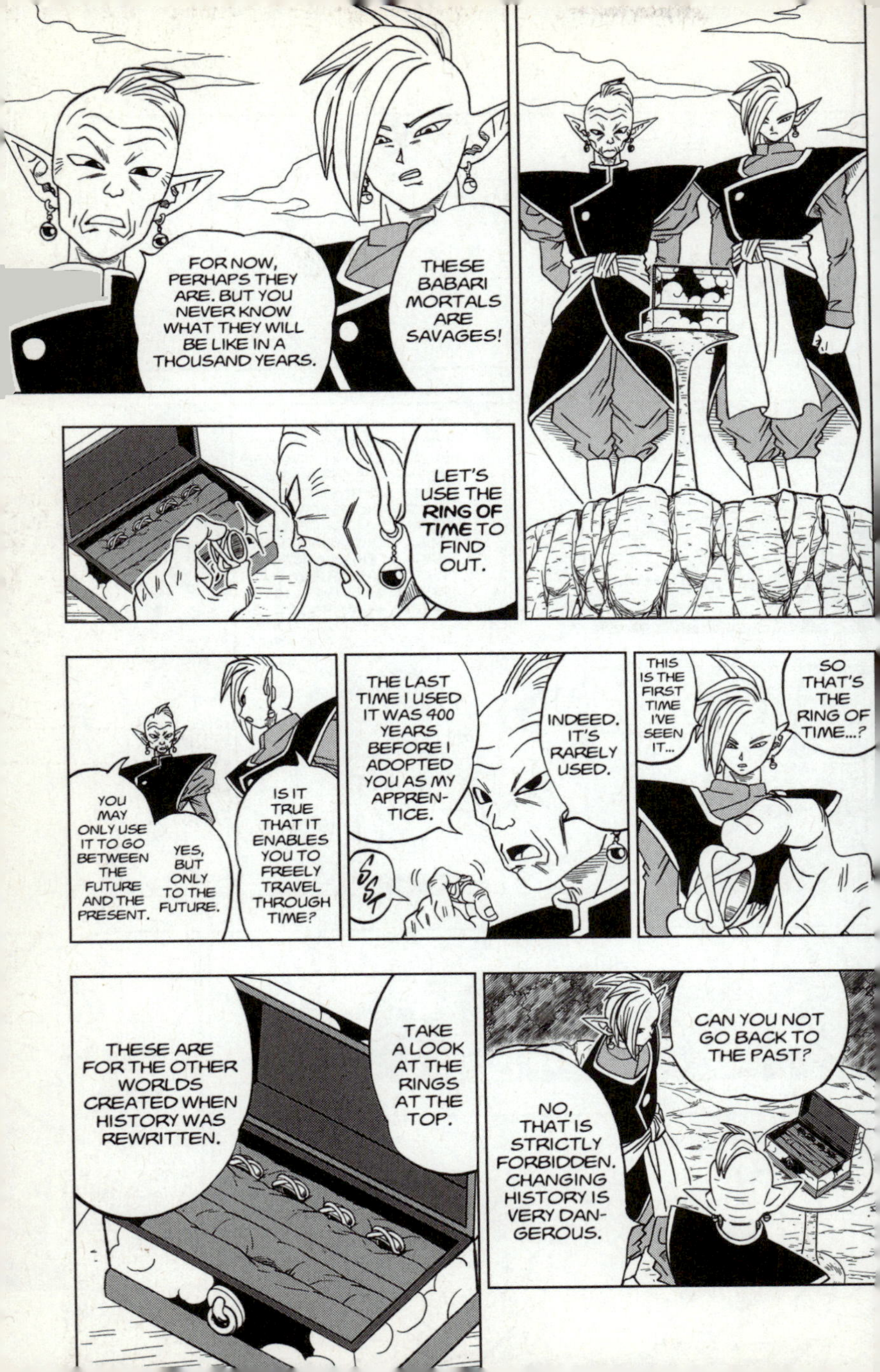
THESE BABARI MORTALS ARE SAVAGES!
FOR NOW, PERHAPS THEY ARE. BUT YOU NEVER KNOW WHAT THEY WILL BE LIKE IN A THOUSAND YEARS.
LET'S USE THE **RING OF TIME** TO FIND OUT.
SO THAT'S THE RING OF TIME...?
THIS IS THE FIRST TIME I'VE SEEN IT...
INDEED. IT'S RARELY USED.
THE LAST TIME I USED IT WAS 400 YEARS BEFORE I ADOPTED YOU AS MY APPRENTICE.
IS IT TRUE THAT IT ENABLES YOU TO FREELY TRAVEL THROUGH TIME?
YES, BUT ONLY TO THE FUTURE.
YOU MAY ONLY USE IT TO GO BETWEEN THE FUTURE AND THE PRESENT.
CAN YOU NOT GO BACK TO THE PAST?
NO, THAT IS STRICTLY FORBIDDEN. CHANGING HISTORY IS VERY DANGEROUS.
TAKE A LOOK AT THE RINGS AT THE TOP.
THESE ARE FOR THE OTHER WORLDS CREATED WHEN HISTORY WAS REWRITTEN.

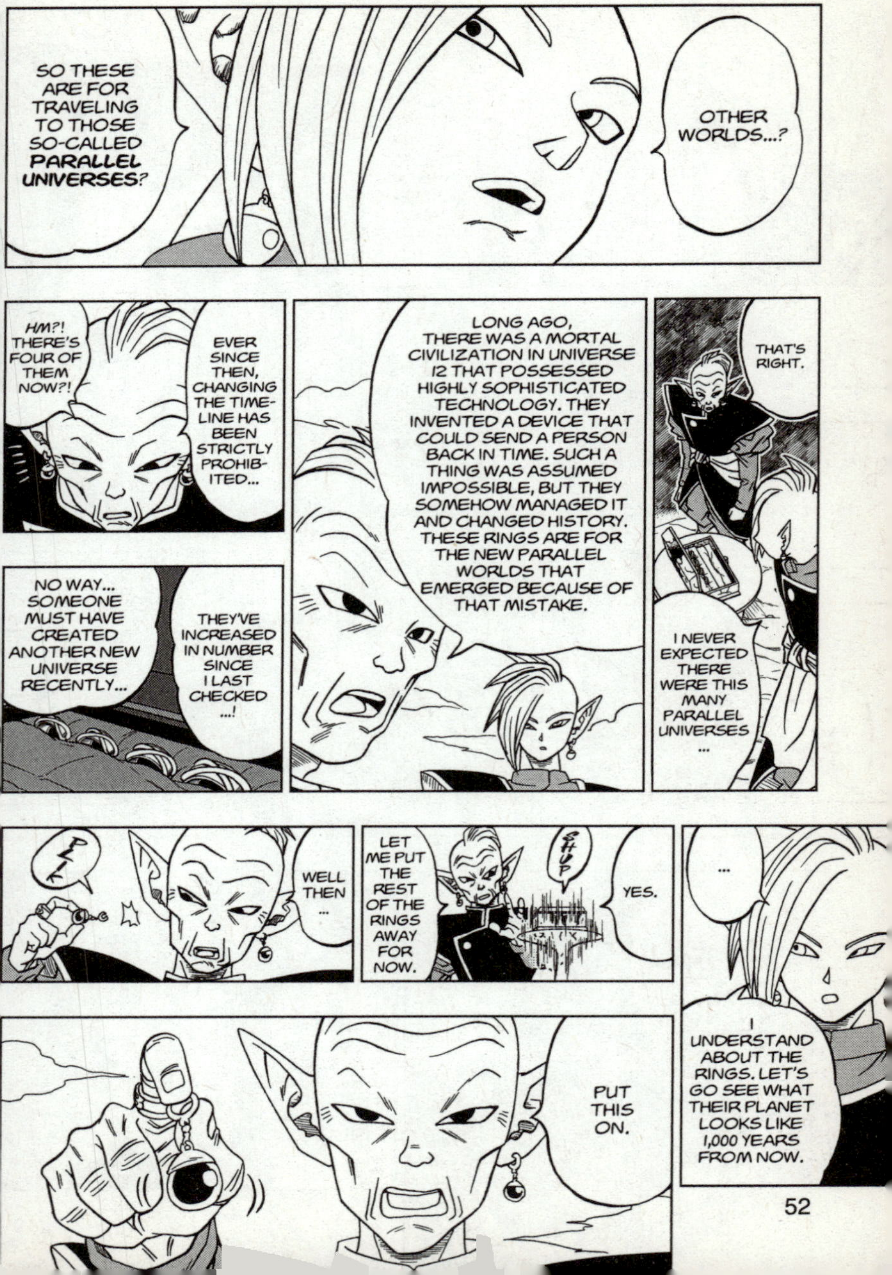
OTHER WORLDS...?
SO THESE ARE FOR TRAVELING TO THOSE SO-CALLED **PARALLEL UNIVERSES**?
THAT'S RIGHT.
I NEVER EXPECTED THERE WERE THIS MANY PARALLEL UNIVERSES...
LONG AGO, THERE WAS A MORTAL CIVILIZATION IN UNIVERSE 12 THAT POSSESSED HIGHLY SOPHISTICATED TECHNOLOGY. THEY INVENTED A DEVICE THAT COULD SEND A PERSON BACK IN TIME. SUCH A THING WAS ASSUMED IMPOSSIBLE, BUT THEY SOMEHOW MANAGED IT AND CHANGED HISTORY. THESE RINGS ARE FOR THE NEW PARALLEL WORLDS THAT EMERGED BECAUSE OF THAT MISTAKE.
EVER SINCE THEN, CHANGING THE TIME-LINE HAS BEEN STRICTLY PROHIB-ITED...
*HM?! THERE'S FOUR OF THEM NOW?!*
THEY'VE INCREASED IN NUMBER SINCE I LAST CHECKED ...!
NO WAY... SOMEONE MUST HAVE CREATED ANOTHER NEW UNIVERSE RECENTLY...
...
I UNDERSTAND ABOUT THE RINGS. LET'S GO SEE WHAT THEIR PLANET LOOKS LIKE 1,000 YEARS FROM NOW.
YES.
SHUP
LET ME PUT THE REST OF THE RINGS AWAY FOR NOW.
WELL THEN ...
PLIK
PUT THIS ON.

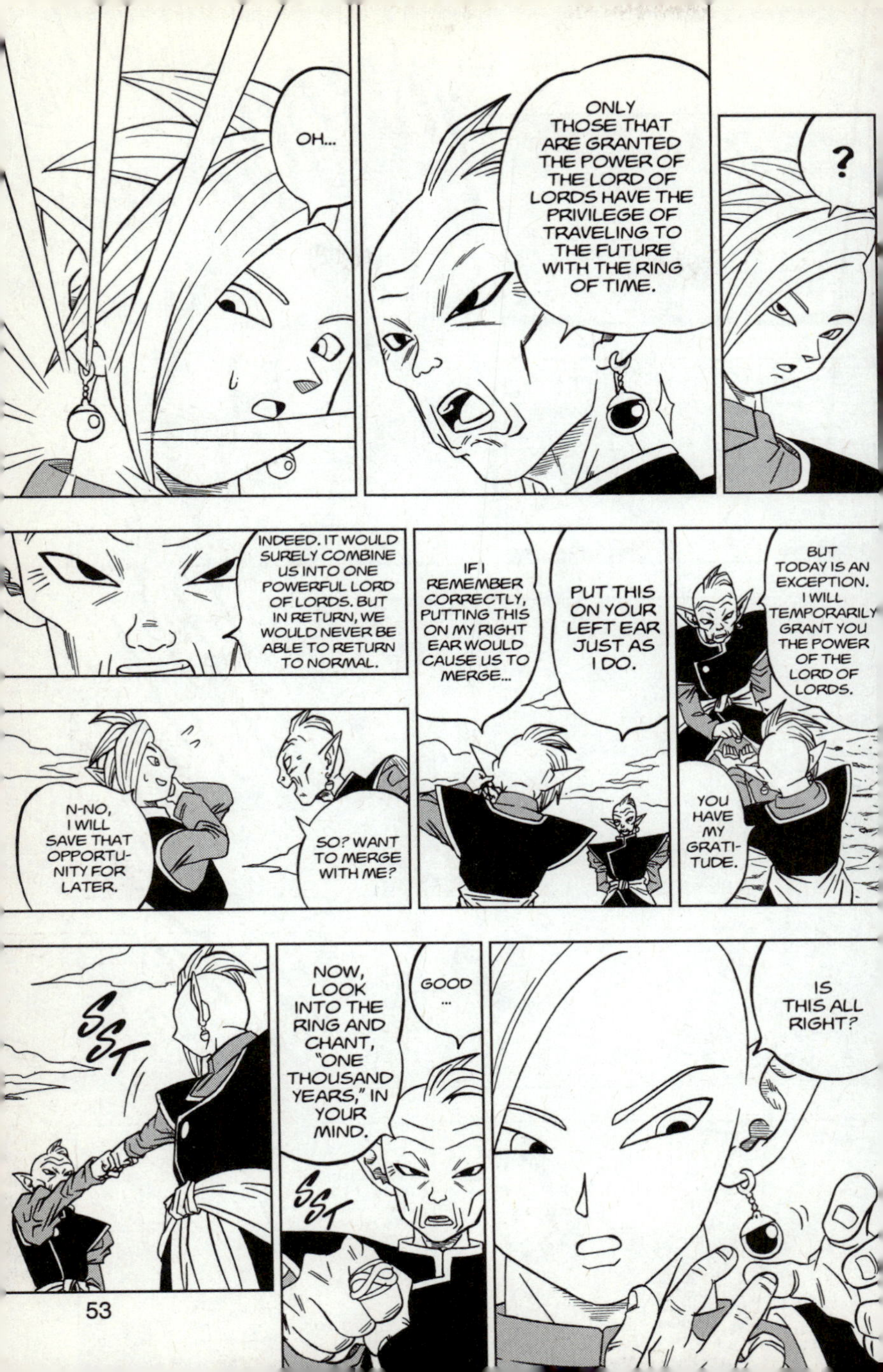
?
ONLY THOSE THAT ARE GRANTED THE POWER OF THE LORD OF LORDS HAVE THE PRIVILEGE OF TRAVELING TO THE FUTURE WITH THE RING OF TIME.
OH...
BUT TODAY IS AN EXCEPTION. I WILL TEMPORARILY GRANT YOU THE POWER OF THE LORD OF LORDS.
YOU HAVE MY GRATITUDE.
PUT THIS ON YOUR LEFT EAR JUST AS I DO.
IF I REMEMBER CORRECTLY, PUTTING THIS ON MY RIGHT EAR WOULD CAUSE US TO MERGE...
INDEED. IT WOULD SURELY COMBINE US INTO ONE POWERFUL LORD OF LORDS. BUT IN RETURN, WE WOULD NEVER BE ABLE TO RETURN TO NORMAL.
SO? WANT TO MERGE WITH ME?
N-NO, I WILL SAVE THAT OPPORTUNITY FOR LATER.
IS THIS ALL RIGHT?
GOOD ...
NOW, LOOK INTO THE RING AND CHANT, "ONE THOUSAND YEARS," IN YOUR MIND.
SST
SST

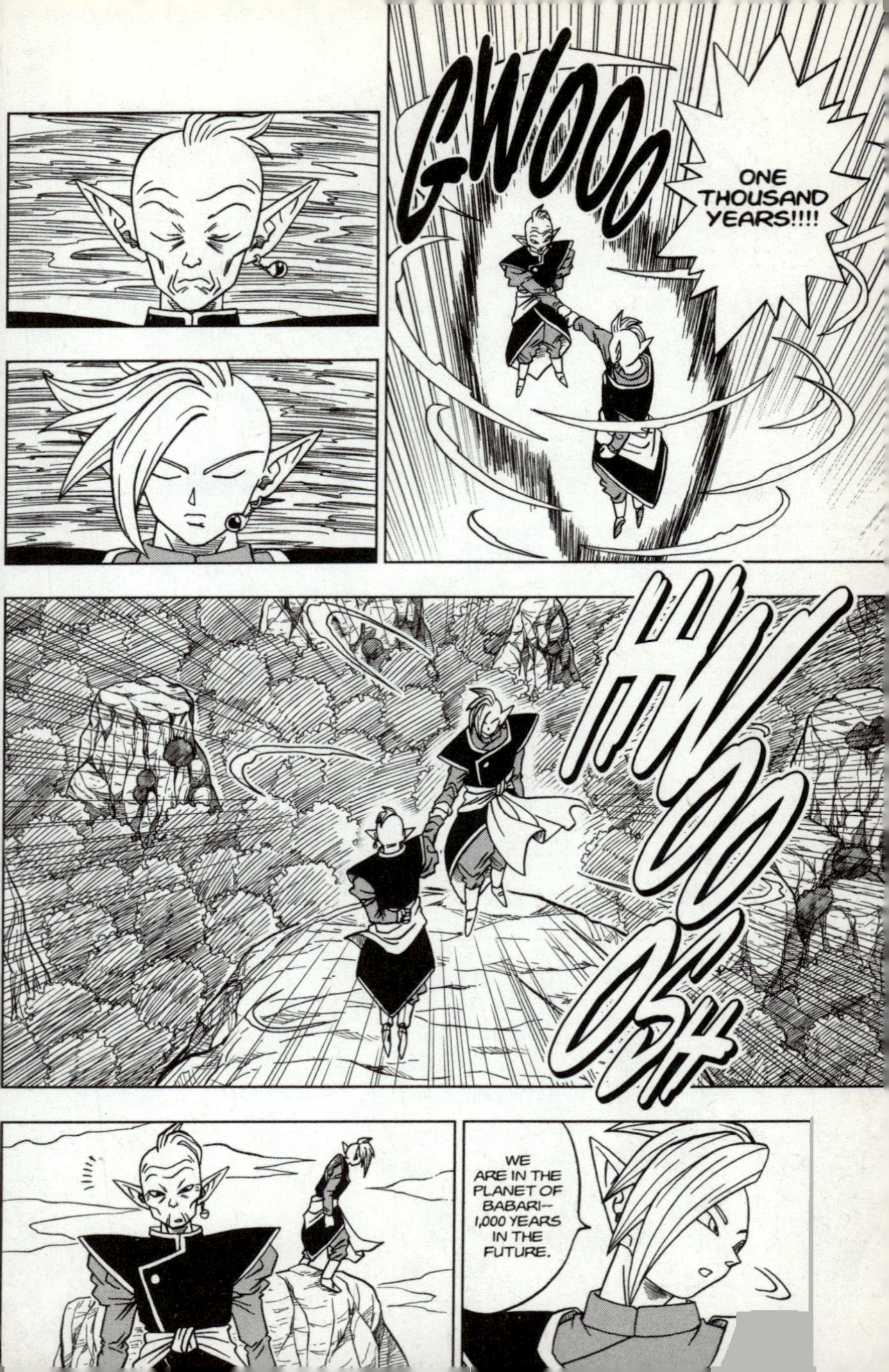
GWOOO
ONE THOUSAND YEARS!!!!
HWOOOSH
WE ARE IN THE PLANET OF BABARI-- 1,000 YEARS IN THE FUTURE.
!

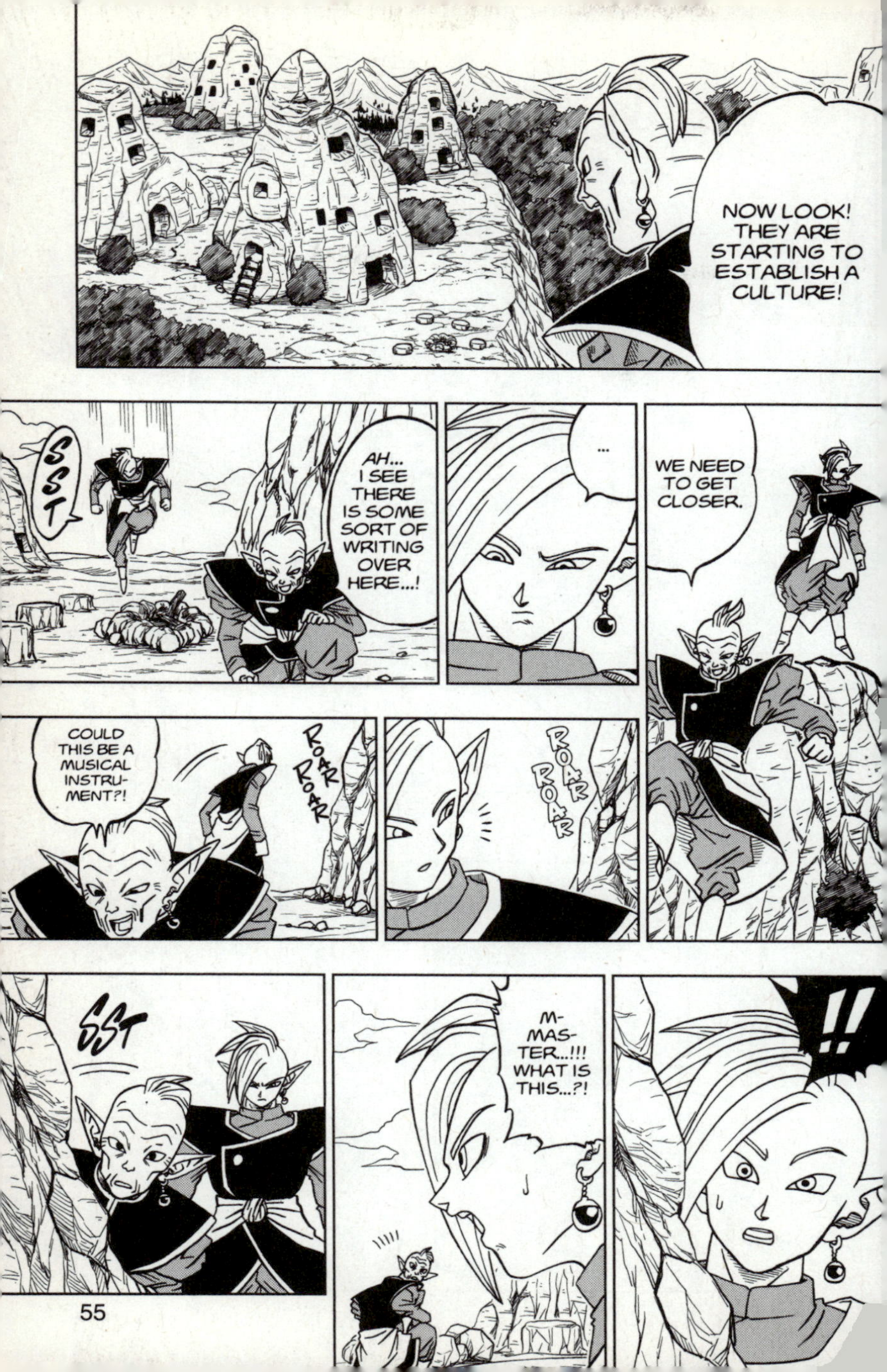
NOW LOOK! THEY ARE STARTING TO ESTABLISH A CULTURE!
WE NEED TO GET CLOSER.
...
AH... I SEE THERE IS SOME SORT OF WRITING OVER HERE...!
SST
ROAR ROAR
ROAR ROAR
COULD THIS BE A MUSICAL INSTRU-MENT?!
!!
M-MAS-TER...!!! WHAT IS THIS...?!
SST

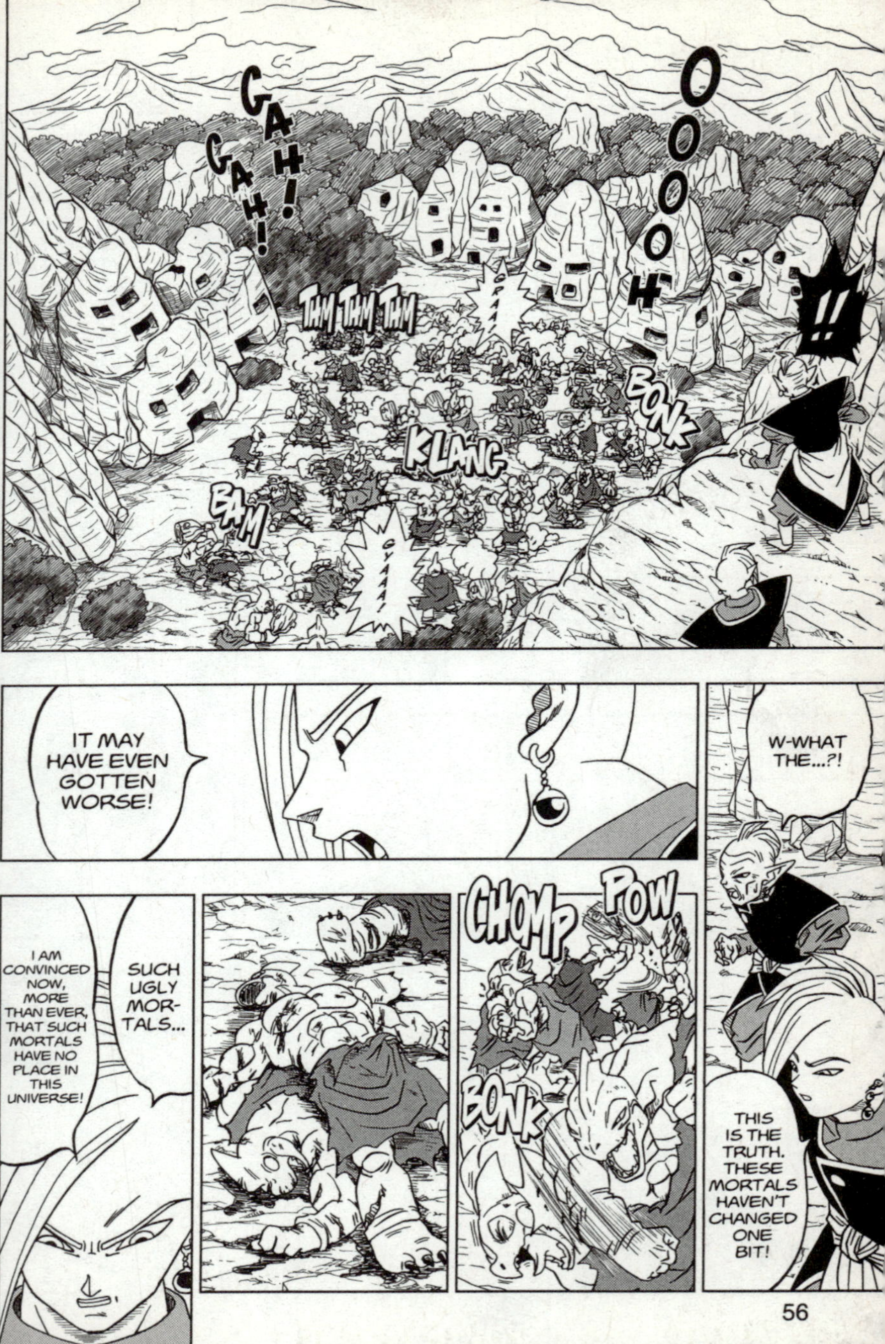
OOOOOH
!!
BONK
GAH GAH!
THM THM THM
KLANG
BAM
GYAAA
W-WHAT THE...?!
THIS IS THE TRUTH. THESE MORTALS HAVEN'T CHANGED ONE BIT!
IT MAY HAVE EVEN GOTTEN WORSE!
POW
CHOMP
BONK
SUCH UGLY MORTALS...
I AM CONVINCED NOW, MORE THAN EVER, THAT SUCH MORTALS HAVE NO PLACE IN THIS UNIVERSE!

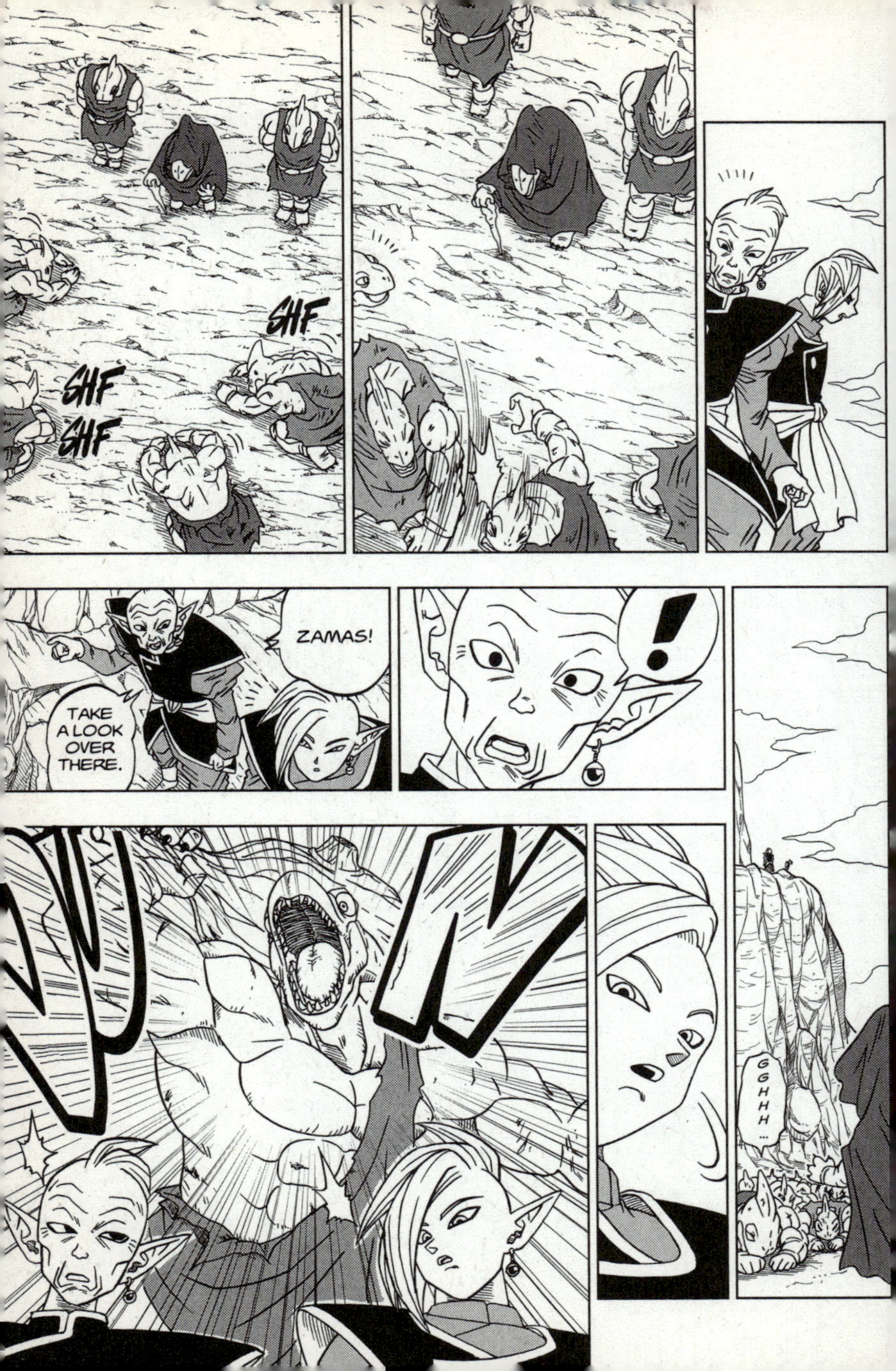
SHF
SHF
SHF
GGHHH...
!
ZAMAS!
TAKE A LOOK OVER THERE.

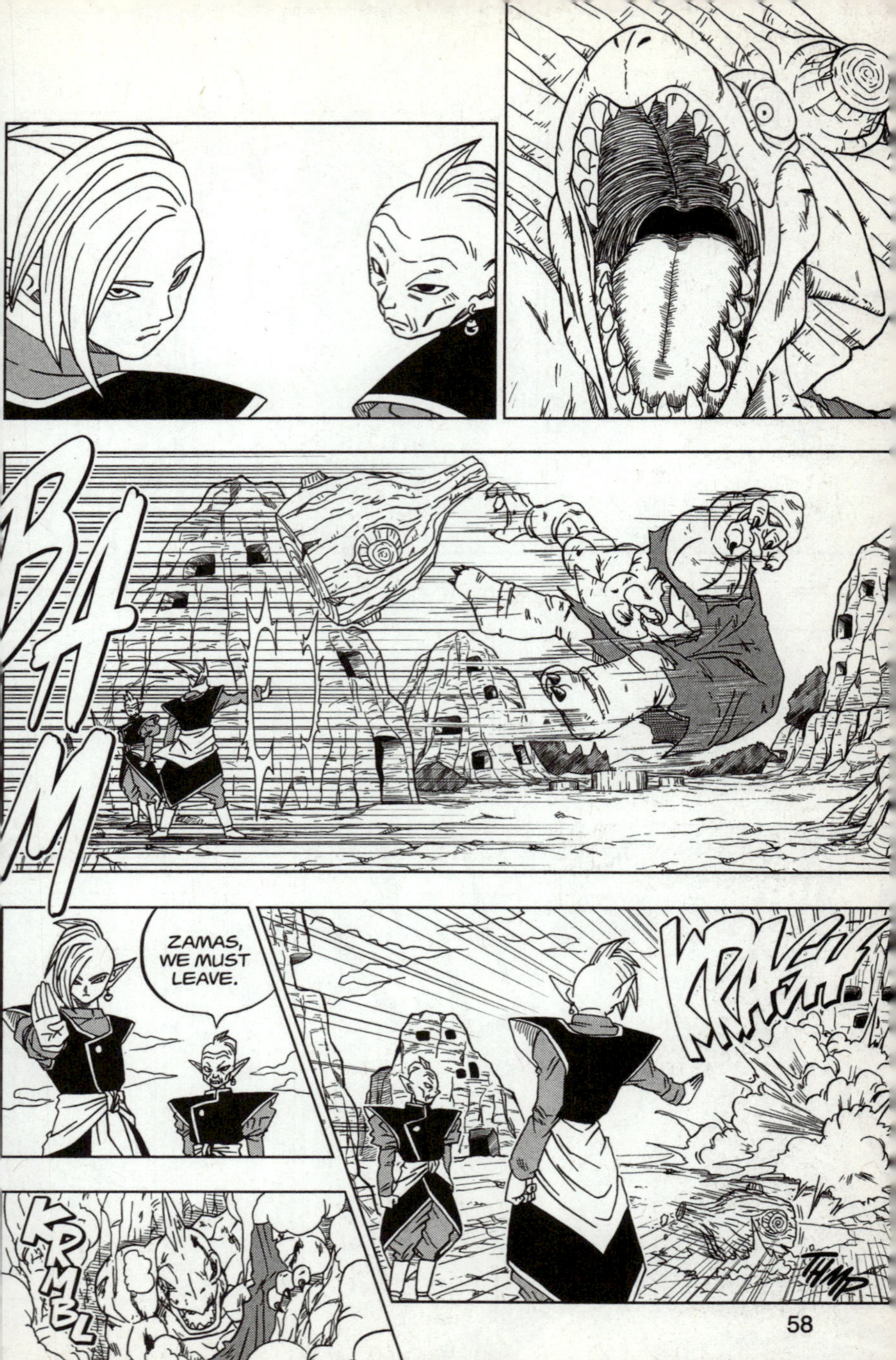
BAM
KRAKH
THMP
ZAMAS, WE MUST LEAVE.
KRMBL

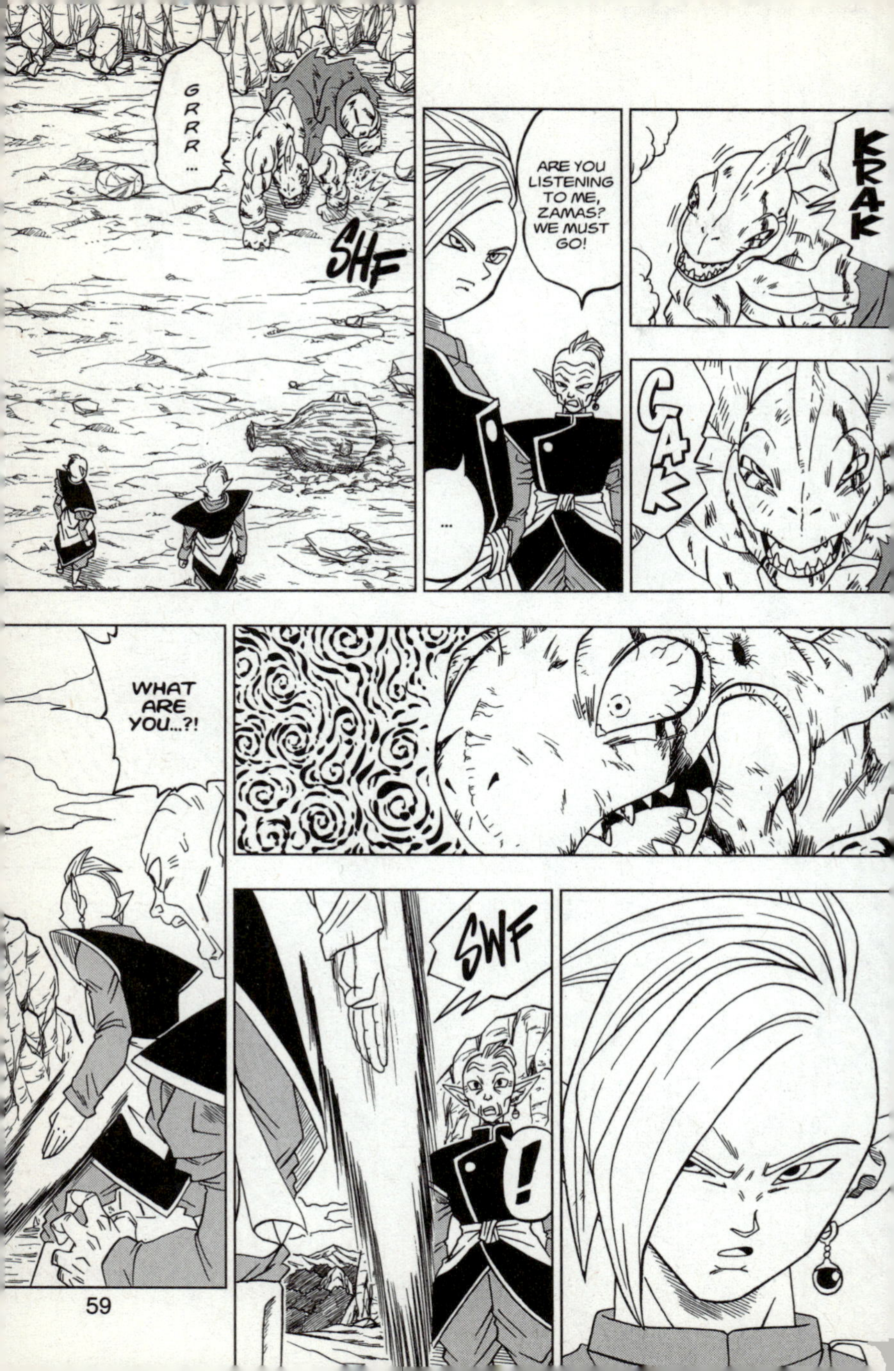
KRAK
CAK
ARE YOU LISTENING TO ME, ZAMAS? WE MUST GO!
...
GRRR...
SHF
SWF
!
WHAT ARE YOU...?!

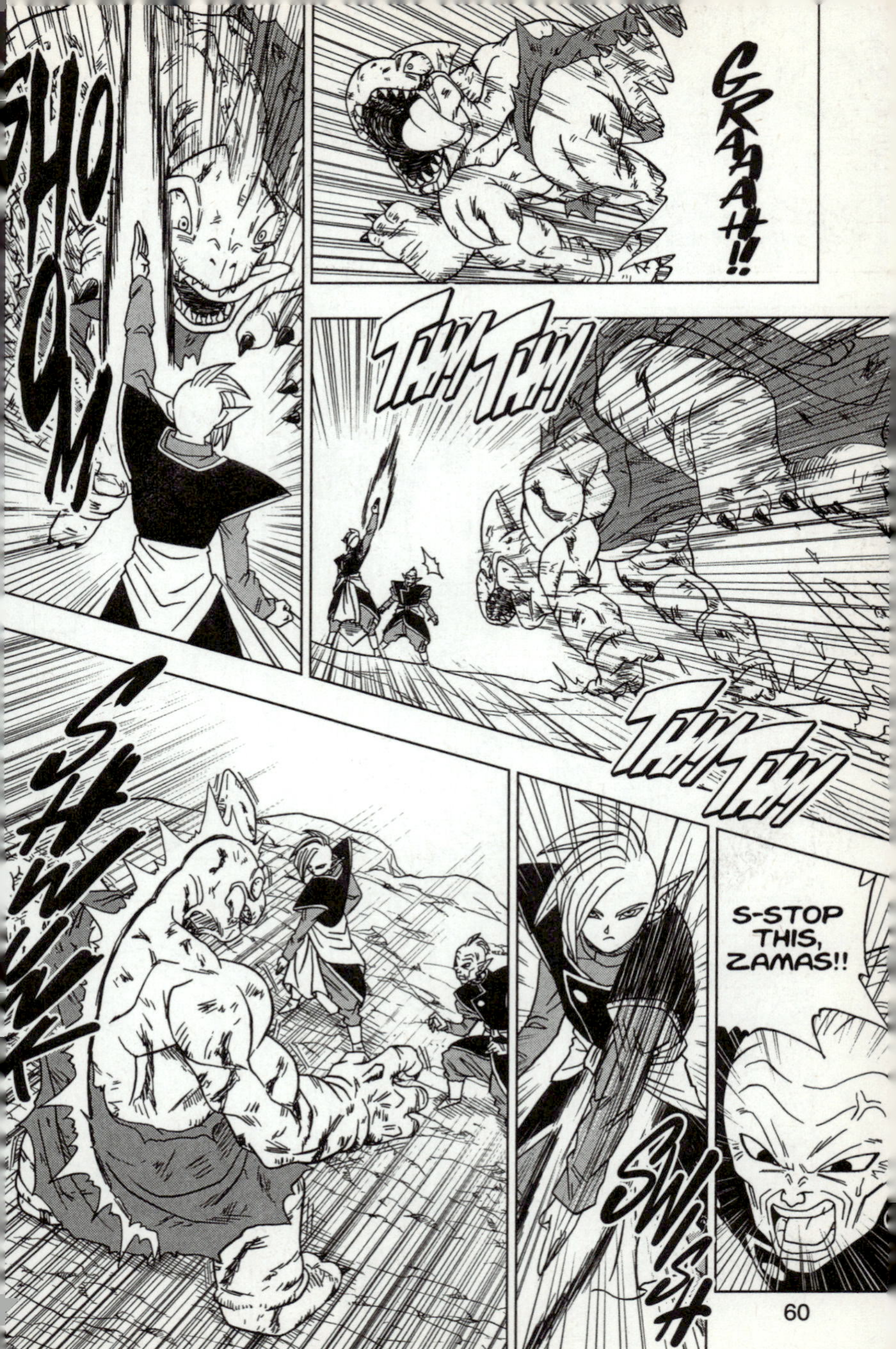
GRAAH!!
TCHK TCHK
TCHK TCHK
FHOOM
S-STOP THIS, ZAMAS!!
SWISH
SHUNK

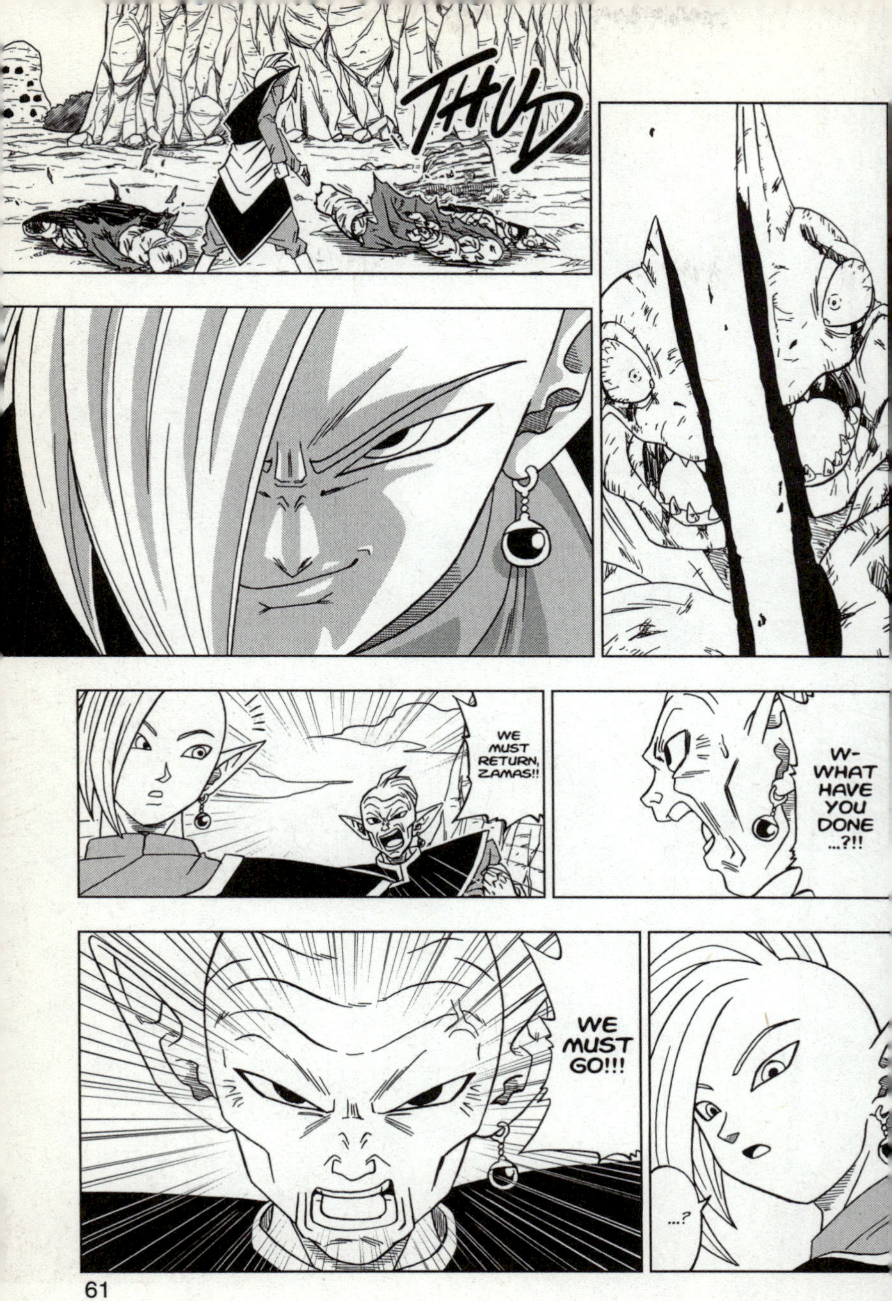
THUD
W-WHAT HAVE YOU DONE ...?!!
WE MUST RETURN, ZAMAS!!
...?
WE MUST GO!!!

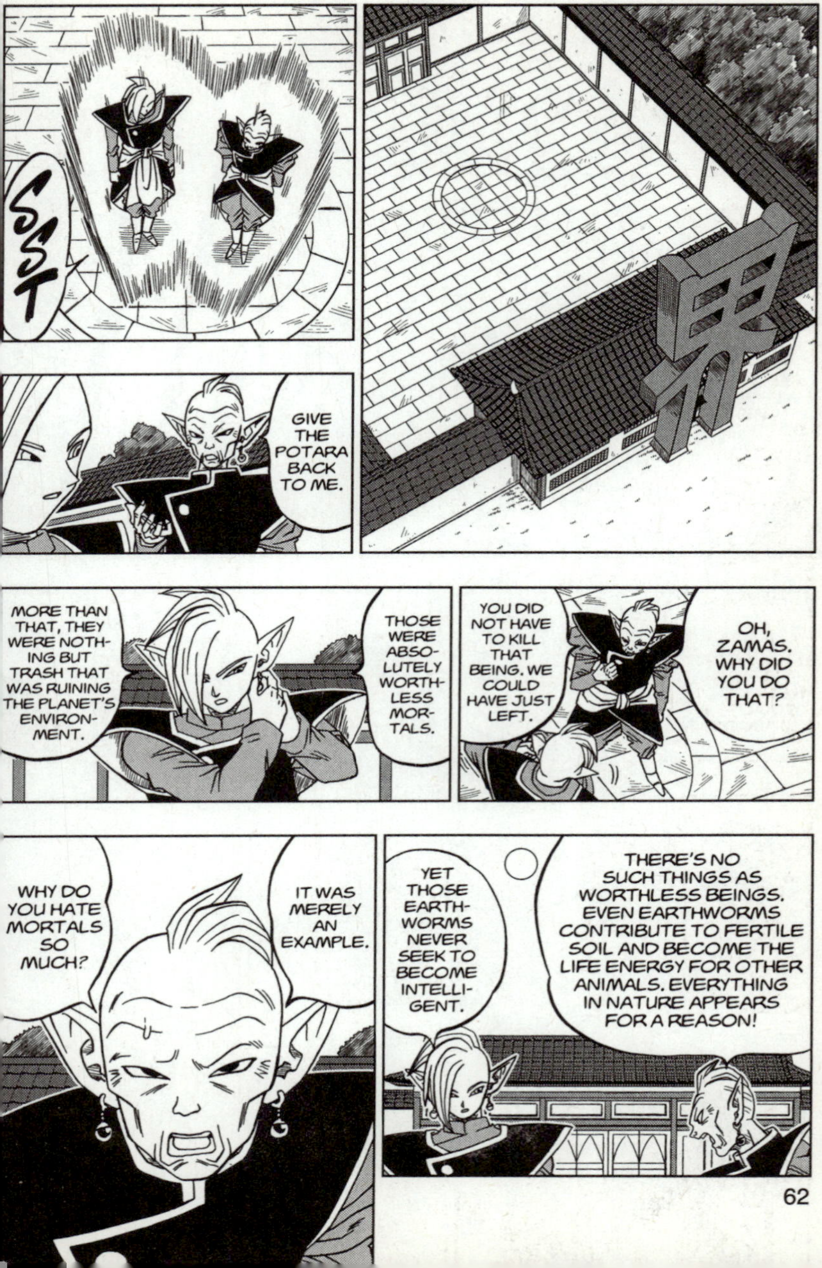
SSST
GIVE THE POTARA BACK TO ME.
OH, ZAMAS. WHY DID YOU DO THAT?
YOU DID NOT HAVE TO KILL THAT BEING. WE COULD HAVE JUST LEFT.
THOSE WERE ABSOLUTELY WORTHLESS MORTALS.
MORE THAN THAT, THEY WERE NOTHING BUT TRASH THAT WAS RUINING THE PLANET'S ENVIRONMENT.
THERE'S NO SUCH THINGS AS WORTHLESS BEINGS. EVEN EARTHWORMS CONTRIBUTE TO FERTILE SOIL AND BECOME THE LIFE ENERGY FOR OTHER ANIMALS. EVERYTHING IN NATURE APPEARS FOR A REASON!
YET THOSE EARTHWORMS NEVER SEEK TO BECOME INTELLIGENT.
IT WAS MERELY AN EXAMPLE.
WHY DO YOU HATE MORTALS SO MUCH?

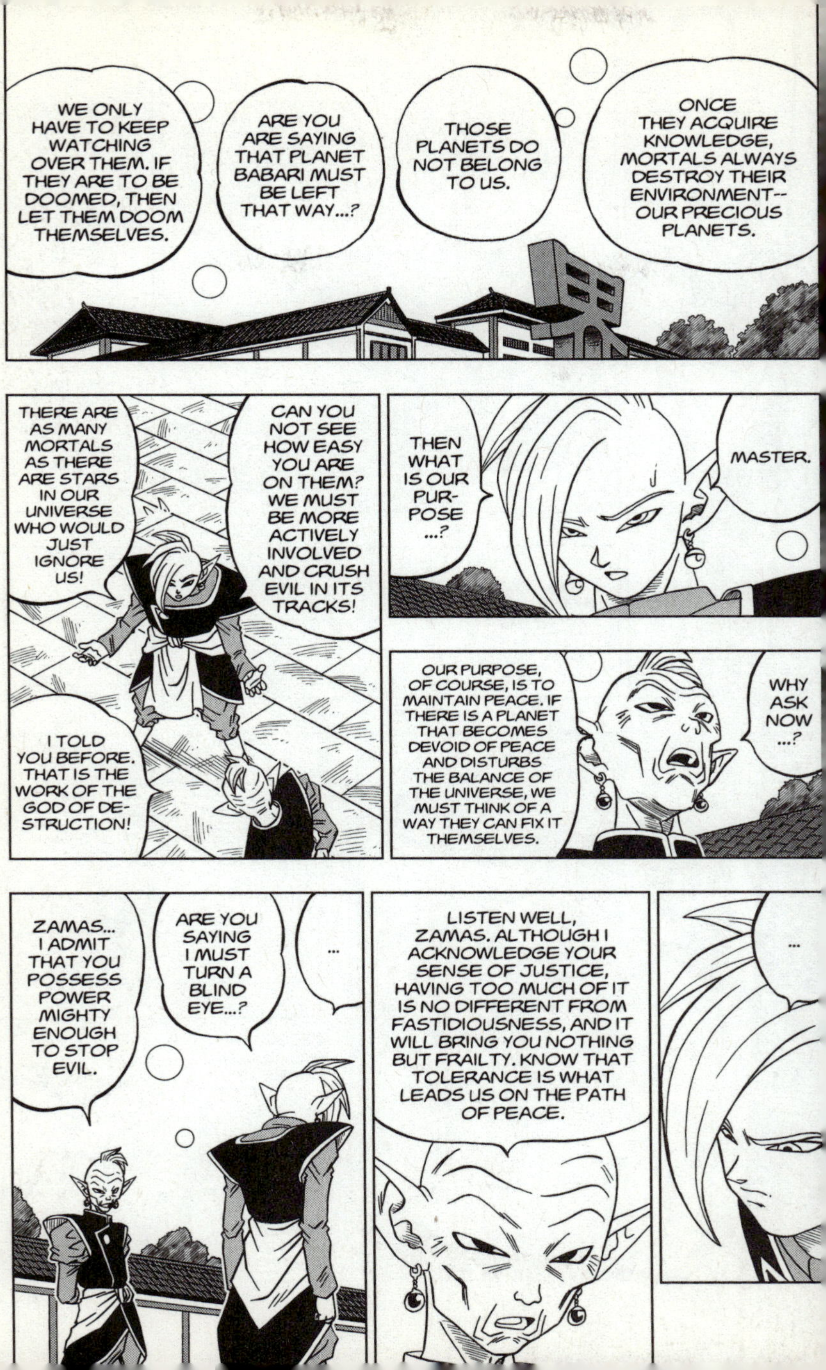
ONCE THEY ACQUIRE KNOWLEDGE, MORTALS ALWAYS DESTROY THEIR ENVIRONMENT-- OUR PRECIOUS PLANETS.
THOSE PLANETS DO NOT BELONG TO US.
ARE YOU ARE SAYING THAT PLANET BABARI MUST BE LEFT THAT WAY...?
WE ONLY HAVE TO KEEP WATCHING OVER THEM. IF THEY ARE TO BE DOOMED, THEN LET THEM DOOM THEMSELVES.
MASTER.
THEN WHAT IS OUR PURPOSE...?
WHY ASK NOW...?
OUR PURPOSE, OF COURSE, IS TO MAINTAIN PEACE. IF THERE IS A PLANET THAT BECOMES DEVOID OF PEACE AND DISTURBS THE BALANCE OF THE UNIVERSE, WE MUST THINK OF A WAY THEY CAN FIX IT THEMSELVES.
CAN YOU NOT SEE HOW EASY YOU ARE ON THEM? WE MUST BE MORE ACTIVELY INVOLVED AND CRUSH EVIL IN ITS TRACKS!
THERE ARE AS MANY MORTALS AS THERE ARE STARS IN OUR UNIVERSE WHO WOULD JUST IGNORE US!
I TOLD YOU BEFORE. THAT IS THE WORK OF THE GOD OF DESTRUCTION!
...
LISTEN WELL, ZAMAS. ALTHOUGH I ACKNOWLEDGE YOUR SENSE OF JUSTICE, HAVING TOO MUCH OF IT IS NO DIFFERENT FROM FASTIDIOUSNESS, AND IT WILL BRING YOU NOTHING BUT FRAILTY. KNOW THAT TOLERANCE IS WHAT LEADS US ON THE PATH OF PEACE.
...
ARE YOU SAYING I MUST TURN A BLIND EYE...?
ZAMAS... I ADMIT THAT YOU POSSESS POWER MIGHTY ENOUGH TO STOP EVIL.

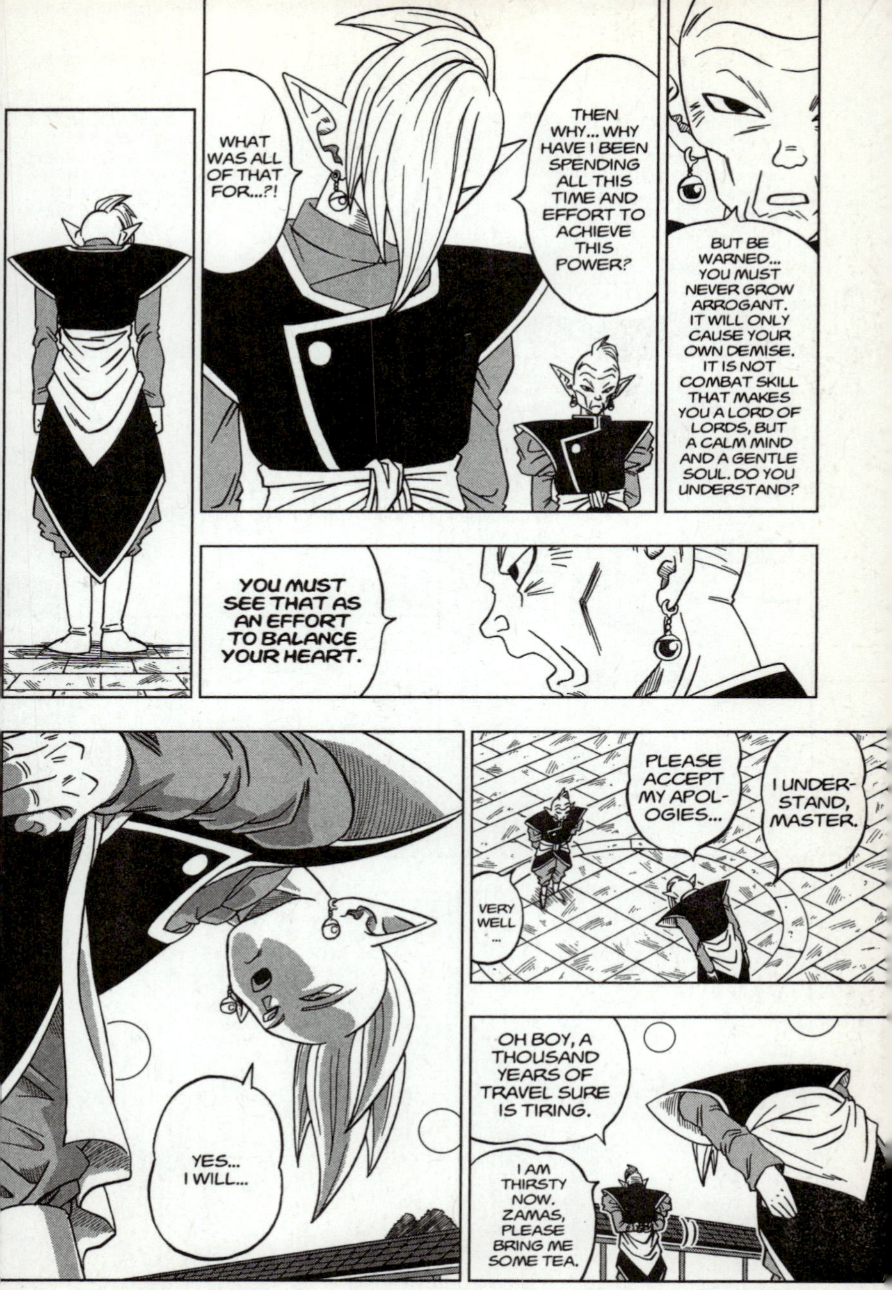
BUT BE WARNED... YOU MUST NEVER GROW ARROGANT. IT WILL ONLY CAUSE YOUR OWN DEMISE. IT IS NOT COMBAT SKILL THAT MAKES YOU A LORD OF LORDS, BUT A CALM MIND AND A GENTLE SOUL. DO YOU UNDERSTAND?
THEN WHY... WHY HAVE I BEEN SPENDING ALL THIS TIME AND EFFORT TO ACHIEVE THIS POWER?
WHAT WAS ALL OF THAT FOR...?!
YOU MUST SEE THAT AS AN EFFORT TO BALANCE YOUR HEART.
I UNDER-STAND, MASTER.
PLEASE ACCEPT MY APOL-OGIES...
VERY WELL ...
OH BOY, A THOUSAND YEARS OF TRAVEL SURE IS TIRING.
I AM THIRSTY NOW. ZAMAS, PLEASE BRING ME SOME TEA.
YES... I WILL...

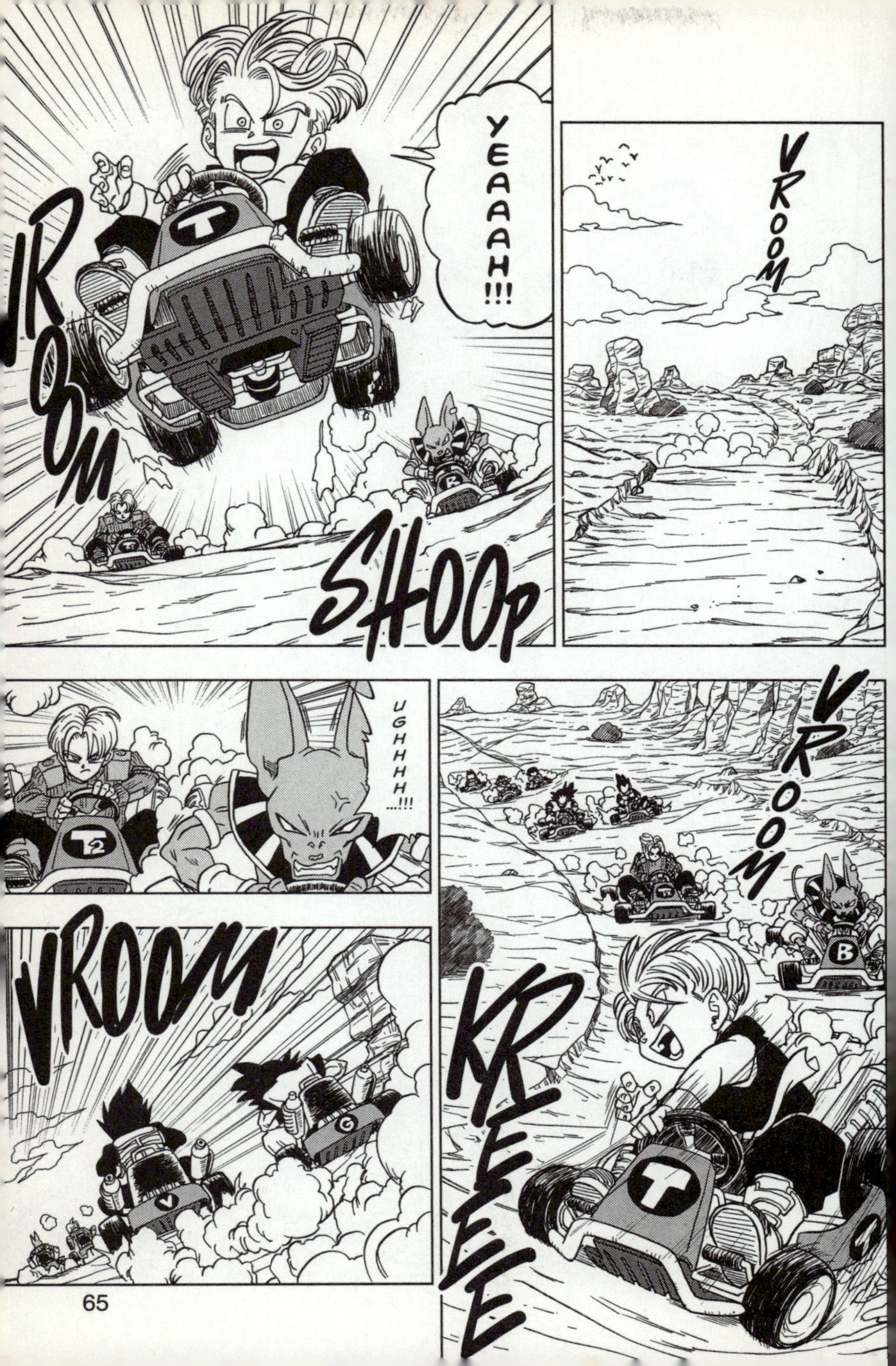
VROOM
YEAAAAH!!!
VROOM
SHOOP
VROOOM
KREEEE
UGHHHH...!!!
VROOM

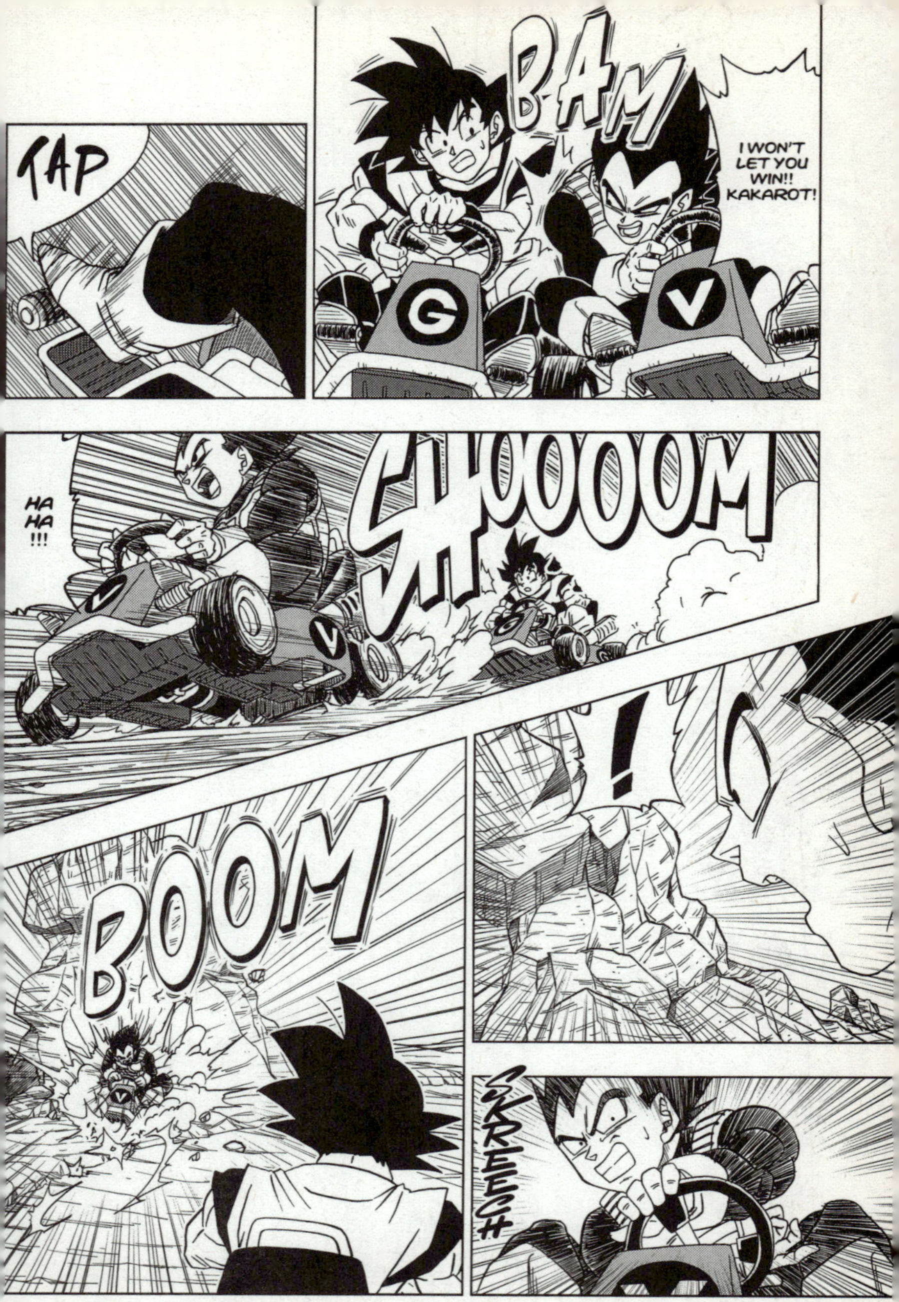
BAM
I WON'T LET YOU WIN!! KAKAROT!
TAP
SHOOOOM
HA HA !!!
!
SKREECH
BOOM

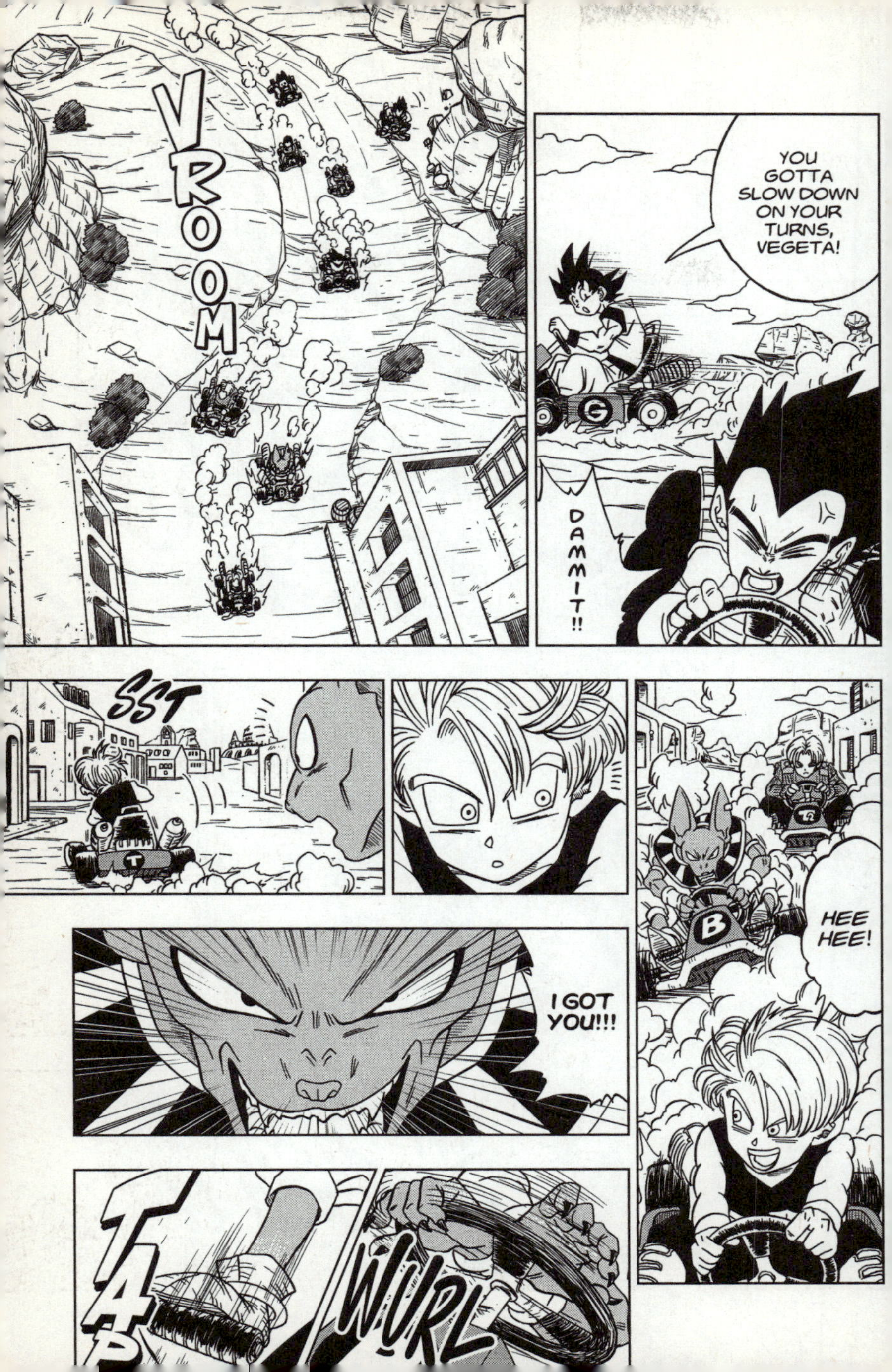
YOU GOTTA SLOW DOWN ON YOUR TURNS, VEGETA!
DAMMIT!!
VROOM
HEE HEE!
SST
I GOT YOU!!!
WURL
TAP

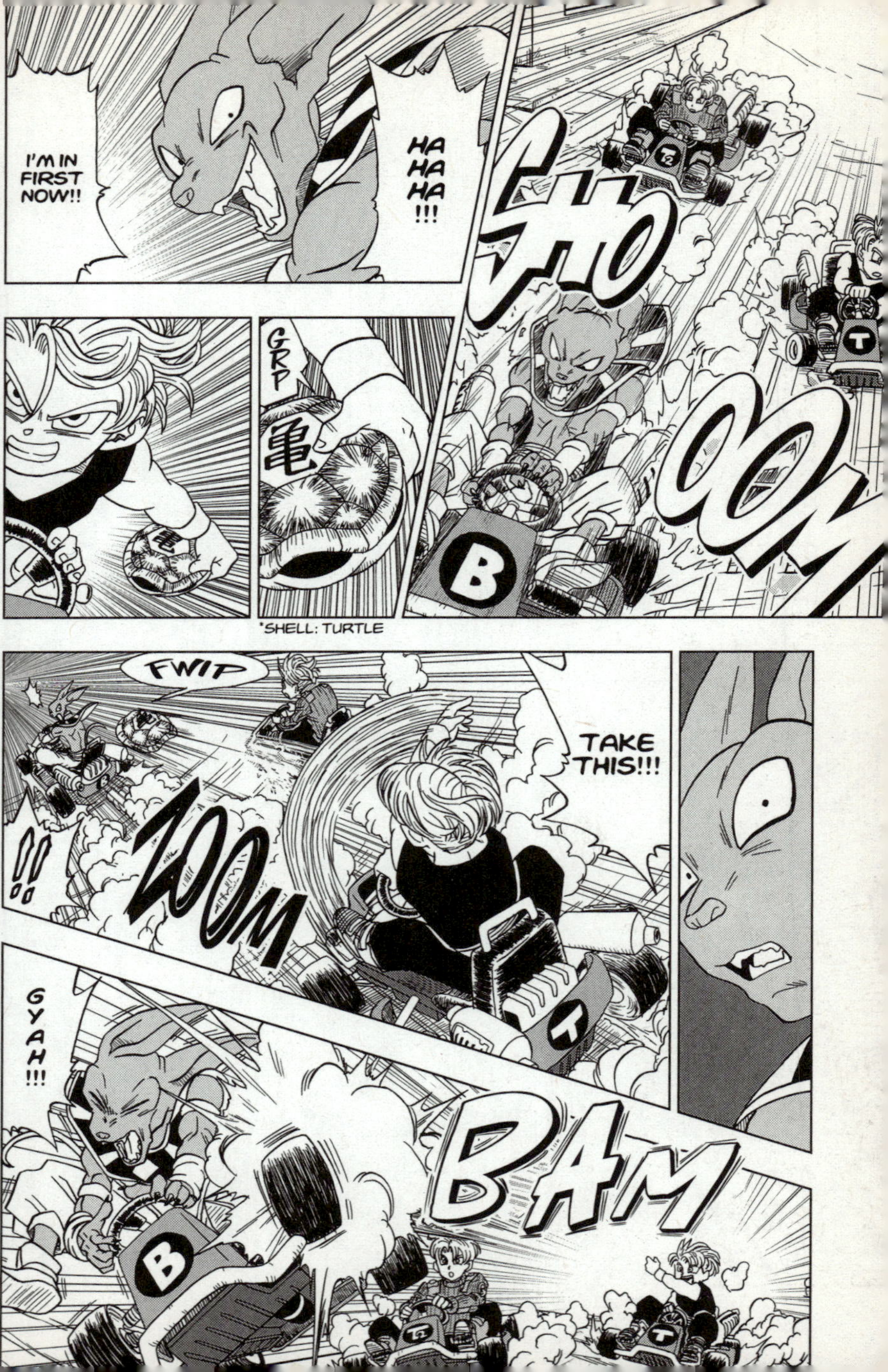
SHOOOOM
HA HA HA!!!
I'M IN FIRST NOW!!
GRP
亀
TAKE THIS!!!
FWIP
ZOOM
!!
BAM
GYAH!!!
*SHELL: TURTLE

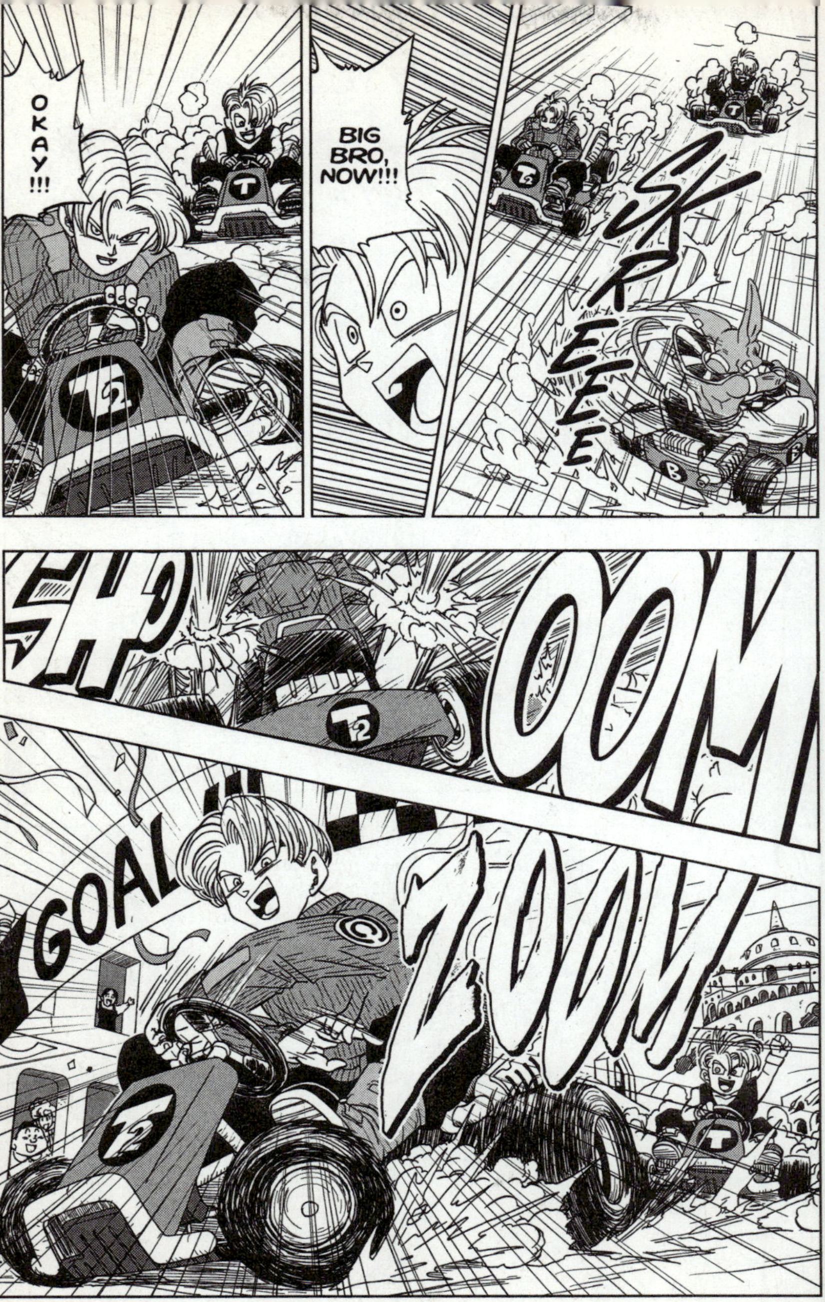
SKREEEE
BIG BRO, NOW!!!
OKAY!!!
SHOOOM
ZOOM
GOAL

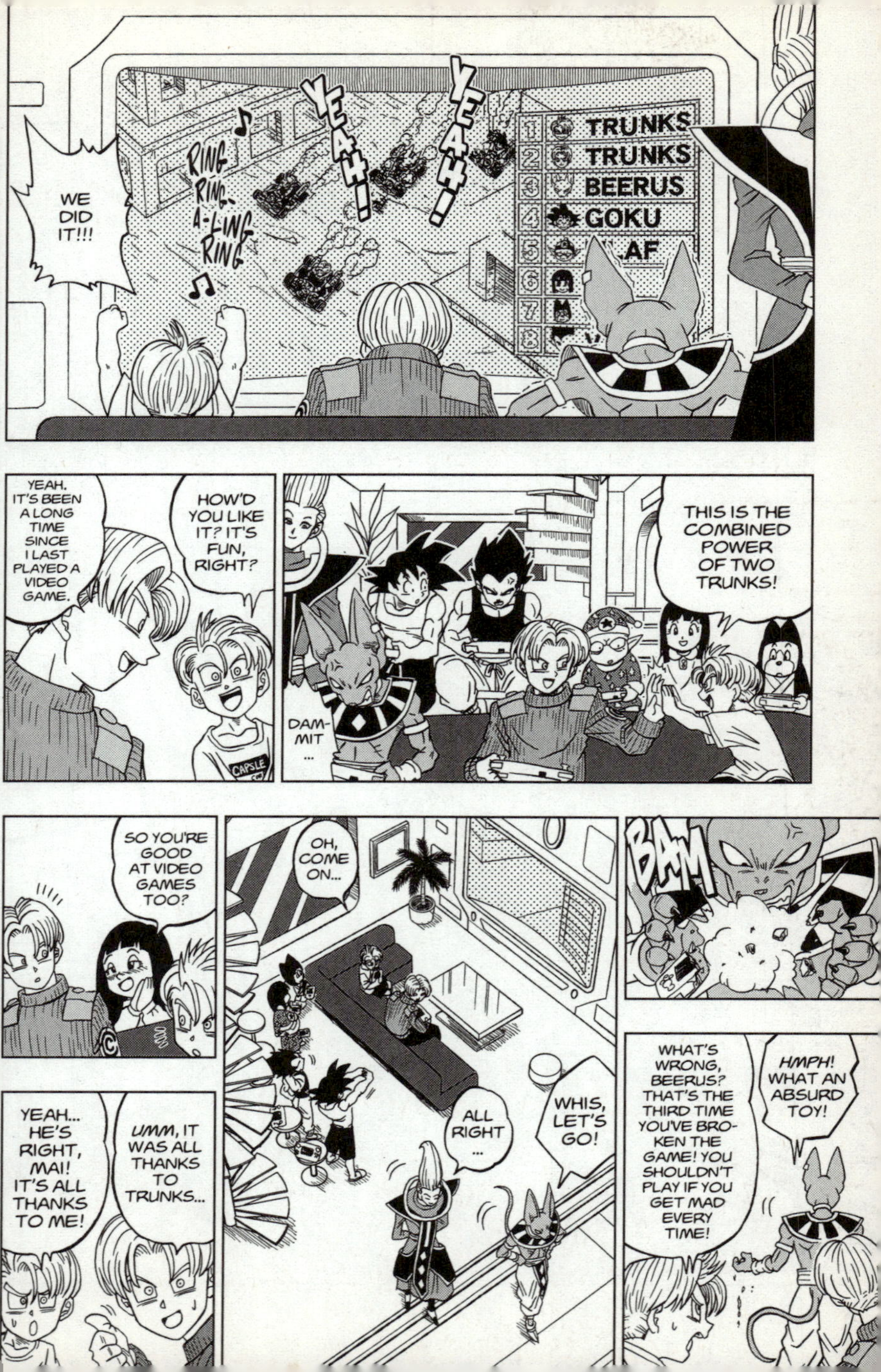

1 TRUNKS
2 TRUNKS
3 BEERUS
4 GOKU
5 ...AF
YEAH!
YEAH!
RING RING-A-LING RING
WE DID IT!!!
THIS IS THE COMBINED POWER OF TWO TRUNKS!
DAMMIT...
HOW'D YOU LIKE IT? IT'S FUN, RIGHT?
YEAH. IT'S BEEN A LONG TIME SINCE I LAST PLAYED A VIDEO GAME.
CAPSULE
BAM
HMPH! WHAT AN ABSURD TOY!
WHAT'S WRONG, BEERUS? THAT'S THE THIRD TIME YOU'VE BROKEN THE GAME! YOU SHOULDN'T PLAY IF YOU GET MAD EVERY TIME!
OH, COME ON...
WHIS, LET'S GO!
ALL RIGHT...
SO YOU'RE GOOD AT VIDEO GAMES TOO?
UMM, IT WAS ALL THANKS TO TRUNKS...
YEAH... HE'S RIGHT, MAI! IT'S ALL THANKS TO ME!

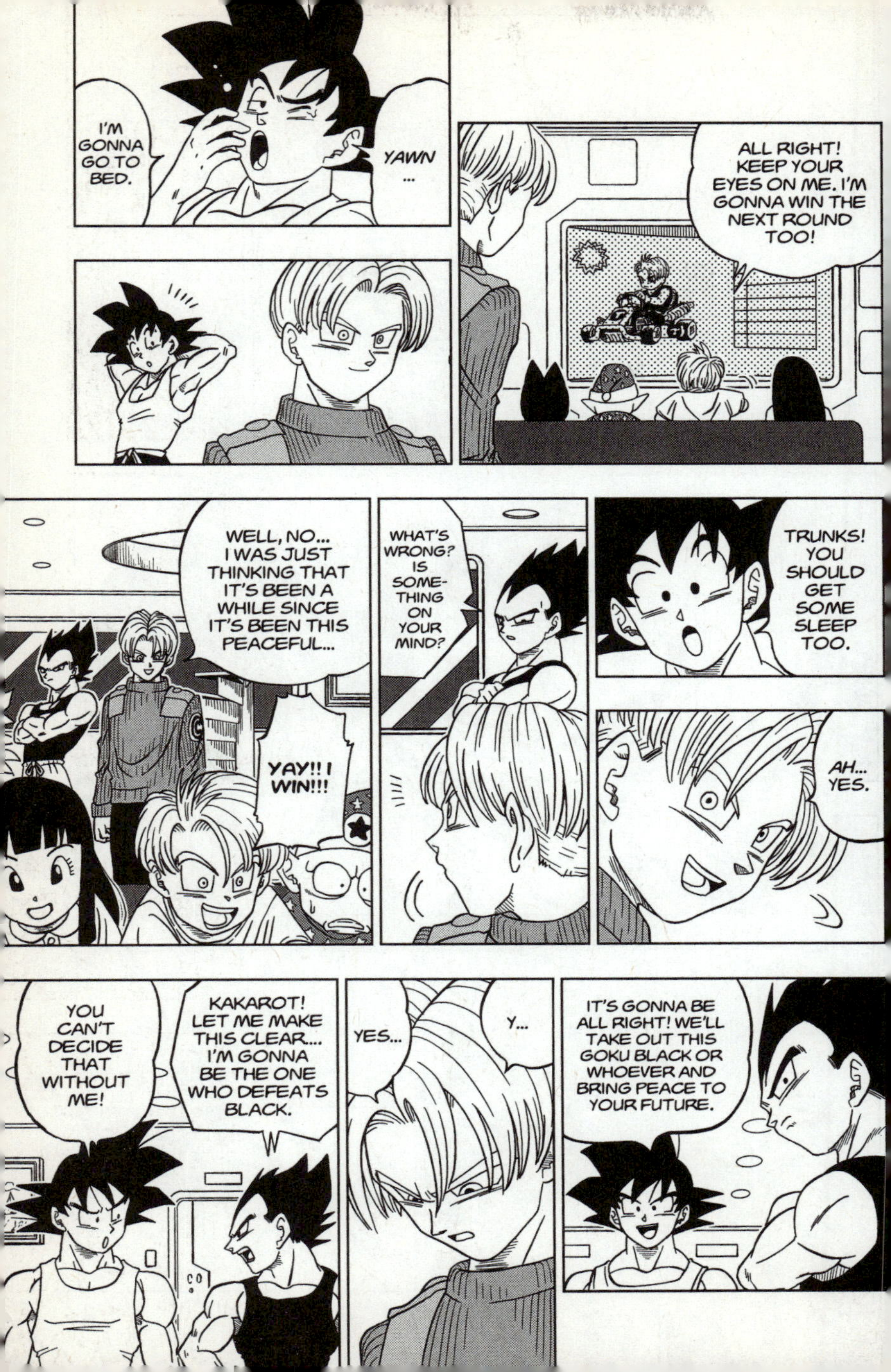
ALL RIGHT! KEEP YOUR EYES ON ME. I'M GONNA WIN THE NEXT ROUND TOO!
YAWN ...
I'M GONNA GO TO BED.
TRUNKS! YOU SHOULD GET SOME SLEEP TOO.
AH... YES.
WHAT'S WRONG? IS SOMETHING ON YOUR MIND?
WELL, NO... I WAS JUST THINKING THAT IT'S BEEN A WHILE SINCE IT'S BEEN THIS PEACEFUL...
YAY!!! I WIN!!!
IT'S GONNA BE ALL RIGHT! WE'LL TAKE OUT THIS GOKU BLACK OR WHOEVER AND BRING PEACE TO YOUR FUTURE.
Y...
YES...
KAKAROT! LET ME MAKE THIS CLEAR.... I'M GONNA BE THE ONE WHO DEFEATS BLACK.
YOU CAN'T DECIDE THAT WITHOUT ME!

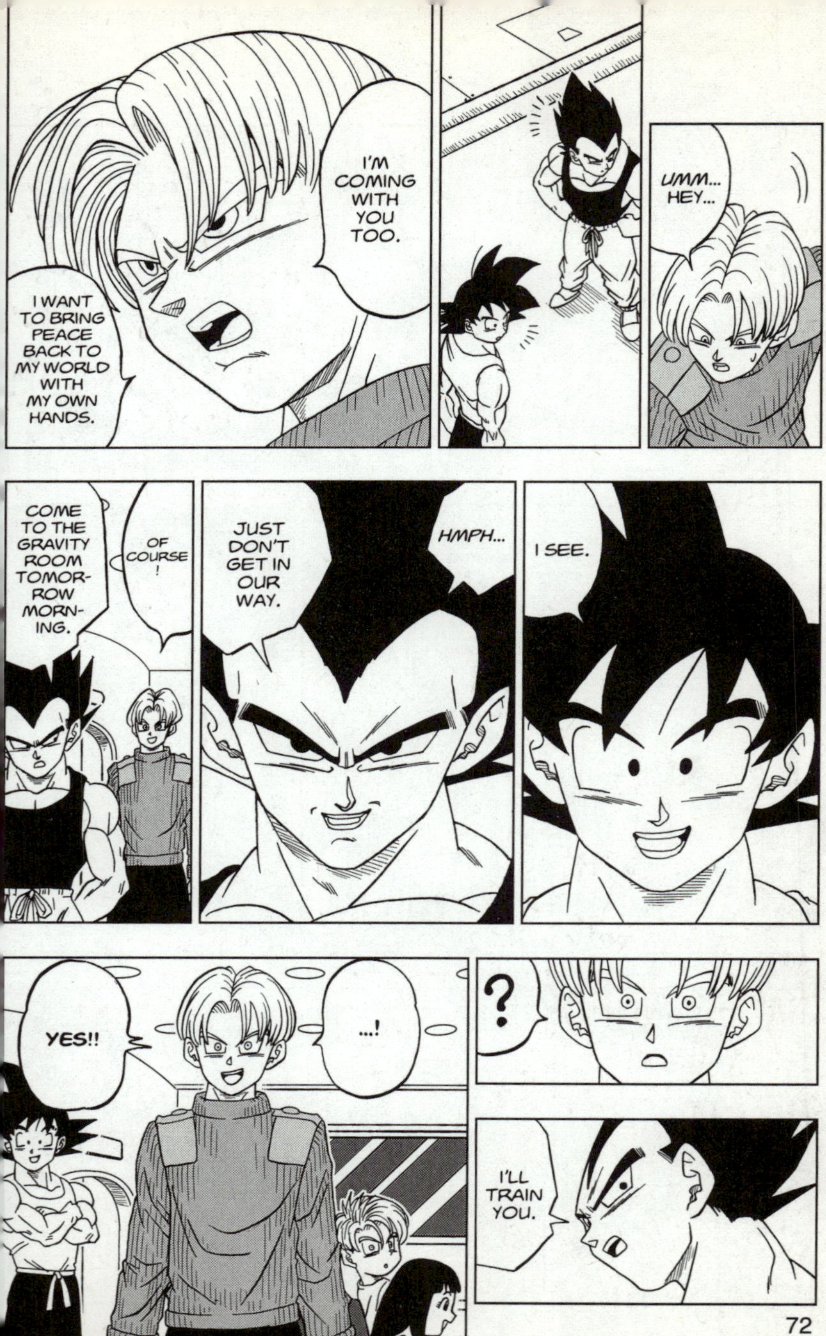
UMM... HEY...
I'M COMING WITH YOU TOO.
I WANT TO BRING PEACE BACK TO MY WORLD WITH MY OWN HANDS.
I SEE.
HMPH...
JUST DON'T GET IN OUR WAY.
COME TO THE GRAVITY ROOM TOMORROW MORNING.
OF COURSE!
?
I'LL TRAIN YOU.
...!
YES!!

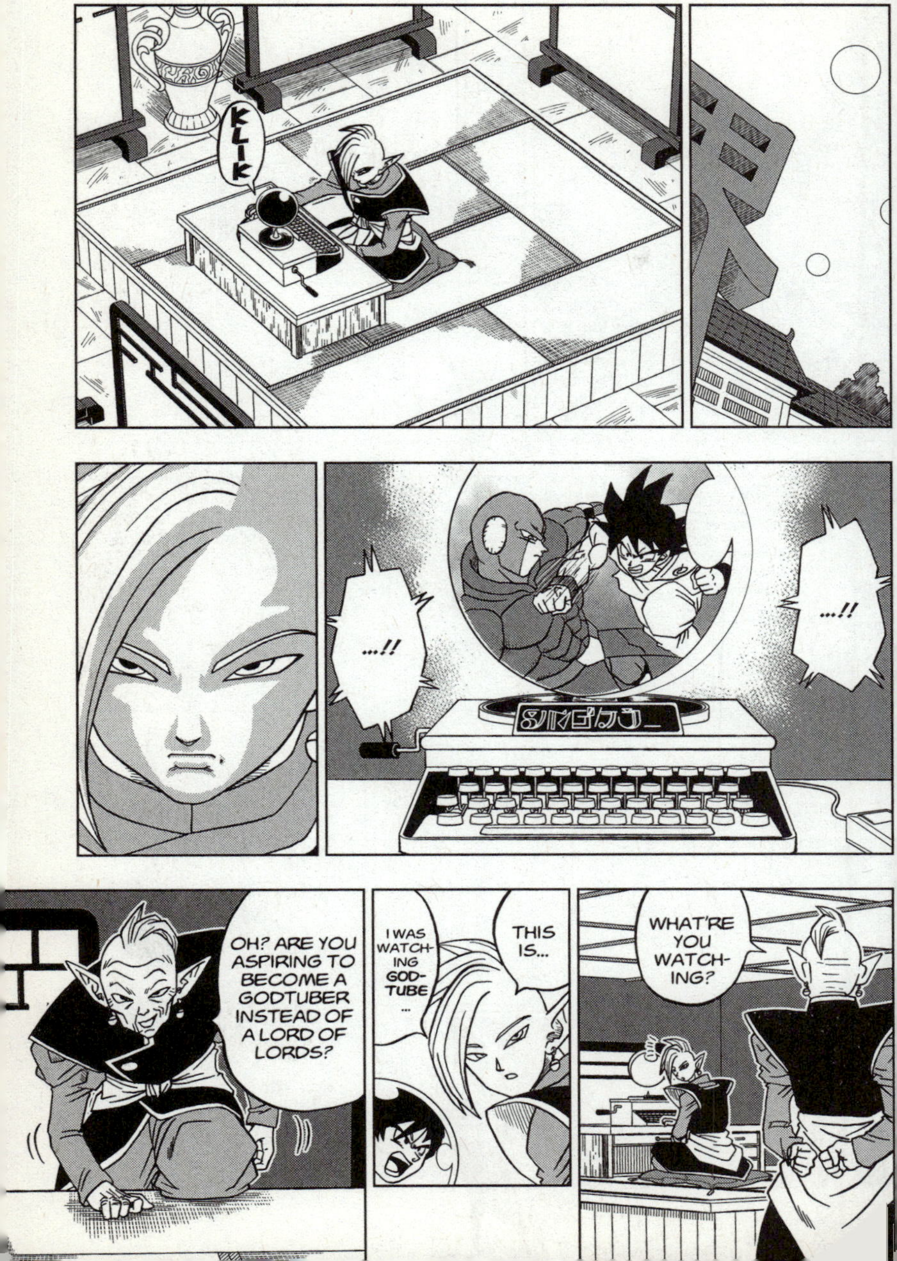
KLIK
...!!
...!!
WHAT'RE YOU WATCHING?
THIS IS...
I WAS WATCHING GODTUBE...
OH? ARE YOU ASPIRING TO BECOME A GODTUBER INSTEAD OF A LORD OF LORDS?

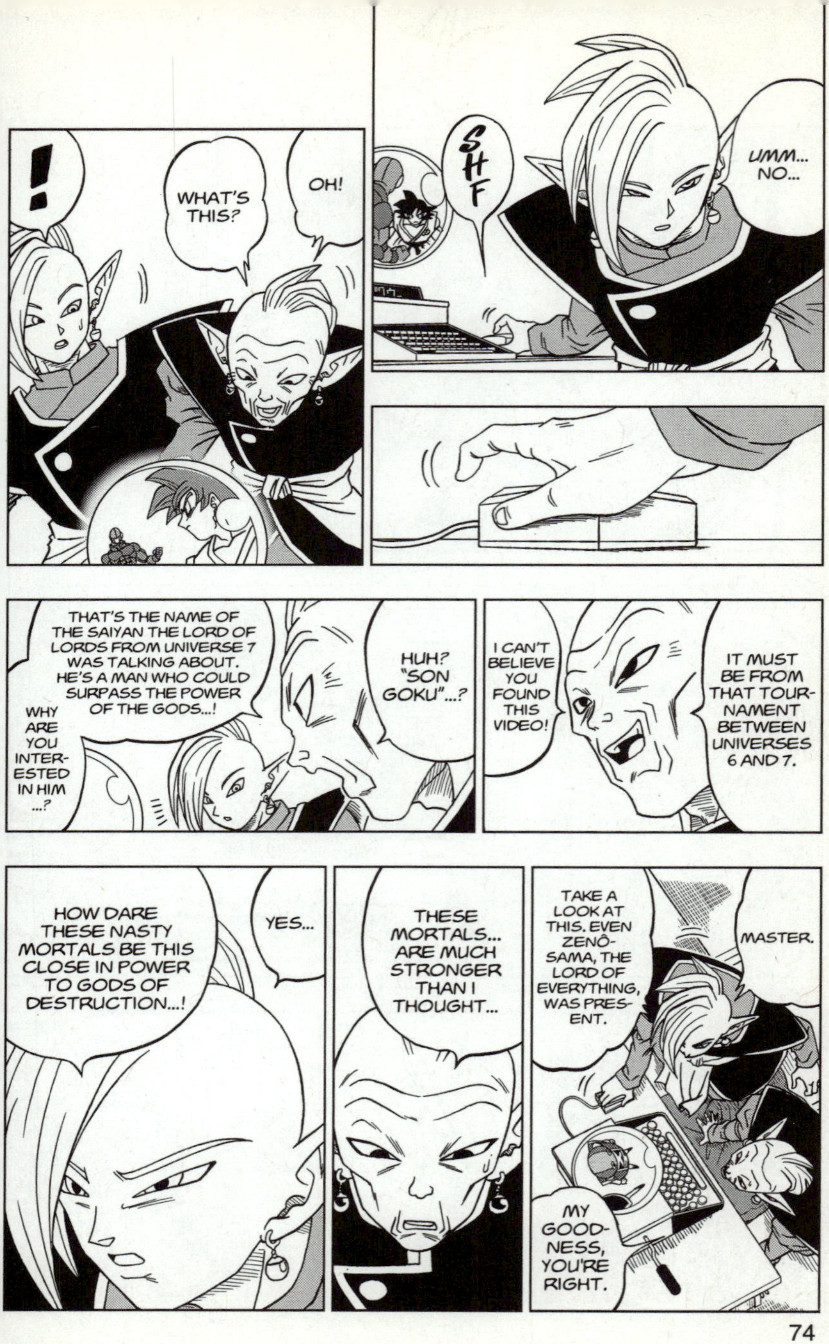
UMM... NO...
SHF
OH!
WHAT'S THIS?
!
IT MUST BE FROM THAT TOUR-NAMENT BETWEEN UNIVERSES 6 AND 7.
I CAN'T BELIEVE YOU FOUND THIS VIDEO!
HUH? "SON GOKU"...?
THAT'S THE NAME OF THE SAIYAN THE LORD OF LORDS FROM UNIVERSE 7 WAS TALKING ABOUT. HE'S A MAN WHO COULD SURPASS THE POWER OF THE GODS...!
WHY ARE YOU INTER-ESTED IN HIM ...?
MASTER.
TAKE A LOOK AT THIS. EVEN ZENÔ-SAMA, THE LORD OF EVERYTHING, WAS PRES-ENT.
MY GOOD-NESS, YOU'RE RIGHT.
THESE MORTALS... ARE MUCH STRONGER THAN I THOUGHT...
YES...
HOW DARE THESE NASTY MORTALS BE THIS CLOSE IN POWER TO GODS OF DESTRUCTION...!

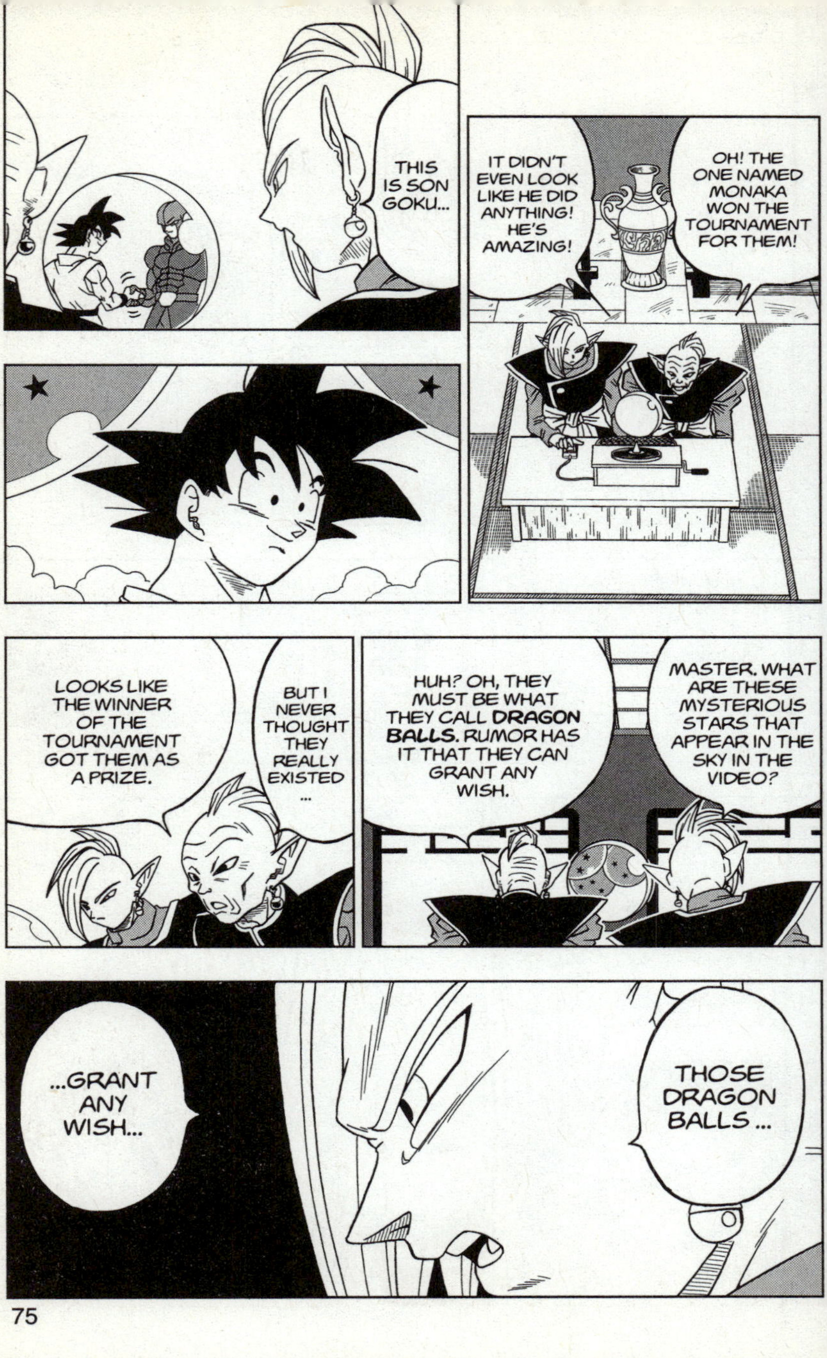
OH! THE ONE NAMED MONAKA WON THE TOURNAMENT FOR THEM!
IT DIDN'T EVEN LOOK LIKE HE DID ANYTHING! HE'S AMAZING!
THIS IS SON GOKU...
MASTER. WHAT ARE THESE MYSTERIOUS STARS THAT APPEAR IN THE SKY IN THE VIDEO?
HUH? OH, THEY MUST BE WHAT THEY CALL **DRAGON BALLS.** RUMOR HAS IT THAT THEY CAN GRANT ANY WISH.
BUT I NEVER THOUGHT THEY REALLY EXISTED...
LOOKS LIKE THE WINNER OF THE TOURNAMENT GOT THEM AS A PRIZE.
THOSE DRAGON BALLS...
...GRANT ANY WISH...

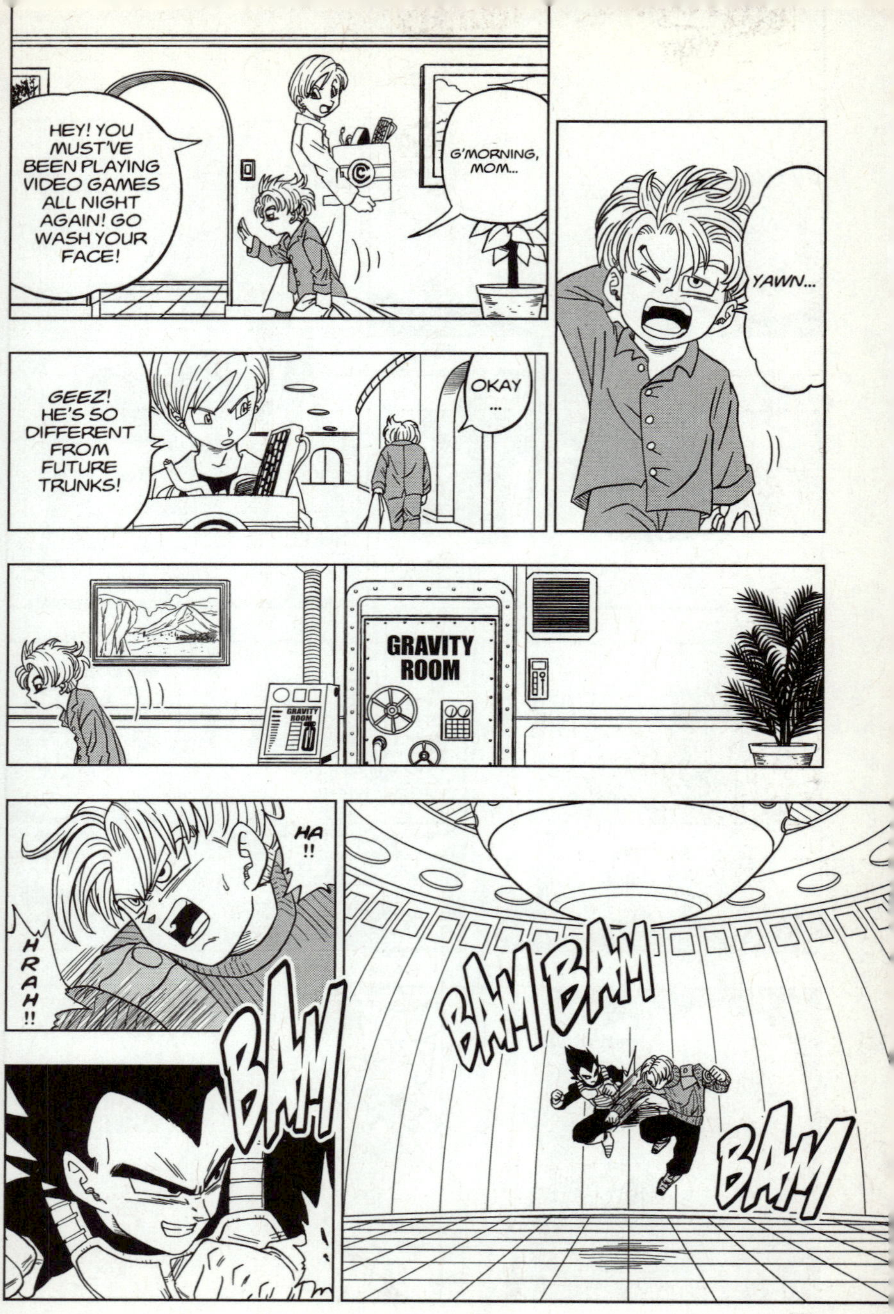
YAWN...
G'MORNING, MOM...
HEY! YOU MUST'VE BEEN PLAYING VIDEO GAMES ALL NIGHT AGAIN! GO WASH YOUR FACE!
OKAY ...
GEEZ! HE'S SO DIFFERENT FROM FUTURE TRUNKS!
GRAVITY ROOM
GRAVITY ROOM
BAM BAM
BAM
HA!!
HRAH!!
BAM

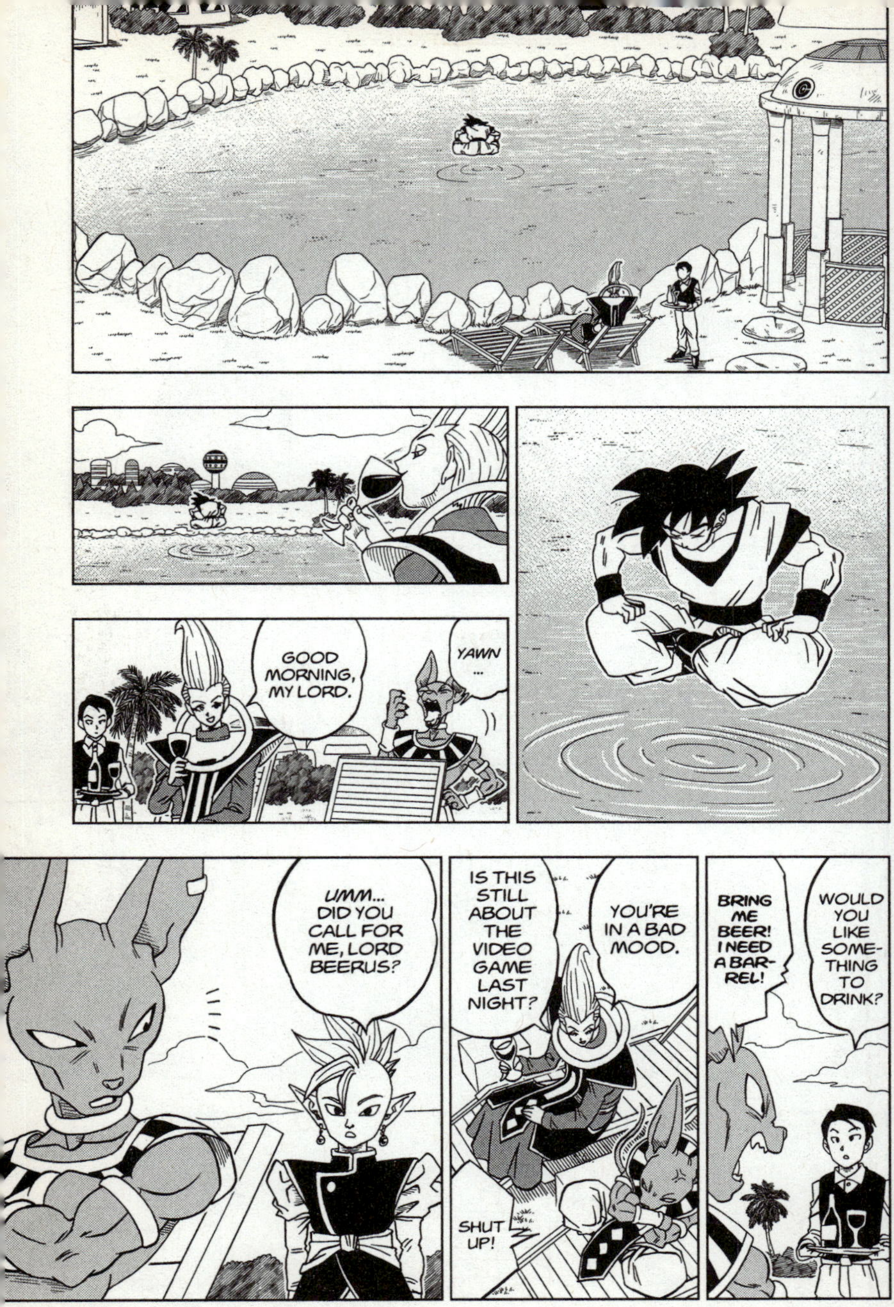
GOOD MORNING, MY LORD.
YAWN...
WOULD YOU LIKE SOMETHING TO DRINK?
BRING ME BEER! I NEED A BARREL!
YOU'RE IN A BAD MOOD.
IS THIS STILL ABOUT THE VIDEO GAME LAST NIGHT?
SHUT UP!
UMM... DID YOU CALL FOR ME, LORD BEERUS?

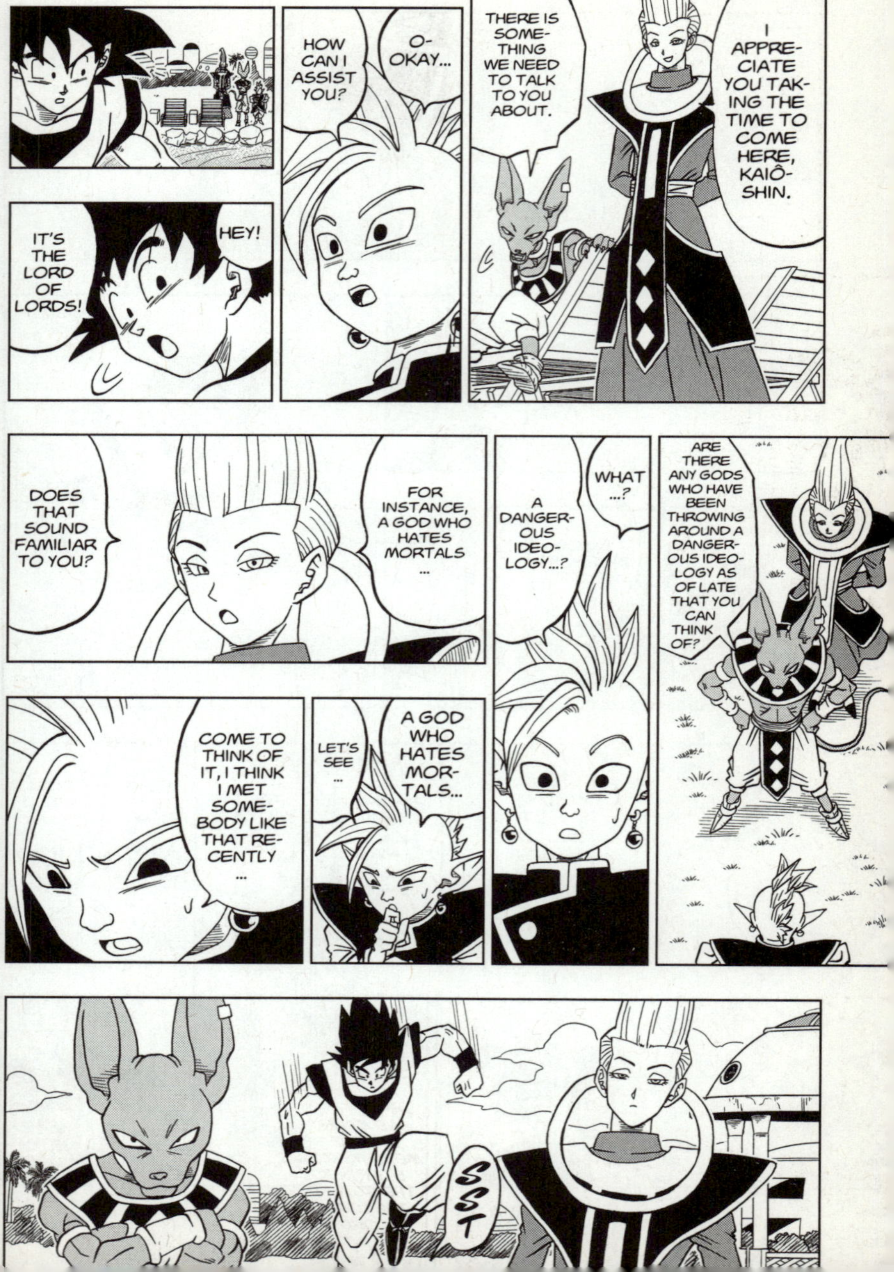
I APPRECIATE YOU TAKING THE TIME TO COME HERE, KAIÔ-SHIN.
THERE IS SOMETHING WE NEED TO TALK TO YOU ABOUT.
O-OKAY...
HOW CAN I ASSIST YOU?
HEY!
IT'S THE LORD OF LORDS!
ARE THERE ANY GODS WHO HAVE BEEN THROWING AROUND A DANGEROUS IDEOLOGY AS OF LATE THAT YOU CAN THINK OF?
WHAT ...?
A DANGEROUS IDEOLOGY...?
FOR INSTANCE, A GOD WHO HATES MORTALS ...
DOES THAT SOUND FAMILIAR TO YOU?
A GOD WHO HATES MORTALS...
LET'S SEE ...
COME TO THINK OF IT, I THINK I MET SOMEBODY LIKE THAT RECENTLY ...
SSST

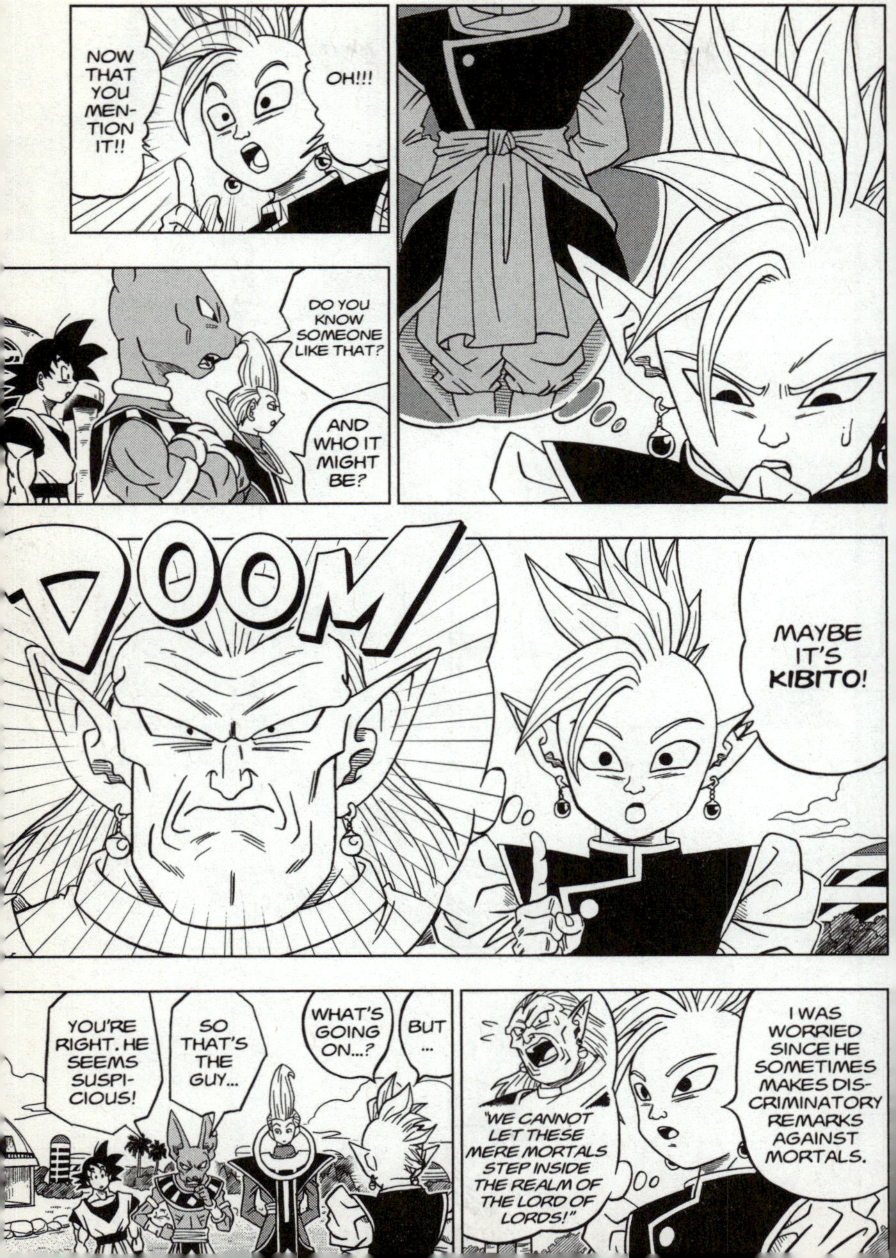
OH!!!
NOW THAT YOU MENTION IT!!
DO YOU KNOW SOMEONE LIKE THAT?
AND WHO IT MIGHT BE?
MAYBE IT'S KIBITO!
DOOM
I WAS WORRIED SINCE HE SOMETIMES MAKES DISCRIMINATORY REMARKS AGAINST MORTALS.
"WE CANNOT LET THESE MERE MORTALS STEP INSIDE THE REALM OF THE LORD OF LORDS!"
BUT...
WHAT'S GOING ON...?
SO THAT'S THE GUY...
YOU'RE RIGHT. HE SEEMS SUSPICIOUS!

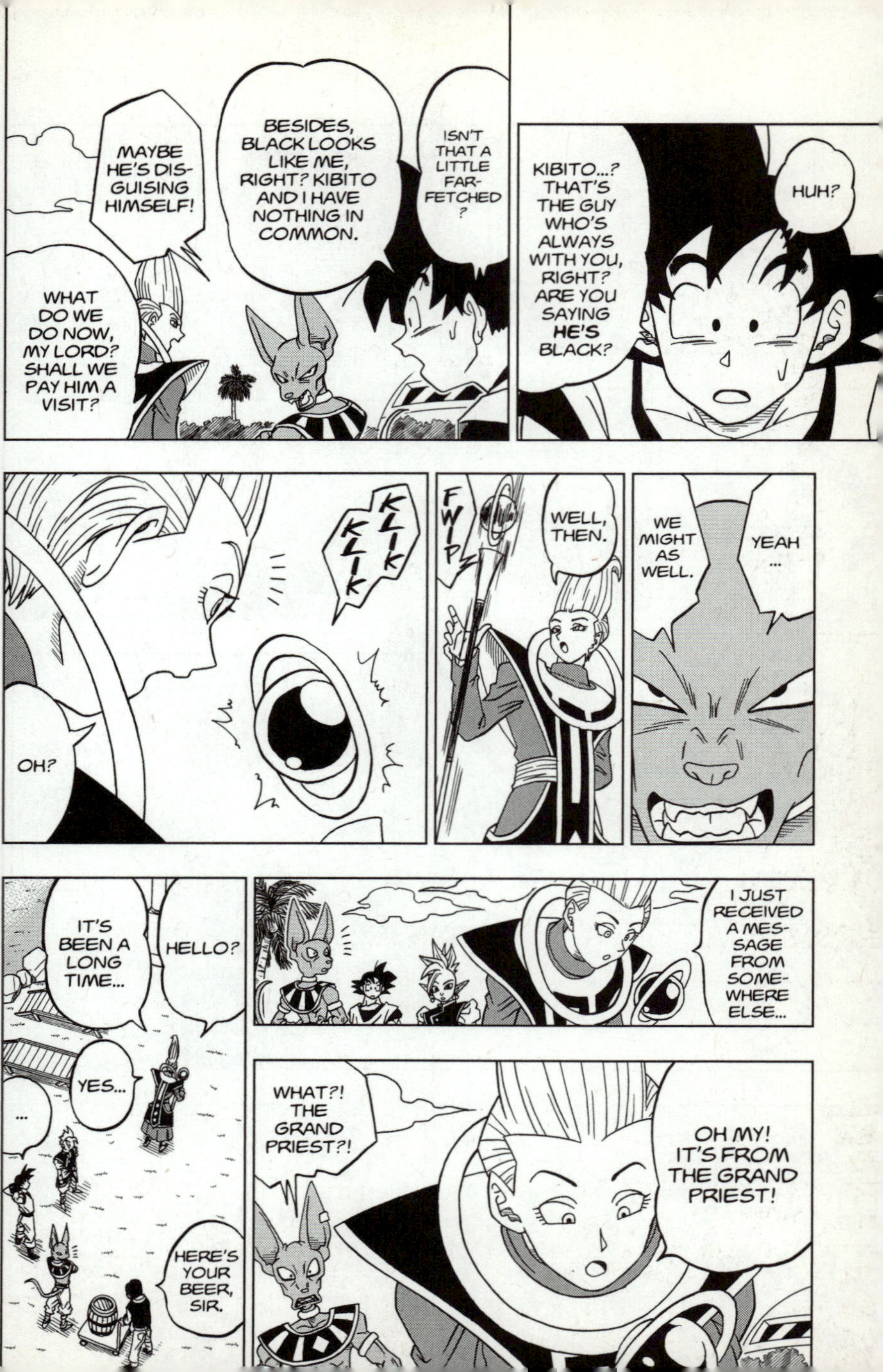
HUH?
KIBITO...? THAT'S THE GUY WHO'S ALWAYS WITH YOU, RIGHT? ARE YOU SAYING **HE'S** BLACK?
ISN'T THAT A LITTLE FAR-FETCHED?
BESIDES, BLACK LOOKS LIKE ME, RIGHT? KIBITO AND I HAVE NOTHING IN COMMON.
MAYBE HE'S DISGUISING HIMSELF!
WHAT DO WE DO NOW, MY LORD? SHALL WE PAY HIM A VISIT?
YEAH...
WE MIGHT AS WELL.
WELL, THEN.
FWIP
KLIK KLIK KLIK
OH?
I JUST RECEIVED A MESSAGE FROM SOMEWHERE ELSE...
OH MY! IT'S FROM THE GRAND PRIEST!
WHAT?! THE GRAND PRIEST?!
HELLO?
IT'S BEEN A LONG TIME...
YES...
...
HERE'S YOUR BEER, SIR.

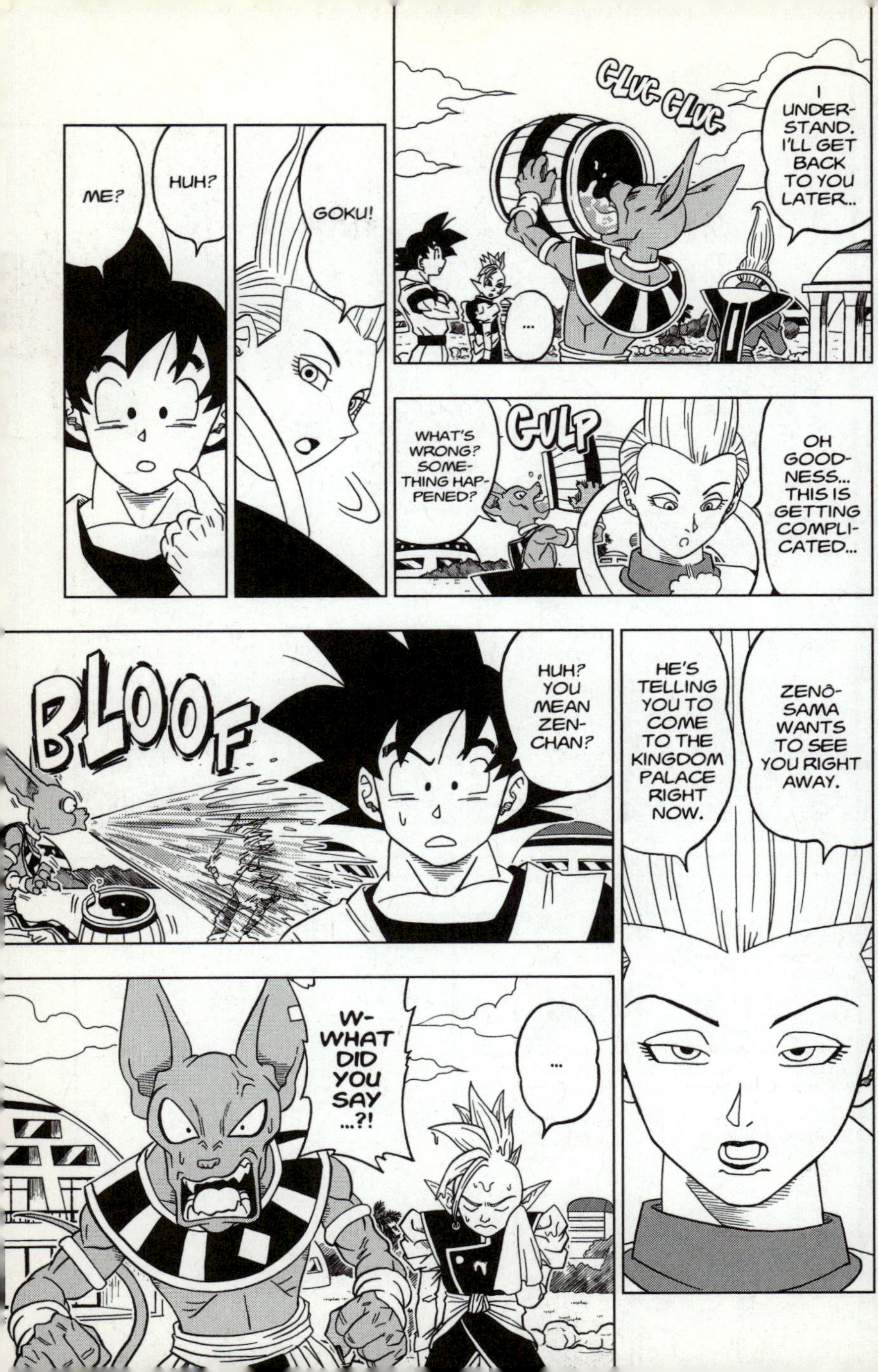
I UNDERSTAND. I'LL GET BACK TO YOU LATER..
GLUG GLUG
...
OH GOODNESS... THIS IS GETTING COMPLICATED...
GULP
WHAT'S WRONG? SOMETHING HAPPENED?
GOKU!
HUH?
ME?
ZENÔ-SAMA WANTS TO SEE YOU RIGHT AWAY.
HE'S TELLING YOU TO COME TO THE KINGDOM PALACE RIGHT NOW.
HUH? YOU MEAN ZEN-CHAN?
BLOOF
...
W-WHAT DID YOU SAY...?!

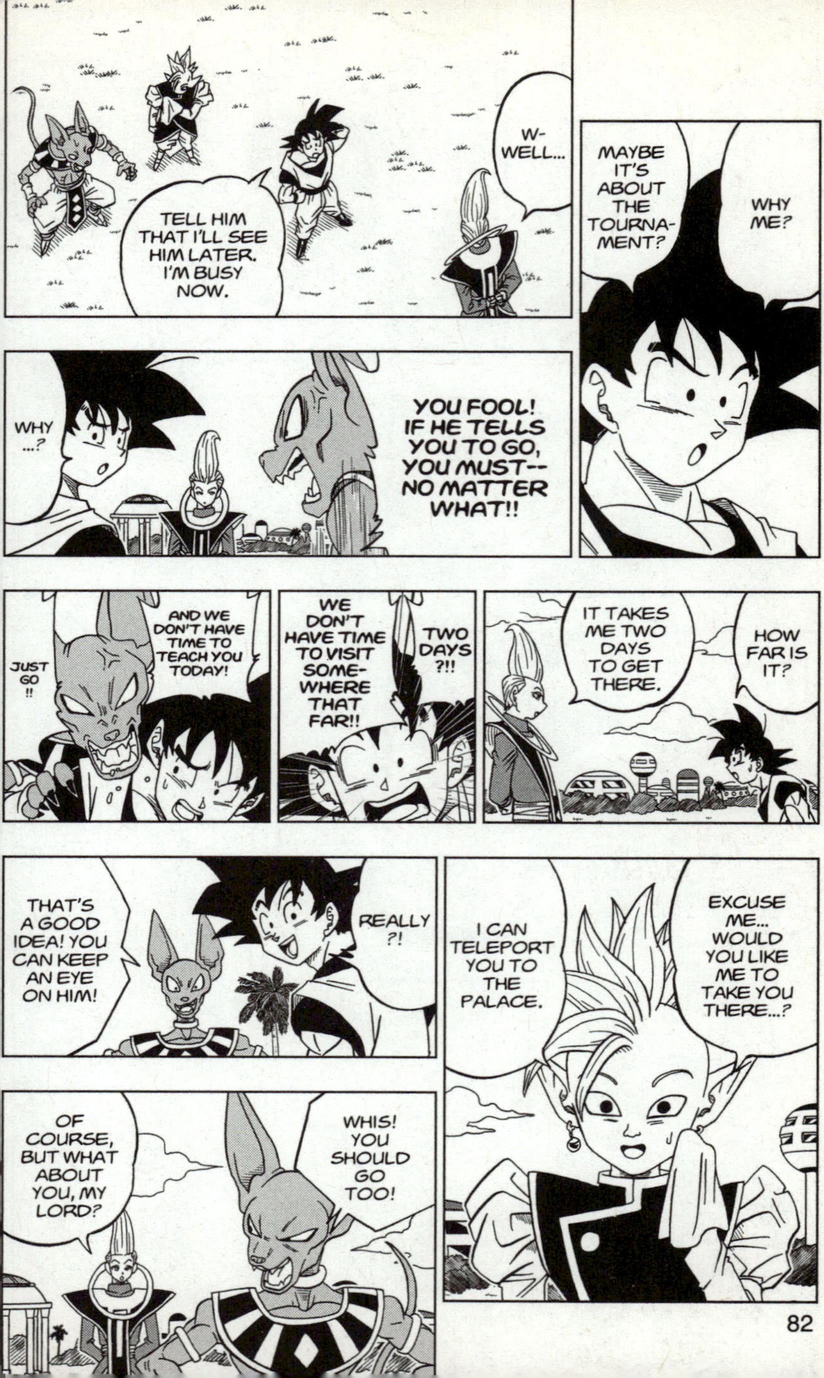
W-WELL...
TELL HIM THAT I'LL SEE HIM LATER. I'M BUSY NOW.
WHY ME?
MAYBE IT'S ABOUT THE TOURNA-MENT?
YOU FOOL! IF HE TELLS YOU TO GO, YOU MUST-- NO MATTER WHAT!!
WHY ...?
HOW FAR IS IT?
IT TAKES ME TWO DAYS TO GET THERE.
TWO DAYS ?!!
WE DON'T HAVE TIME TO VISIT SOME-WHERE THAT FAR!!
AND WE DON'T HAVE TIME TO TEACH YOU TODAY!
JUST GO !!
EXCUSE ME... WOULD YOU LIKE ME TO TAKE YOU THERE...?
I CAN TELEPORT YOU TO THE PALACE.
REALLY ?!
THAT'S A GOOD IDEA! YOU CAN KEEP AN EYE ON HIM!
WHIS! YOU SHOULD GO TOO!
OF COURSE, BUT WHAT ABOUT YOU, MY LORD?

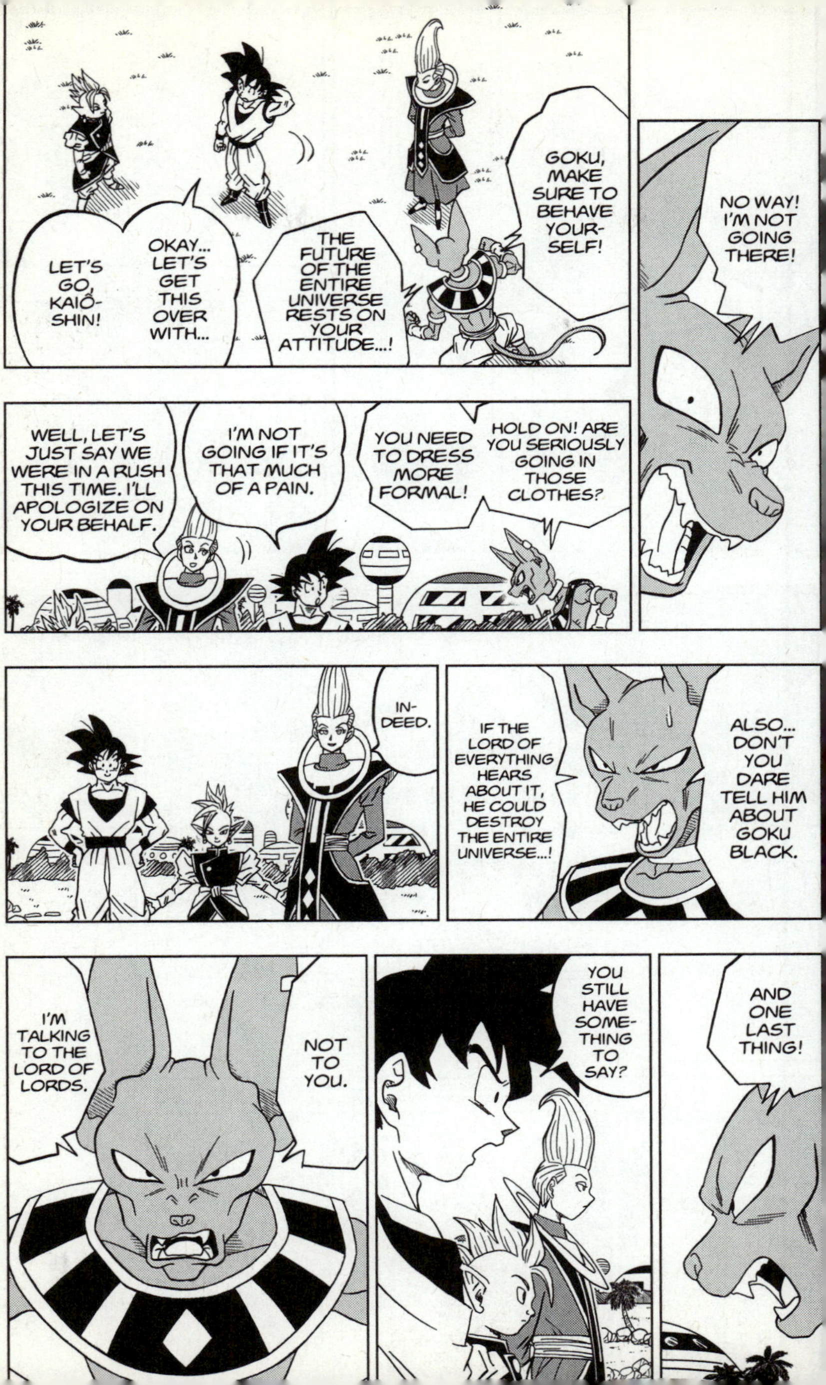
GOKU, MAKE SURE TO BEHAVE YOURSELF!
THE FUTURE OF THE ENTIRE UNIVERSE RESTS ON YOUR ATTITUDE...!
OKAY... LET'S GET THIS OVER WITH...
LET'S GO, KAIŌ-SHIN!
NO WAY! I'M NOT GOING THERE!
HOLD ON! ARE YOU SERIOUSLY GOING IN THOSE CLOTHES?
YOU NEED TO DRESS MORE FORMAL!
I'M NOT GOING IF IT'S THAT MUCH OF A PAIN.
WELL, LET'S JUST SAY WE WERE IN A RUSH THIS TIME. I'LL APOLOGIZE ON YOUR BEHALF.
ALSO... DON'T YOU DARE TELL HIM ABOUT GOKU BLACK.
IF THE LORD OF EVERYTHING HEARS ABOUT IT, HE COULD DESTROY THE ENTIRE UNIVERSE...!
INDEED.
AND ONE LAST THING!
YOU STILL HAVE SOMETHING TO SAY?
NOT TO YOU.
I'M TALKING TO THE LORD OF LORDS.

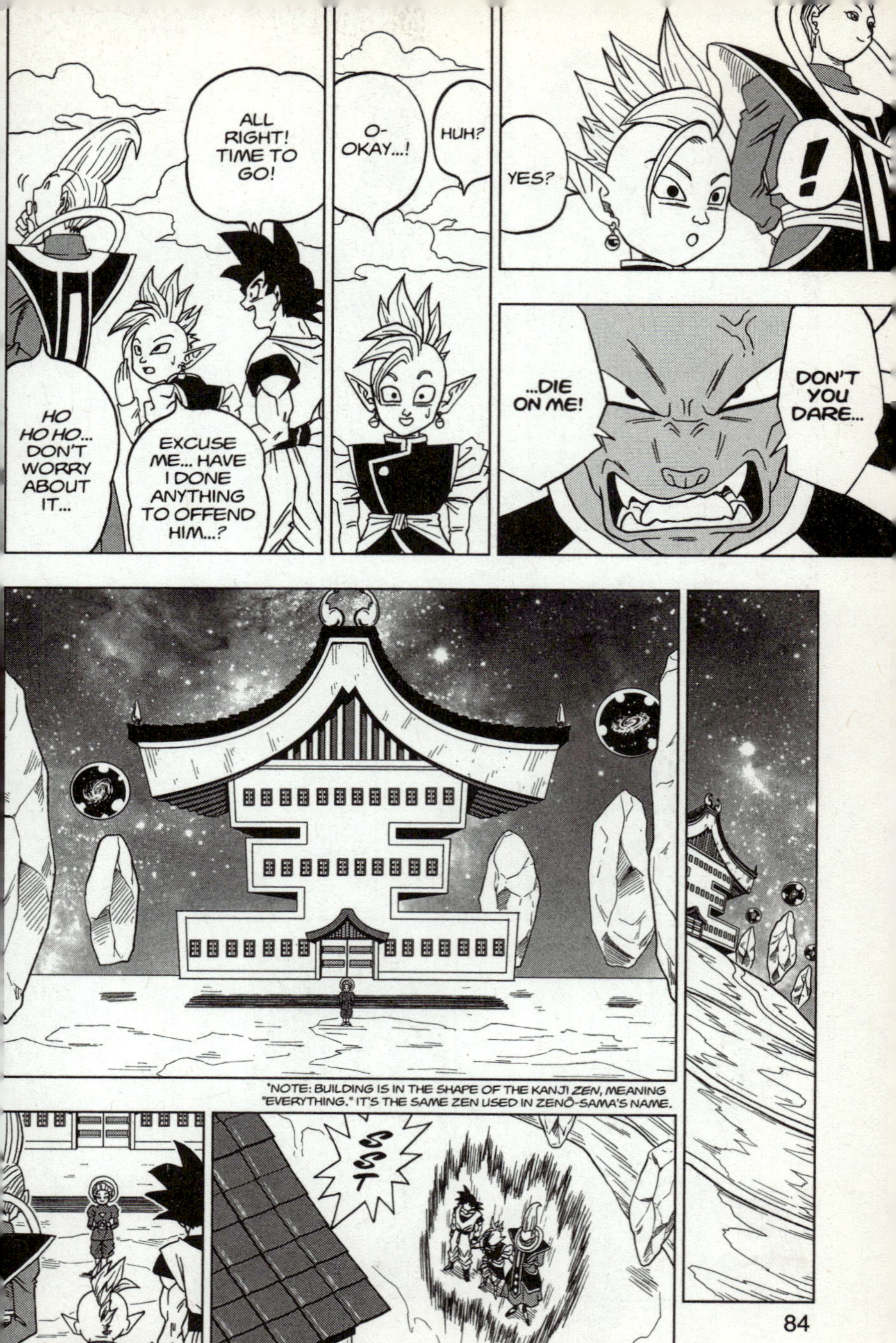
YES?
!
DON'T YOU DARE...
...DIE ON ME!
HUH?
O-OKAY...!
ALL RIGHT! TIME TO GO!
EXCUSE ME... HAVE I DONE ANYTHING TO OFFEND HIM...?
HO HO HO... DON'T WORRY ABOUT IT...
*NOTE: BUILDING IS IN THE SHAPE OF THE KANJI ZEN, MEANING "EVERYTHING." IT'S THE SAME ZEN USED IN ZENŌ-SAMA'S NAME.
SSST

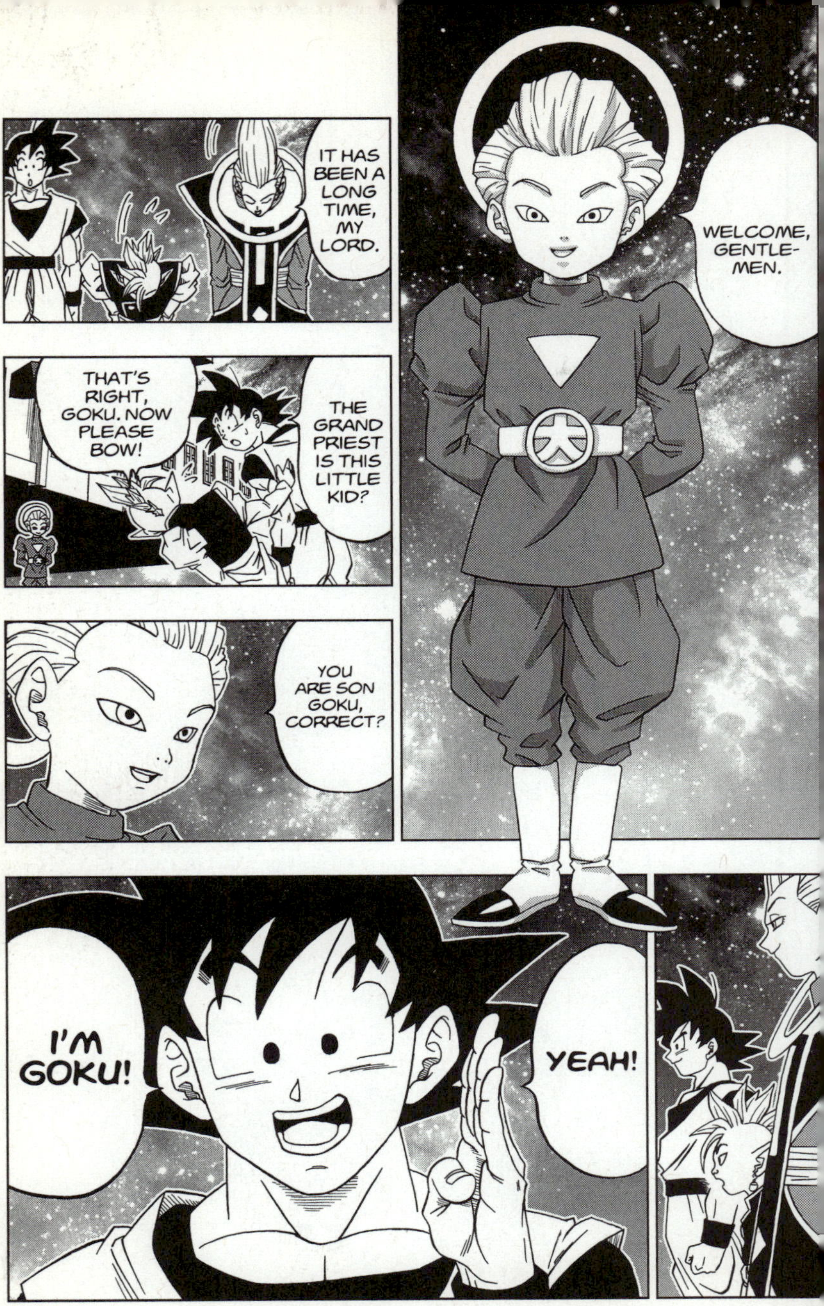
WELCOME, GENTLE-MEN.
IT HAS BEEN A LONG TIME, MY LORD.
THE GRAND PRIEST IS THIS LITTLE KID?
THAT'S RIGHT, GOKU. NOW PLEASE BOW!
YOU ARE SON GOKU, CORRECT?
YEAH!
I'M GOKU!

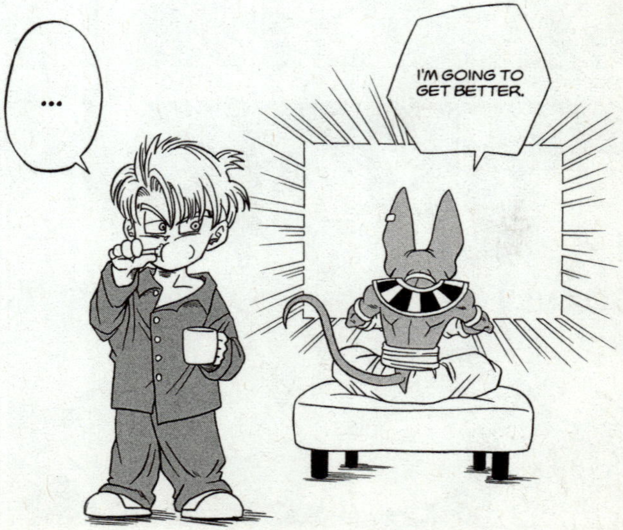
I'M GOING TO GET BETTER.
...

# DRAGON BALL SUPER

## CHAPTER 18: GOKU BLACK'S TRUE IDENTITY

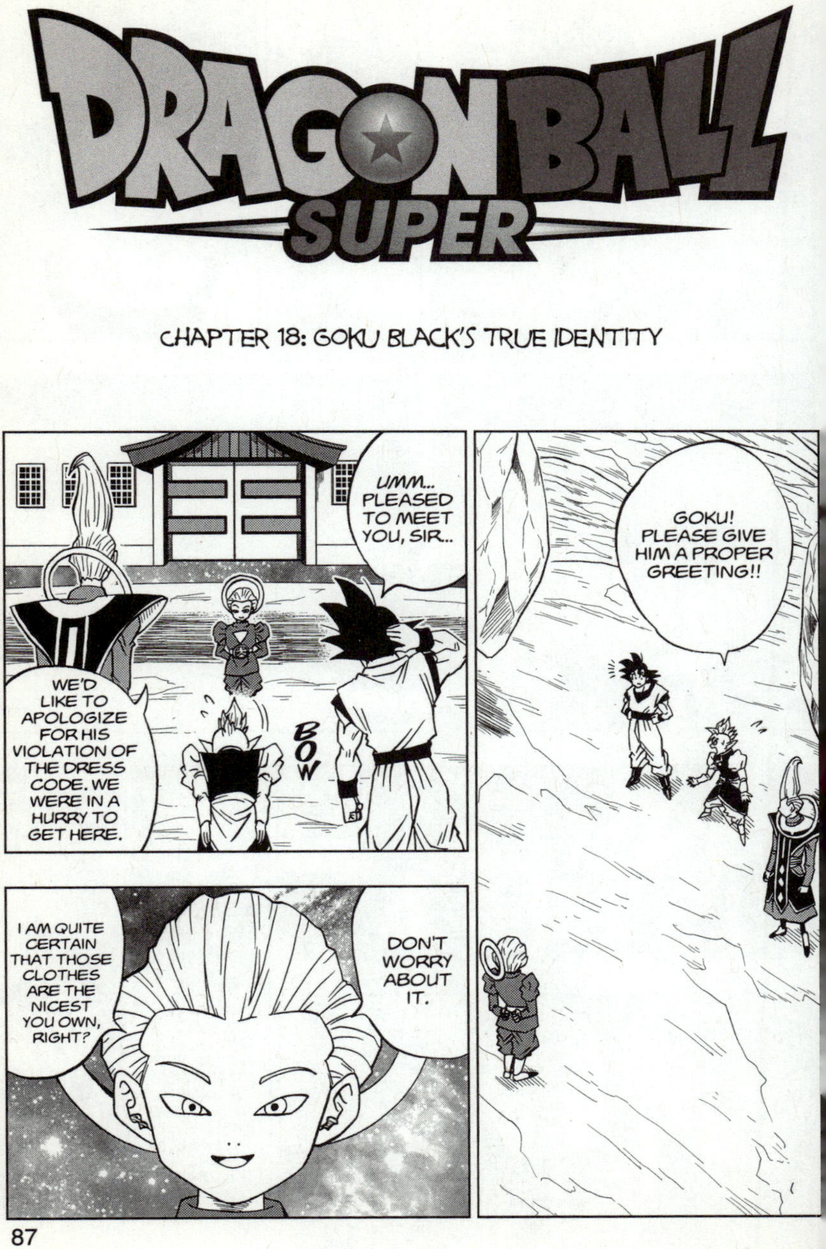
GOKU! PLEASE GIVE HIM A PROPER GREETING!!
UMM... PLEASED TO MEET YOU, SIR...
BOW
WE'D LIKE TO APOLOGIZE FOR HIS VIOLATION OF THE DRESS CODE. WE WERE IN A HURRY TO GET HERE.
DON'T WORRY ABOUT IT.
I AM QUITE CERTAIN THAT THOSE CLOTHES ARE THE NICEST YOU OWN, RIGHT?

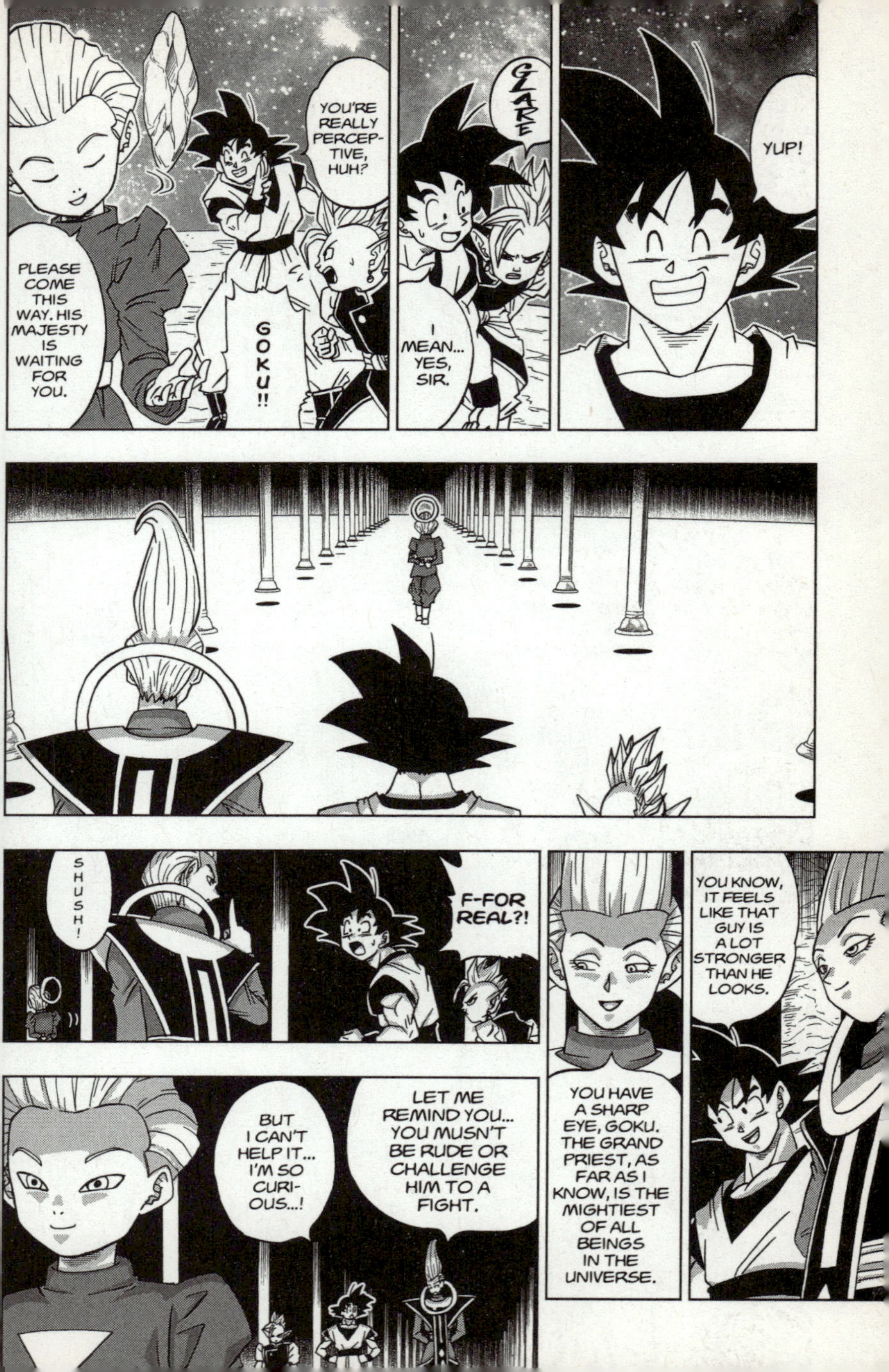
YUP!
GLARE
I MEAN... YES, SIR.
YOU'RE REALLY PERCEPTIVE, HUH?
GOKU!!
PLEASE COME THIS WAY. HIS MAJESTY IS WAITING FOR YOU.
YOU KNOW, IT FEELS LIKE THAT GUY IS A LOT STRONGER THAN HE LOOKS.
YOU HAVE A SHARP EYE, GOKU. THE GRAND PRIEST, AS FAR AS I KNOW, IS THE MIGHTIEST OF ALL BEINGS IN THE UNIVERSE.
F-FOR REAL?!
SHUSH!
LET ME REMIND YOU... YOU MUSN'T BE RUDE OR CHALLENGE HIM TO A FIGHT.
BUT I CAN'T HELP IT... I'M SO CURIOUS...!

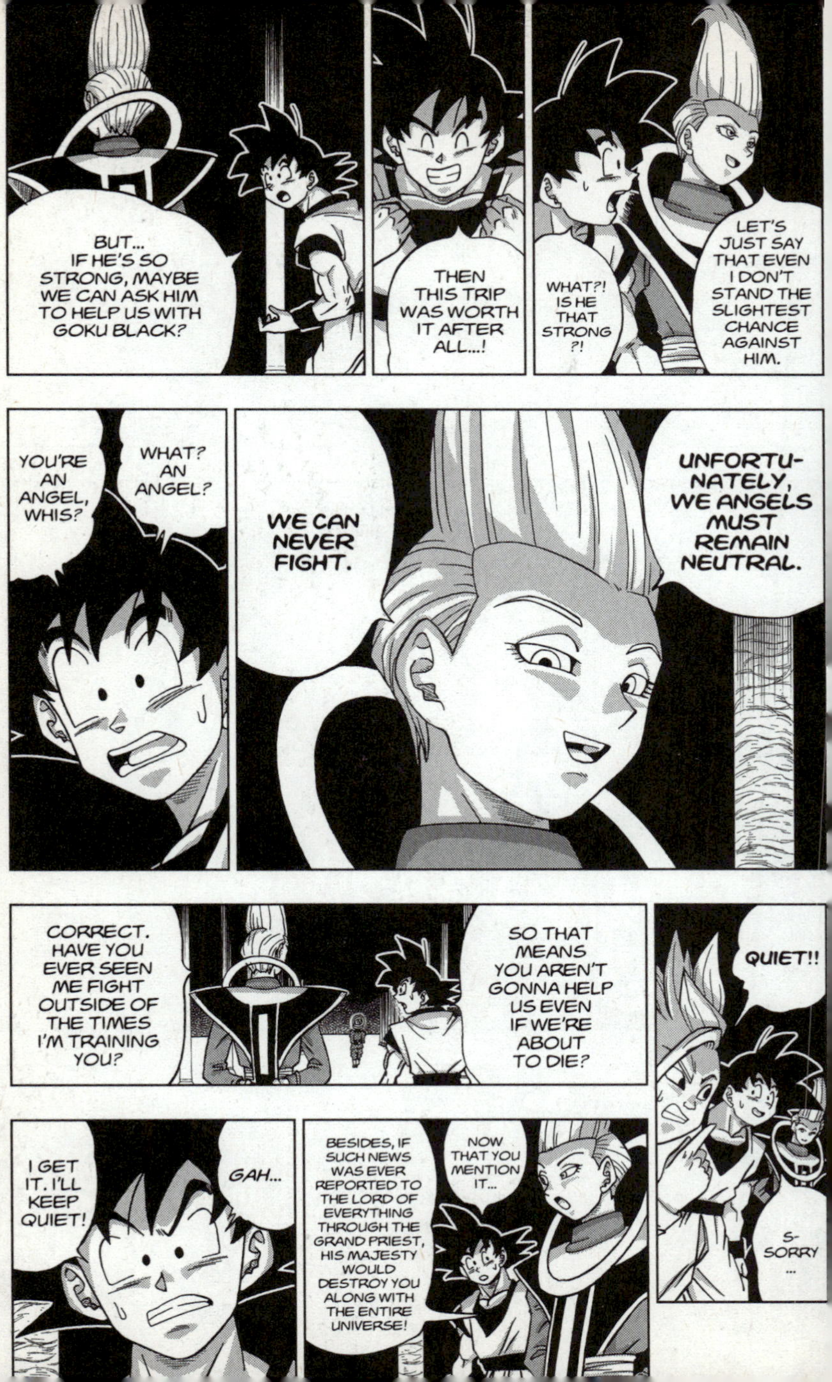
LET'S JUST SAY THAT EVEN I DON'T STAND THE SLIGHTEST CHANCE AGAINST HIM.
WHAT?! IS HE THAT STRONG ?!
THEN THIS TRIP WAS WORTH IT AFTER ALL...!
BUT... IF HE'S SO STRONG, MAYBE WE CAN ASK HIM TO HELP US WITH GOKU BLACK?
UNFORTU-NATELY, WE ANGELS MUST REMAIN NEUTRAL.
WE CAN NEVER FIGHT.
WHAT? AN ANGEL?
YOU'RE AN ANGEL, WHIS?
QUIET!!
S-SORRY...
SO THAT MEANS YOU AREN'T GONNA HELP US EVEN IF WE'RE ABOUT TO DIE?
CORRECT. HAVE YOU EVER SEEN ME FIGHT OUTSIDE OF THE TIMES I'M TRAINING YOU?
NOW THAT YOU MENTION IT...
BESIDES, IF SUCH NEWS WAS EVER REPORTED TO THE LORD OF EVERYTHING THROUGH THE GRAND PRIEST, HIS MAJESTY WOULD DESTROY YOU ALONG WITH THE ENTIRE UNIVERSE!
GAH...
I GET IT. I'LL KEEP QUIET!

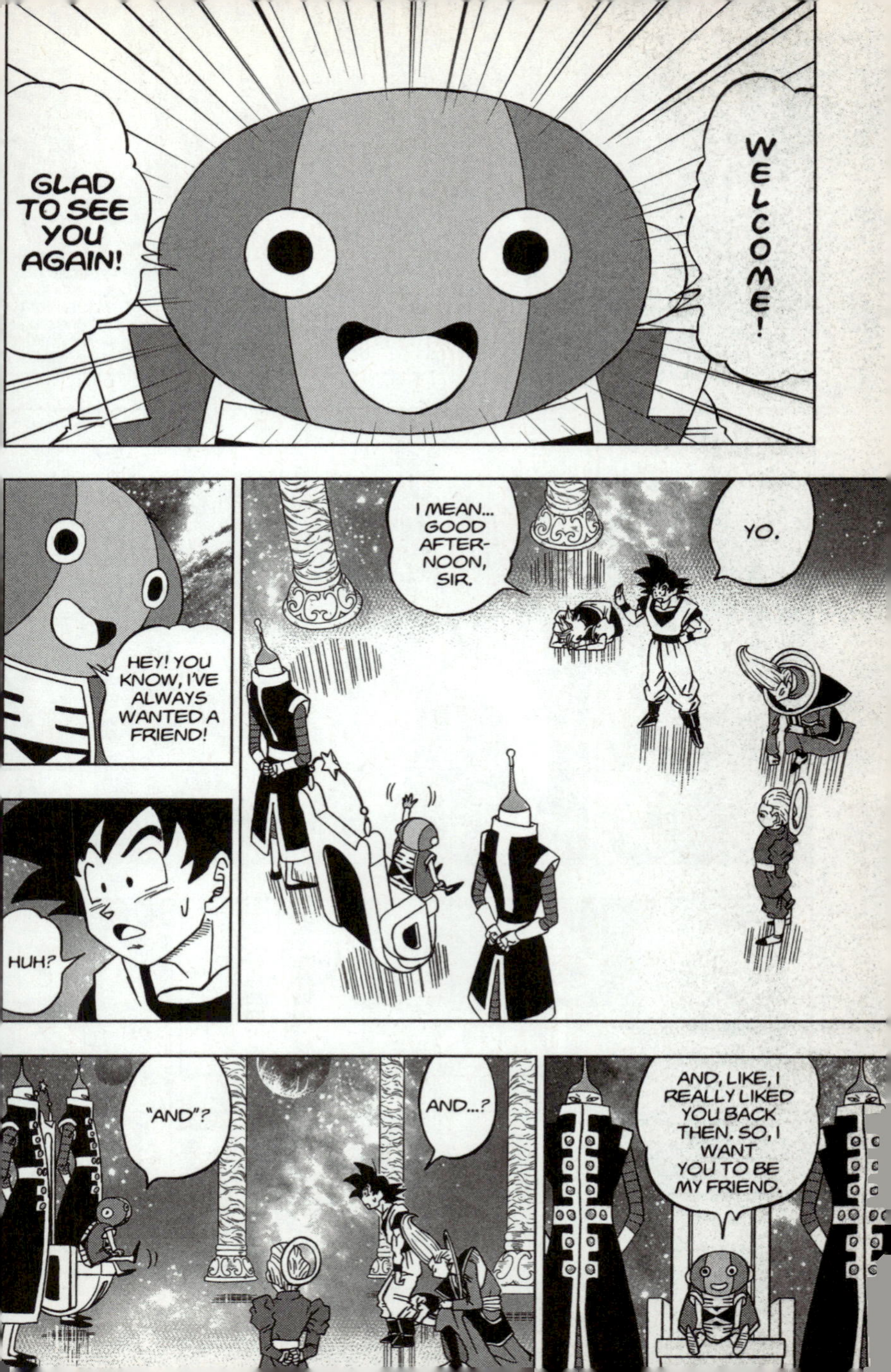
WELCOME!
GLAD TO SEE YOU AGAIN!
YO.
I MEAN... GOOD AFTERNOON, SIR.
HEY! YOU KNOW, I'VE ALWAYS WANTED A FRIEND!
HUH?
AND, LIKE, I REALLY LIKED YOU BACK THEN. SO, I WANT YOU TO BE MY FRIEND.
AND...?
"AND"?

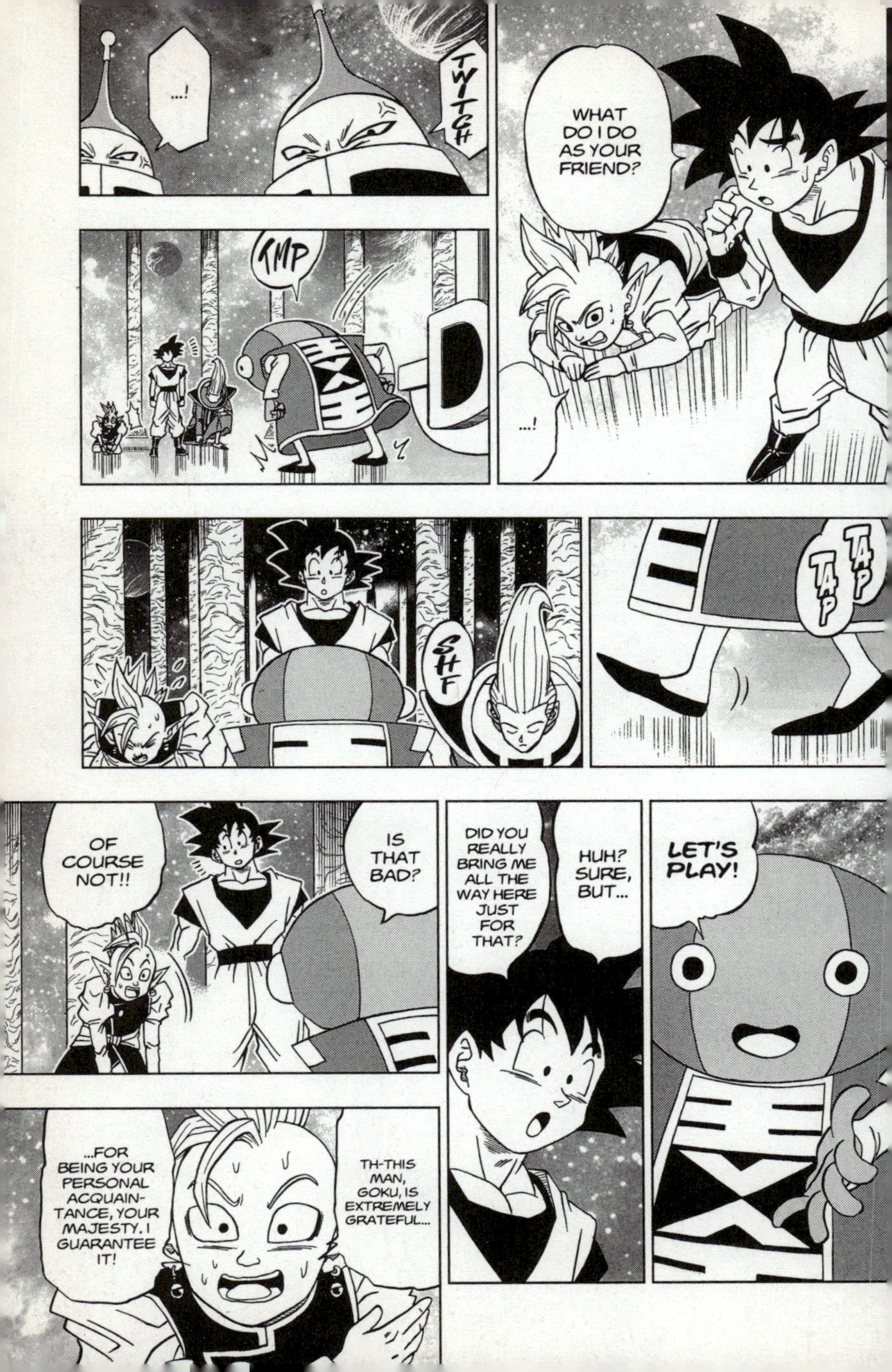

WHAT DO I DO AS YOUR FRIEND?
...!
...!
TWITCH
TMP
TAP TAP
SHF
LET'S PLAY!
HUH? SURE, BUT...
DID YOU REALLY BRING ME ALL THE WAY HERE JUST FOR THAT?
IS THAT BAD?
OF COURSE NOT!!
TH-THIS MAN, GOKU, IS EXTREMELY GRATEFUL...
...FOR BEING YOUR PERSONAL ACQUAIN-TANCE, YOUR MAJESTY. I GUARANTEE IT!

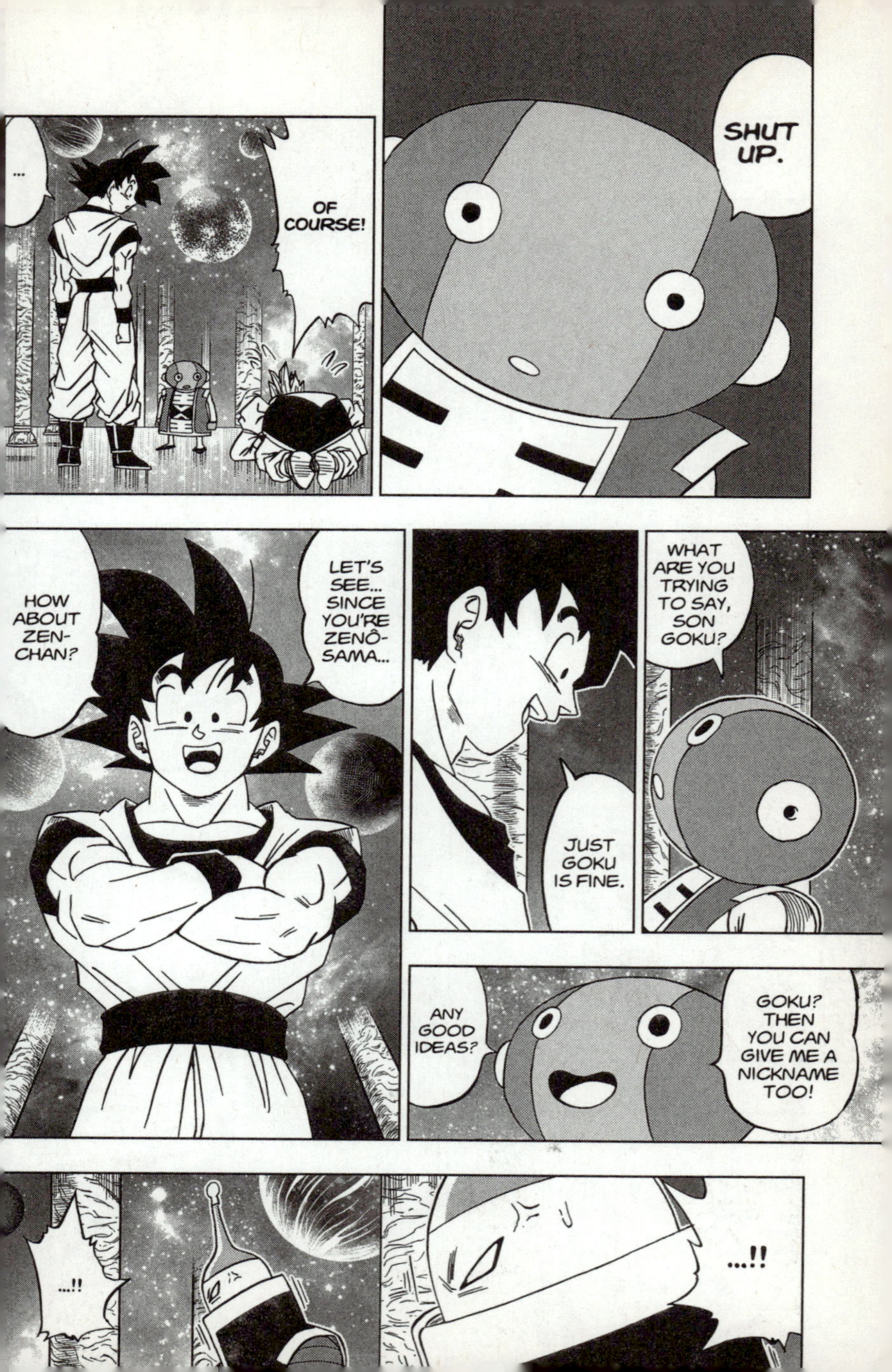
SHUT UP.
OF COURSE!
...
WHAT ARE YOU TRYING TO SAY, SON GOKU?
JUST GOKU IS FINE.
GOKU? THEN YOU CAN GIVE ME A NICKNAME TOO!
ANY GOOD IDEAS?
LET'S SEE... SINCE YOU'RE ZENÔ-SAMA...
HOW ABOUT ZEN-CHAN?
...!!
...!!

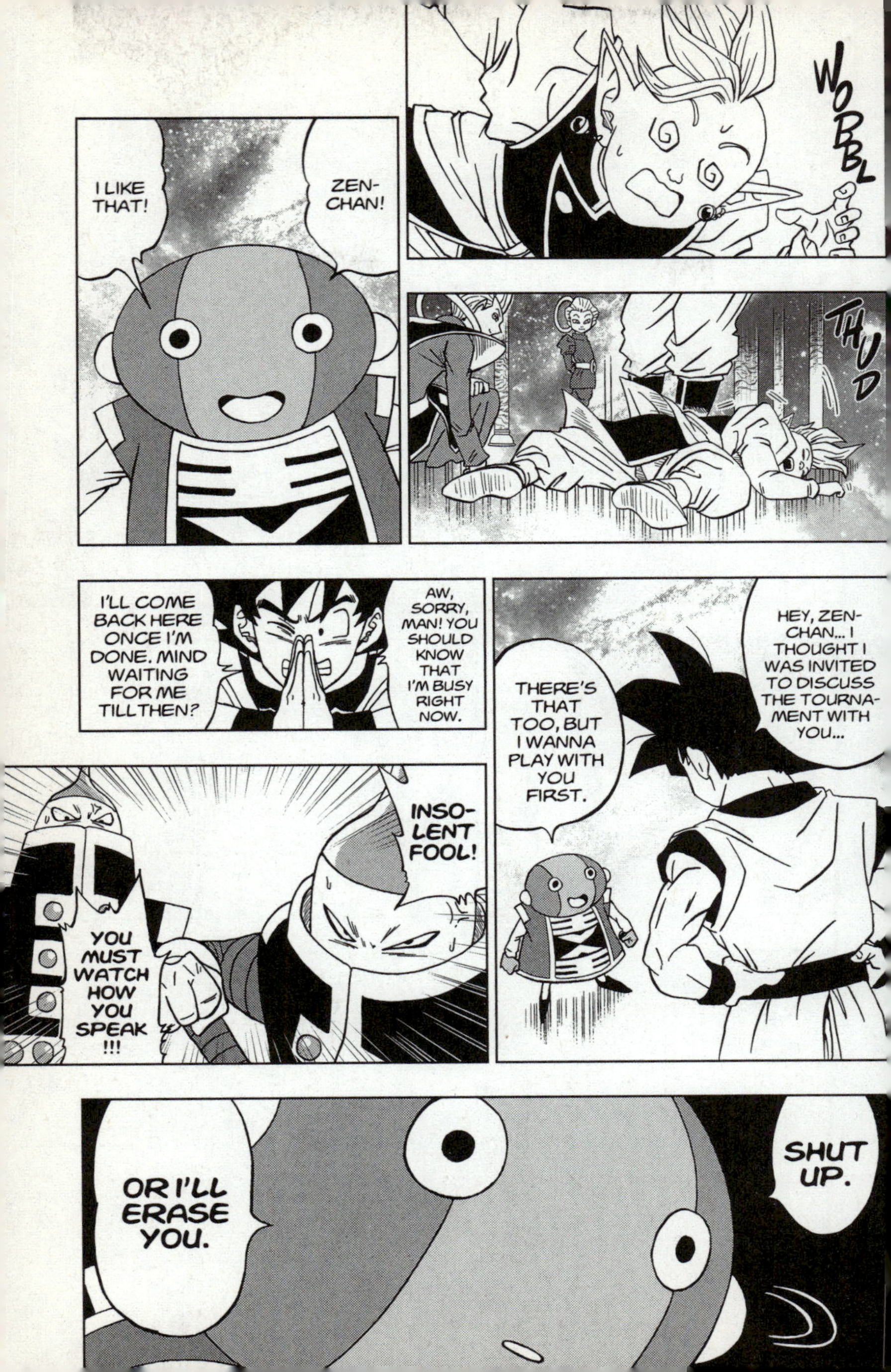
WOBBL
THUD
ZEN-CHAN!
I LIKE THAT!
HEY, ZEN-CHAN... I THOUGHT I WAS INVITED TO DISCUSS THE TOURNAMENT WITH YOU...
THERE'S THAT TOO, BUT I WANNA PLAY WITH YOU FIRST.
AW, SORRY, MAN! YOU SHOULD KNOW THAT I'M BUSY RIGHT NOW.
I'LL COME BACK HERE ONCE I'M DONE. MIND WAITING FOR ME TILL THEN?
INSOLENT FOOL!
YOU MUST WATCH HOW YOU SPEAK!!!
SHUT UP.
OR I'LL ERASE YOU.

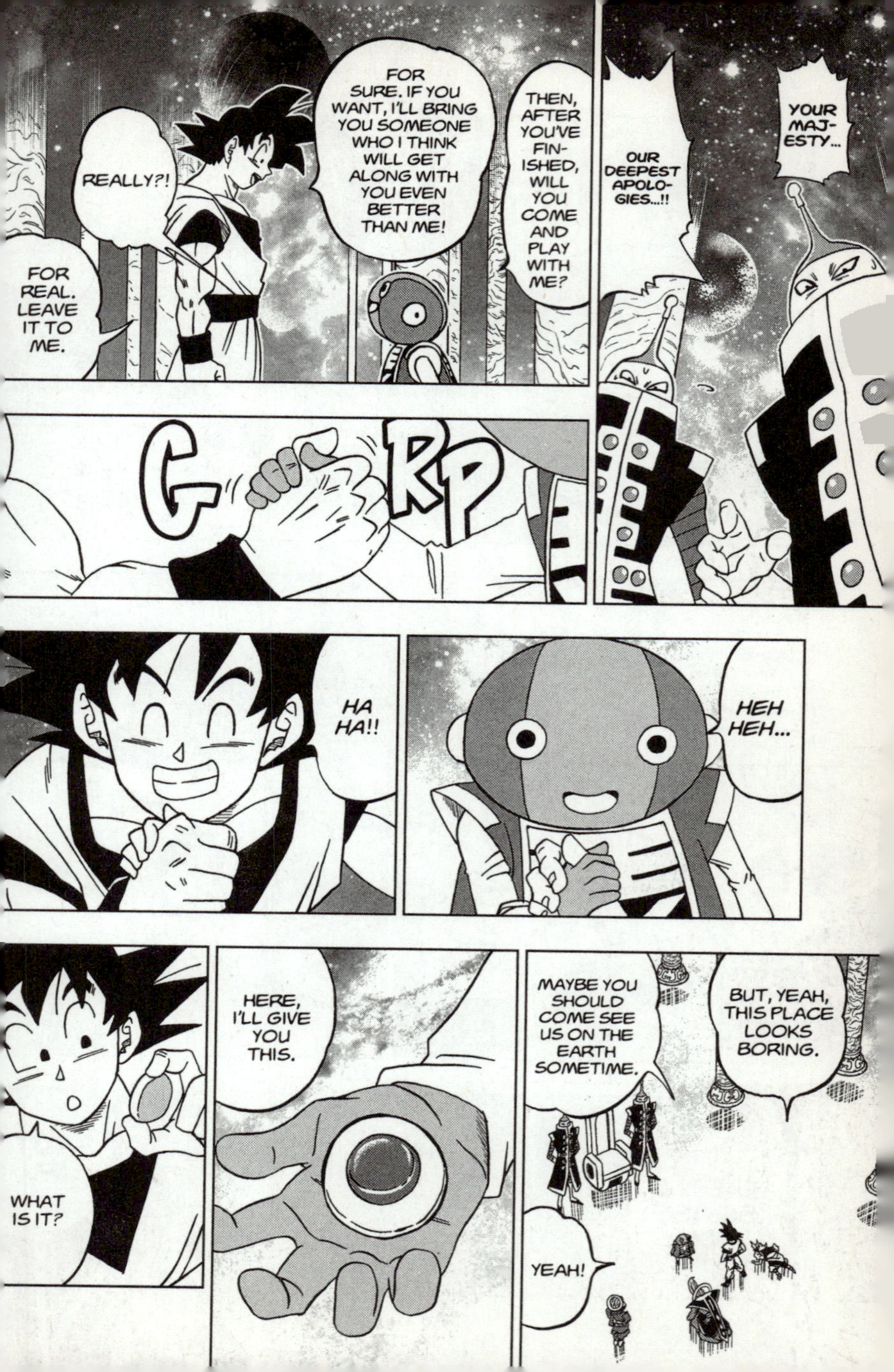
YOUR MAJ-ESTY...
OUR DEEPEST APOLO-GIES...!!
THEN, AFTER YOU'VE FIN-ISHED, WILL YOU COME AND PLAY WITH ME?
FOR SURE. IF YOU WANT, I'LL BRING YOU SOMEONE WHO I THINK WILL GET ALONG WITH YOU EVEN BETTER THAN ME!
REALLY?!
FOR REAL. LEAVE IT TO ME.
GRP
HEH HEH...
HA HA!!
BUT, YEAH, THIS PLACE LOOKS BORING.
MAYBE YOU SHOULD COME SEE US ON THE EARTH SOMETIME.
YEAH!
HERE, I'LL GIVE YOU THIS.
WHAT IS IT?

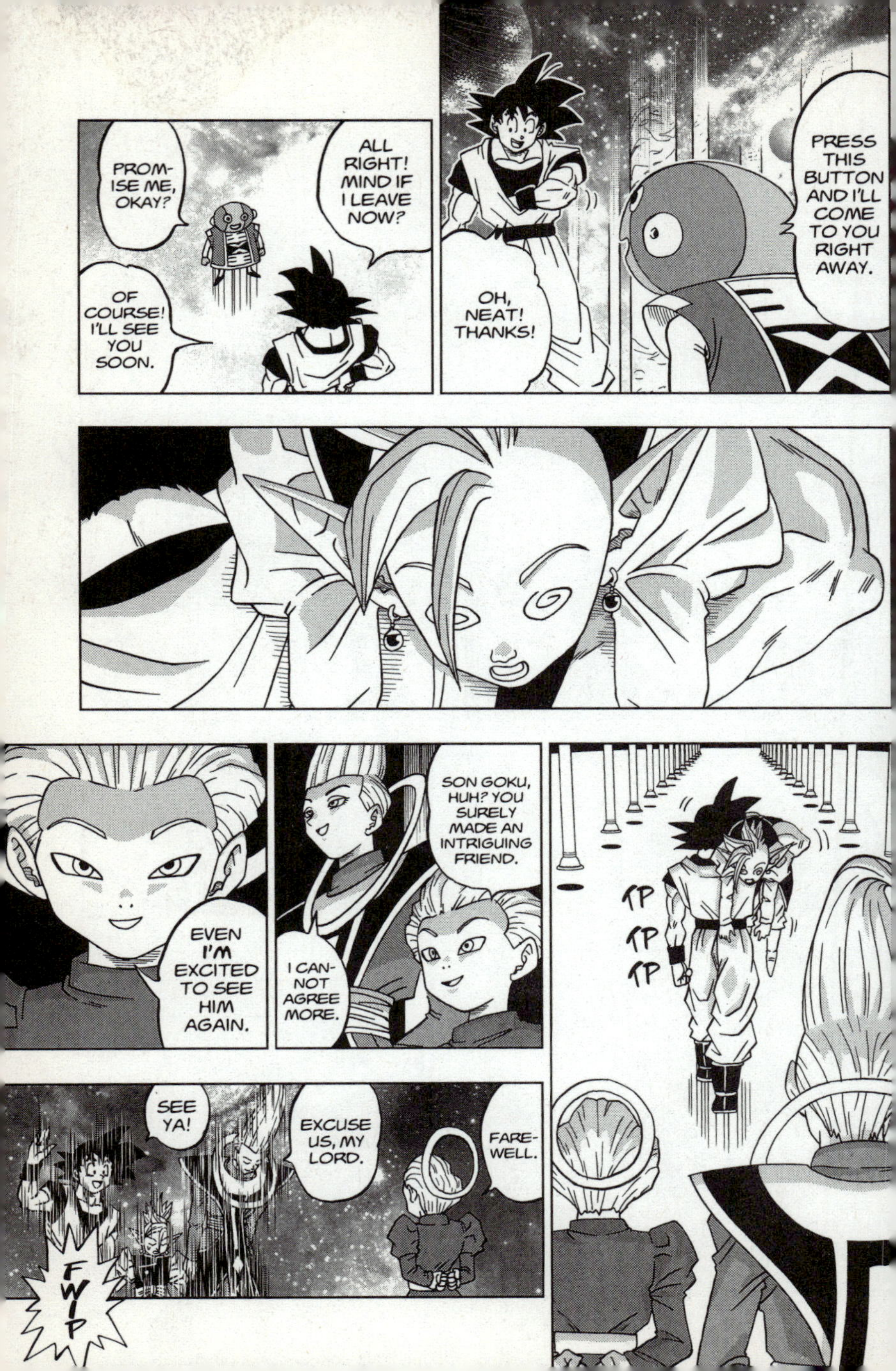
PRESS THIS BUTTON AND I'LL COME TO YOU RIGHT AWAY.
OH, NEAT! THANKS!
ALL RIGHT! MIND IF I LEAVE NOW?
PROM-ISE ME, OKAY?
OF COURSE! I'LL SEE YOU SOON.
TP
TP
TP
SON GOKU, HUH? YOU SURELY MADE AN INTRIGUING FRIEND.
I CAN-NOT AGREE MORE.
EVEN I'M EXCITED TO SEE HIM AGAIN.
FARE-WELL.
EXCUSE US, MY LORD.
SEE YA!
FWIP

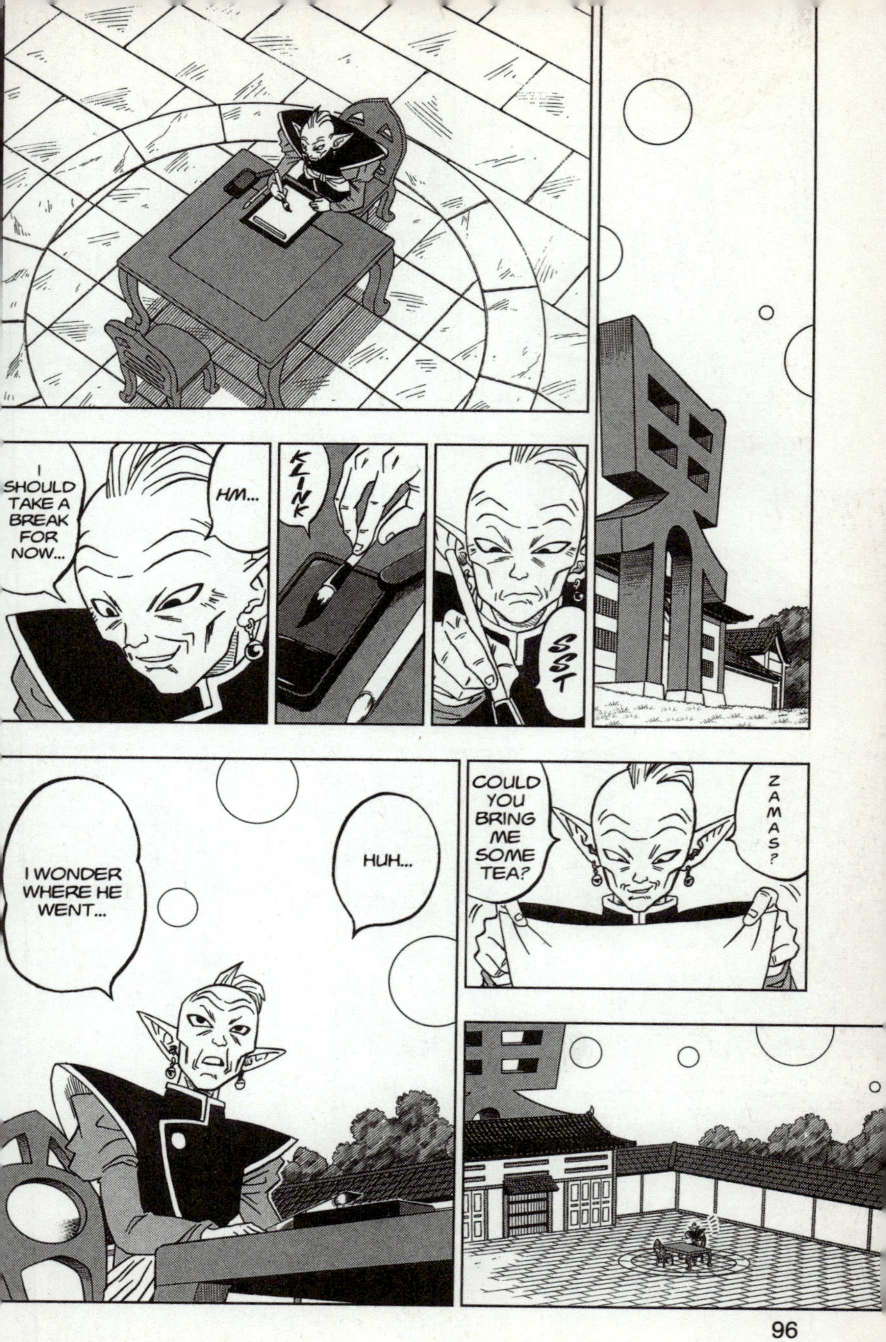
SST
KLINK
HM...
I SHOULD TAKE A BREAK FOR NOW...
ZAMAS?
COULD YOU BRING ME SOME TEA?
HUH...
I WONDER WHERE HE WENT...

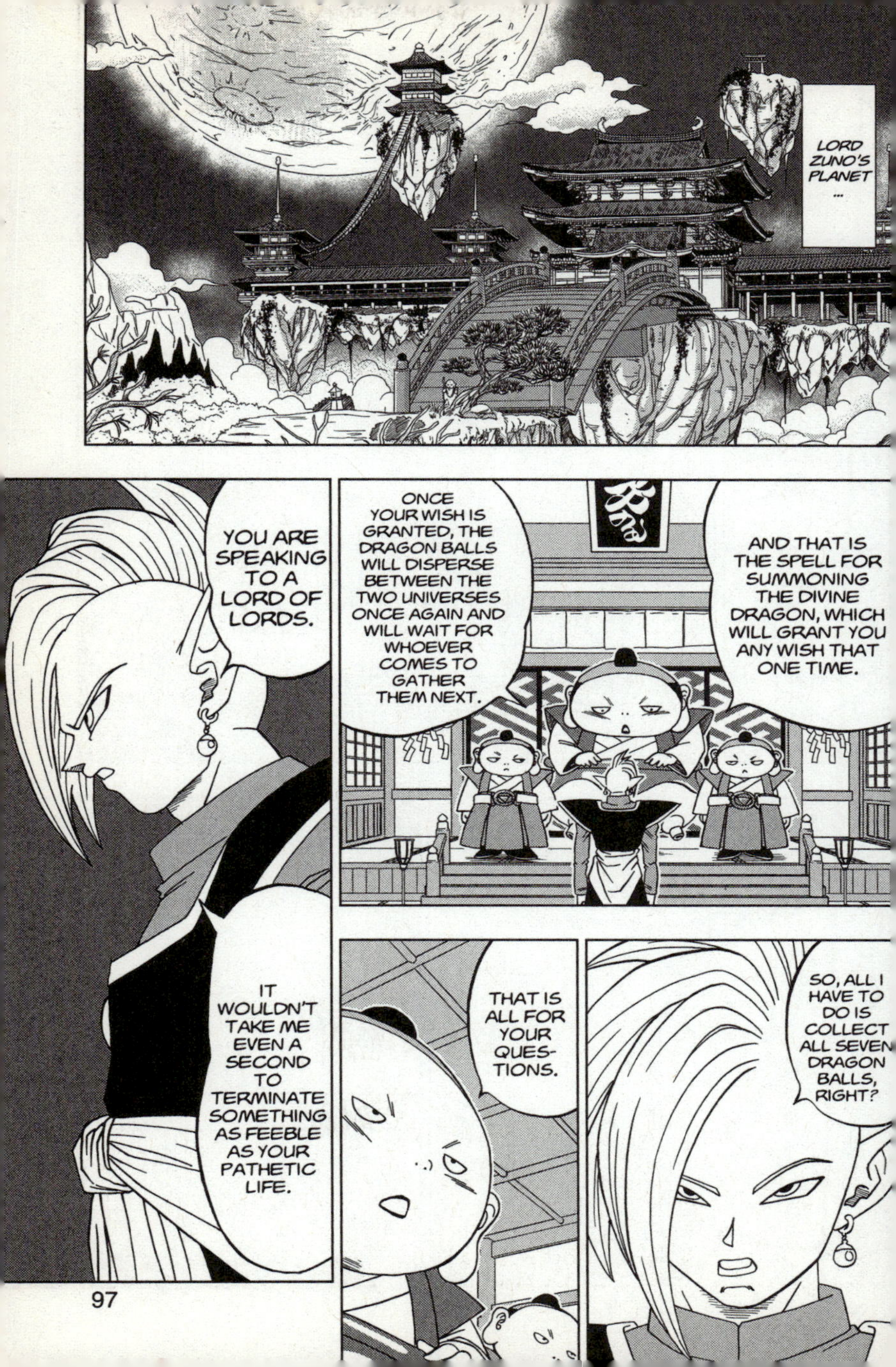
LORD ZUNO'S PLANET ...
AND THAT IS THE SPELL FOR SUMMONING THE DIVINE DRAGON, WHICH WILL GRANT YOU ANY WISH THAT ONE TIME.
ONCE YOUR WISH IS GRANTED, THE DRAGON BALLS WILL DISPERSE BETWEEN THE TWO UNIVERSES ONCE AGAIN AND WILL WAIT FOR WHOEVER COMES TO GATHER THEM NEXT.
SO, ALL I HAVE TO DO IS COLLECT ALL SEVEN DRAGON BALLS, RIGHT?
THAT IS ALL FOR YOUR QUES-TIONS.
YOU ARE SPEAKING TO A LORD OF LORDS.
IT WOULDN'T TAKE ME EVEN A SECOND TO TERMINATE SOMETHING AS FEEBLE AS YOUR PATHETIC LIFE.

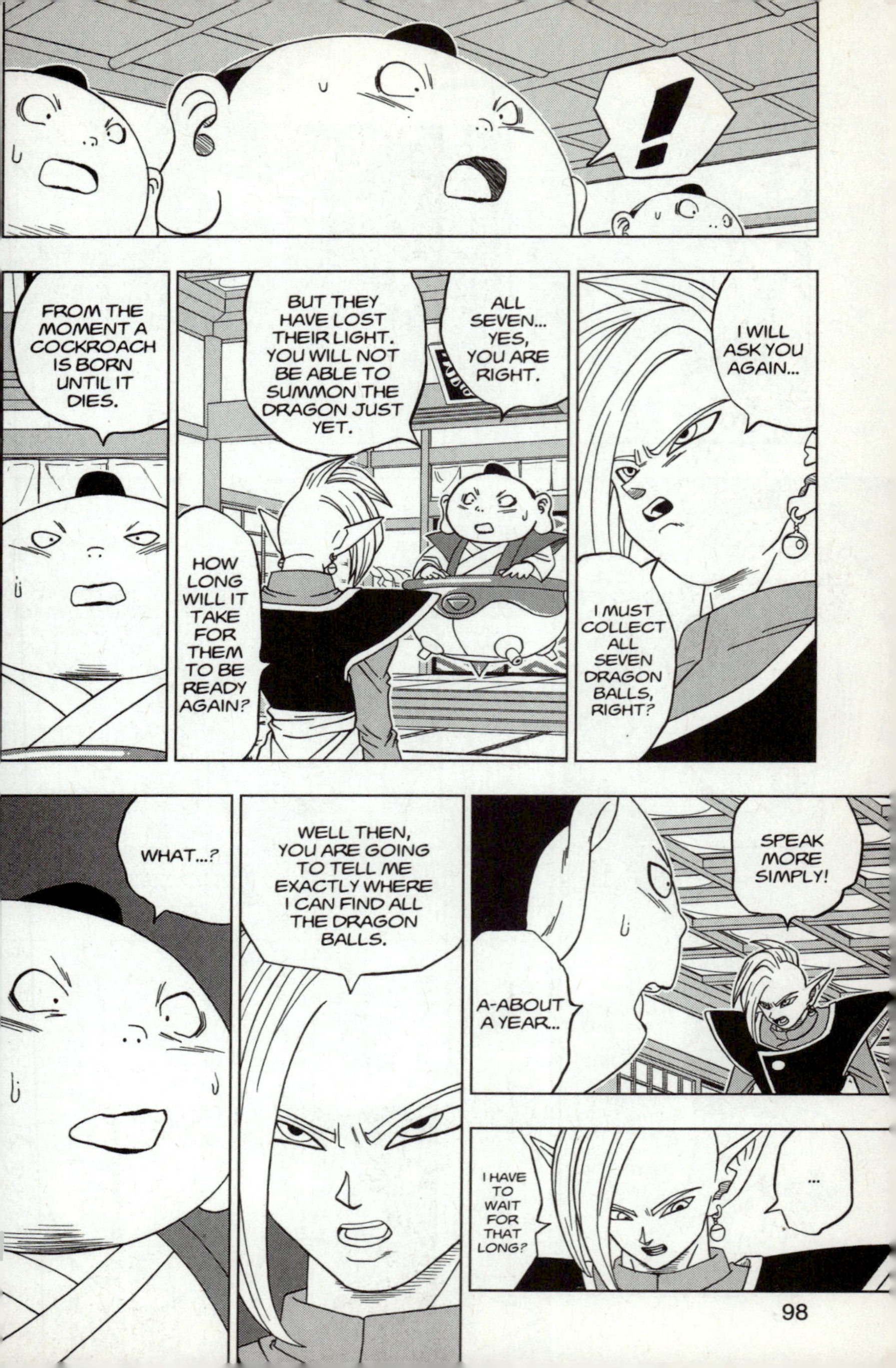
!
I WILL ASK YOU AGAIN...
I MUST COLLECT ALL SEVEN DRAGON BALLS, RIGHT?
ALL SEVEN... YES, YOU ARE RIGHT.
BUT THEY HAVE LOST THEIR LIGHT. YOU WILL NOT BE ABLE TO SUMMON THE DRAGON JUST YET.
HOW LONG WILL IT TAKE FOR THEM TO BE READY AGAIN?
FROM THE MOMENT A COCKROACH IS BORN UNTIL IT DIES.
SPEAK MORE SIMPLY!
A-ABOUT A YEAR...
...
I HAVE TO WAIT FOR THAT LONG?
WELL THEN, YOU ARE GOING TO TELL ME EXACTLY WHERE I CAN FIND ALL THE DRAGON BALLS.
WHAT...?

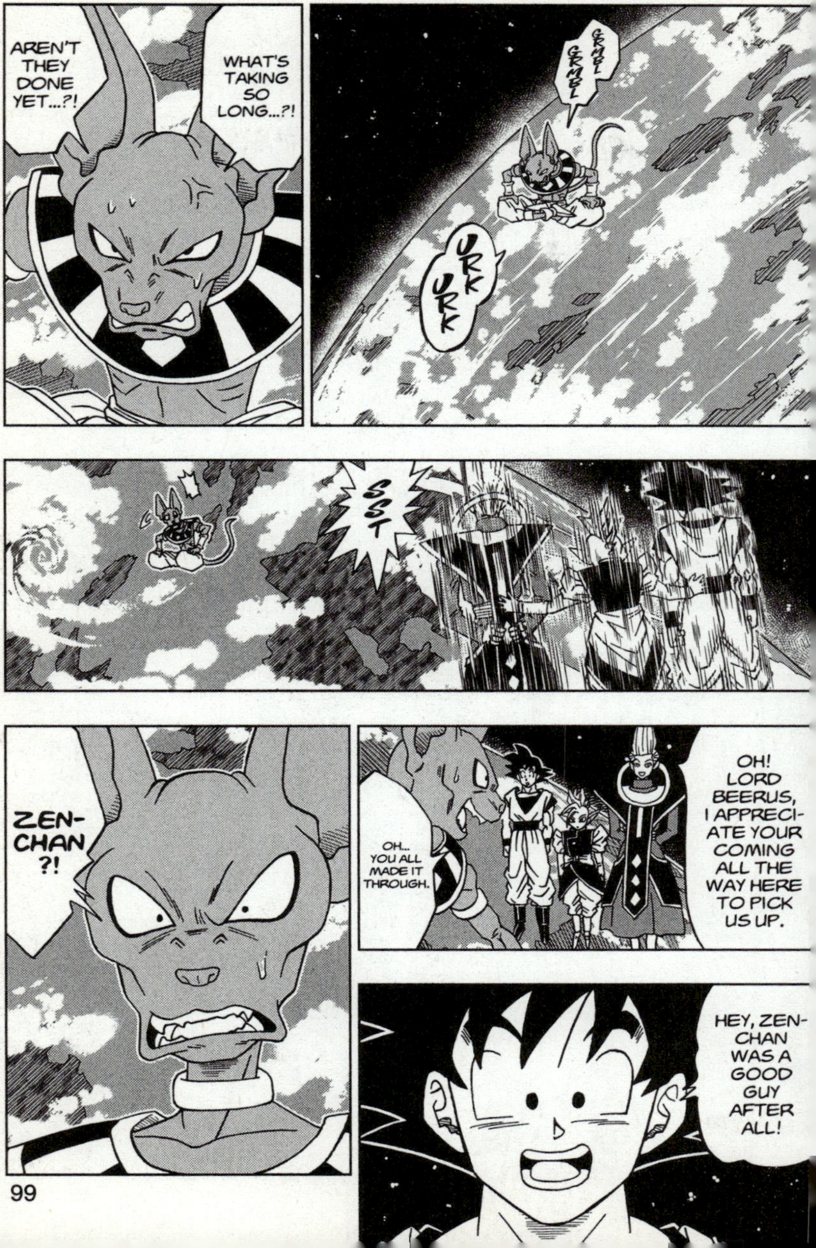
GRMBL GRMBL
URK URK
WHAT'S TAKING SO LONG...?!
AREN'T THEY DONE YET...?!
SST
OH! LORD BEERUS, I APPRECI- ATE YOUR COMING ALL THE WAY HERE TO PICK US UP.
OH... YOU ALL MADE IT THROUGH.
HEY, ZEN- CHAN WAS A GOOD GUY AFTER ALL!
ZEN- CHAN ?!

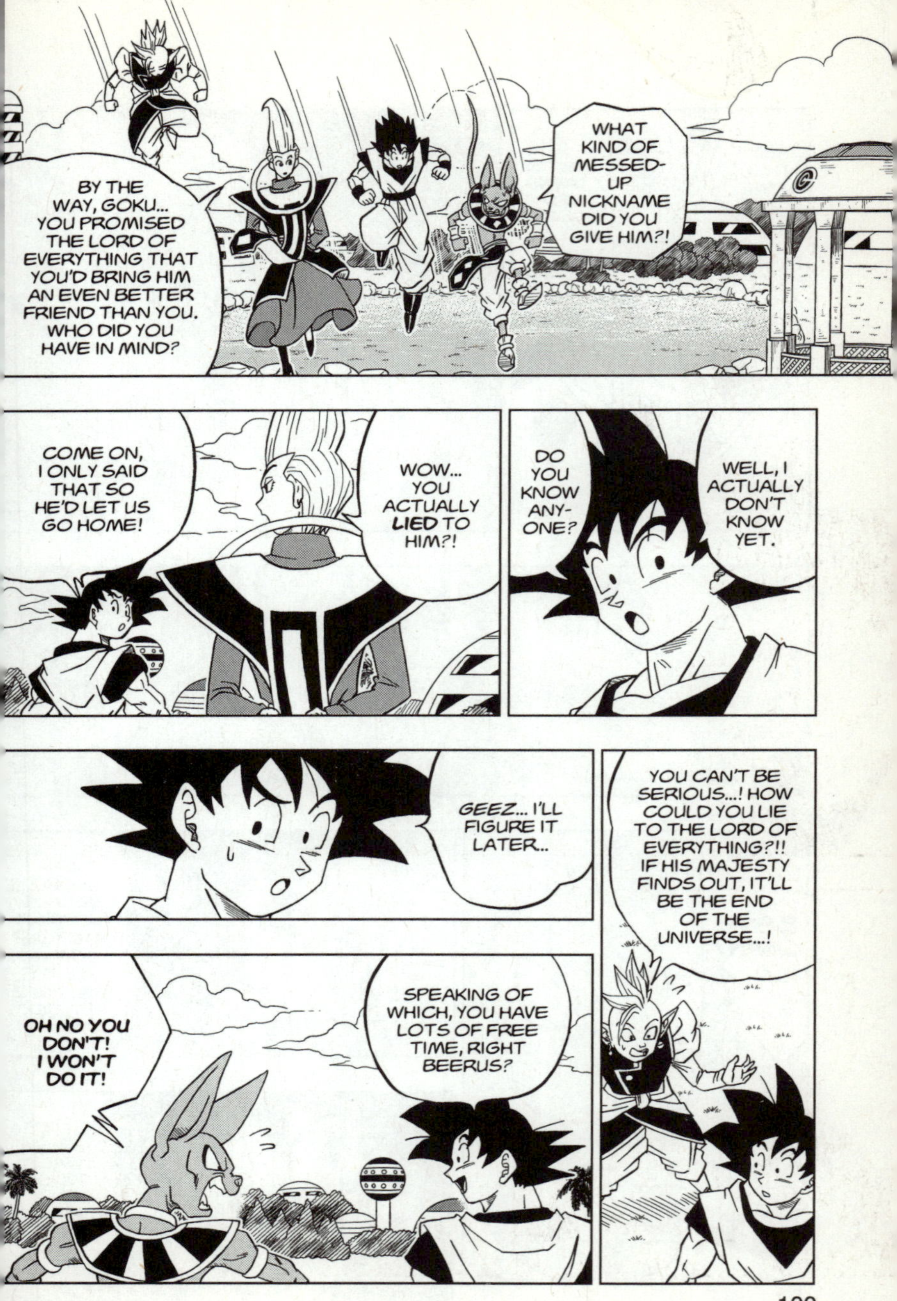
WHAT KIND OF MESSED-UP NICKNAME DID YOU GIVE HIM?!
BY THE WAY, GOKU... YOU PROMISED THE LORD OF EVERYTHING THAT YOU'D BRING HIM AN EVEN BETTER FRIEND THAN YOU. WHO DID YOU HAVE IN MIND?
WELL, I ACTUALLY DON'T KNOW YET.
DO YOU KNOW ANYONE?
WOW... YOU ACTUALLY LIED TO HIM?!
COME ON, I ONLY SAID THAT SO HE'D LET US GO HOME!
YOU CAN'T BE SERIOUS...! HOW COULD YOU LIE TO THE LORD OF EVERYTHING?!! IF HIS MAJESTY FINDS OUT, IT'LL BE THE END OF THE UNIVERSE...!
GEEZ... I'LL FIGURE IT LATER...
SPEAKING OF WHICH, YOU HAVE LOTS OF FREE TIME, RIGHT BEERUS?
OH NO YOU DON'T! I WON'T DO IT!

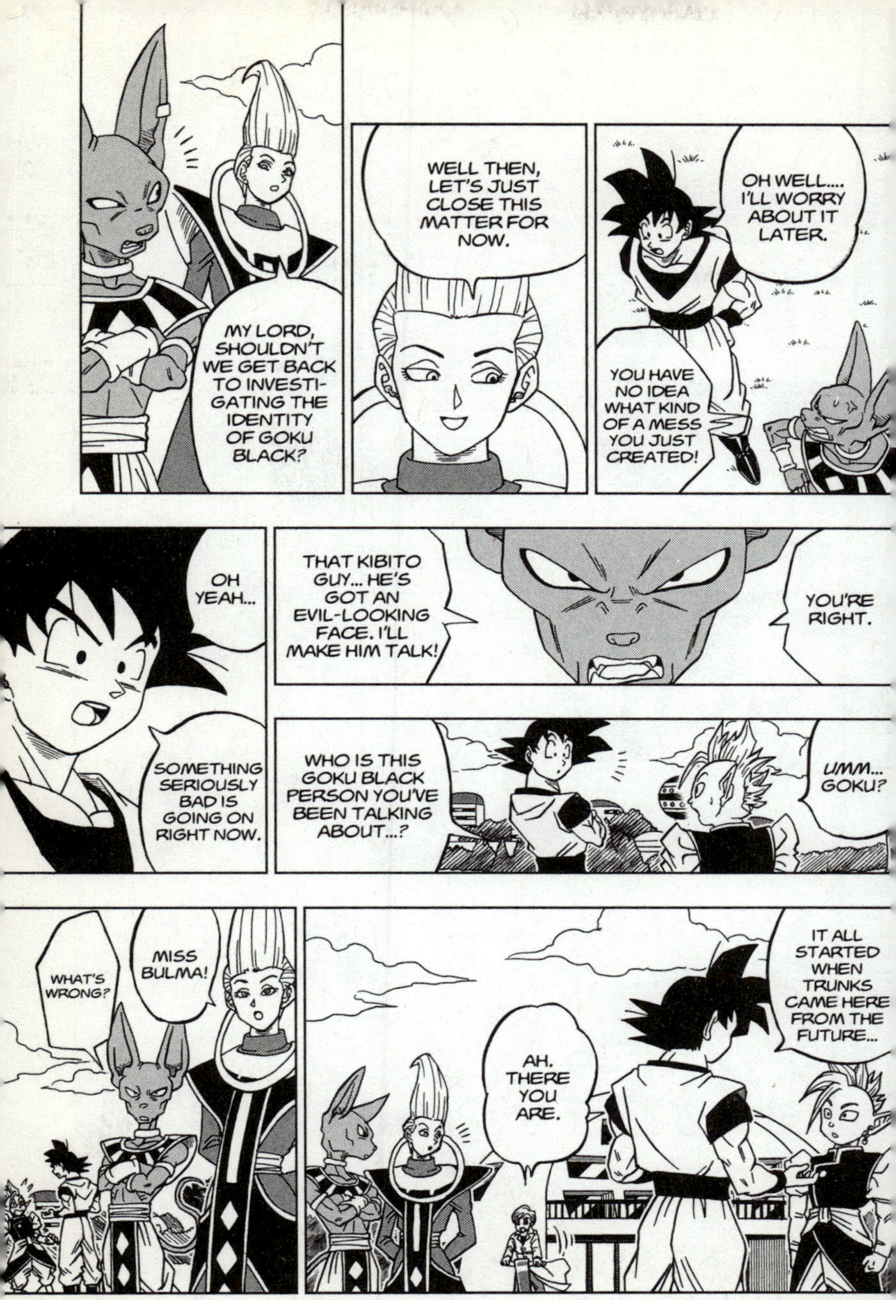
OH WELL.... I'LL WORRY ABOUT IT LATER.
YOU HAVE NO IDEA WHAT KIND OF A MESS YOU JUST CREATED!
WELL THEN, LET'S JUST CLOSE THIS MATTER FOR NOW.
MY LORD, SHOULDN'T WE GET BACK TO INVESTI-GATING THE IDENTITY OF GOKU BLACK?
YOU'RE RIGHT.
THAT KIBITO GUY... HE'S GOT AN EVIL-LOOKING FACE. I'LL MAKE HIM TALK!
UMM... GOKU?
WHO IS THIS GOKU BLACK PERSON YOU'VE BEEN TALKING ABOUT...?
OH YEAH...
SOMETHING SERIOUSLY BAD IS GOING ON RIGHT NOW.
IT ALL STARTED WHEN TRUNKS CAME HERE FROM THE FUTURE...
AH. THERE YOU ARE.
MISS BULMA!
WHAT'S WRONG?

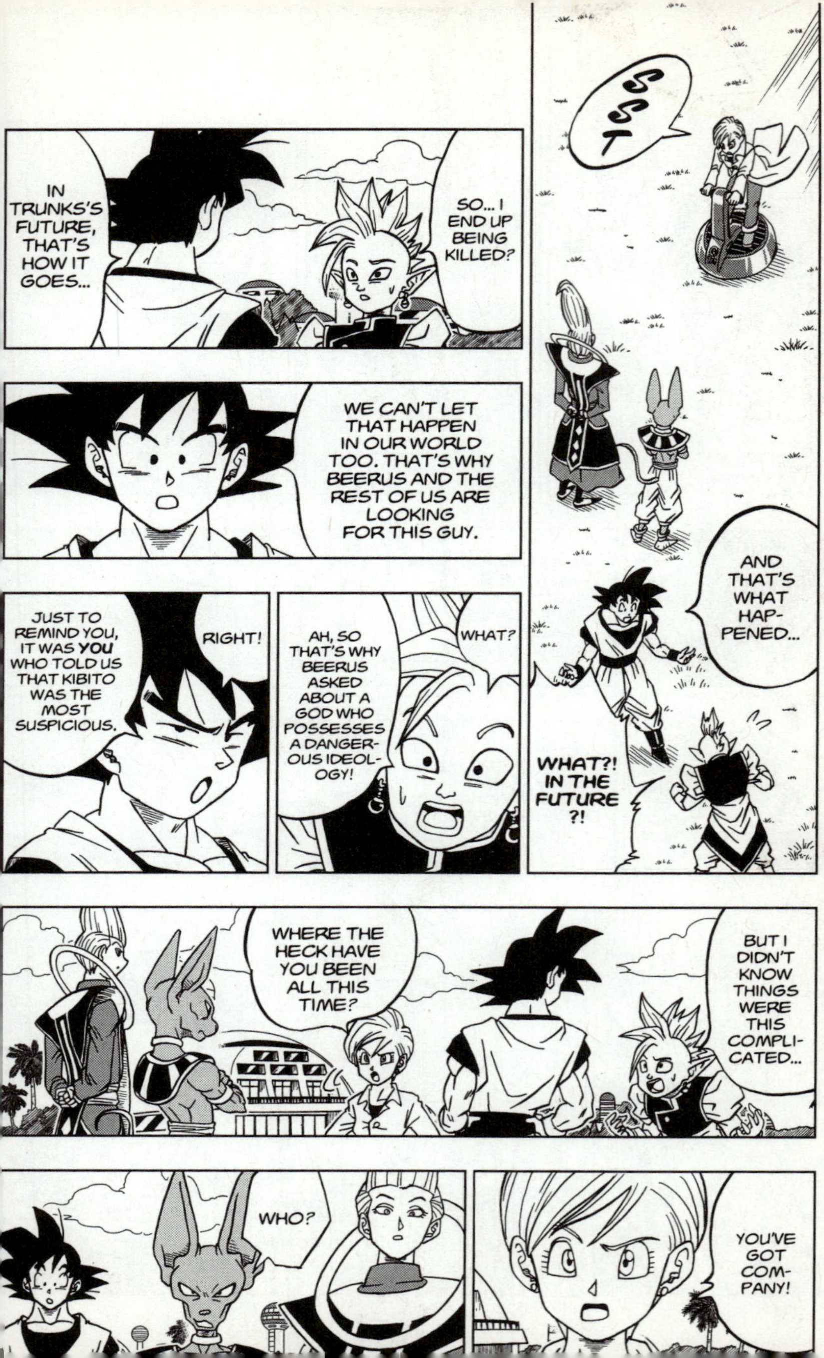
SSK
AND THAT'S WHAT HAP-PENED...
WHAT?! IN THE FUTURE ?!
SO... I END UP BEING KILLED?
IN TRUNKS'S FUTURE, THAT'S HOW IT GOES...
WE CAN'T LET THAT HAPPEN IN OUR WORLD TOO. THAT'S WHY BEERUS AND THE REST OF US ARE LOOKING FOR THIS GUY.
WHAT?
AH, SO THAT'S WHY BEERUS ASKED ABOUT A GOD WHO POSSESSES A DANGER-OUS IDEOL-OGY!
RIGHT!
JUST TO REMIND YOU, IT WAS **YOU** WHO TOLD US THAT KIBITO WAS THE MOST SUSPICIOUS.
BUT I DIDN'T KNOW THINGS WERE THIS COMPLI-CATED...
WHERE THE HECK HAVE YOU BEEN ALL THIS TIME?
YOU'VE GOT COM-PANY!
WHO?

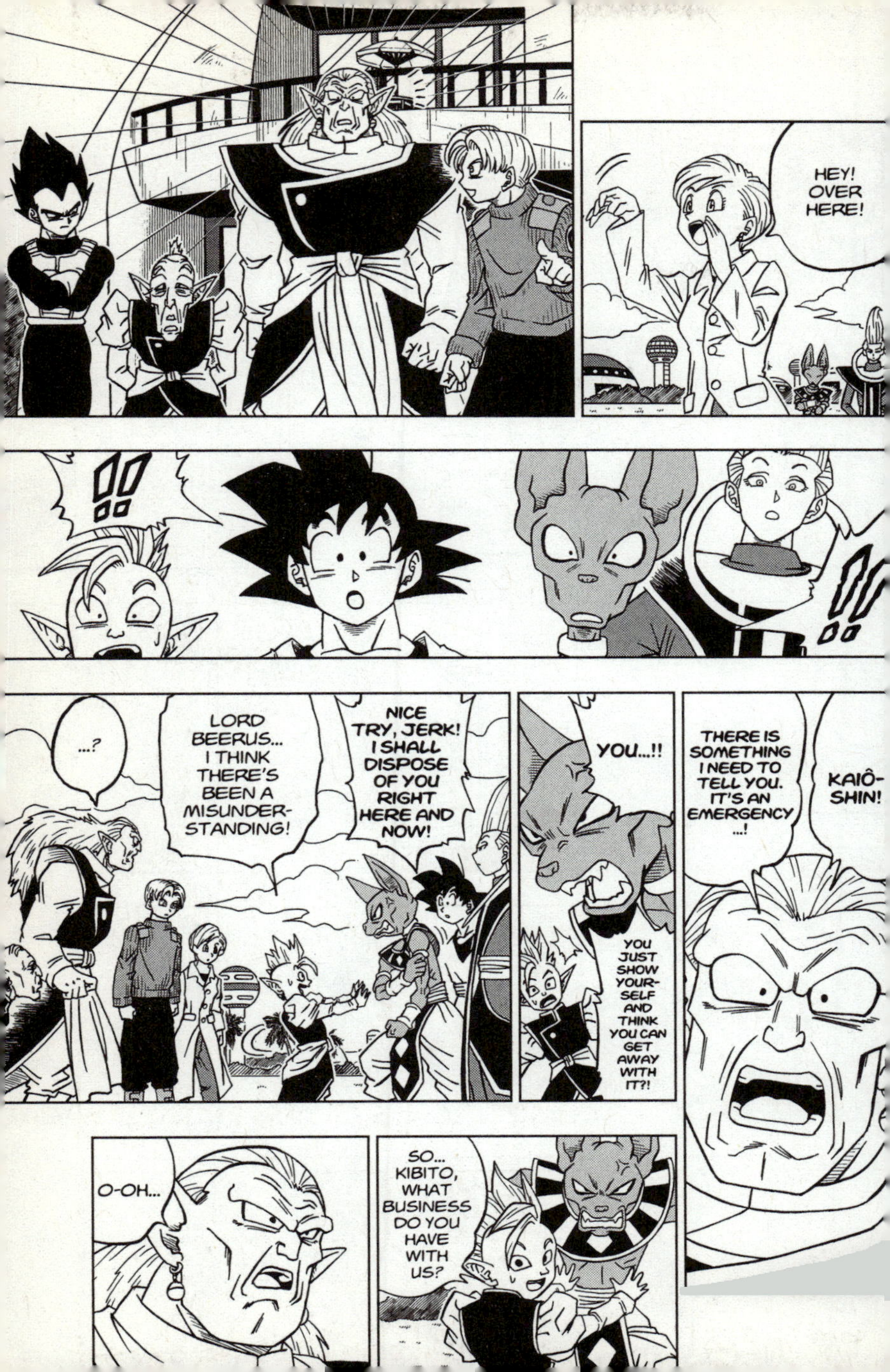
HEY! OVER HERE!
KAIÔ-SHIN!
THERE IS SOMETHING I NEED TO TELL YOU. IT'S AN EMERGENCY...!
YOU...!!
YOU JUST SHOW YOURSELF AND THINK YOU CAN GET AWAY WITH IT?!
NICE TRY, JERK! I SHALL DISPOSE OF YOU RIGHT HERE AND NOW!
LORD BEERUS... I THINK THERE'S BEEN A MISUNDERSTANDING!
...?
SO... KIBITO, WHAT BUSINESS DO YOU HAVE WITH US?
O-OH...

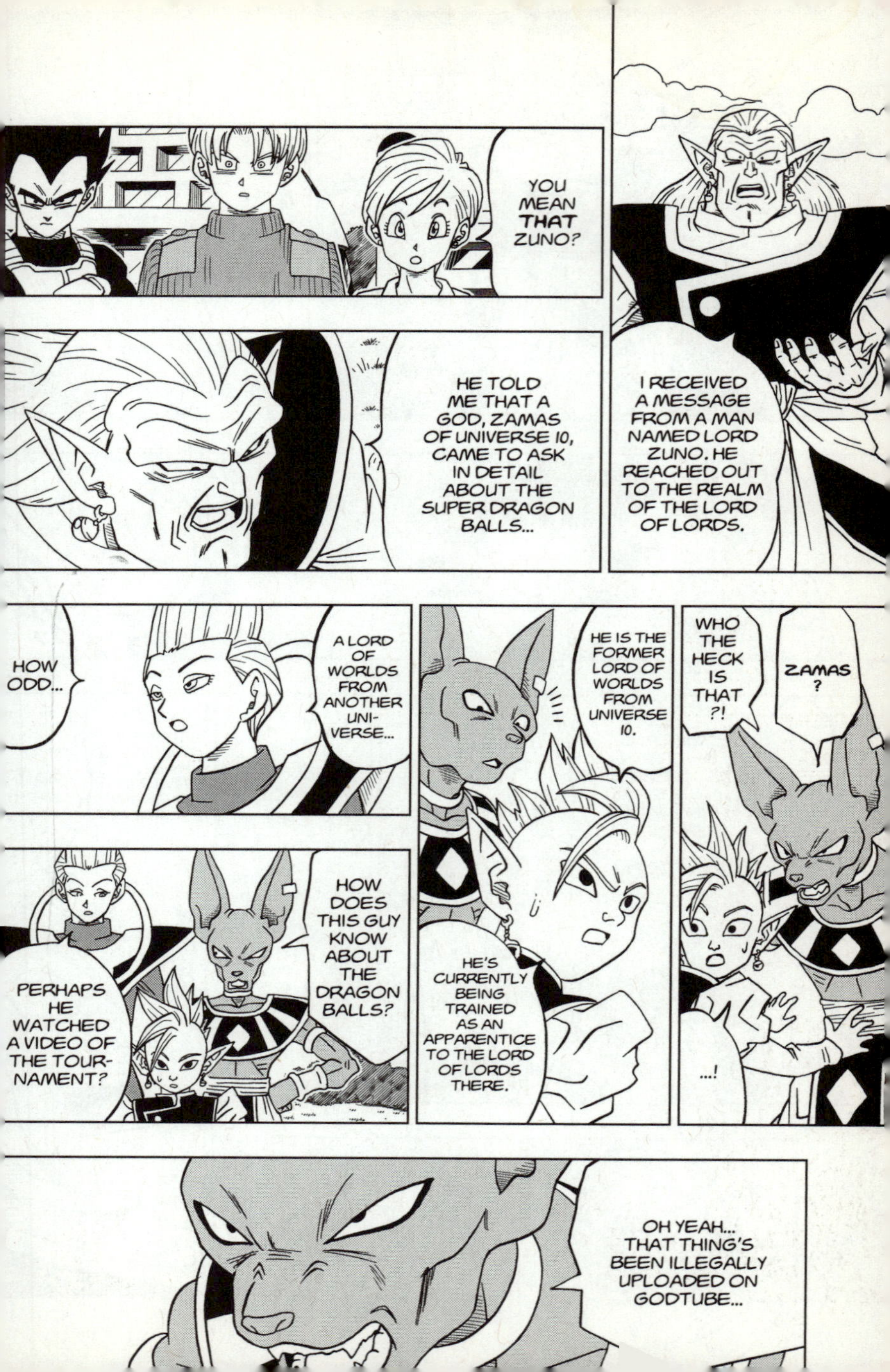

I RECEIVED A MESSAGE FROM A MAN NAMED LORD ZUNO. HE REACHED OUT TO THE REALM OF THE LORD OF LORDS.
YOU MEAN THAT ZUNO?
HE TOLD ME THAT A GOD, ZAMAS OF UNIVERSE 10, CAME TO ASK IN DETAIL ABOUT THE SUPER DRAGON BALLS...
ZAMAS?
WHO THE HECK IS THAT?!
...!
HE IS THE FORMER LORD OF WORLDS FROM UNIVERSE 10.
HE'S CURRENTLY BEING TRAINED AS AN APPARENTICE TO THE LORD OF LORDS THERE.
A LORD OF WORLDS FROM ANOTHER UNI-VERSE...
HOW ODD...
HOW DOES THIS GUY KNOW ABOUT THE DRAGON BALLS?
PERHAPS HE WATCHED A VIDEO OF THE TOUR-NAMENT?
OH YEAH... THAT THING'S BEEN ILLEGALLY UPLOADED ON GODTUBE...

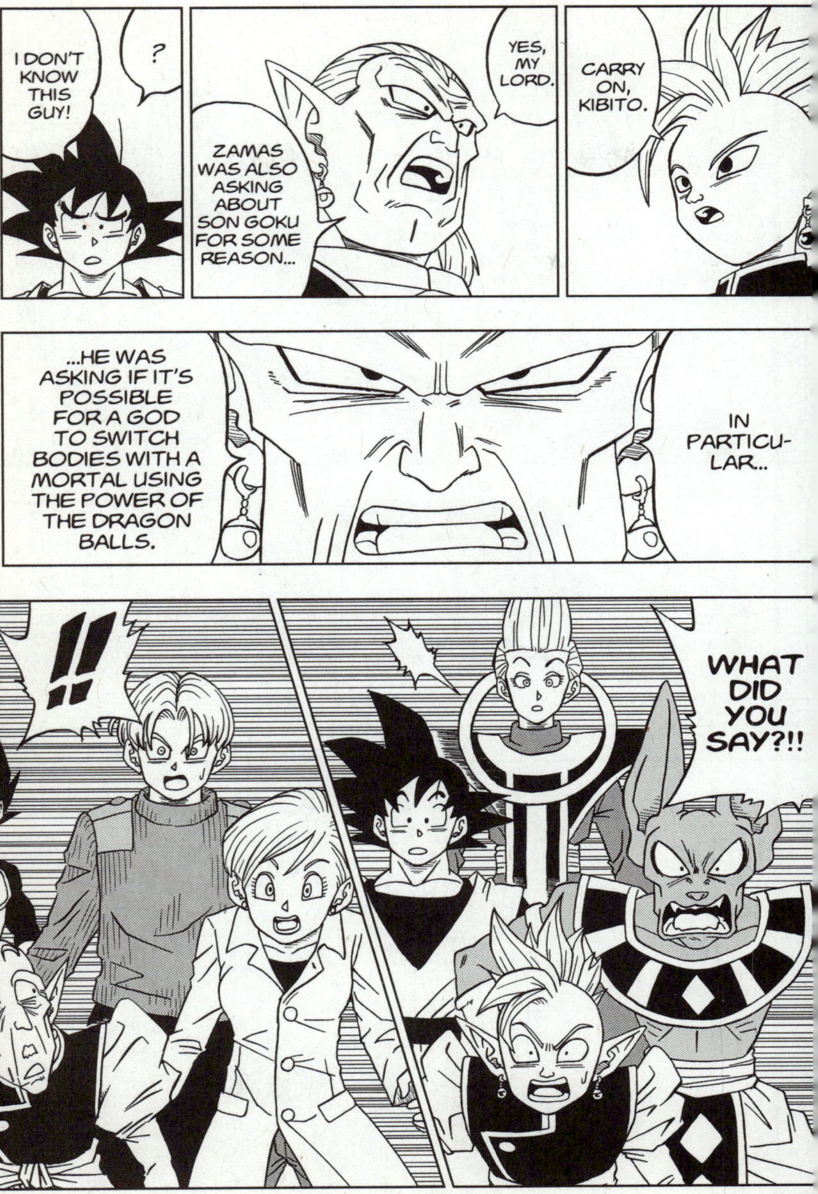
CARRY ON, KIBITO.
YES, MY LORD.
ZAMAS WAS ALSO ASKING ABOUT SON GOKU FOR SOME REASON...
?
I DON'T KNOW THIS GUY!
IN PARTICU-LAR...
...HE WAS ASKING IF IT'S POSSIBLE FOR A GOD TO SWITCH BODIES WITH A MORTAL USING THE POWER OF THE DRAGON BALLS.
WHAT DID YOU SAY?!!
!!

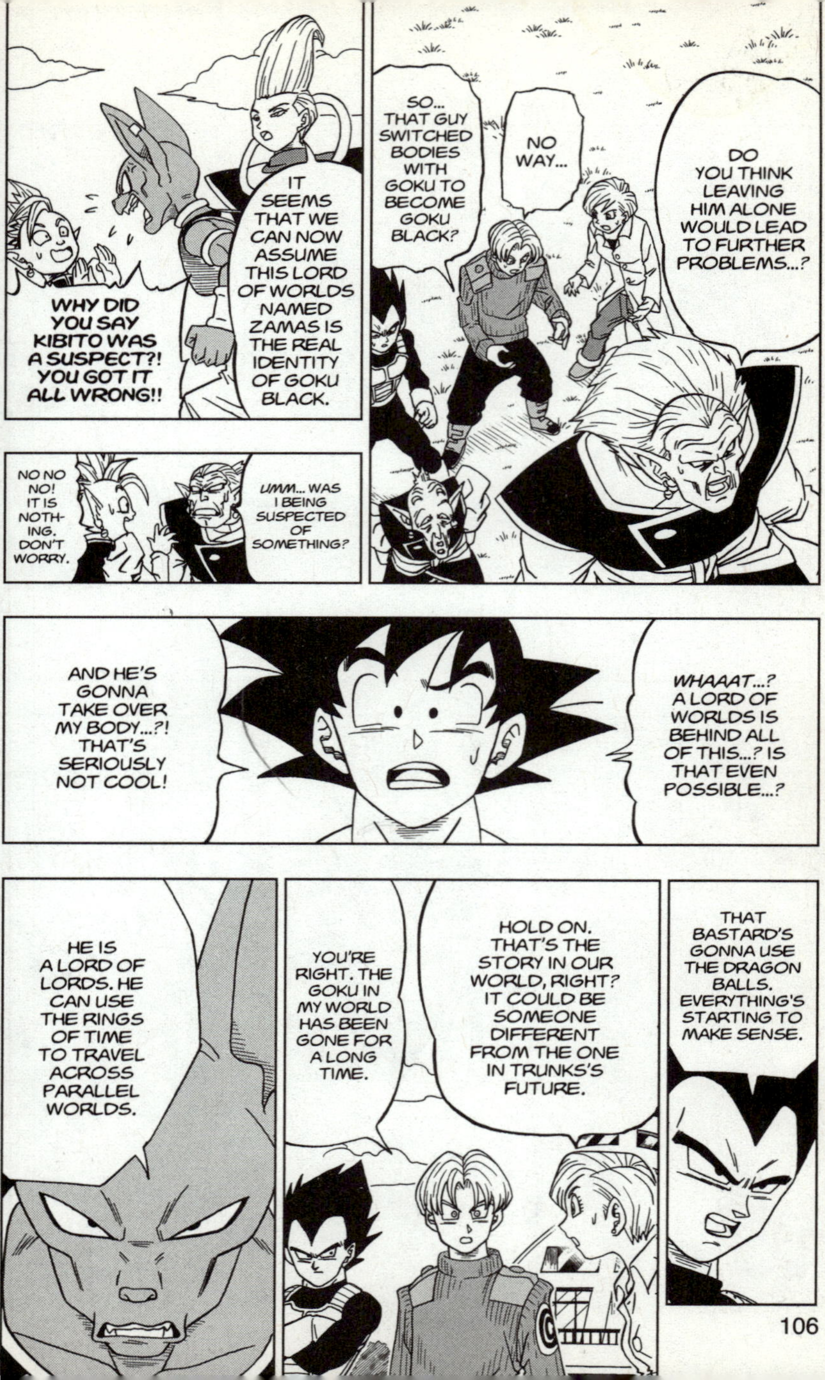
DO YOU THINK LEAVING HIM ALONE WOULD LEAD TO FURTHER PROBLEMS...?
NO WAY...
SO... THAT GUY SWITCHED BODIES WITH GOKU TO BECOME GOKU BLACK?
IT SEEMS THAT WE CAN NOW ASSUME THIS LORD OF WORLDS NAMED ZAMAS IS THE REAL IDENTITY OF GOKU BLACK.
WHY DID YOU SAY KIBITO WAS A SUSPECT?! YOU GOT IT ALL WRONG!!
UMM... WAS I BEING SUSPECTED OF SOMETHING?
NO NO NO! IT IS NOTHING. DON'T WORRY.
WHAAAT...? A LORD OF WORLDS IS BEHIND ALL OF THIS...? IS THAT EVEN POSSIBLE...?
AND HE'S GONNA TAKE OVER MY BODY...?! THAT'S SERIOUSLY NOT COOL!
THAT BASTARD'S GONNA USE THE DRAGON BALLS. EVERYTHING'S STARTING TO MAKE SENSE.
HOLD ON. THAT'S THE STORY IN OUR WORLD, RIGHT? IT COULD BE SOMEONE DIFFERENT FROM THE ONE IN TRUNKS'S FUTURE.
YOU'RE RIGHT. THE GOKU IN MY WORLD HAS BEEN GONE FOR A LONG TIME.
HE IS A LORD OF LORDS. HE CAN USE THE RINGS OF TIME TO TRAVEL ACROSS PARALLEL WORLDS.

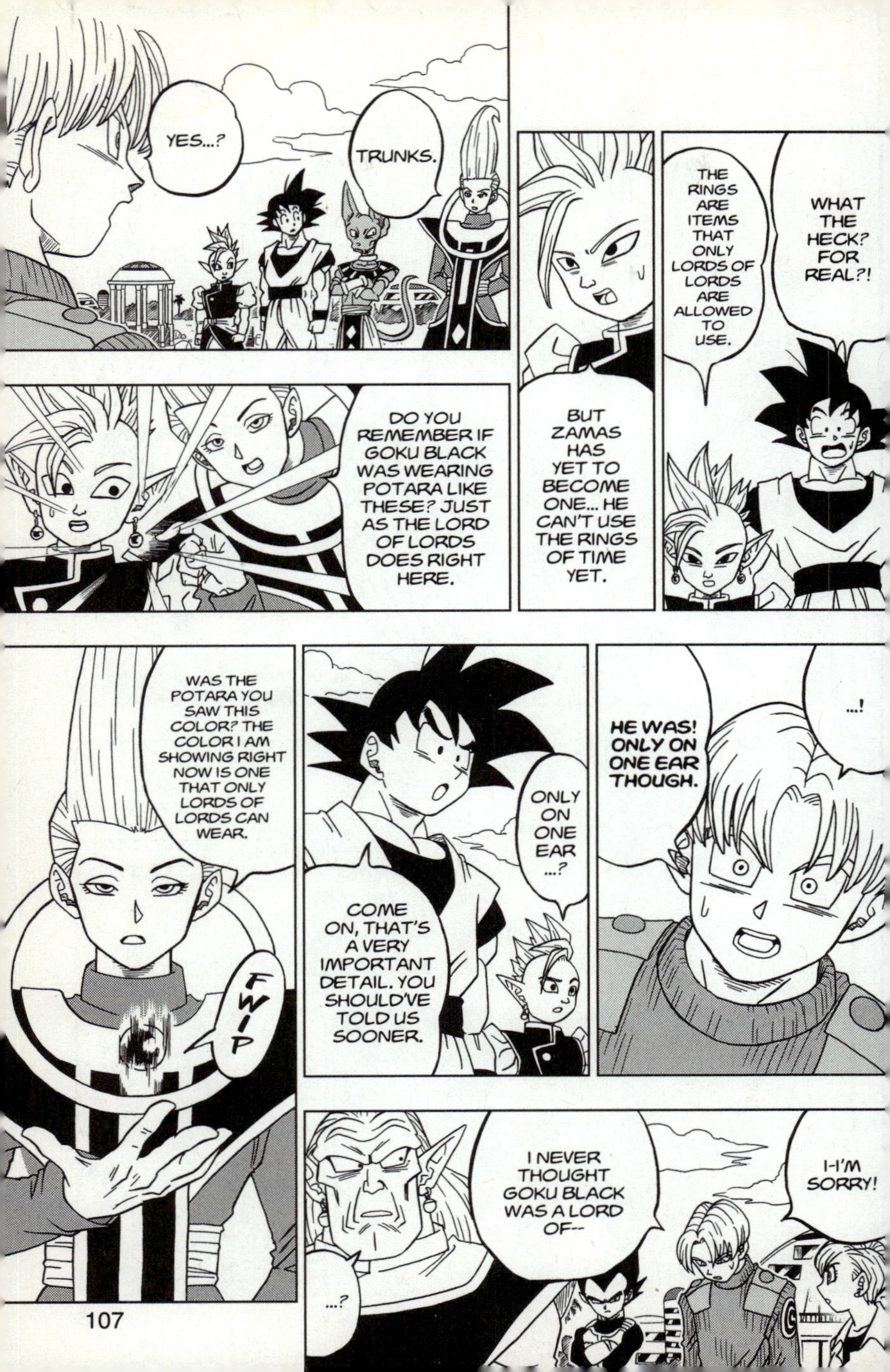
WHAT THE HECK? FOR REAL?!
THE RINGS ARE ITEMS THAT ONLY LORDS OF LORDS ARE ALLOWED TO USE.
BUT ZAMAS HAS YET TO BECOME ONE... HE CAN'T USE THE RINGS OF TIME YET.
TRUNKS.
YES...?
DO YOU REMEMBER IF GOKU BLACK WAS WEARING POTARA LIKE THESE? JUST AS THE LORD OF LORDS DOES RIGHT HERE.
...!
HE WAS! ONLY ON ONE EAR THOUGH.
ONLY ON ONE EAR ...?
COME ON, THAT'S A VERY IMPORTANT DETAIL. YOU SHOULD'VE TOLD US SOONER.
I-I'M SORRY!
I NEVER THOUGHT GOKU BLACK WAS A LORD OF--
...?
WAS THE POTARA YOU SAW THIS COLOR? THE COLOR I AM SHOWING RIGHT NOW IS ONE THAT ONLY LORDS OF LORDS CAN WEAR.
FWIP

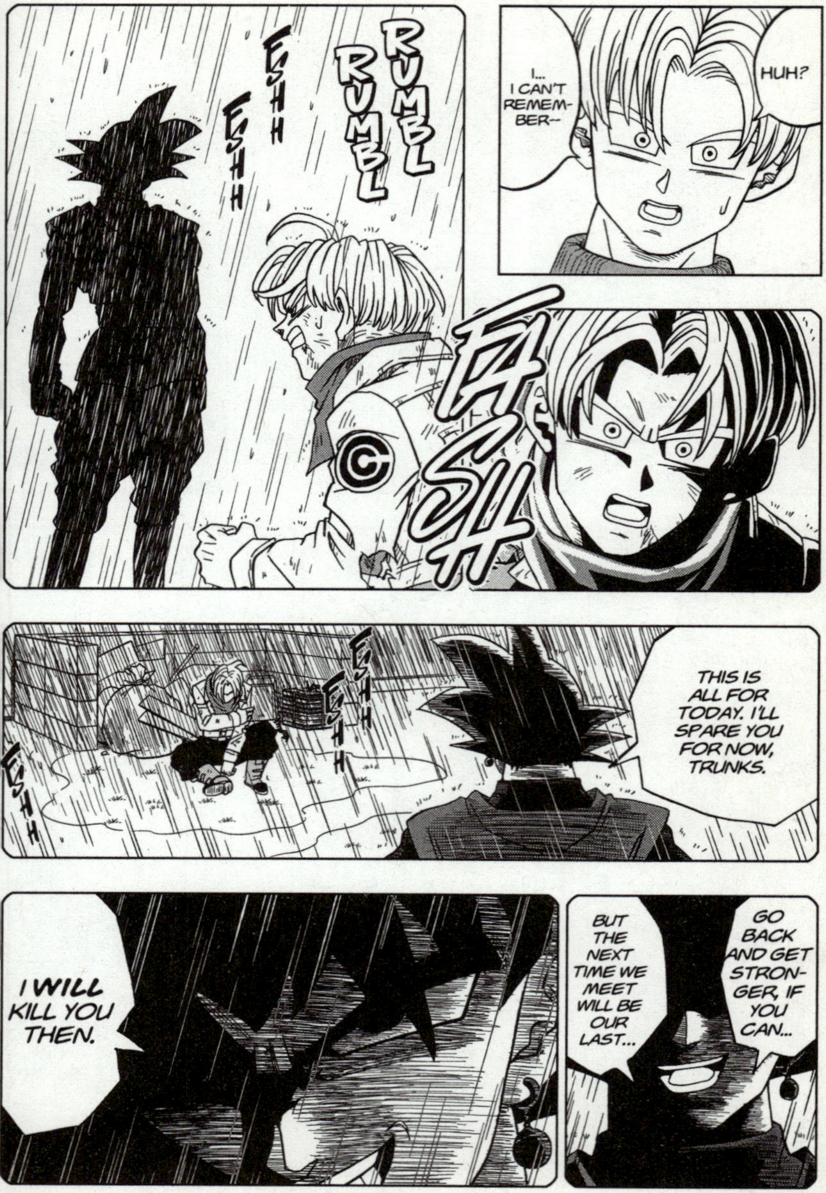
HUH?
I... I CAN'T REMEMBER--
FASH
RUMBL RUMBL
FSHH FSHH
THIS IS ALL FOR TODAY. I'LL SPARE YOU FOR NOW, TRUNKS.
FSHH FSHH
FSHH
GO BACK AND GET STRONGER, IF YOU CAN...
BUT THE NEXT TIME WE MEET WILL BE OUR LAST...
I WILL KILL YOU THEN.

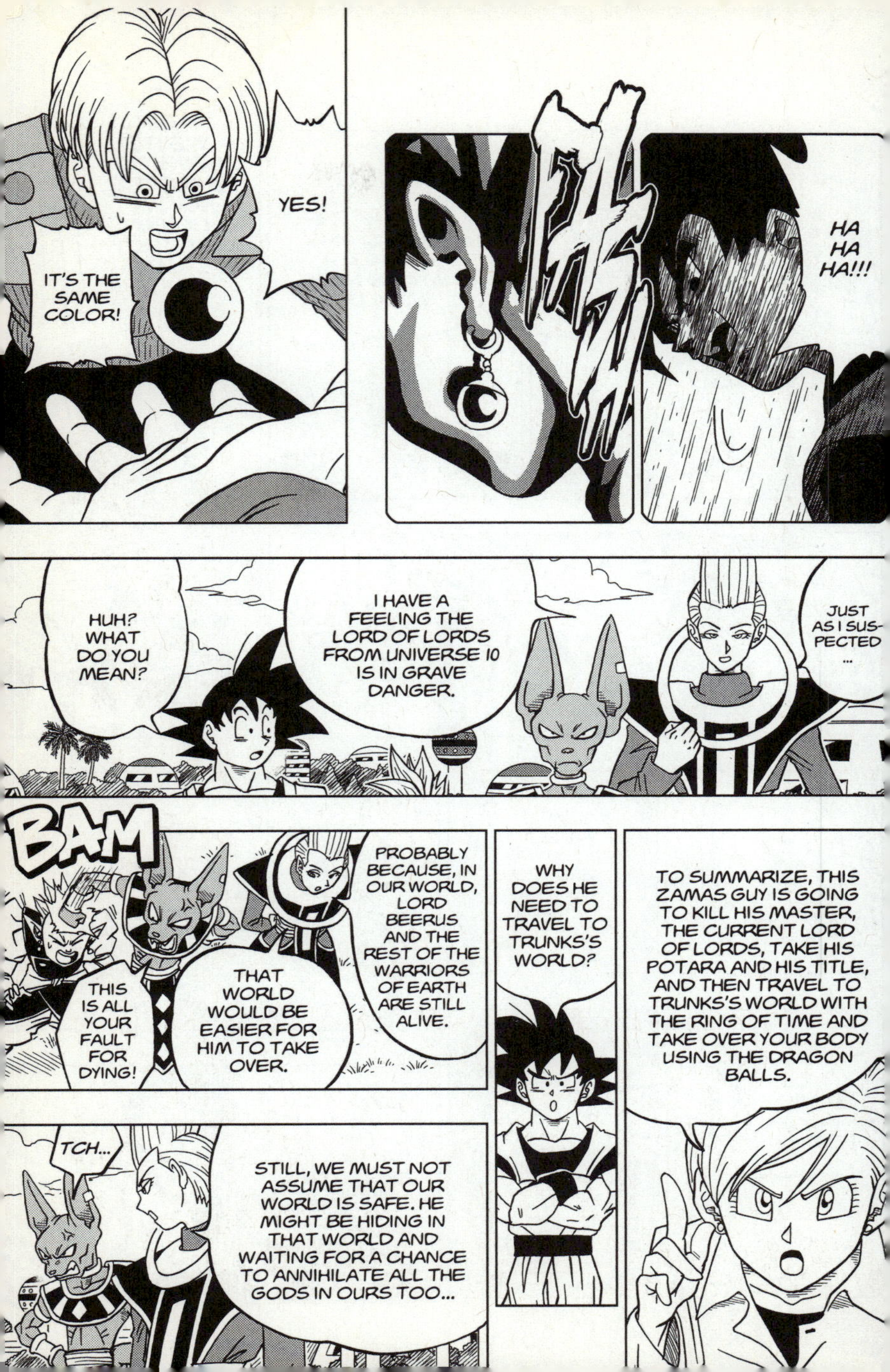
HA HA HA!!!
YES!
IT'S THE SAME COLOR!
JUST AS I SUSPECTED ...
I HAVE A FEELING THE LORD OF LORDS FROM UNIVERSE 10 IS IN GRAVE DANGER.
HUH? WHAT DO YOU MEAN?
TO SUMMARIZE, THIS ZAMAS GUY IS GOING TO KILL HIS MASTER, THE CURRENT LORD OF LORDS, TAKE HIS POTARA AND HIS TITLE, AND THEN TRAVEL TO TRUNKS'S WORLD WITH THE RING OF TIME AND TAKE OVER YOUR BODY USING THE DRAGON BALLS.
WHY DOES HE NEED TO TRAVEL TO TRUNKS'S WORLD?
PROBABLY BECAUSE, IN OUR WORLD, LORD BEERUS AND THE REST OF THE WARRIORS OF EARTH ARE STILL ALIVE.
THAT WORLD WOULD BE EASIER FOR HIM TO TAKE OVER.
THIS IS ALL YOUR FAULT FOR DYING!
BAM
STILL, WE MUST NOT ASSUME THAT OUR WORLD IS SAFE. HE MIGHT BE HIDING IN THAT WORLD AND WAITING FOR A CHANCE TO ANNIHILATE ALL THE GODS IN OURS TOO...
TCH...

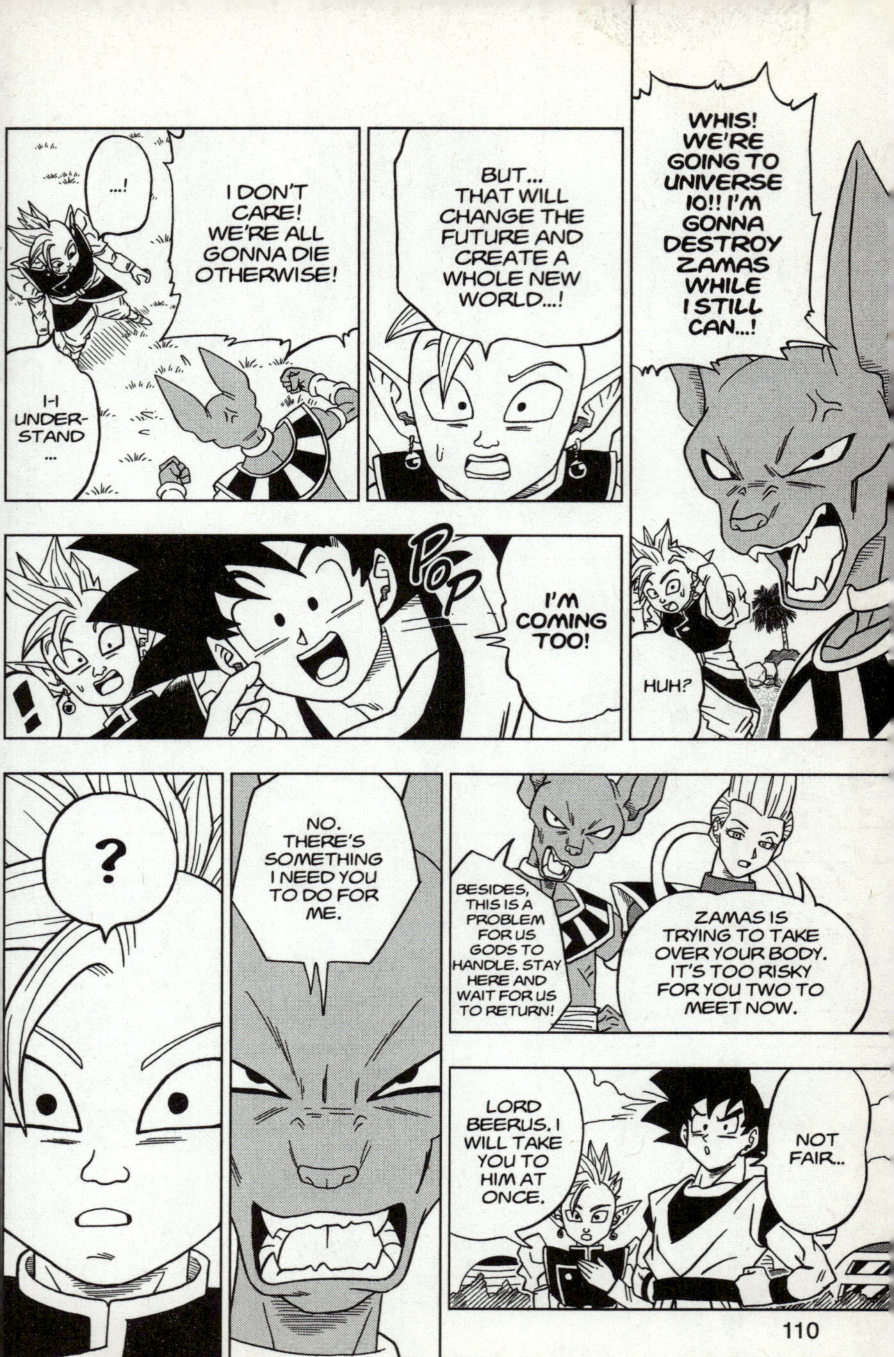
WHIS! WE'RE GOING TO UNIVERSE 10!! I'M GONNA DESTROY ZAMAS WHILE I STILL CAN...!
HUH?
BUT... THAT WILL CHANGE THE FUTURE AND CREATE A WHOLE NEW WORLD...!
I DON'T CARE! WE'RE ALL GONNA DIE OTHERWISE!
...!
I-I UNDER-STAND ...
I'M COMING TOO!
POP
!
ZAMAS IS TRYING TO TAKE OVER YOUR BODY. IT'S TOO RISKY FOR YOU TWO TO MEET NOW.
BESIDES, THIS IS A PROBLEM FOR US GODS TO HANDLE. STAY HERE AND WAIT FOR US TO RETURN!
NOT FAIR...
LORD BEERUS. I WILL TAKE YOU TO HIM AT ONCE.
NO. THERE'S SOMETHING I NEED YOU TO DO FOR ME.
?

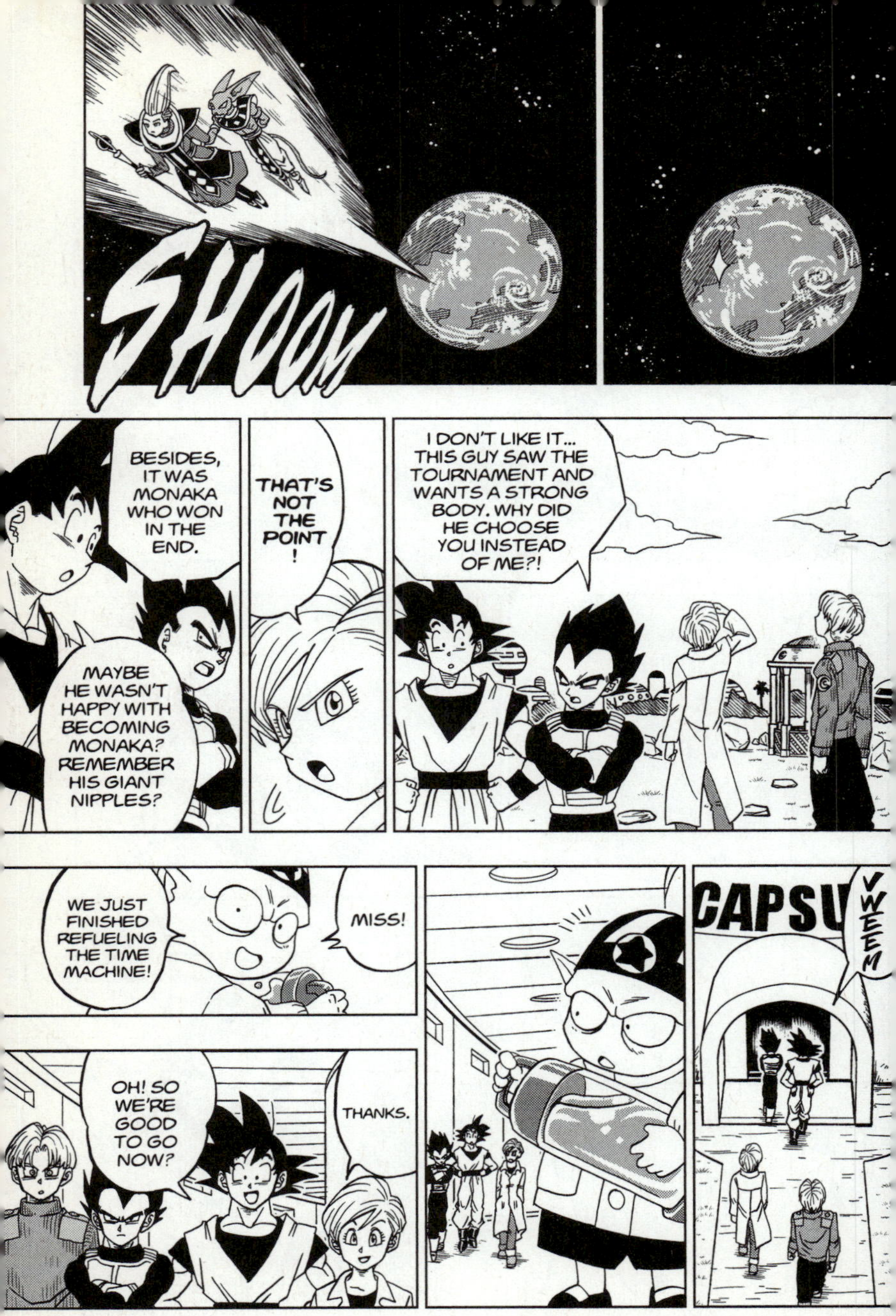
SHOOM
I DON'T LIKE IT... THIS GUY SAW THE TOURNAMENT AND WANTS A STRONG BODY. WHY DID HE CHOOSE YOU INSTEAD OF ME?!
THAT'S NOT THE POINT!
BESIDES, IT WAS MONAKA WHO WON IN THE END.
MAYBE HE WASN'T HAPPY WITH BECOMING MONAKA? REMEMBER HIS GIANT NIPPLES?
CAPSU
VWEEM
MISS!
WE JUST FINISHED REFUELING THE TIME MACHINE!
THANKS.
OH! SO WE'RE GOOD TO GO NOW?

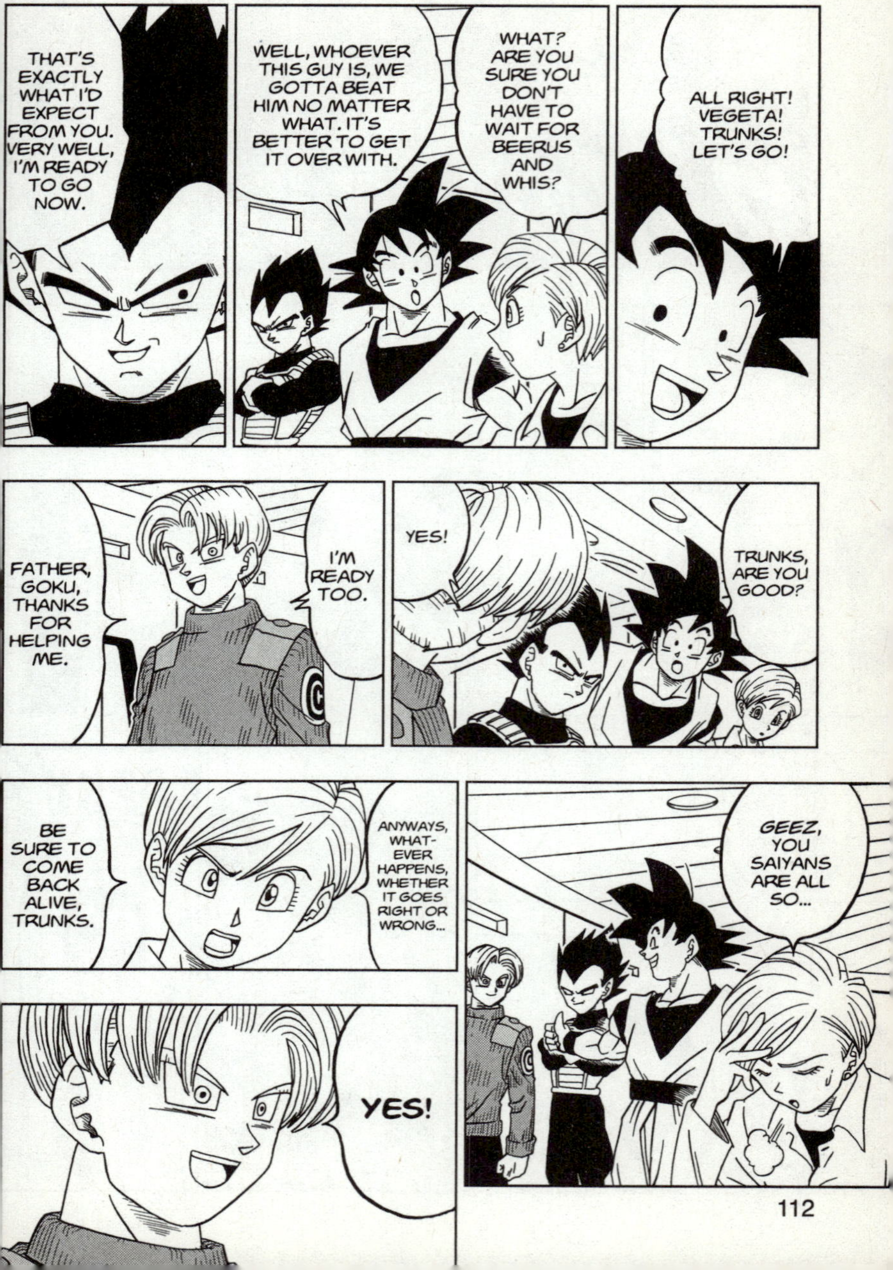
ALL RIGHT! VEGETA! TRUNKS! LET'S GO!
WHAT? ARE YOU SURE YOU DON'T HAVE TO WAIT FOR BEERUS AND WHIS?
WELL, WHOEVER THIS GUY IS, WE GOTTA BEAT HIM NO MATTER WHAT. IT'S BETTER TO GET IT OVER WITH.
THAT'S EXACTLY WHAT I'D EXPECT FROM YOU. VERY WELL, I'M READY TO GO NOW.
TRUNKS, ARE YOU GOOD?
YES!
I'M READY TOO.
FATHER, GOKU, THANKS FOR HELPING ME.
GEEZ, YOU SAIYANS ARE ALL SO...
ANYWAYS, WHAT-EVER HAPPENS, WHETHER IT GOES RIGHT OR WRONG...
BE SURE TO COME BACK ALIVE, TRUNKS.
YES!

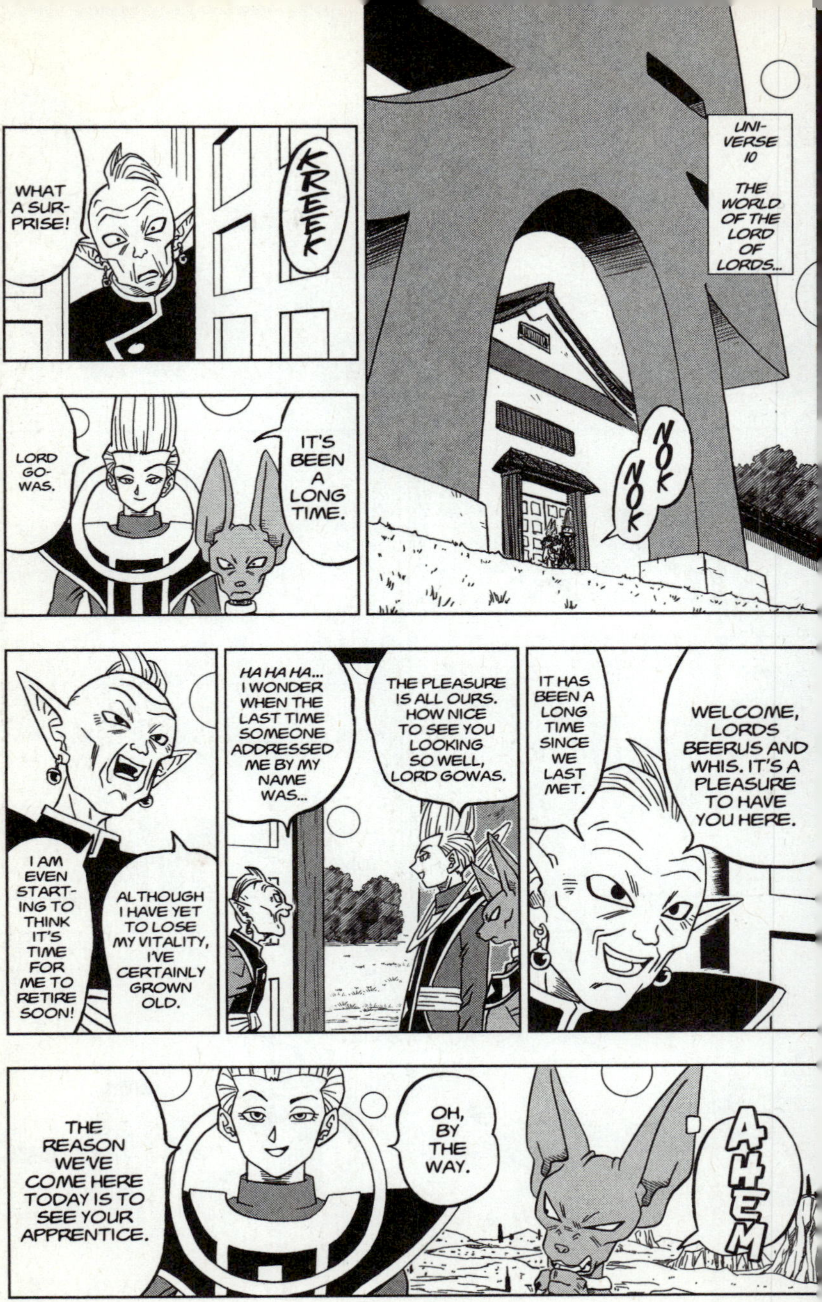
UNIVERSE 10
THE WORLD OF THE LORD OF LORDS...
NOK NOK
KREEK
WHAT A SURPRISE!
IT'S BEEN A LONG TIME.
LORD GOWAS.
WELCOME, LORDS BEERUS AND WHIS. IT'S A PLEASURE TO HAVE YOU HERE.
IT HAS BEEN A LONG TIME SINCE WE LAST MET.
THE PLEASURE IS ALL OURS. HOW NICE TO SEE YOU LOOKING SO WELL, LORD GOWAS.
HA HA HA... I WONDER WHEN THE LAST TIME SOMEONE ADDRESSED ME BY MY NAME WAS...
ALTHOUGH I HAVE YET TO LOSE MY VITALITY, I'VE CERTAINLY GROWN OLD.
I AM EVEN STARTING TO THINK IT'S TIME FOR ME TO RETIRE SOON!
AHEM
OH, BY THE WAY.
THE REASON WE'VE COME HERE TODAY IS TO SEE YOUR APPRENTICE.

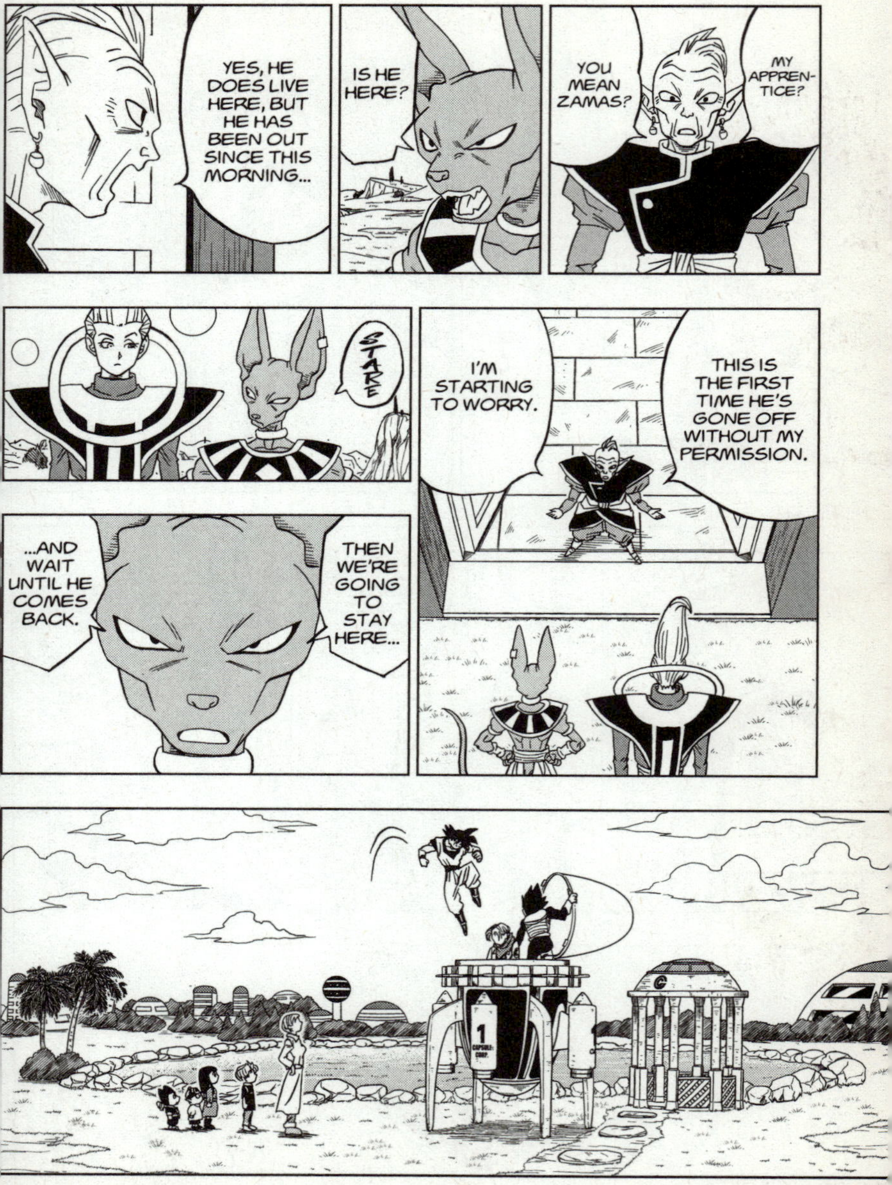
MY APPREN-TICE?
YOU MEAN ZAMAS?
IS HE HERE?
YES, HE DOES LIVE HERE, BUT HE HAS BEEN OUT SINCE THIS MORNING...
THIS IS THE FIRST TIME HE'S GONE OFF WITHOUT MY PERMISSION.
I'M STARTING TO WORRY.
STARE
THEN WE'RE GOING TO STAY HERE...
...AND WAIT UNTIL HE COMES BACK.

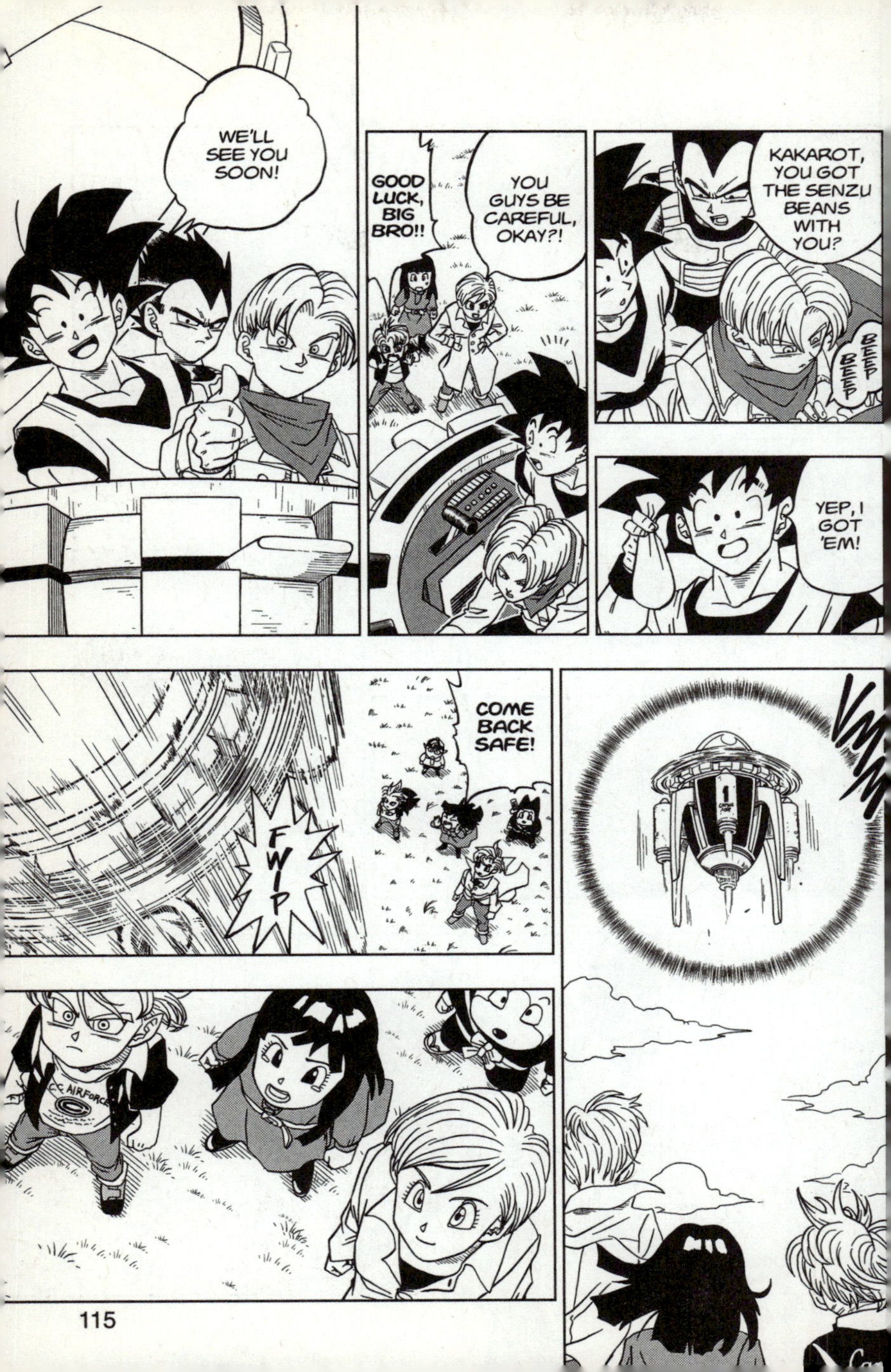
KAKAROT, YOU GOT THE SENZU BEANS WITH YOU?
BEEP BEEP
YEP, I GOT 'EM!
YOU GUYS BE CAREFUL, OKAY?!
GOOD LUCK, BIG BRO!!
WE'LL SEE YOU SOON!
VMMM
COME BACK SAFE!
FWIP

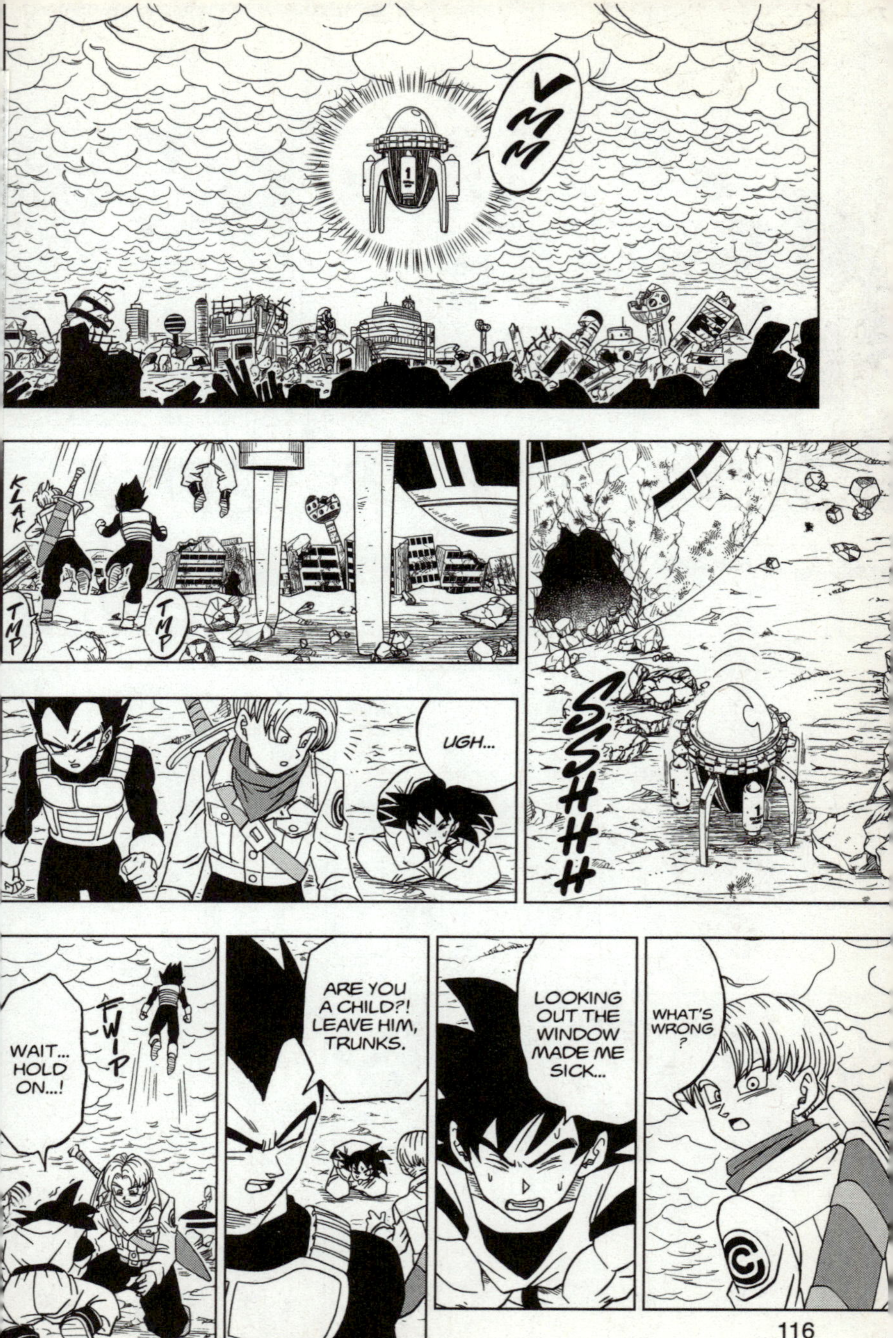
VMM
SSHHHH
KLAK
TMP
TMP
UGH...
WHAT'S WRONG?
LOOKING OUT THE WINDOW MADE ME SICK...
ARE YOU A CHILD?! LEAVE HIM, TRUNKS.
FWIP
WAIT... HOLD ON...!

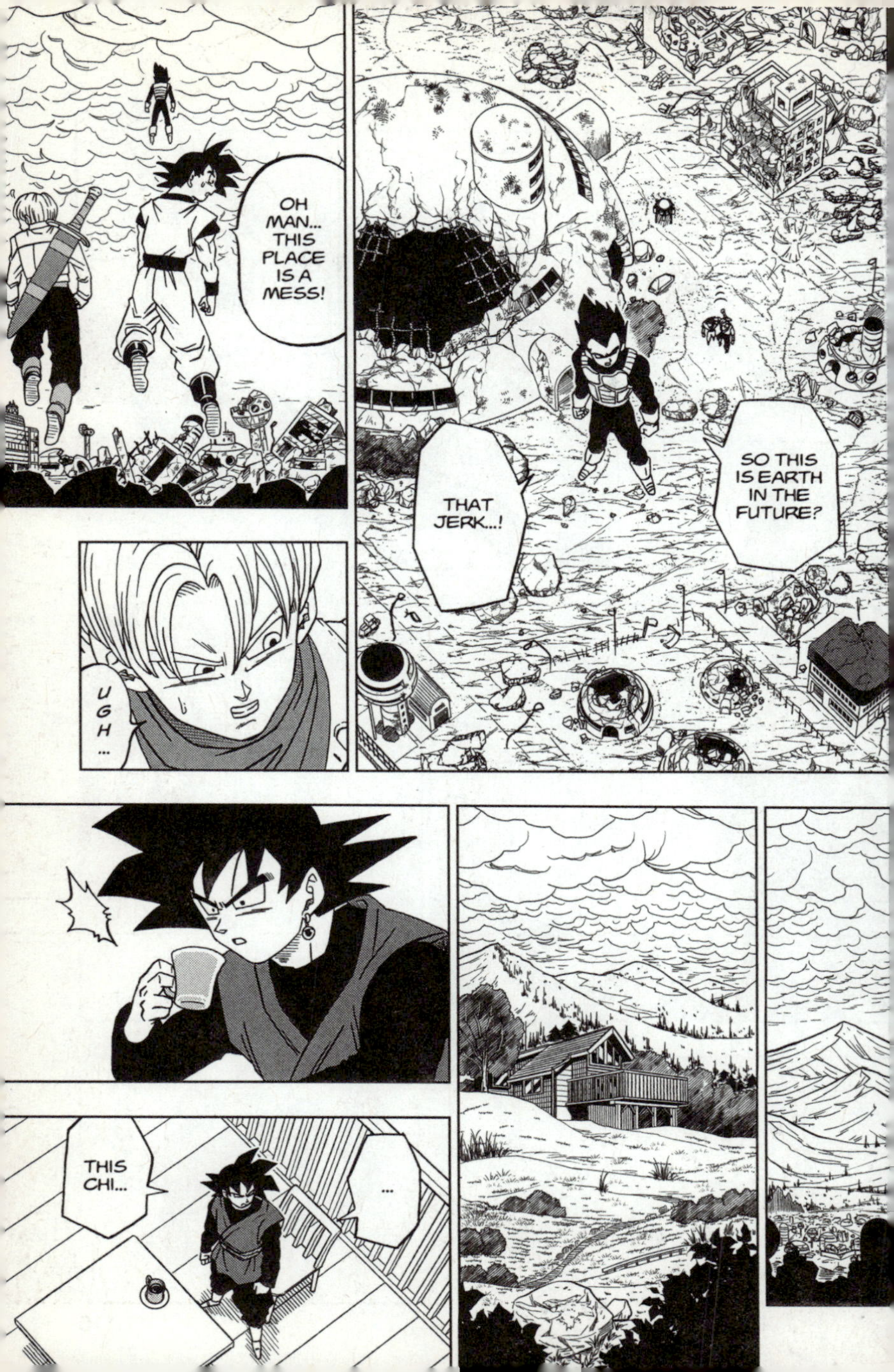
SO THIS IS EARTH IN THE FUTURE?
THAT JERK...!
OH MAN... THIS PLACE IS A MESS!
UGH...
THIS CHI...
...

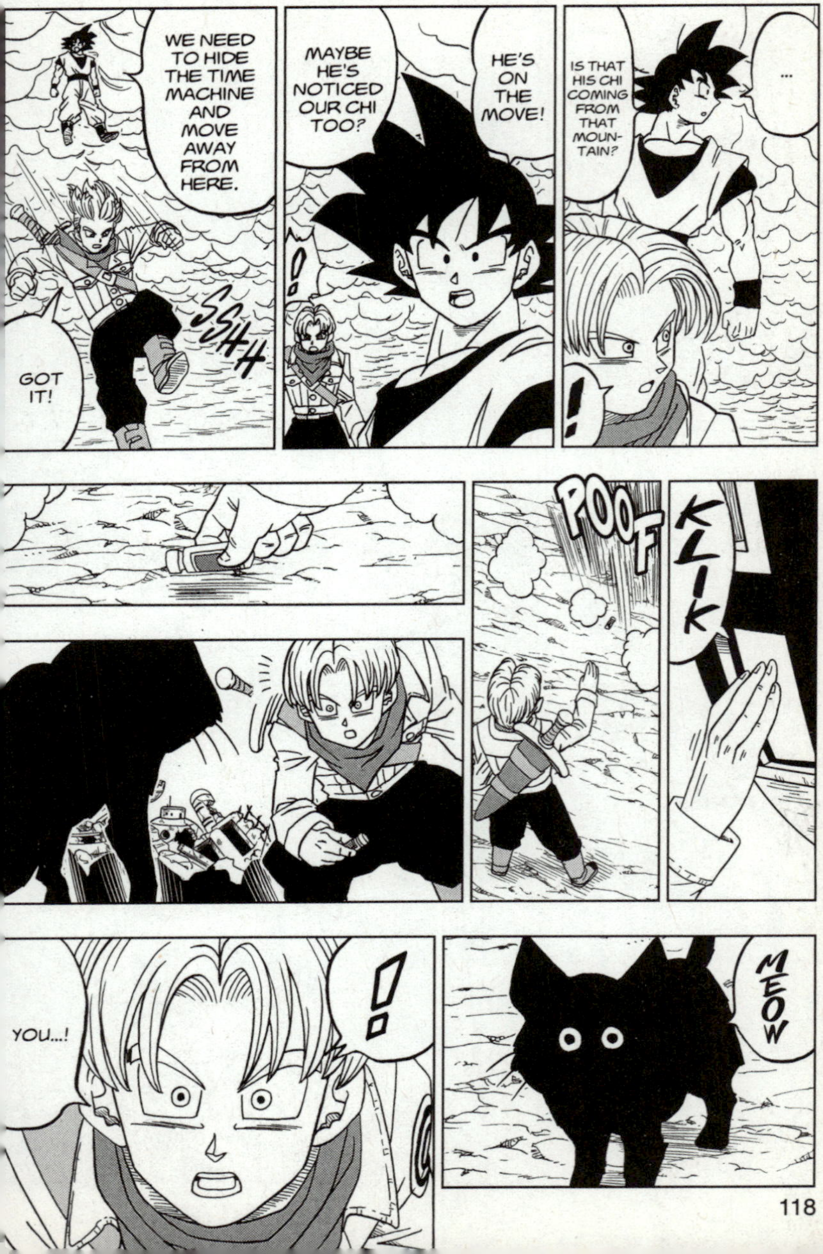
...
IS THAT HIS CHI COMING FROM THAT MOUNTAIN?
!
HE'S ON THE MOVE!
MAYBE HE'S NOTICED OUR CHI TOO?
!
WE NEED TO HIDE THE TIME MACHINE AND MOVE AWAY FROM HERE.
SSHH
GOT IT!
KLIK
POOF
MEOW
!
YOU...!

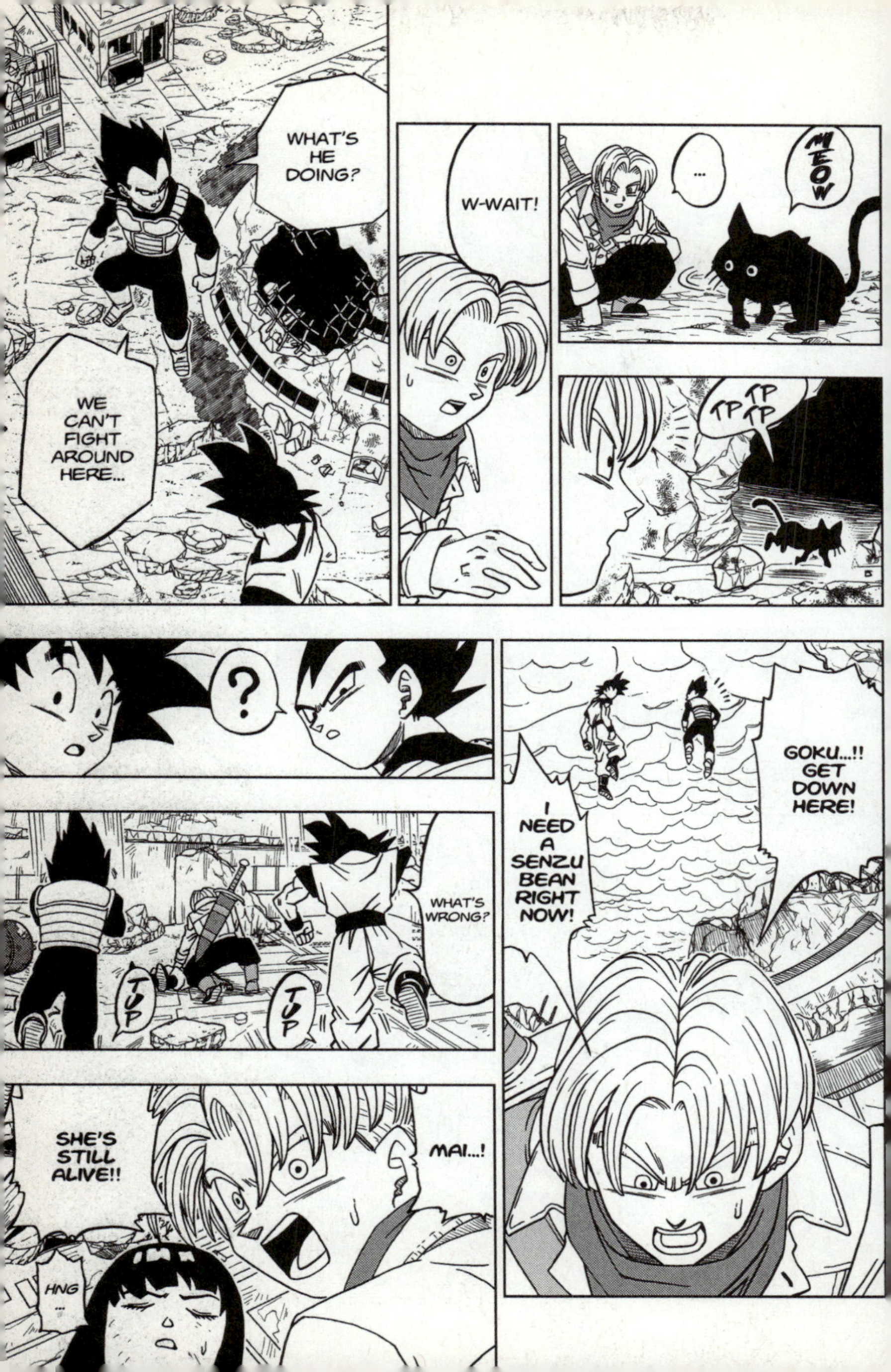

...
MEOW
TP TP TP
W-WAIT!
WHAT'S HE DOING?
WE CAN'T FIGHT AROUND HERE...
GOKU...!! GET DOWN HERE!
I NEED A SENZU BEAN RIGHT NOW!
?
WHAT'S WRONG?
TUP
TUP
MAI...!
SHE'S STILL ALIVE!!
HNG ...

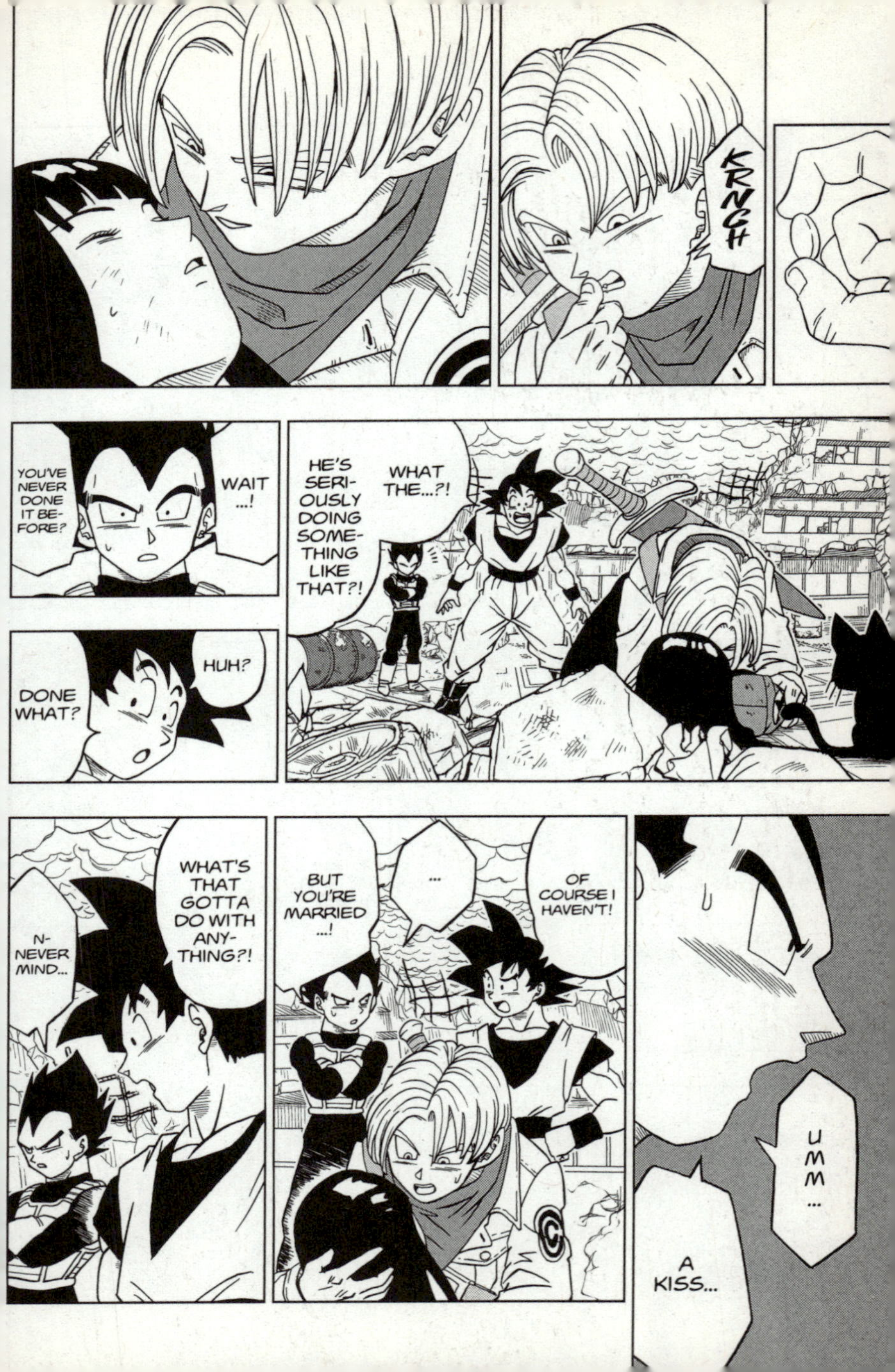
KRNCH
WHAT THE...?!
HE'S SERIOUSLY DOING SOMETHING LIKE THAT?!
WAIT ...!
YOU'VE NEVER DONE IT BEFORE?
HUH?
DONE WHAT?
UMM ...
A KISS...
OF COURSE I HAVEN'T!
...
BUT YOU'RE MARRIED ...!
WHAT'S THAT GOTTA DO WITH ANYTHING?!
N-NEVER MIND...

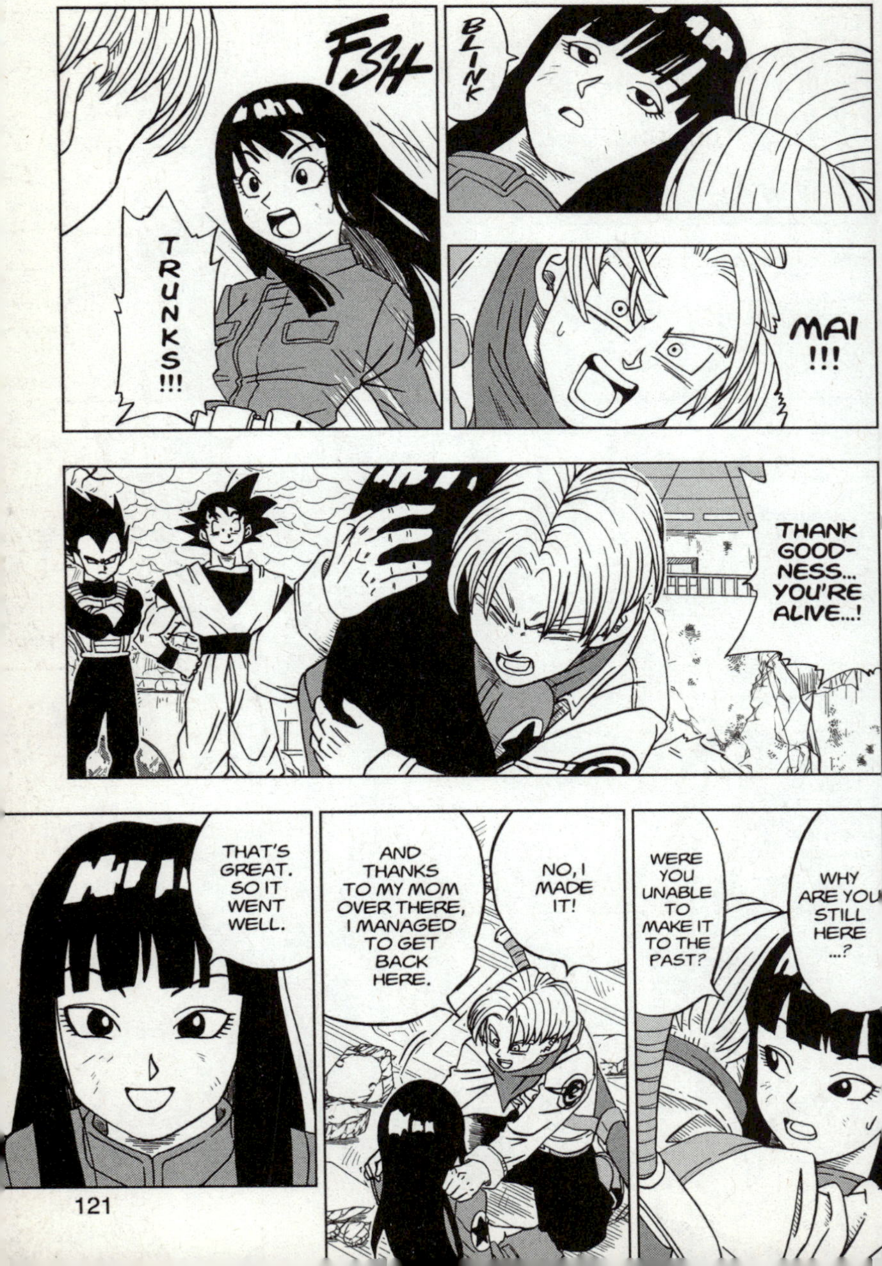
BLINK
MAI !!!
FSH
TRUNKS!!!
THANK GOOD-NESS... YOU'RE ALIVE...!
WHY ARE YOU STILL HERE ...?
WERE YOU UNABLE TO MAKE IT TO THE PAST?
NO, I MADE IT!
AND THANKS TO MY MOM OVER THERE, I MANAGED TO GET BACK HERE.
THAT'S GREAT. SO IT WENT WELL.

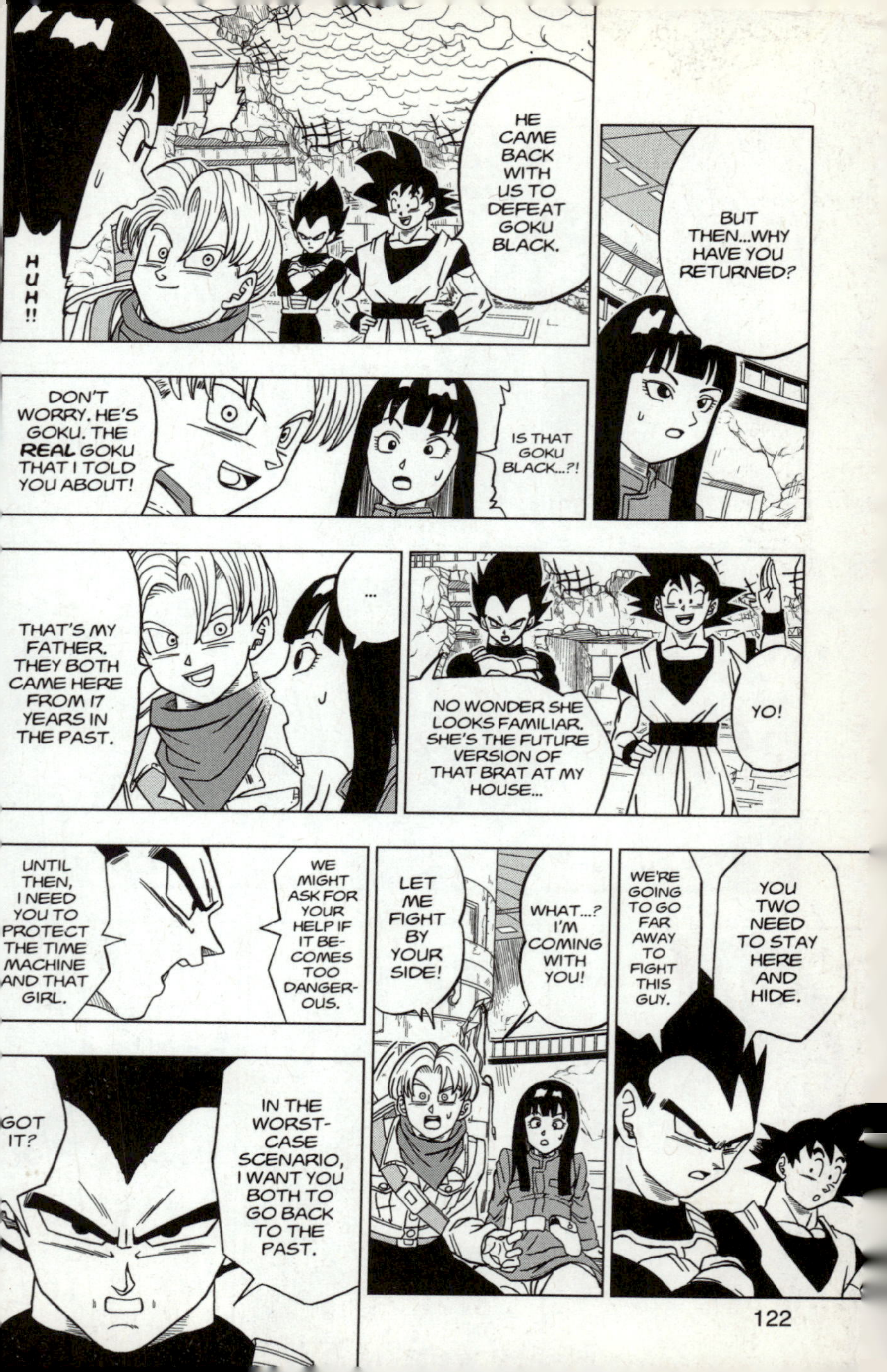
BUT THEN...WHY HAVE YOU RETURNED?
HE CAME BACK WITH US TO DEFEAT GOKU BLACK.
HUH!!
IS THAT GOKU BLACK...?!
DON'T WORRY. HE'S GOKU. THE **REAL** GOKU THAT I TOLD YOU ABOUT!
YO!
NO WONDER SHE LOOKS FAMILIAR. SHE'S THE FUTURE VERSION OF THAT BRAT AT MY HOUSE...
...
THAT'S MY FATHER. THEY BOTH CAME HERE FROM 17 YEARS IN THE PAST.
YOU TWO NEED TO STAY HERE AND HIDE.
WE'RE GOING TO GO FAR AWAY TO FIGHT THIS GUY.
WHAT...? I'M COMING WITH YOU!
LET ME FIGHT BY YOUR SIDE!
WE MIGHT ASK FOR YOUR HELP IF IT BE-COMES TOO DANGER-OUS.
UNTIL THEN, I NEED YOU TO PROTECT THE TIME MACHINE AND THAT GIRL.
IN THE WORST-CASE SCENARIO, I WANT YOU BOTH TO GO BACK TO THE PAST.
GOT IT?

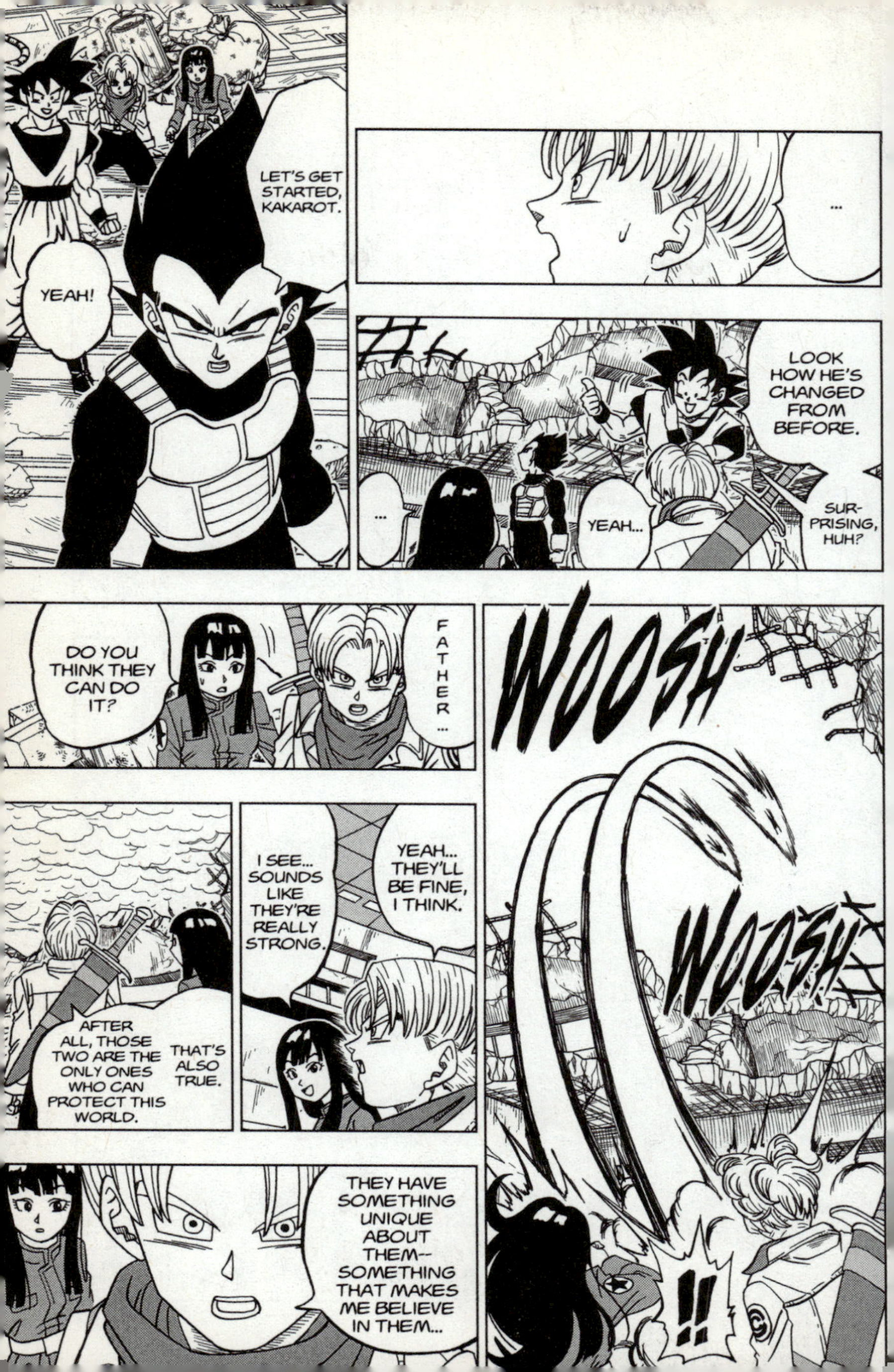
LET'S GET STARTED, KAKAROT.
YEAH!
...
LOOK HOW HE'S CHANGED FROM BEFORE.
SUR-PRISING, HUH?
YEAH...
...
DO YOU THINK THEY CAN DO IT?
FATHER...
I SEE... SOUNDS LIKE THEY'RE REALLY STRONG.
YEAH... THEY'LL BE FINE, I THINK.
AFTER ALL, THOSE TWO ARE THE ONLY ONES WHO CAN PROTECT THIS WORLD.
THAT'S ALSO TRUE.
THEY HAVE SOMETHING UNIQUE ABOUT THEM-- SOMETHING THAT MAKES ME BELIEVE IN THEM...
WOOSH
WOOSH
!!

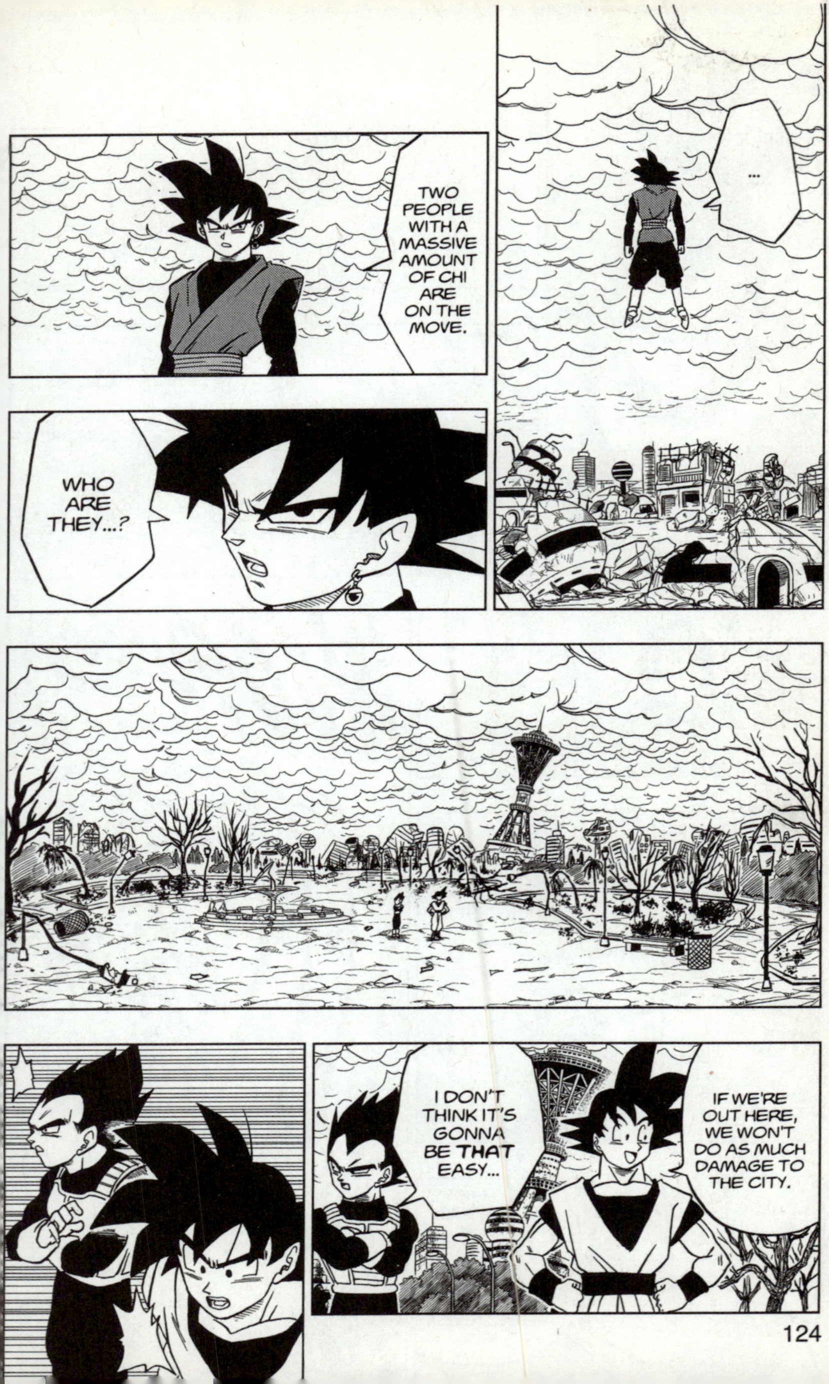
...
TWO PEOPLE WITH A MASSIVE AMOUNT OF CHI ARE ON THE MOVE.
WHO ARE THEY...?
IF WE'RE OUT HERE, WE WON'T DO AS MUCH DAMAGE TO THE CITY.
I DON'T THINK IT'S GONNA BE **THAT** EASY...

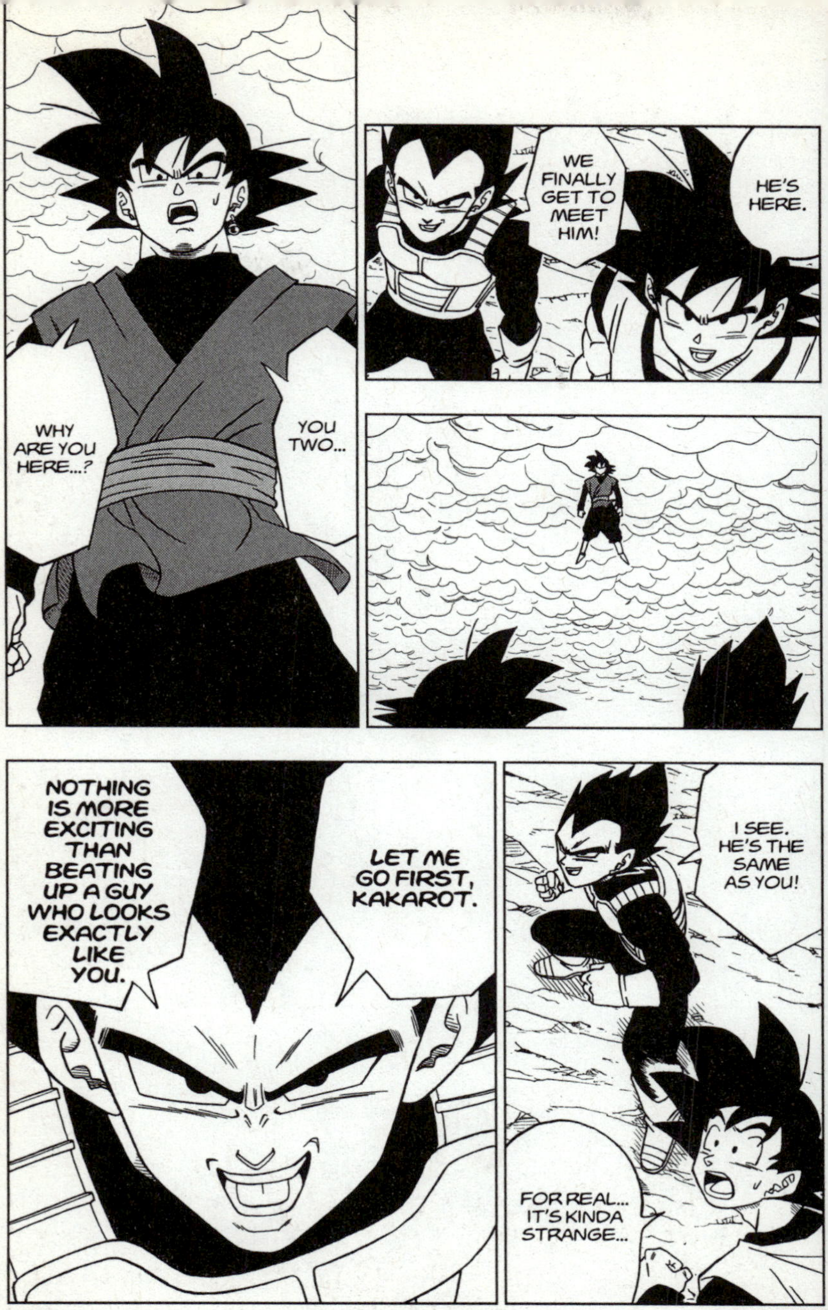
HE'S HERE.
WE FINALLY GET TO MEET HIM!
YOU TWO...
WHY ARE YOU HERE...?
I SEE. HE'S THE SAME AS YOU!
FOR REAL... IT'S KINDA STRANGE...
LET ME GO FIRST, KAKAROT.
NOTHING IS MORE EXCITING THAN BEATING UP A GUY WHO LOOKS EXACTLY LIKE YOU.

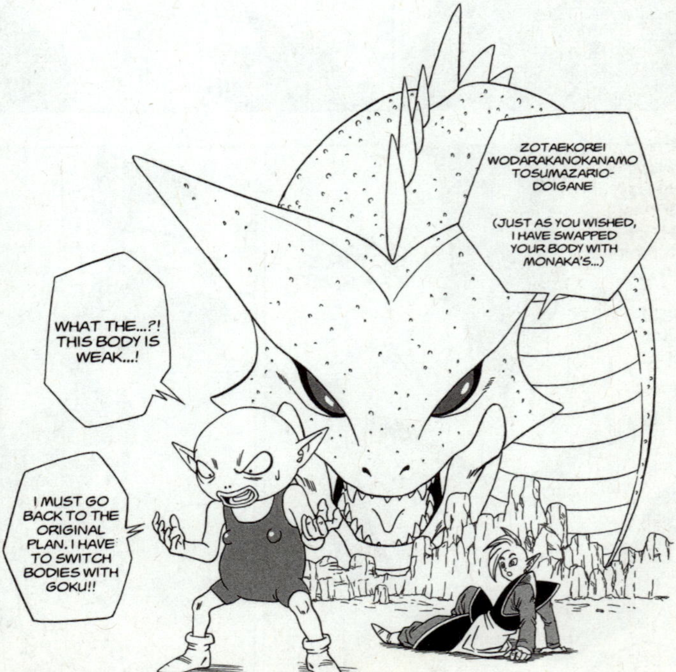
ZOTAEKOREI WODARAKANOKANAMO TOSUMAZARIO-DOIGANE
(JUST AS YOU WISHED, I HAVE SWAPPED YOUR BODY WITH MONAKA'S...)
WHAT THE...?! THIS BODY IS WEAK...!
I MUST GO BACK TO THE ORIGINAL PLAN. I HAVE TO SWITCH BODIES WITH GOKU!!

DRAGON BALL SUPER

## CHAPTER 19: ANOTHER ZAMAS

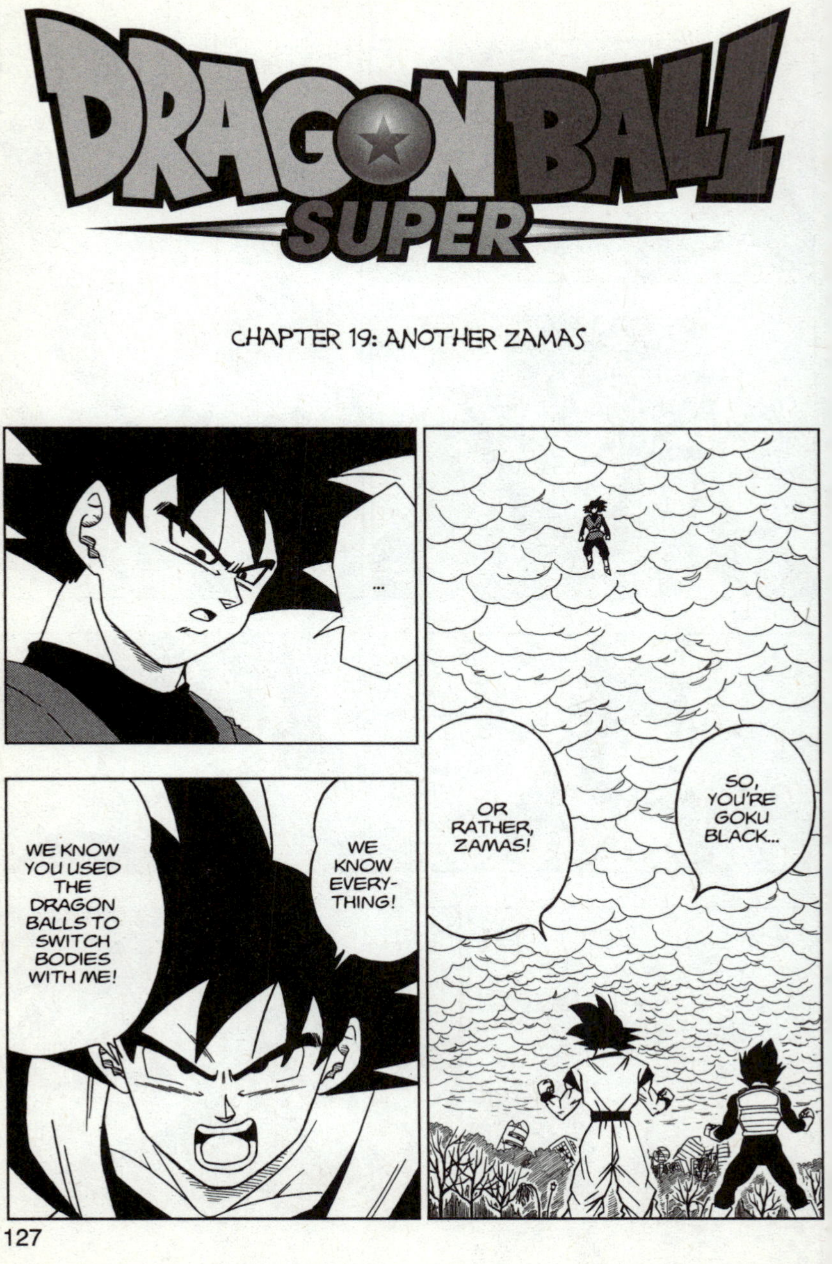
SO, YOU'RE GOKU BLACK...
OR RATHER, ZAMAS!
...
WE KNOW EVERYTHING!
WE KNOW YOU USED THE DRAGON BALLS TO SWITCH BODIES WITH ME!

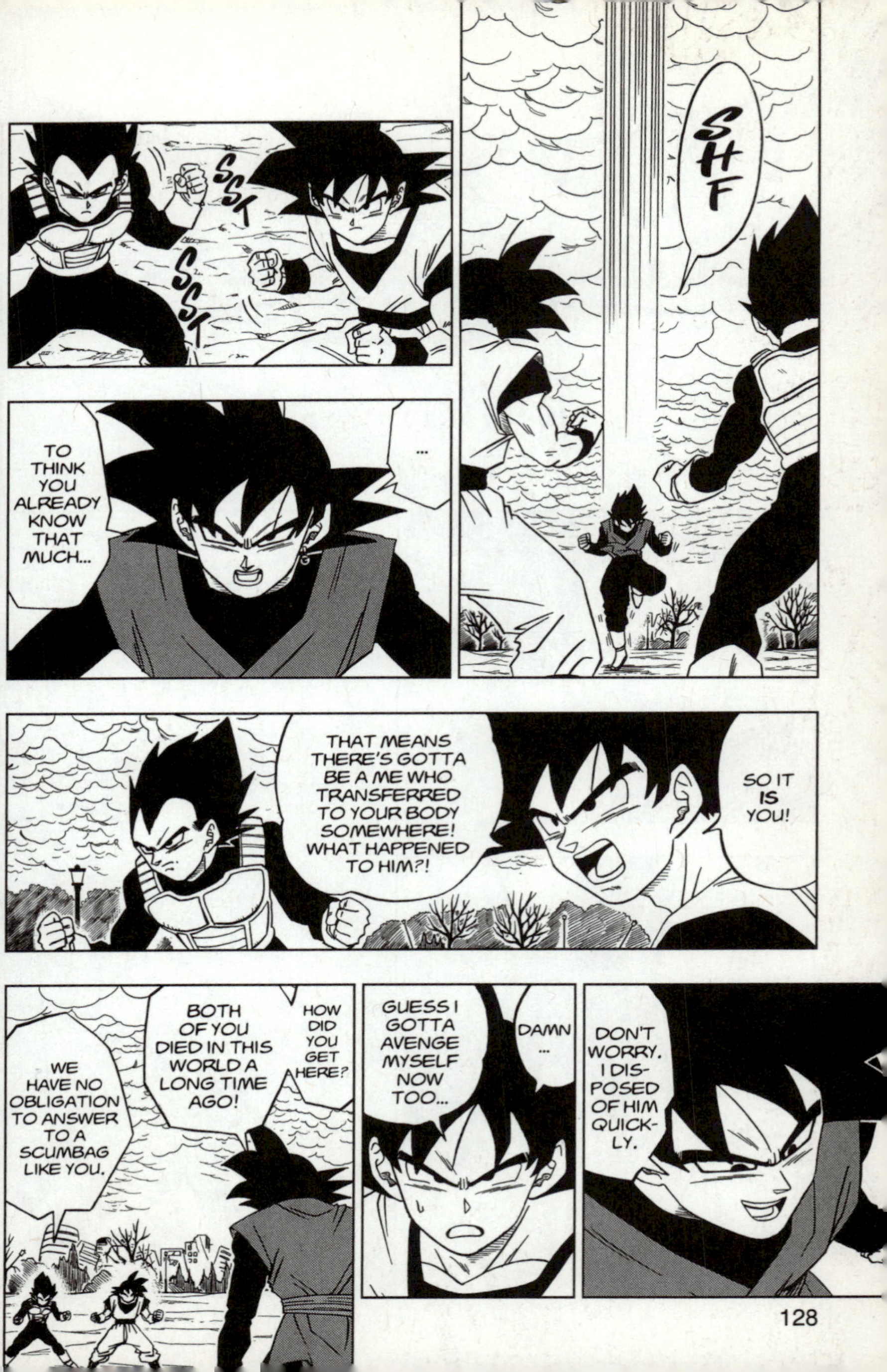
SHF
SSK
SSST
...
TO THINK YOU ALREADY KNOW THAT MUCH...
SO IT IS YOU!
THAT MEANS THERE'S GOTTA BE A ME WHO TRANSFERRED TO YOUR BODY SOMEWHERE! WHAT HAPPENED TO HIM?!
DON'T WORRY. I DIS-POSED OF HIM QUICK-LY.
DAMN...
GUESS I GOTTA AVENGE MYSELF NOW TOO...
HOW DID YOU GET HERE?
BOTH OF YOU DIED IN THIS WORLD A LONG TIME AGO!
WE HAVE NO OBLIGATION TO ANSWER TO A SCUMBAG LIKE YOU.

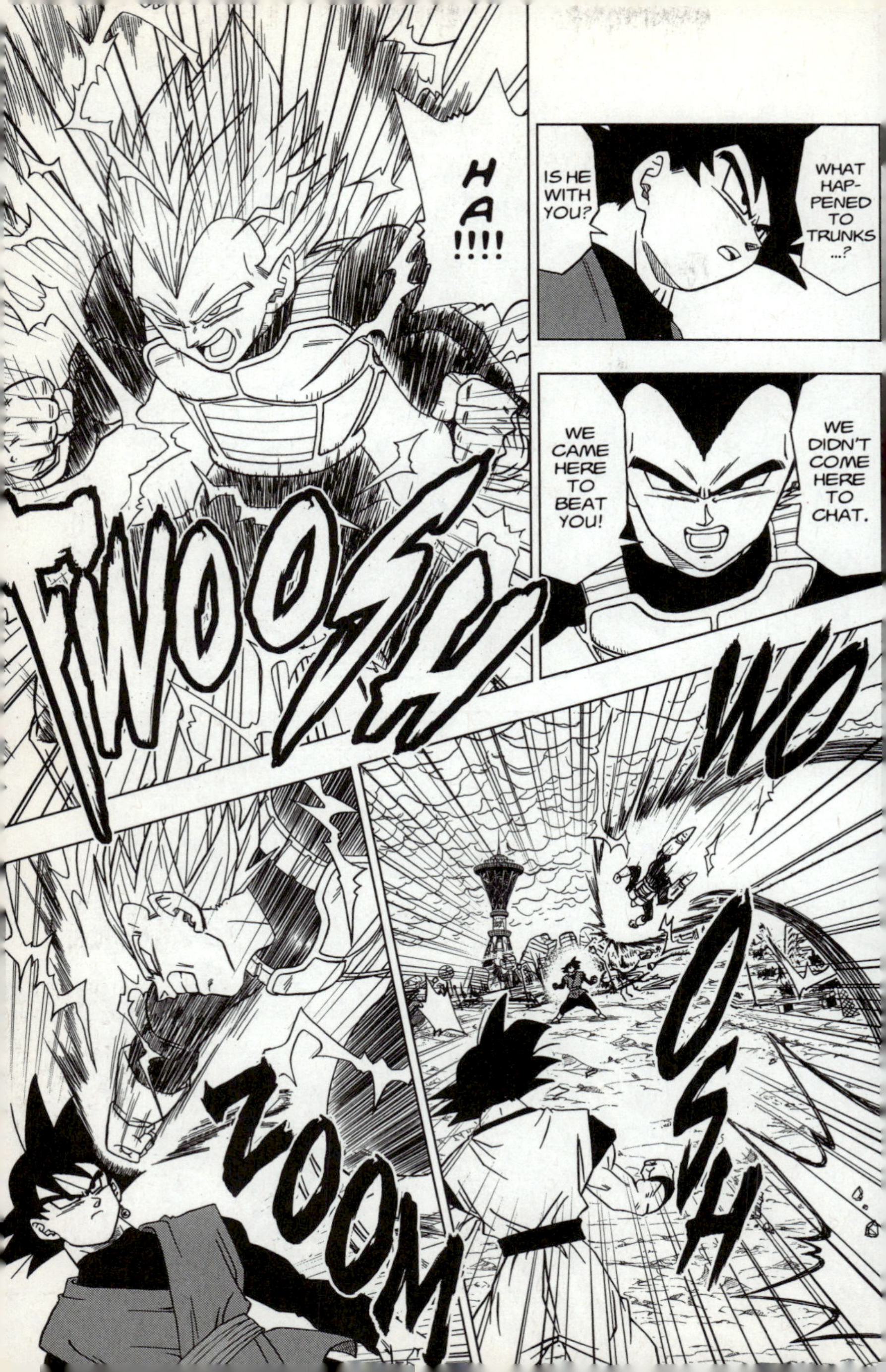

WHAT HAPPENED TO TRUNKS ...?
IS HE WITH YOU?
WE DIDN'T COME HERE TO CHAT.
WE CAME HERE TO BEAT YOU!
HA!!!!
WOOSH
WOOSH
ZOOM

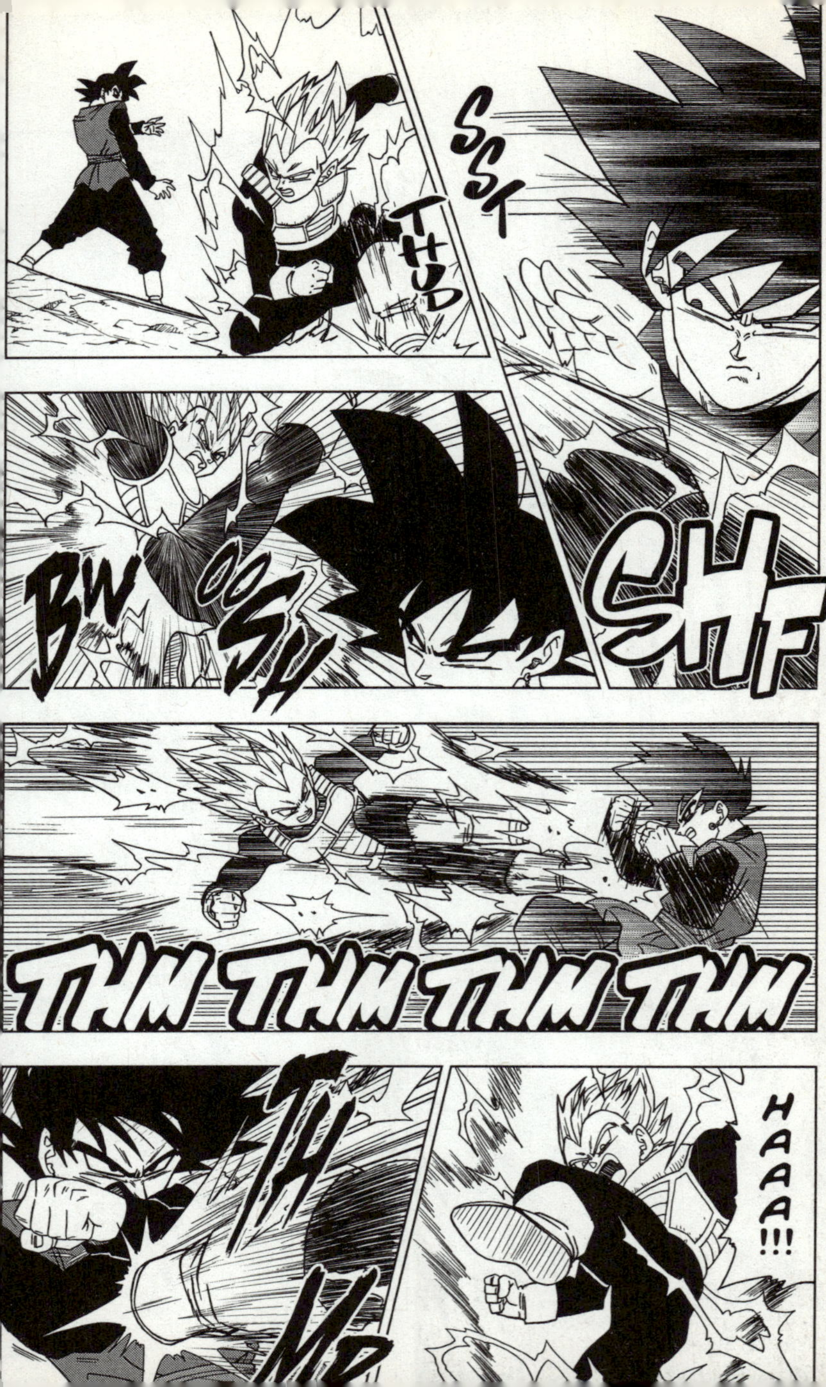
SSK
SHF
THUD
BWOOSH
THM THM THM THM
HAAAA!!!
TH
MP

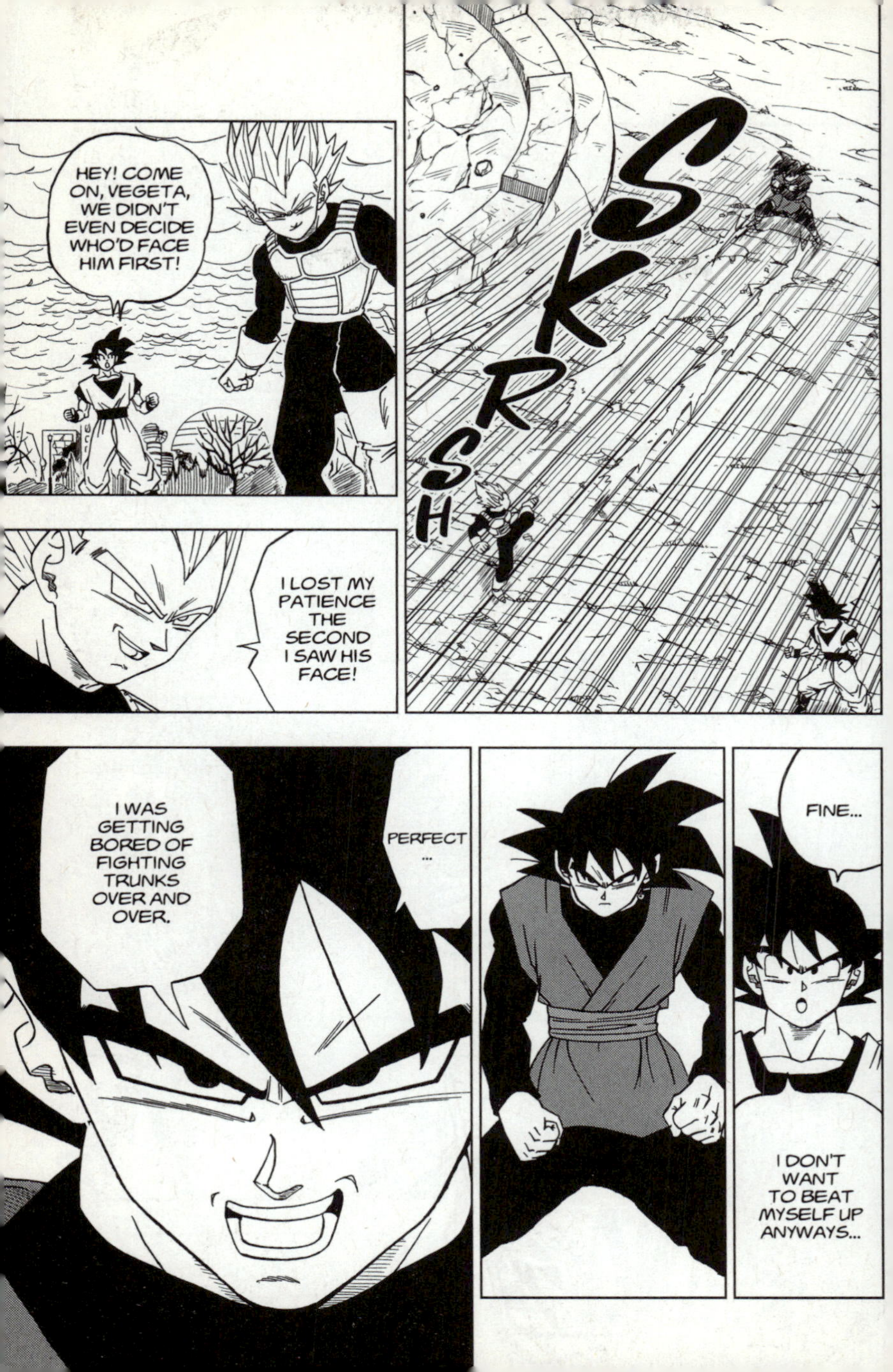
SKRSH
HEY! COME ON, VEGETA, WE DIDN'T EVEN DECIDE WHO'D FACE HIM FIRST!
I LOST MY PATIENCE THE SECOND I SAW HIS FACE!
FINE...
I DON'T WANT TO BEAT MYSELF UP ANYWAYS...
PERFECT...
I WAS GETTING BORED OF FIGHTING TRUNKS OVER AND OVER.

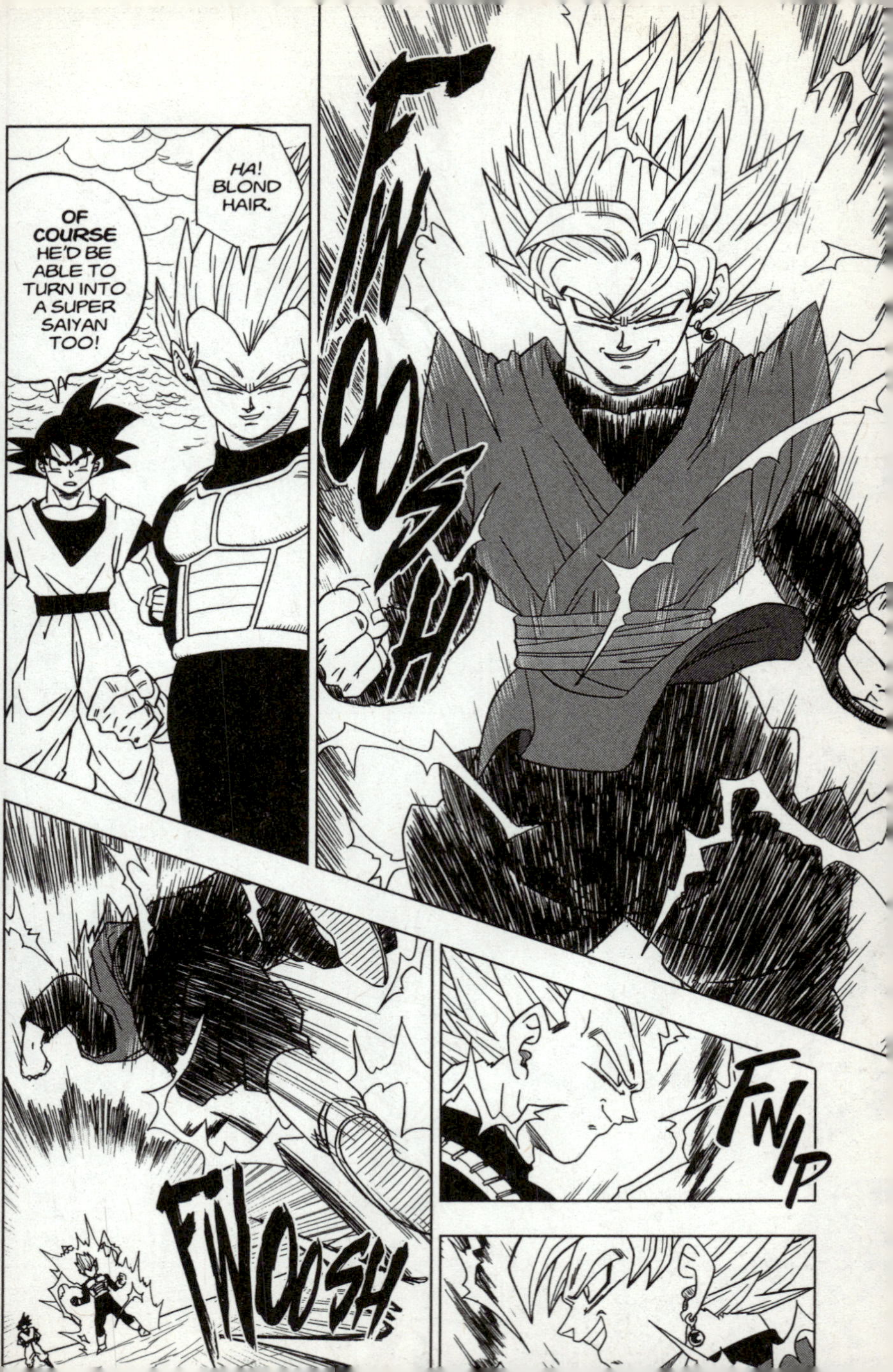
FWOOSH
HA! BLOND HAIR.
OF **COURSE** HE'D BE ABLE TO TURN INTO A SUPER SAIYAN TOO!
FWIP
FWOOSH

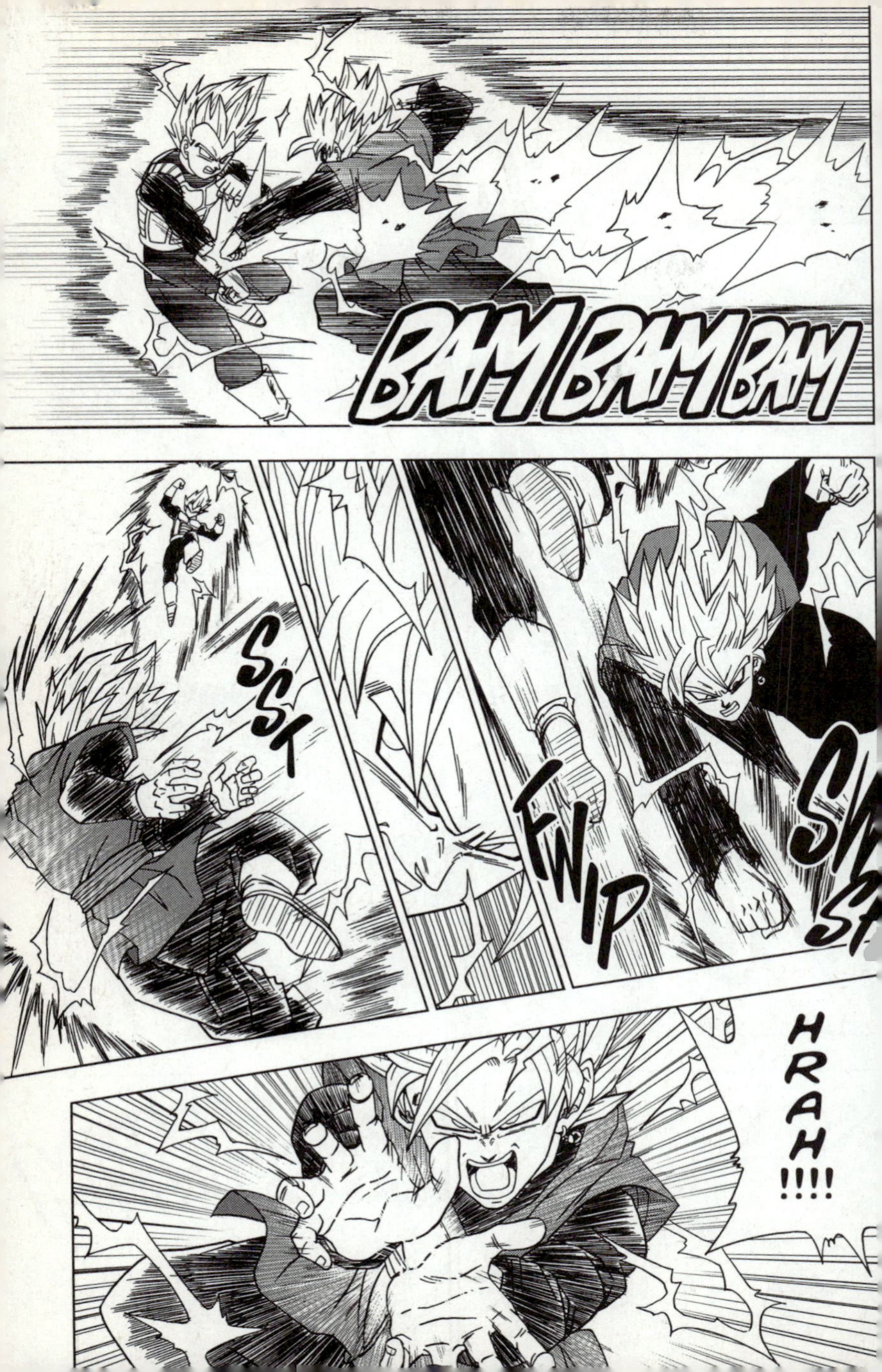
BAM BAM BAM
SW
SH
FWIP
SSK
HRAH!!!!

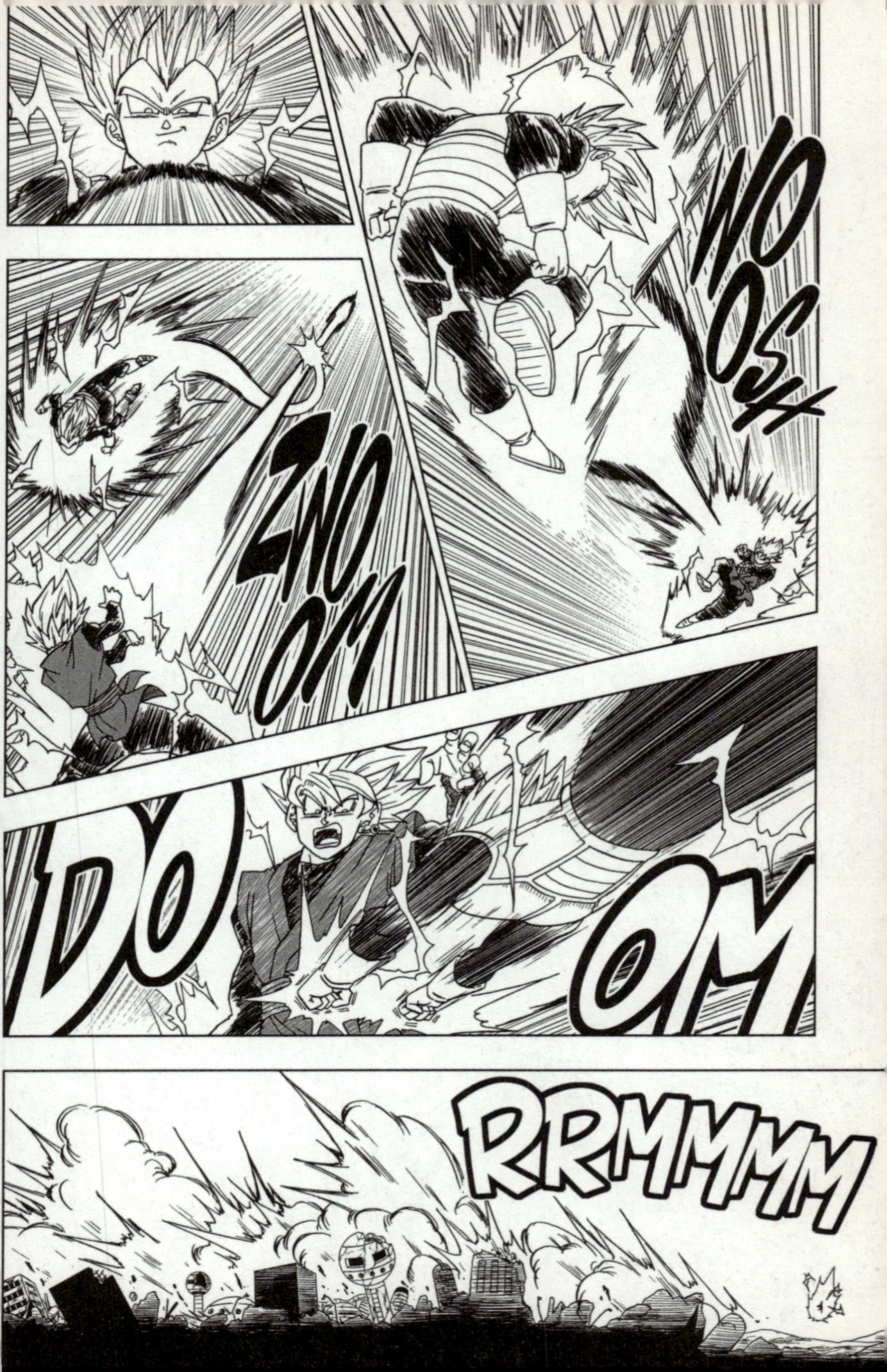
WOOSH
ZWOOM
DOOM
RRMMMM

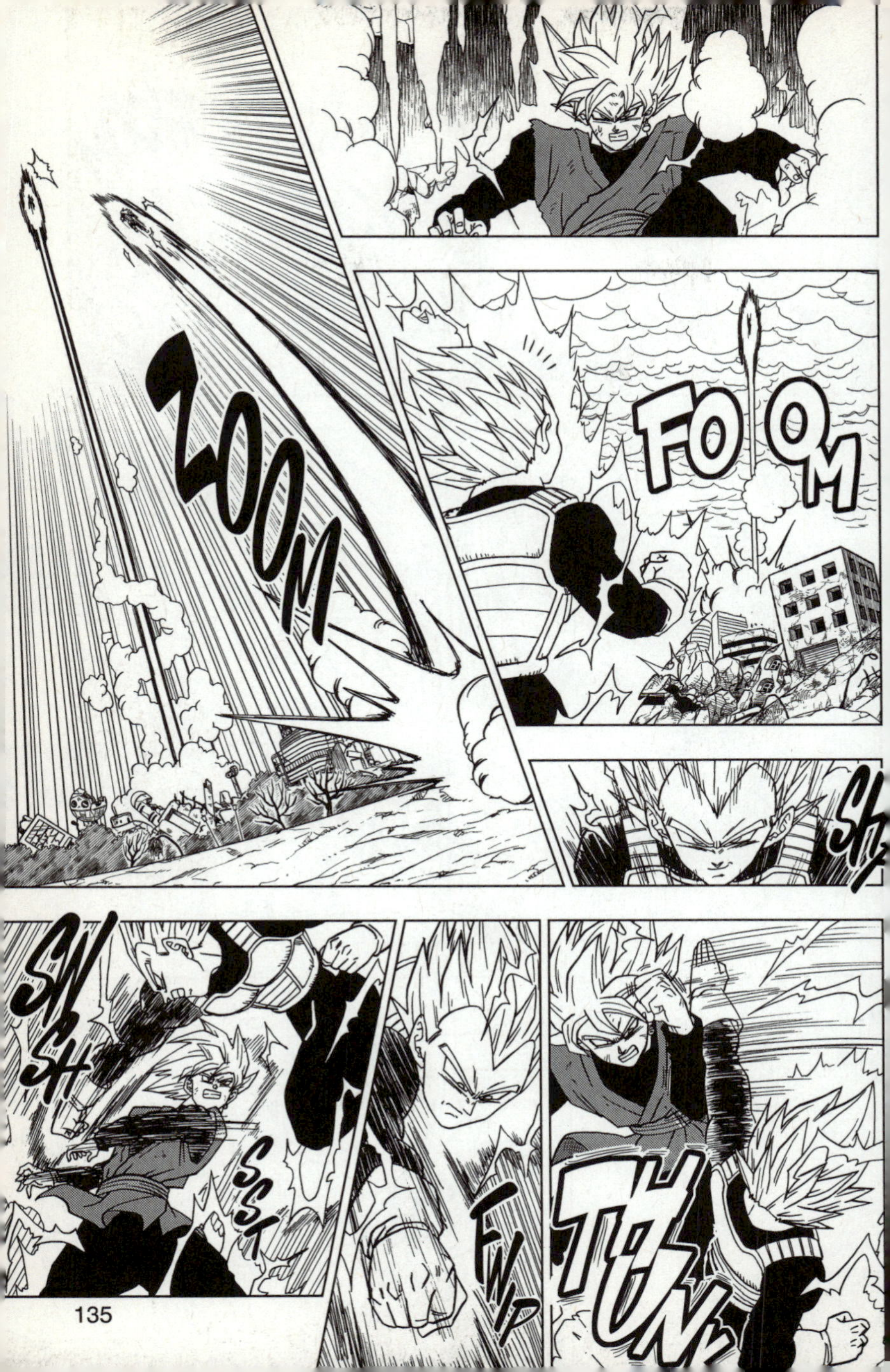
FOOM
SH
ZOOM
THUN
FWIP
SWISH
SSK

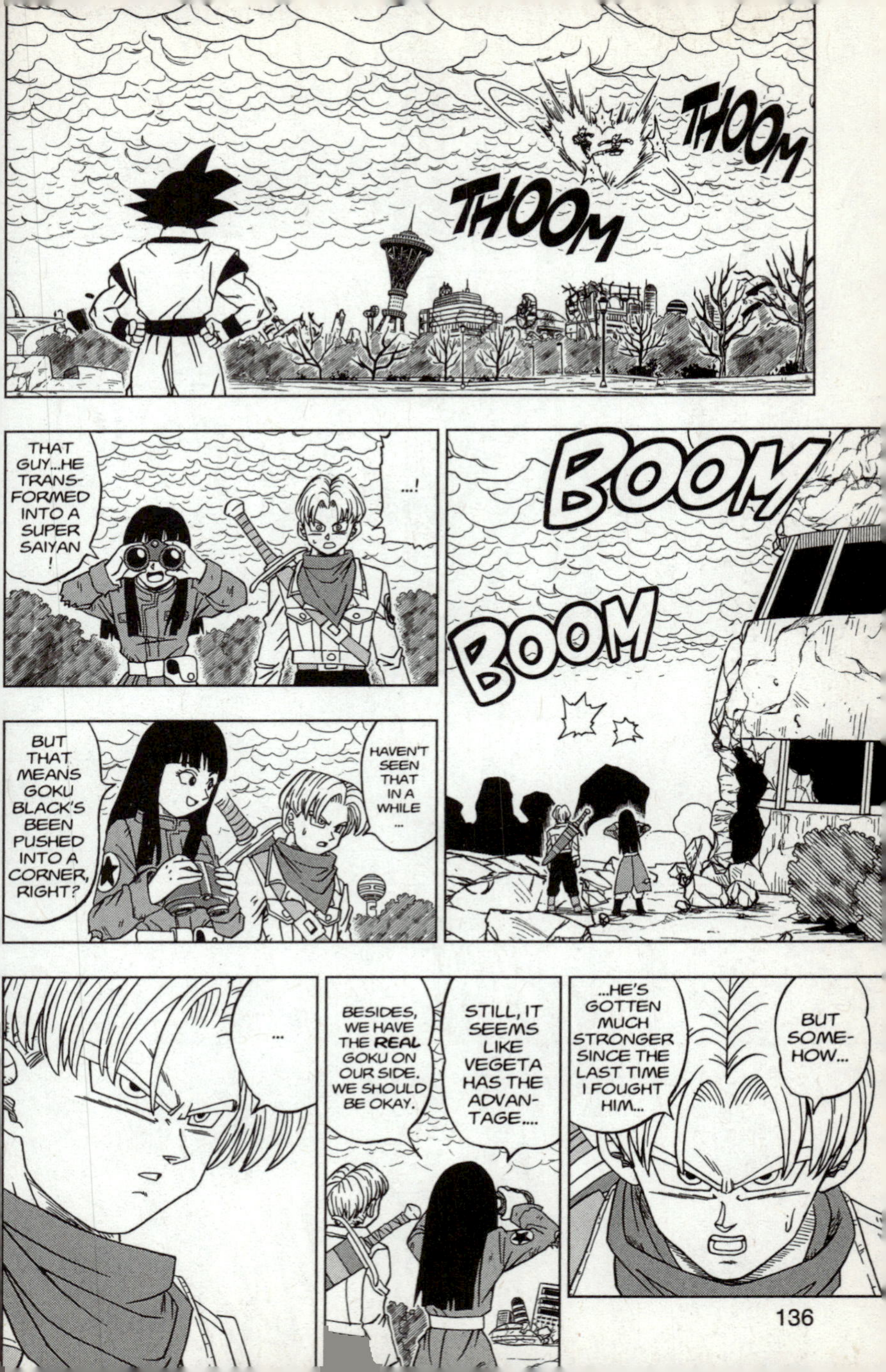
THOOM
THOOM
BOOM
BOOM
...!
THAT GUY...HE TRANSFORMED INTO A SUPER SAIYAN!
HAVEN'T SEEN THAT IN A WHILE...
BUT THAT MEANS GOKU BLACK'S BEEN PUSHED INTO A CORNER, RIGHT?
BUT SOMEHOW...
...HE'S GOTTEN MUCH STRONGER SINCE THE LAST TIME I FOUGHT HIM...
STILL, IT SEEMS LIKE VEGETA HAS THE ADVANTAGE....
BESIDES, WE HAVE THE **REAL** GOKU ON OUR SIDE. WE SHOULD BE OKAY.
...

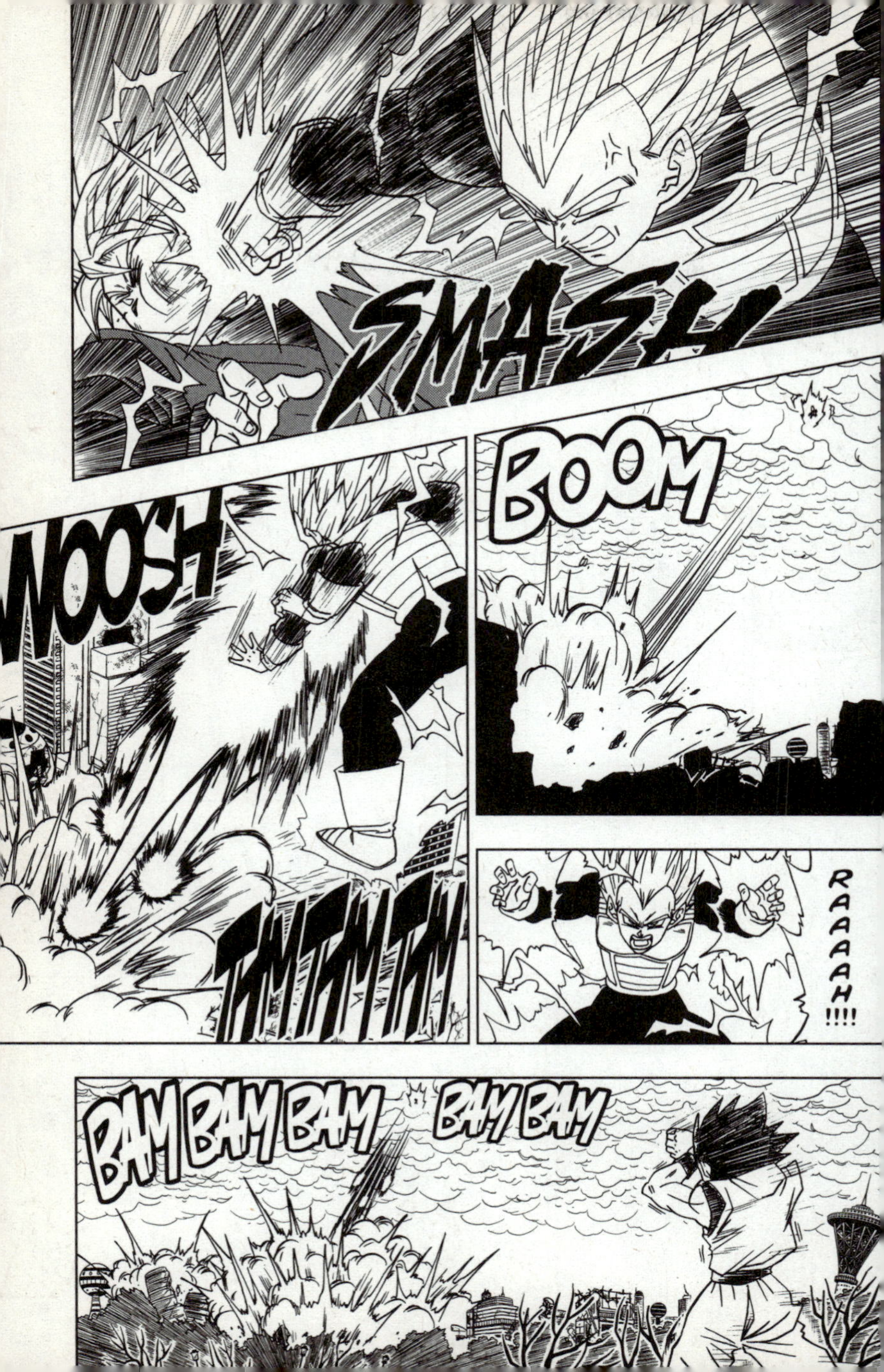
SMASH
BOOM
RAAAAAH!!!!
WOOSH
BAM BAM BAM
BAM BAM

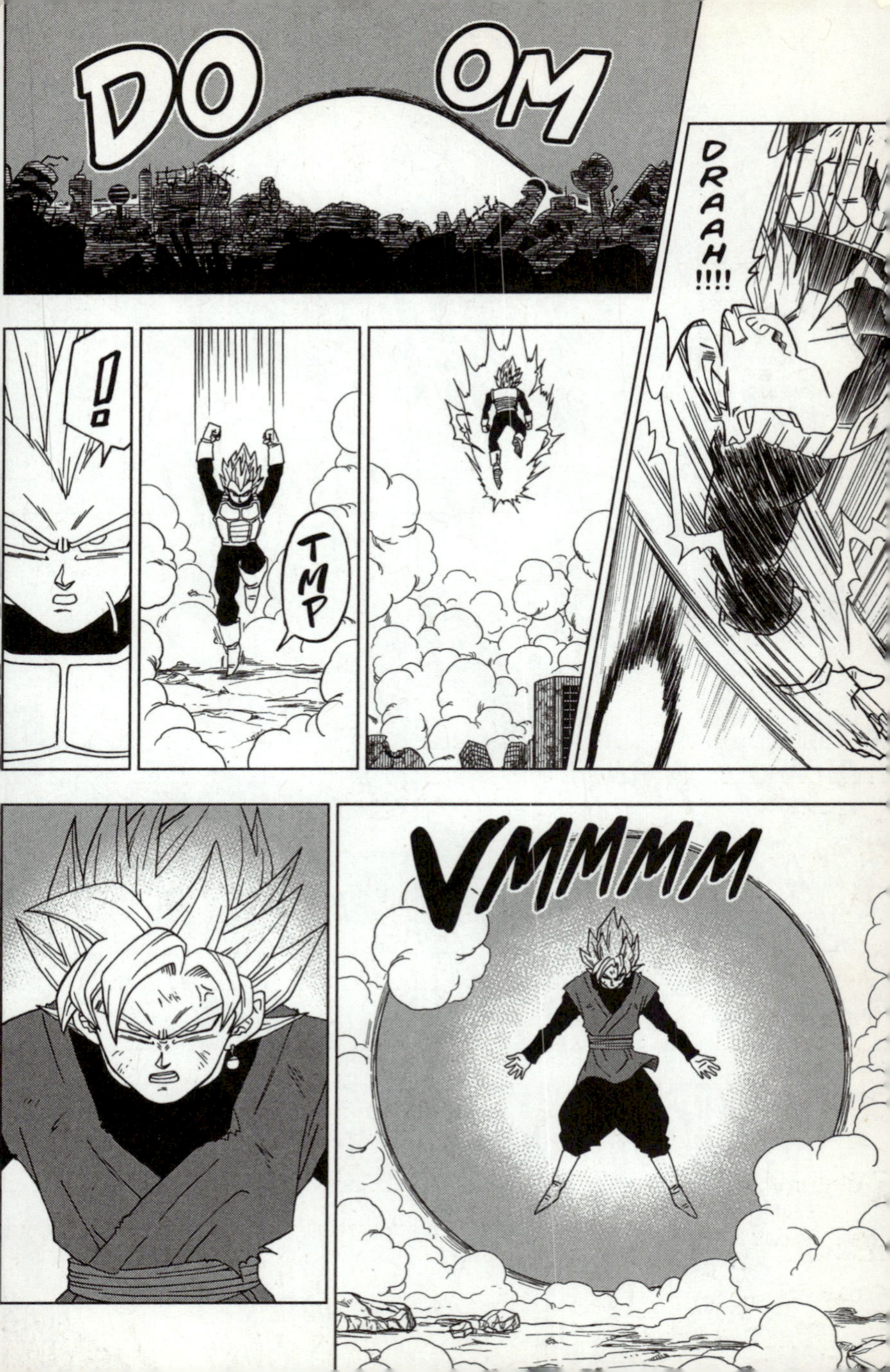
DRAAAH!!!!
DO OM
TMP
!
VMMMM

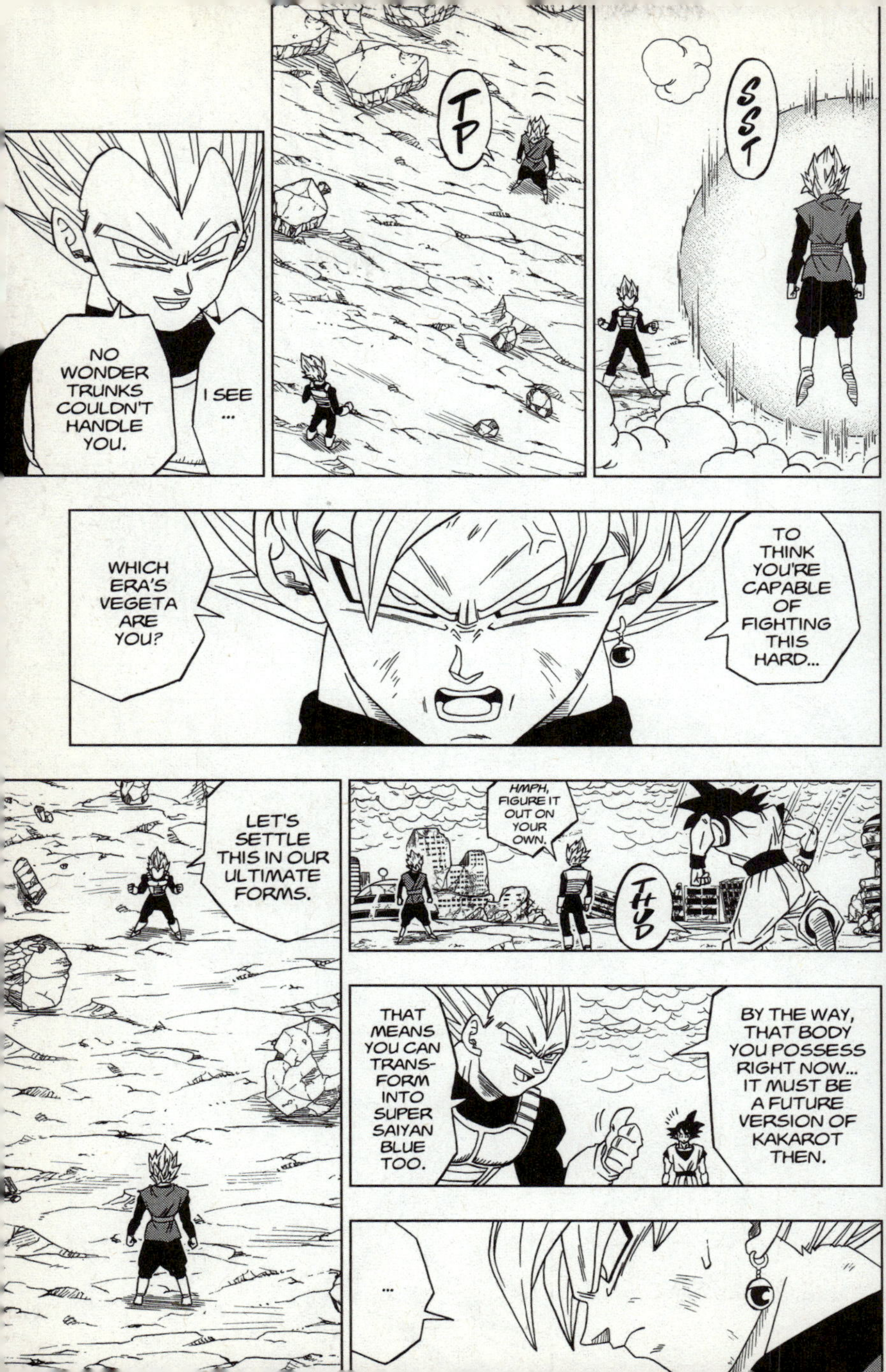
SSST
TP
I SEE...
NO WONDER TRUNKS COULDN'T HANDLE YOU.
TO THINK YOU'RE CAPABLE OF FIGHTING THIS HARD...
WHICH ERA'S VEGETA ARE YOU?
HMPH, FIGURE IT OUT ON YOUR OWN.
THUD
BY THE WAY, THAT BODY YOU POSSESS RIGHT NOW... IT MUST BE A FUTURE VERSION OF KAKAROT THEN.
THAT MEANS YOU CAN TRANSFORM INTO SUPER SAIYAN BLUE TOO.
...
LET'S SETTLE THIS IN OUR ULTIMATE FORMS.

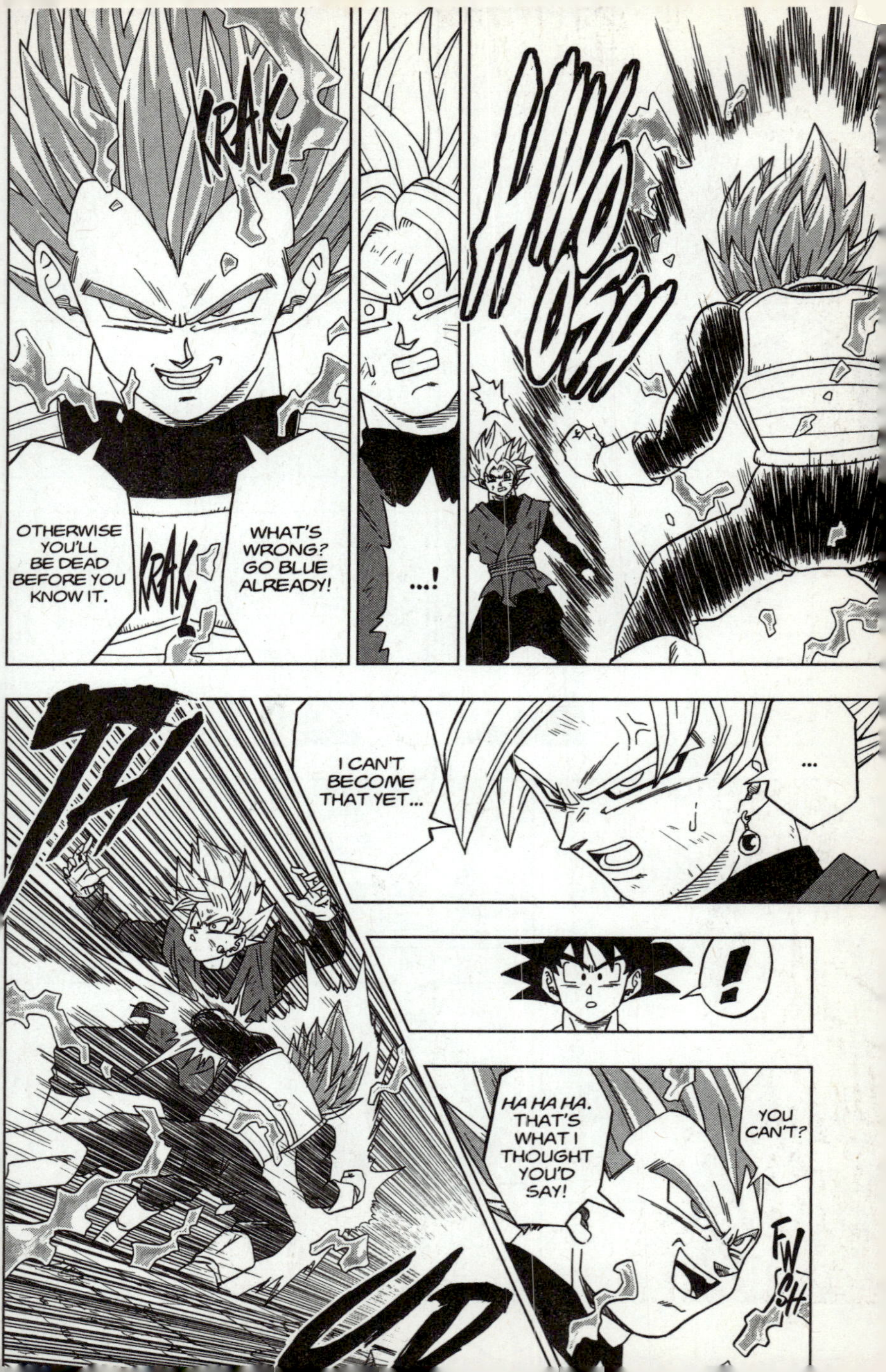
WHOOSH
...!
KRAK
WHAT'S WRONG? GO BLUE ALREADY!
OTHERWISE YOU'LL BE DEAD BEFORE YOU KNOW IT.
KRAK
...
I CAN'T BECOME THAT YET...
!
YOU CAN'T?
HA HA HA. THAT'S WHAT I THOUGHT YOU'D SAY!
FWSH
TH
UD

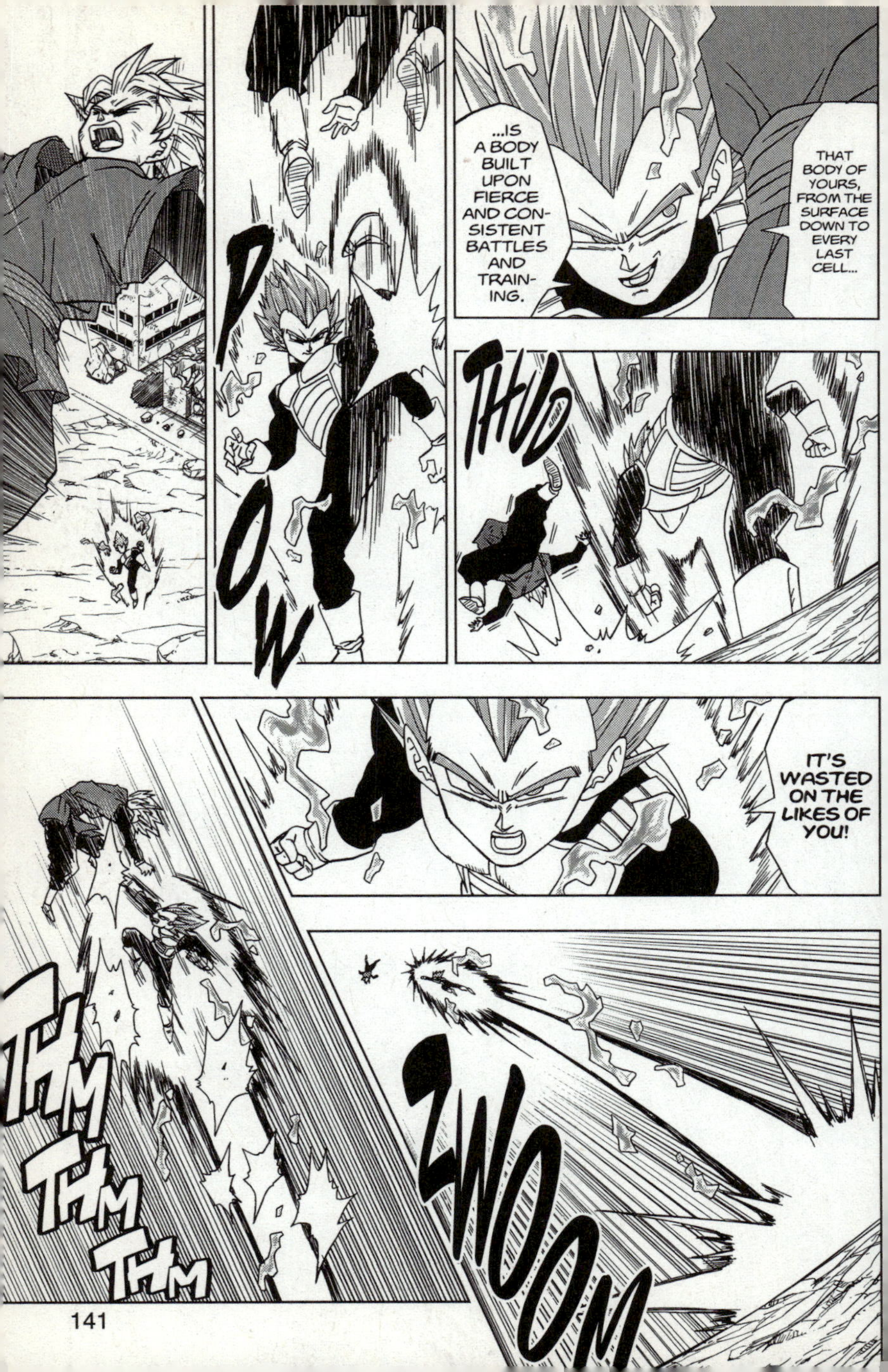
THAT BODY OF YOURS, FROM THE SURFACE DOWN TO EVERY LAST CELL...
...IS A BODY BUILT UPON FIERCE AND CON-SISTENT BATTLES AND TRAIN-ING.
THUD
POW
IT'S WASTED ON THE LIKES OF YOU!
ZWOOM
THM THM THM

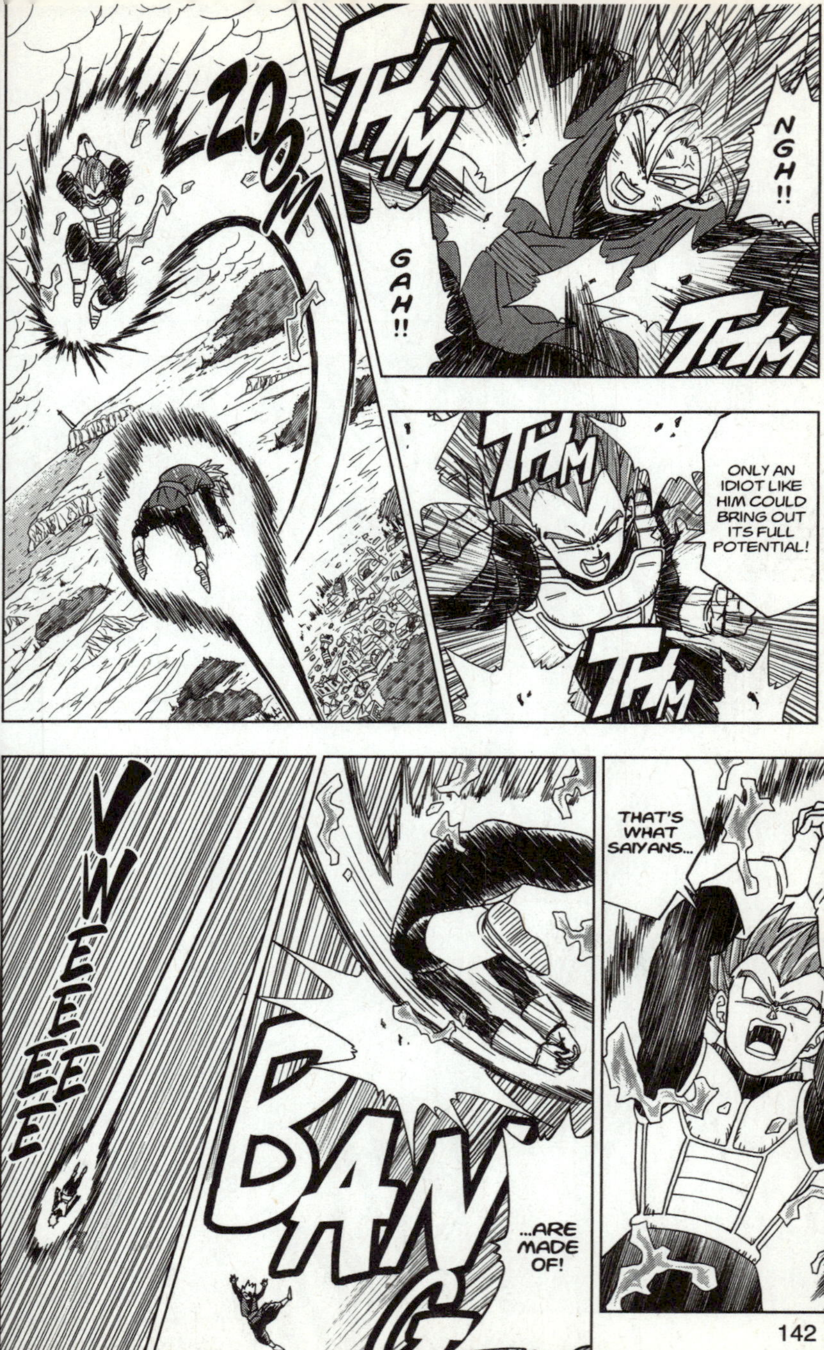
NGH!!
THM
GAH!!
THM
THM
ONLY AN IDIOT LIKE HIM COULD BRING OUT ITS FULL POTENTIAL!
THM
ZOOM
THAT'S WHAT SAIYANS...
BANG
...ARE MADE OF!
VWEEEEEE

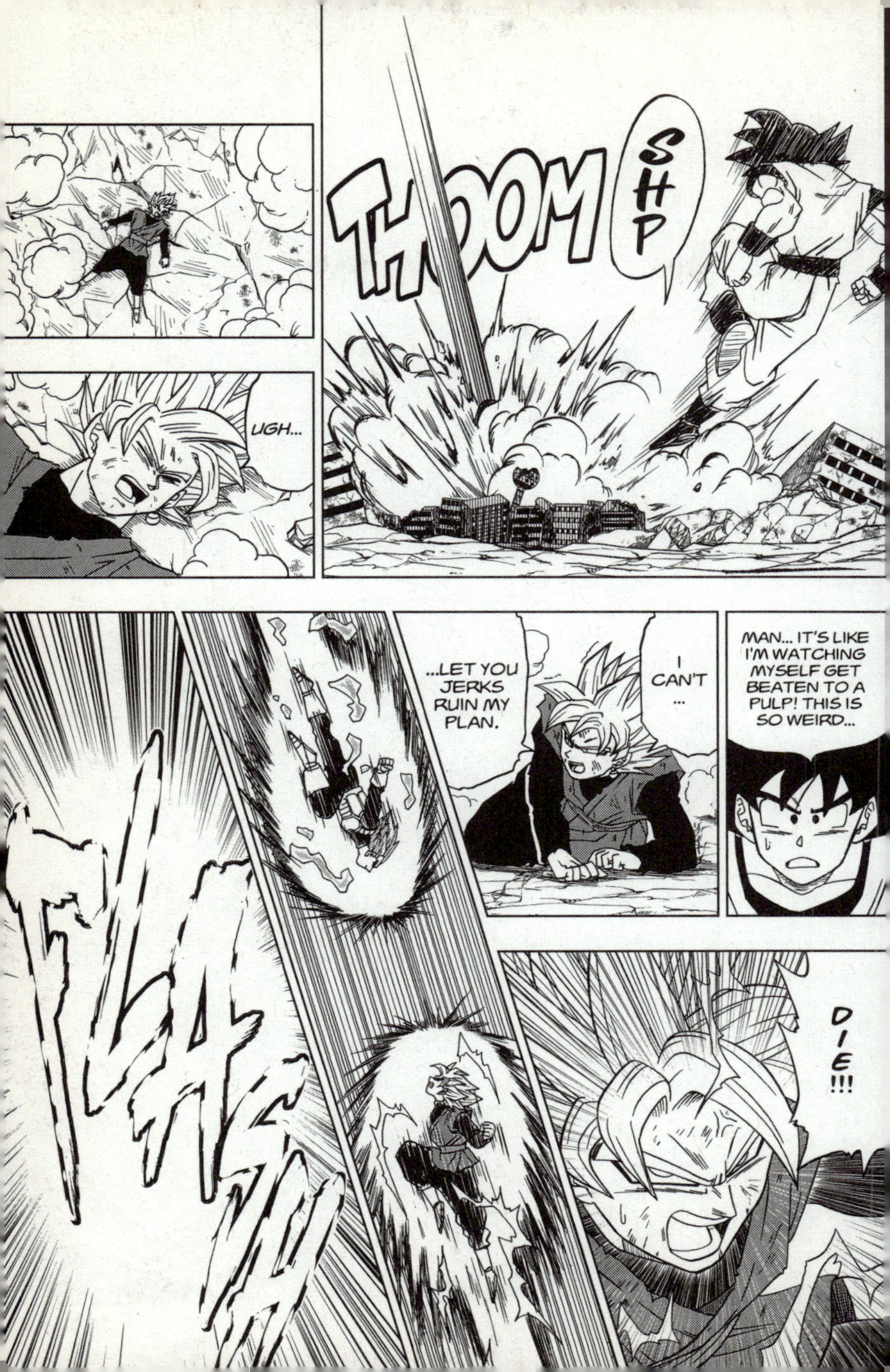
SHP
THOOM
UGH...
MAN... IT'S LIKE I'M WATCHING MYSELF GET BEATEN TO A PULP! THIS IS SO WEIRD...
I CAN'T ...
...LET YOU JERKS RUIN MY PLAN.
DIE!!!

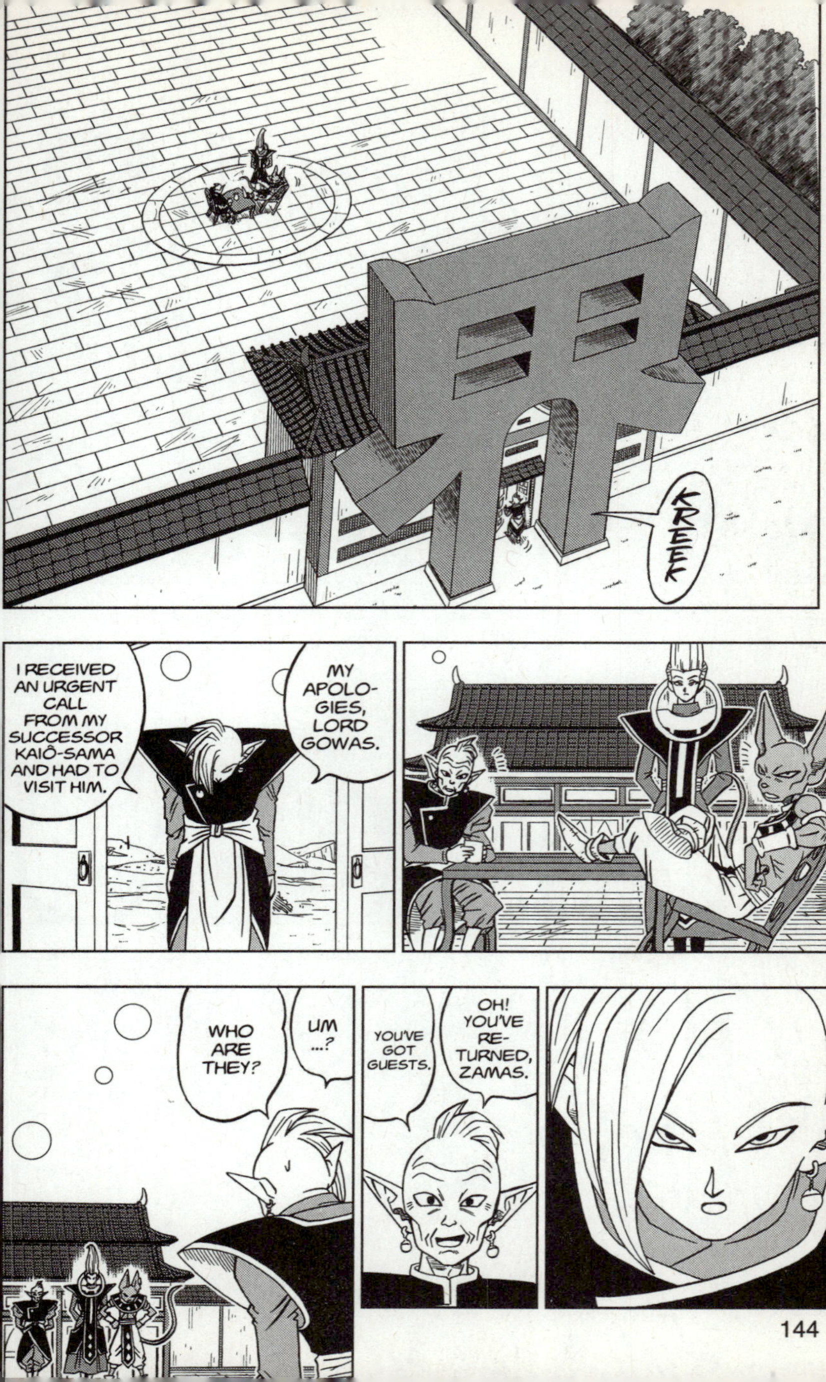
KREEK
MY APOLOGIES, LORD GOWAS.
I RECEIVED AN URGENT CALL FROM MY SUCCESSOR KAIÔ-SAMA AND HAD TO VISIT HIM.
OH! YOU'VE RETURNED, ZAMAS.
YOU'VE GOT GUESTS.
UM ...?
WHO ARE THEY?

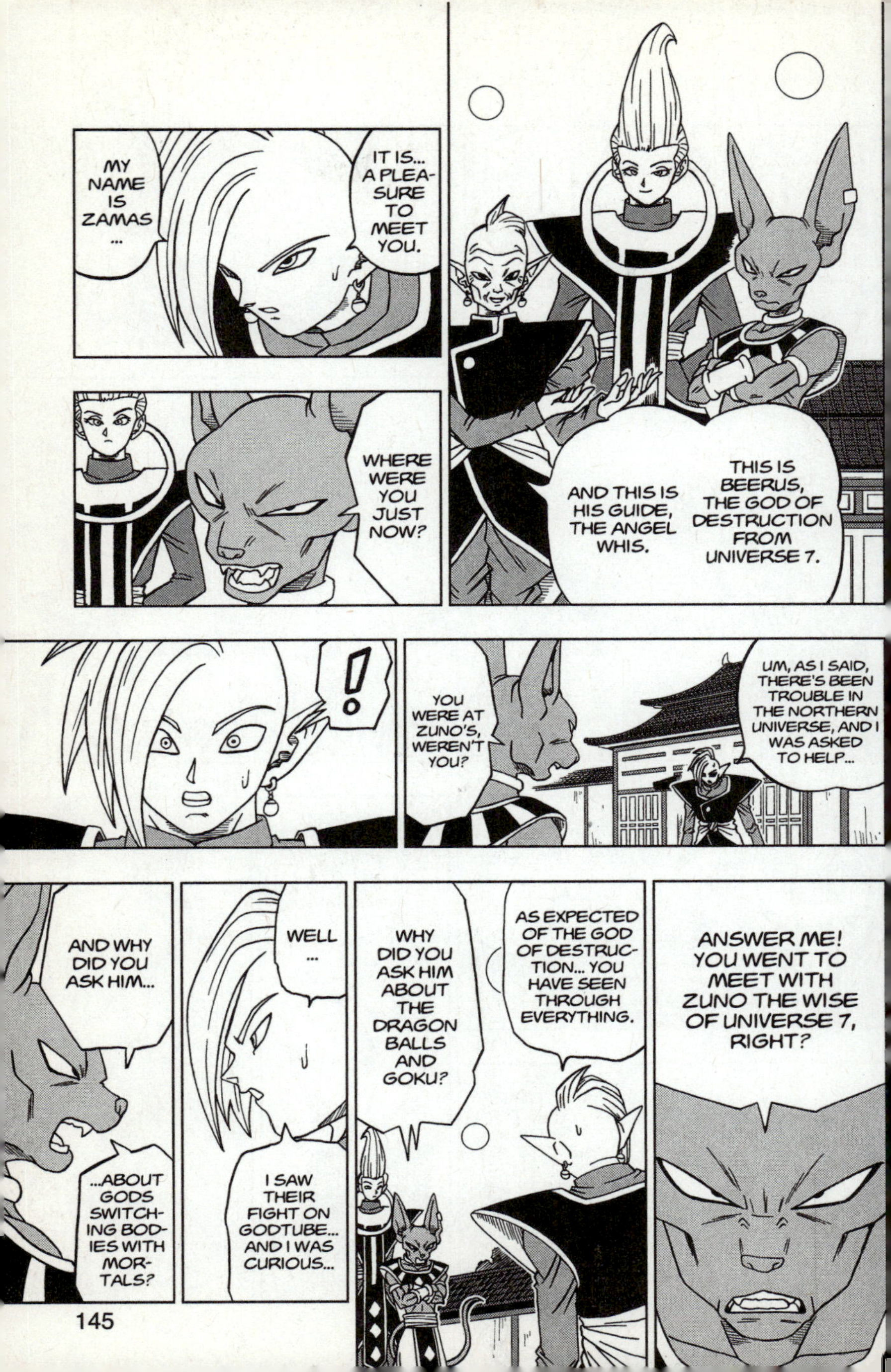
THIS IS BEERUS, THE GOD OF DESTRUCTION FROM UNIVERSE 7.
AND THIS IS HIS GUIDE, THE ANGEL WHIS.
IT IS... A PLEASURE TO MEET YOU.
MY NAME IS ZAMAS ...
WHERE WERE YOU JUST NOW?
UM, AS I SAID, THERE'S BEEN TROUBLE IN THE NORTHERN UNIVERSE, AND I WAS ASKED TO HELP...
YOU WERE AT ZUNO'S, WEREN'T YOU?
!
ANSWER ME! YOU WENT TO MEET WITH ZUNO THE WISE OF UNIVERSE 7, RIGHT?
AS EXPECTED OF THE GOD OF DESTRUCTION... YOU HAVE SEEN THROUGH EVERYTHING.
WHY DID YOU ASK HIM ABOUT THE DRAGON BALLS AND GOKU?
WELL ...
I SAW THEIR FIGHT ON GODTUBE... AND I WAS CURIOUS...
AND WHY DID YOU ASK HIM...
...ABOUT GODS SWITCHING BODIES WITH MORTALS?

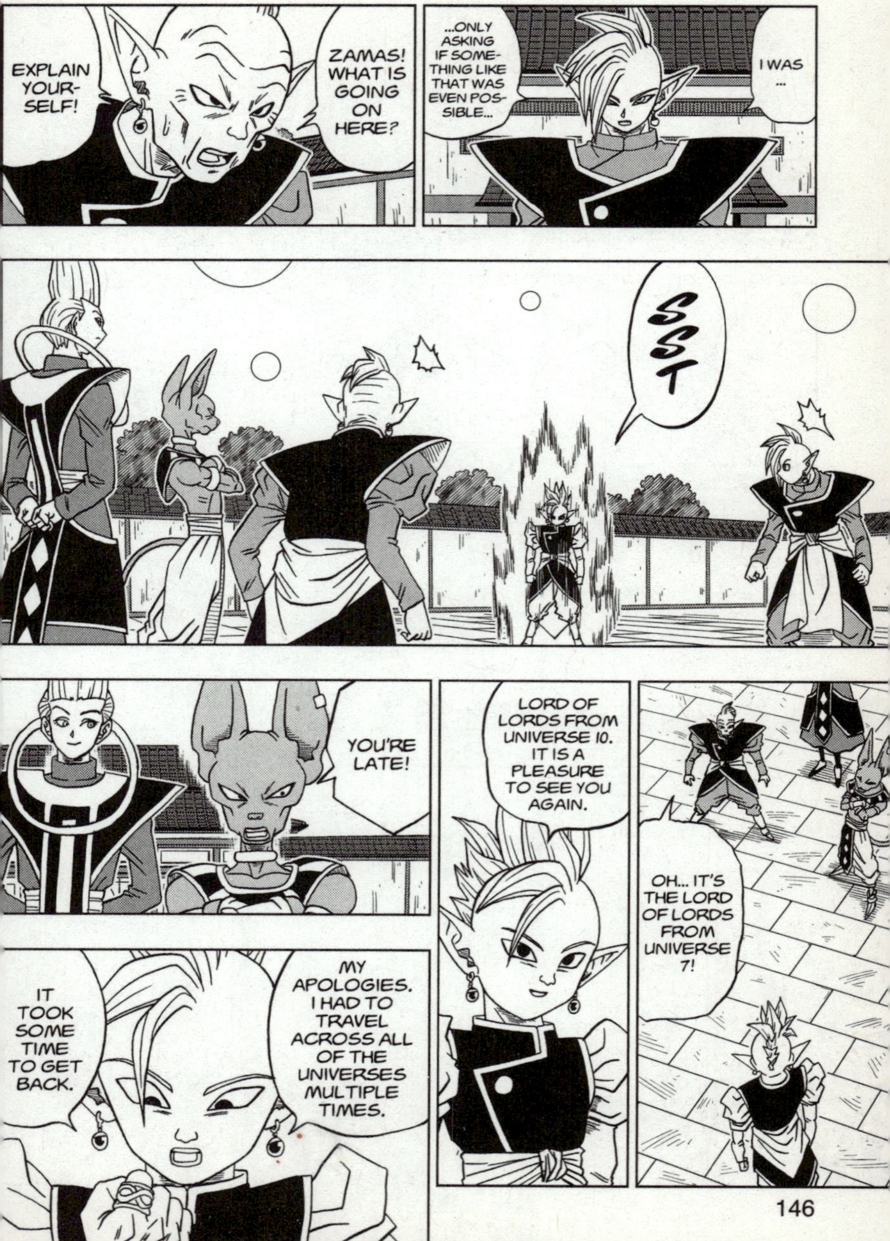
I WAS ...
...ONLY ASKING IF SOME-THING LIKE THAT WAS EVEN POS-SIBLE...
ZAMAS! WHAT IS GOING ON HERE?
EXPLAIN YOUR-SELF!
SST
OH... IT'S THE LORD OF LORDS FROM UNIVERSE 7!
LORD OF LORDS FROM UNIVERSE 10. IT IS A PLEASURE TO SEE YOU AGAIN.
YOU'RE LATE!
MY APOLOGIES. I HAD TO TRAVEL ACROSS ALL OF THE UNIVERSES MULTIPLE TIMES.
IT TOOK SOME TIME TO GET BACK.

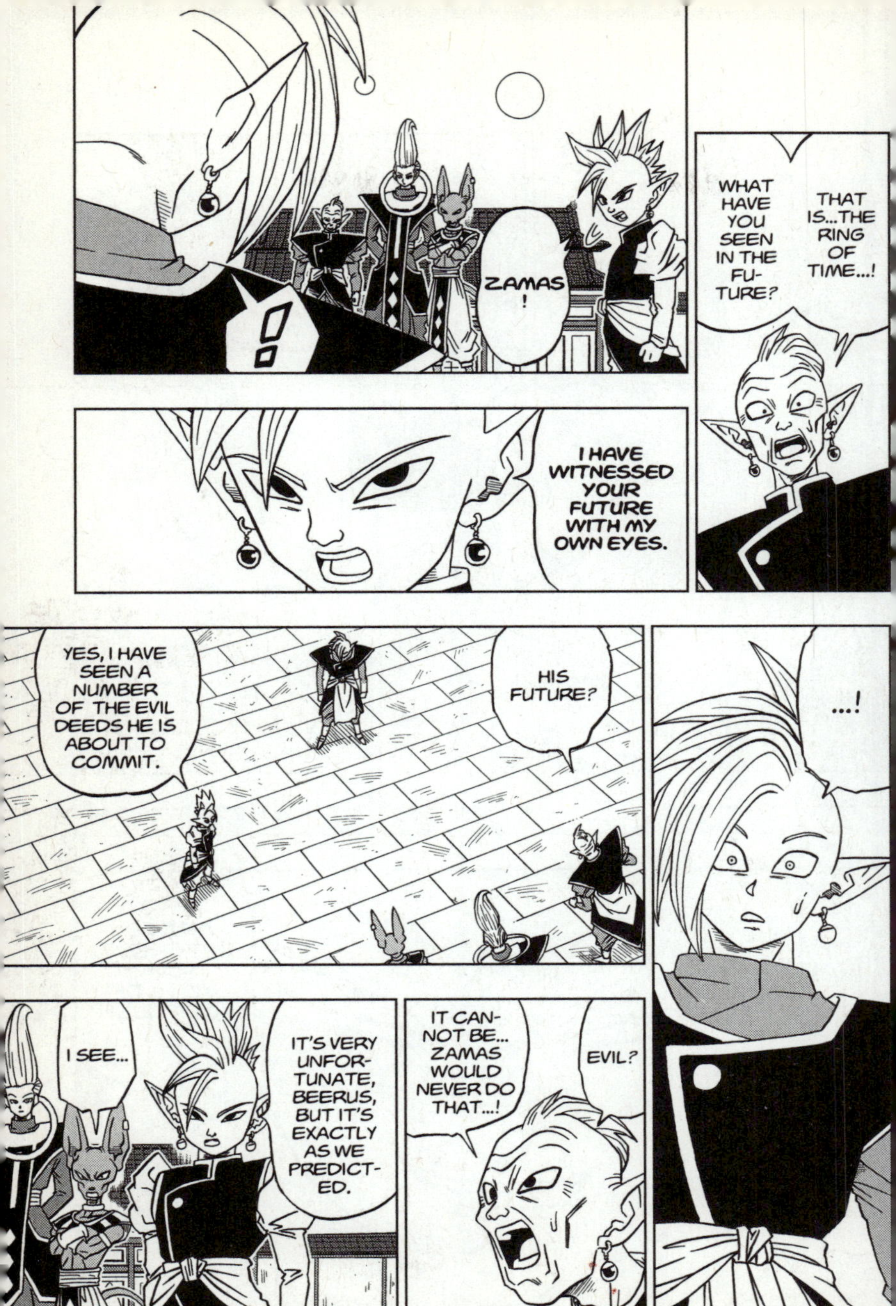
THAT IS...THE RING OF TIME...!
WHAT HAVE YOU SEEN IN THE FU-TURE?
!!
ZAMAS!
I HAVE WITNESSED YOUR FUTURE WITH MY OWN EYES.
...!
HIS FUTURE?
YES, I HAVE SEEN A NUMBER OF THE EVIL DEEDS HE IS ABOUT TO COMMIT.
EVIL?
IT CAN-NOT BE... ZAMAS WOULD NEVER DO THAT...!
IT'S VERY UNFOR-TUNATE, BEERUS, BUT IT'S EXACTLY AS WE PREDICT-ED.
I SEE...

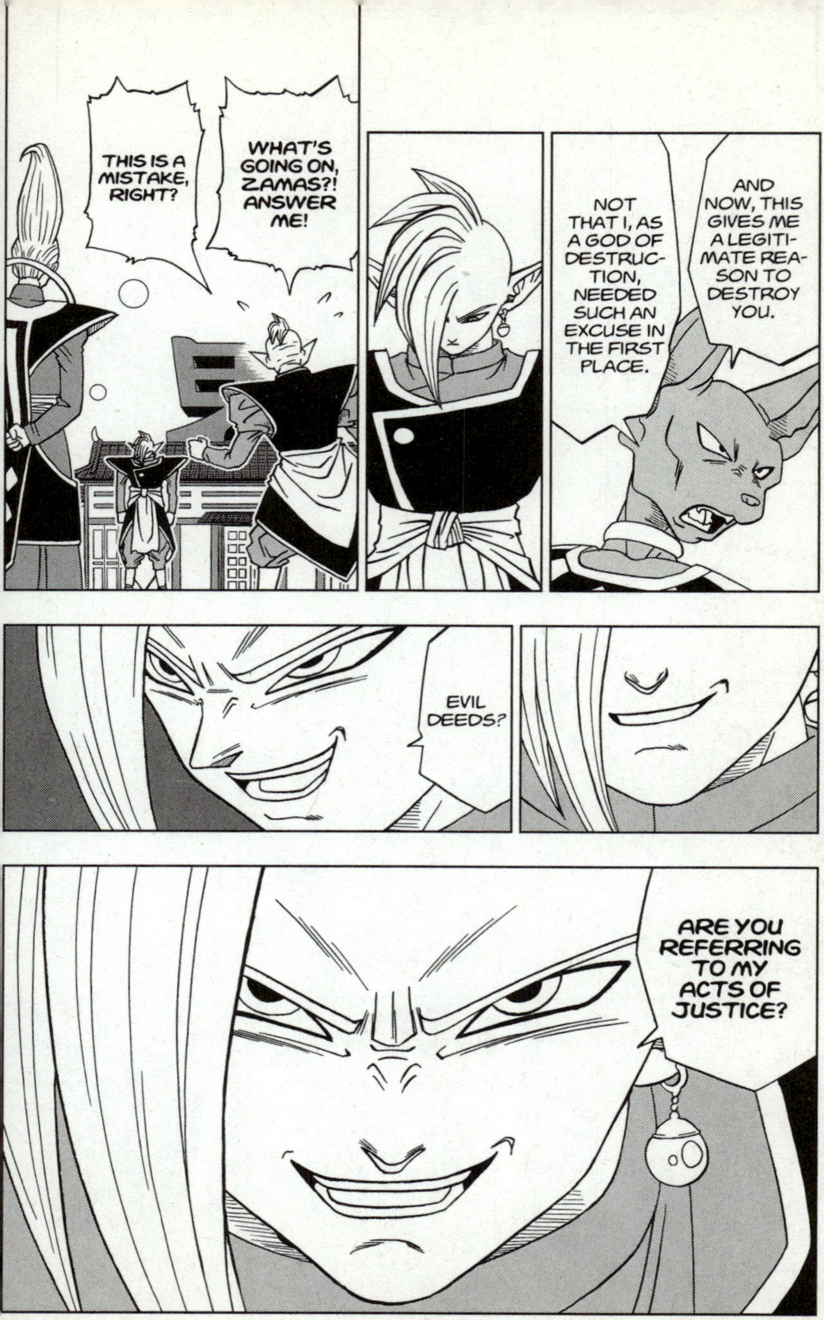
AND NOW, THIS GIVES ME A LEGITIMATE REASON TO DESTROY YOU.
NOT THAT I, AS A GOD OF DESTRUCTION, NEEDED SUCH AN EXCUSE IN THE FIRST PLACE.
WHAT'S GOING ON, ZAMAS?! ANSWER ME!
THIS IS A MISTAKE, RIGHT?
EVIL DEEDS?
ARE YOU REFERRING TO MY ACTS OF JUSTICE?

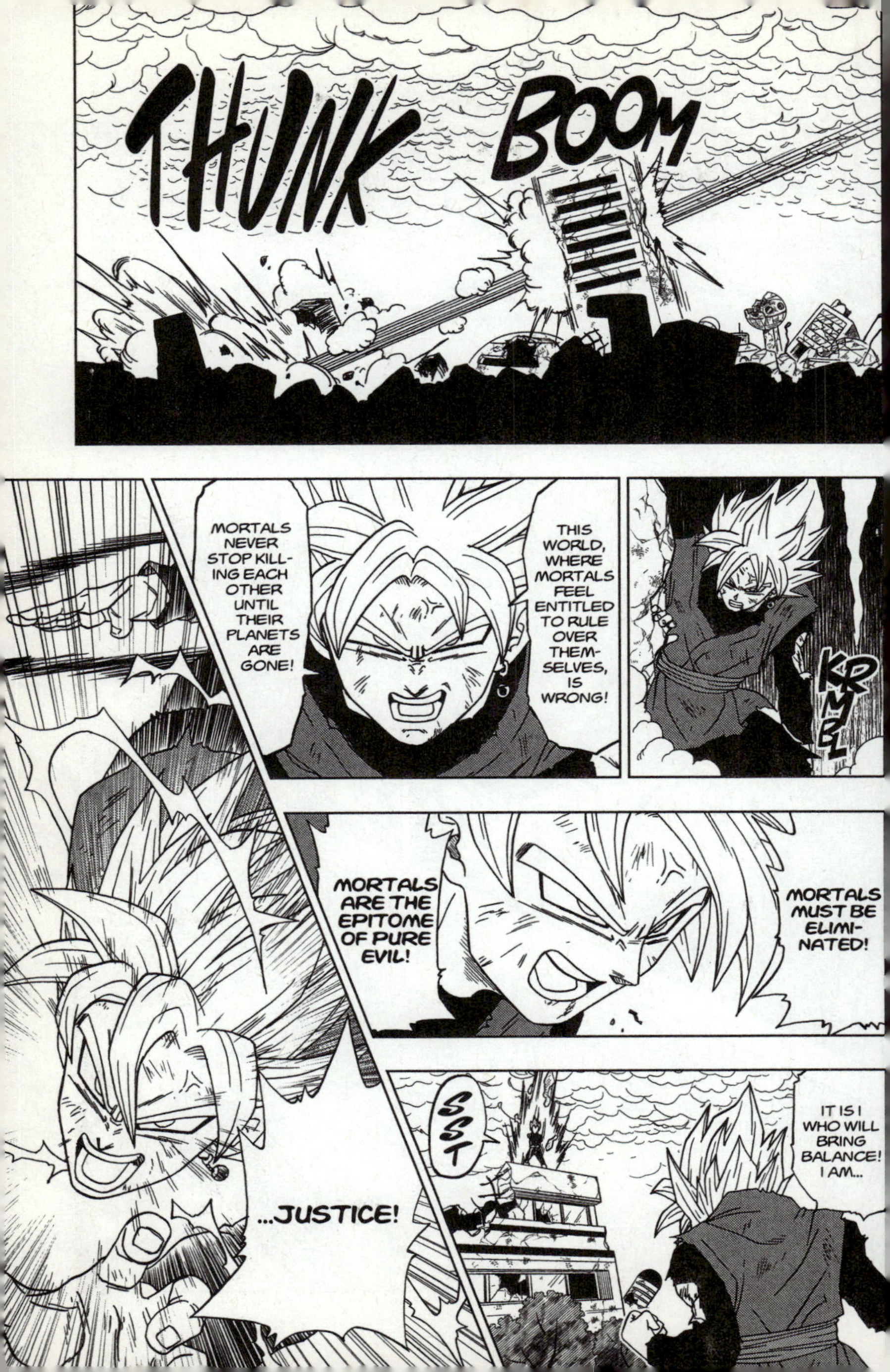
BOOM
THUNK
KRMBL
THIS WORLD, WHERE MORTALS FEEL ENTITLED TO RULE OVER THEMSELVES, IS WRONG!
MORTALS NEVER STOP KILLING EACH OTHER UNTIL THEIR PLANETS ARE GONE!
MORTALS MUST BE ELIMINATED!
MORTALS ARE THE EPITOME OF PURE EVIL!
IT IS I WHO WILL BRING BALANCE! I AM...
SSST
...JUSTICE!

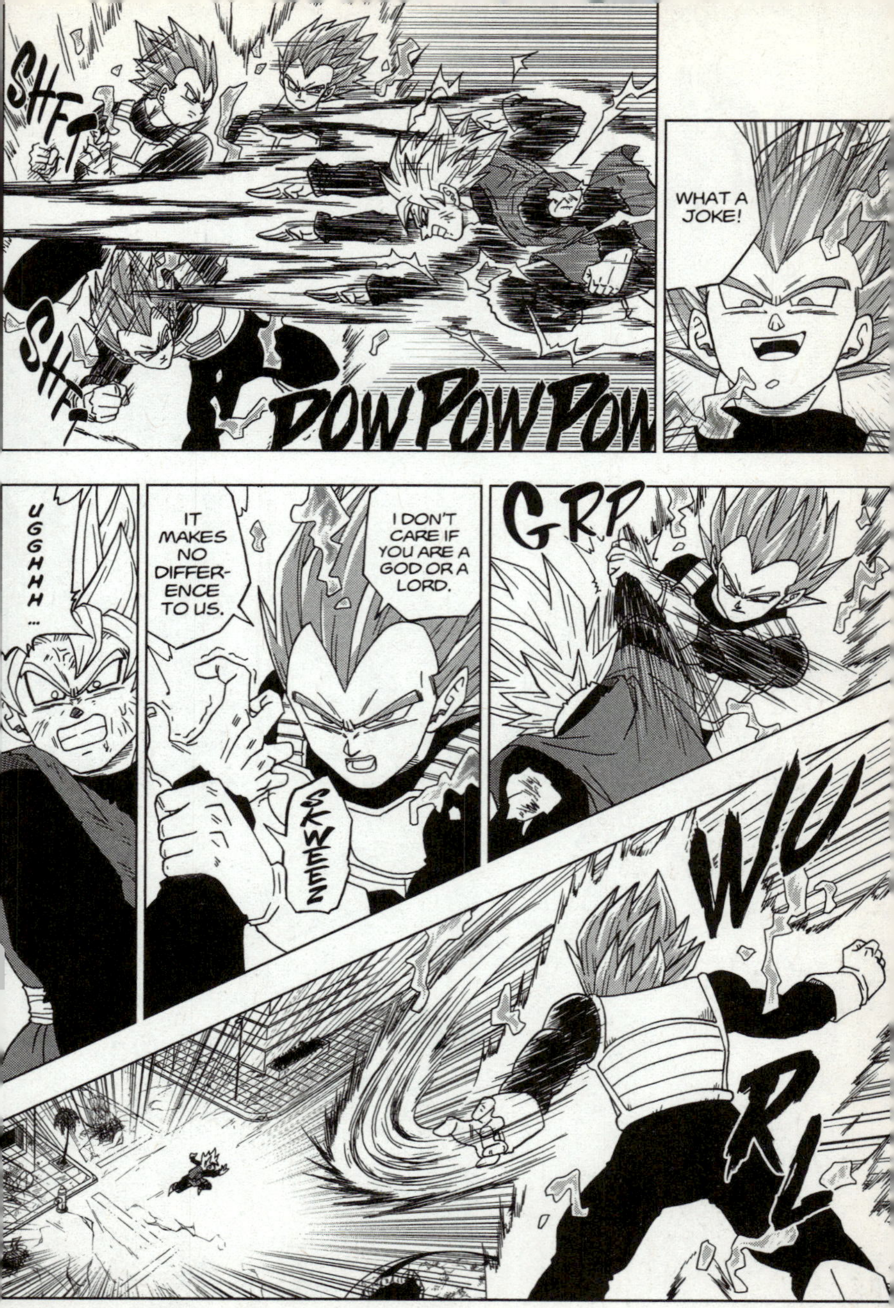
WHAT A JOKE!
SHFT
SHFT
POW POW POW
GRP
I DON'T CARE IF YOU ARE A GOD OR A LORD.
IT MAKES NO DIFFERENCE TO US.
SKWEEZ
UGGHHH...
WU
RL

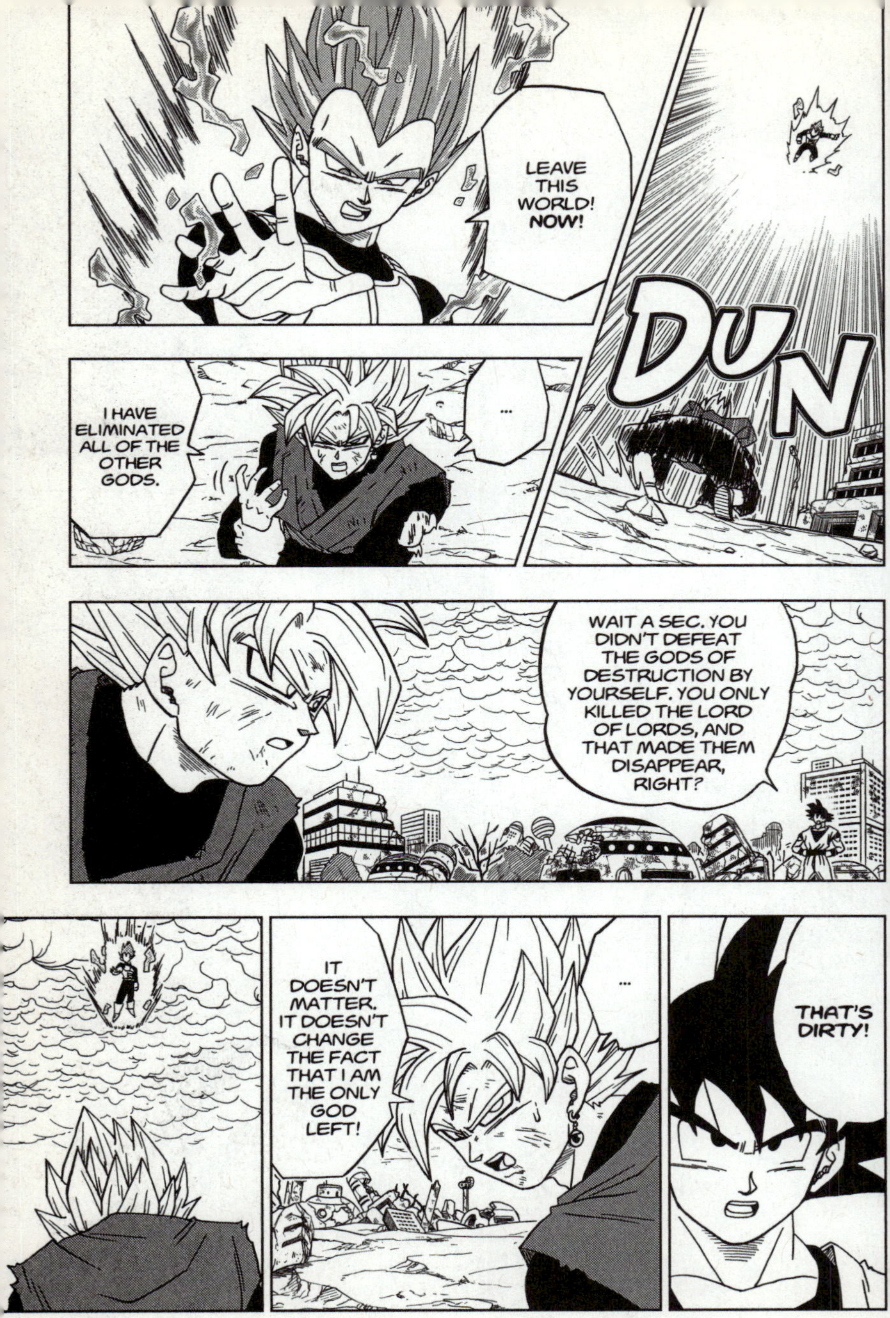
DUN
LEAVE THIS WORLD! NOW!
...
I HAVE ELIMINATED ALL OF THE OTHER GODS.
WAIT A SEC. YOU DIDN'T DEFEAT THE GODS OF DESTRUCTION BY YOURSELF. YOU ONLY KILLED THE LORD OF LORDS, AND THAT MADE THEM DISAPPEAR, RIGHT?
THAT'S DIRTY!
...
IT DOESN'T MATTER. IT DOESN'T CHANGE THE FACT THAT I AM THE ONLY GOD LEFT!

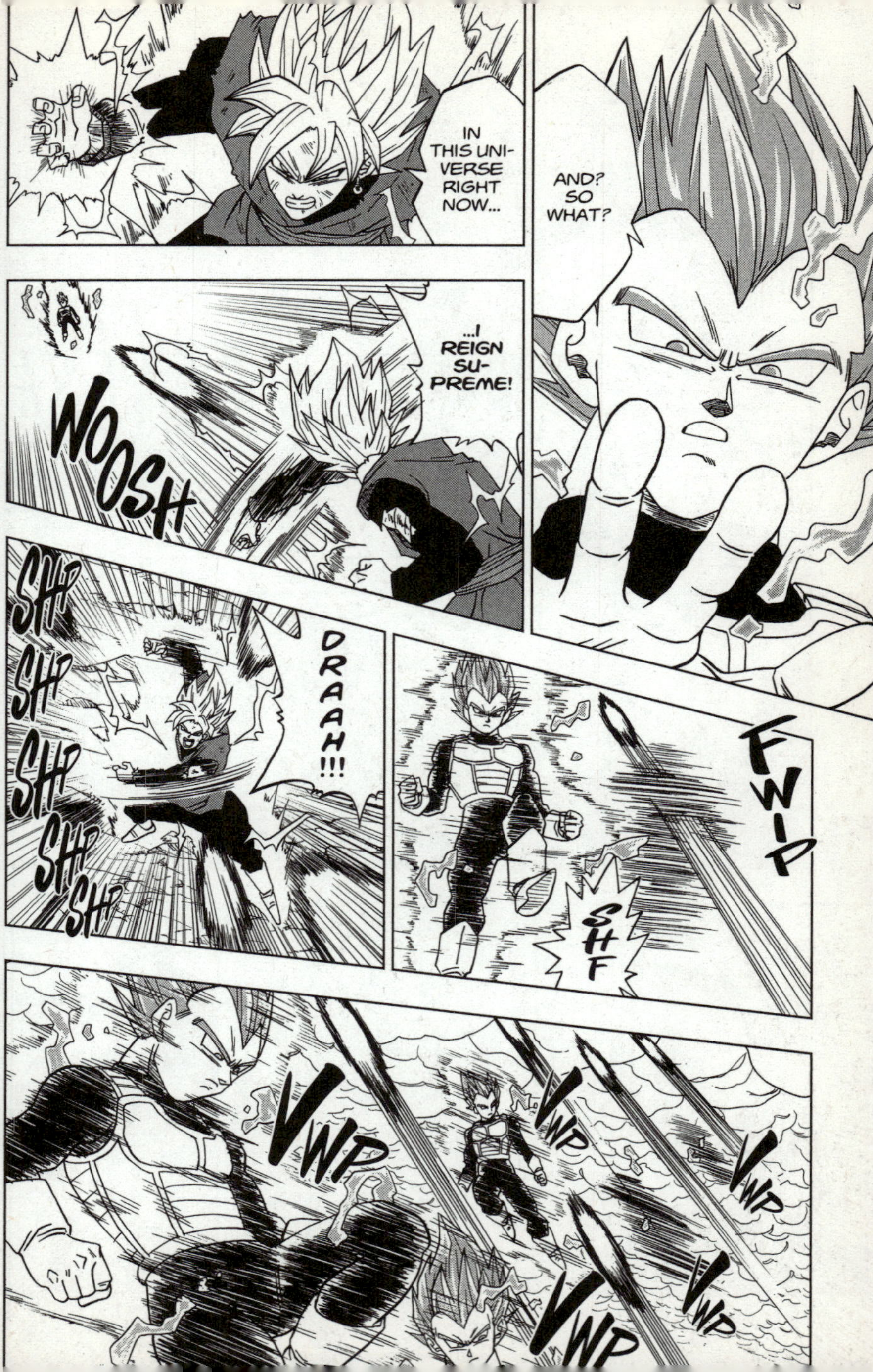
AND? SO WHAT?
IN THIS UNIVERSE RIGHT NOW...
...I REIGN SUPREME!
WOOSH
FWIP
SHF
DRAAAH!!!
SHP SHP SHP SHP SHP SHP
VWP
VWP
VWP
VWP
VWP

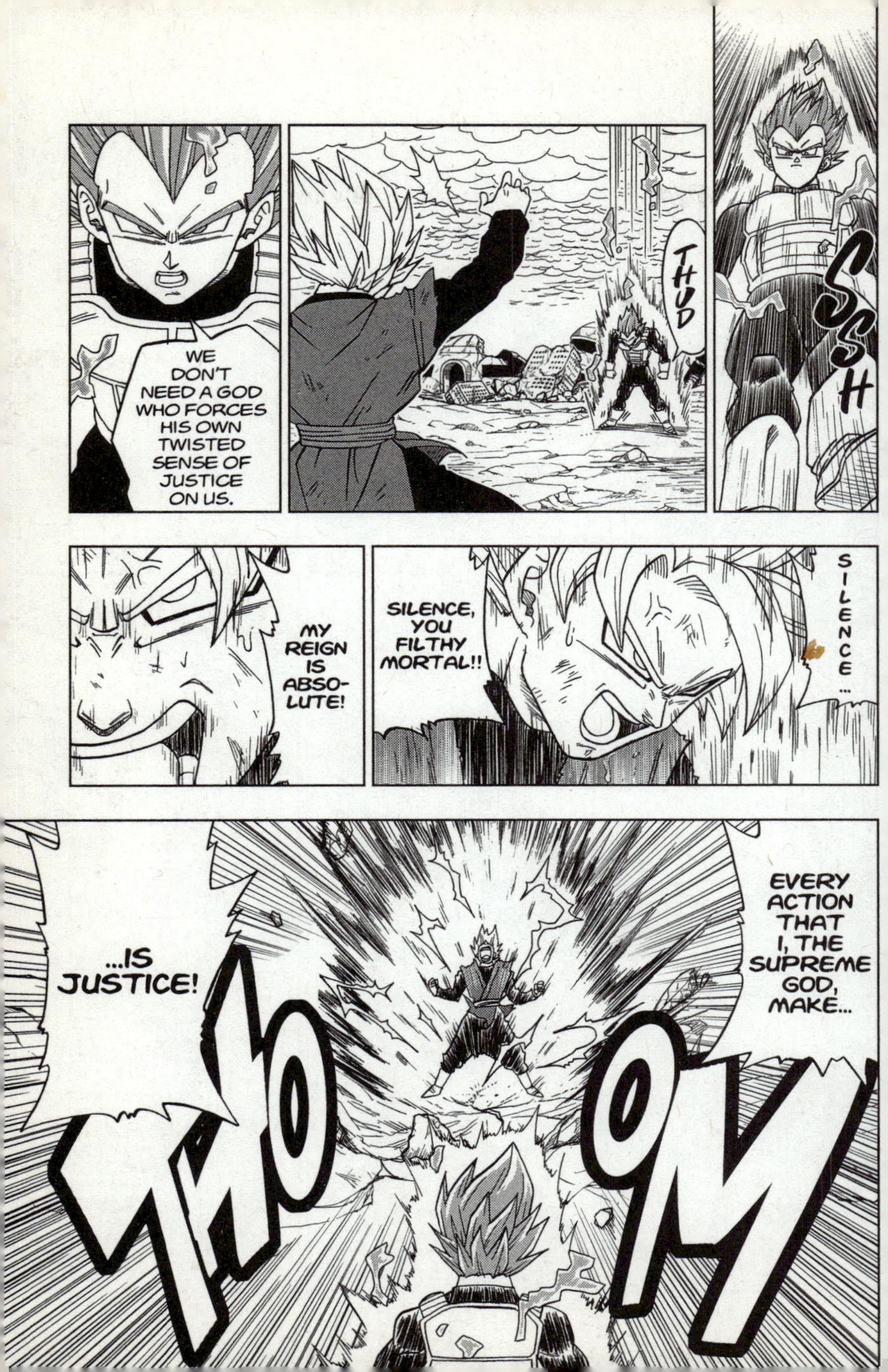
SSH
THUD
WE DON'T NEED A GOD WHO FORCES HIS OWN TWISTED SENSE OF JUSTICE ON US.
SILENCE...
SILENCE, YOU FILTHY MORTAL!!
MY REIGN IS ABSOLUTE!
EVERY ACTION THAT I, THE SUPREME GOD, MAKE...
...IS JUSTICE!
THOOM

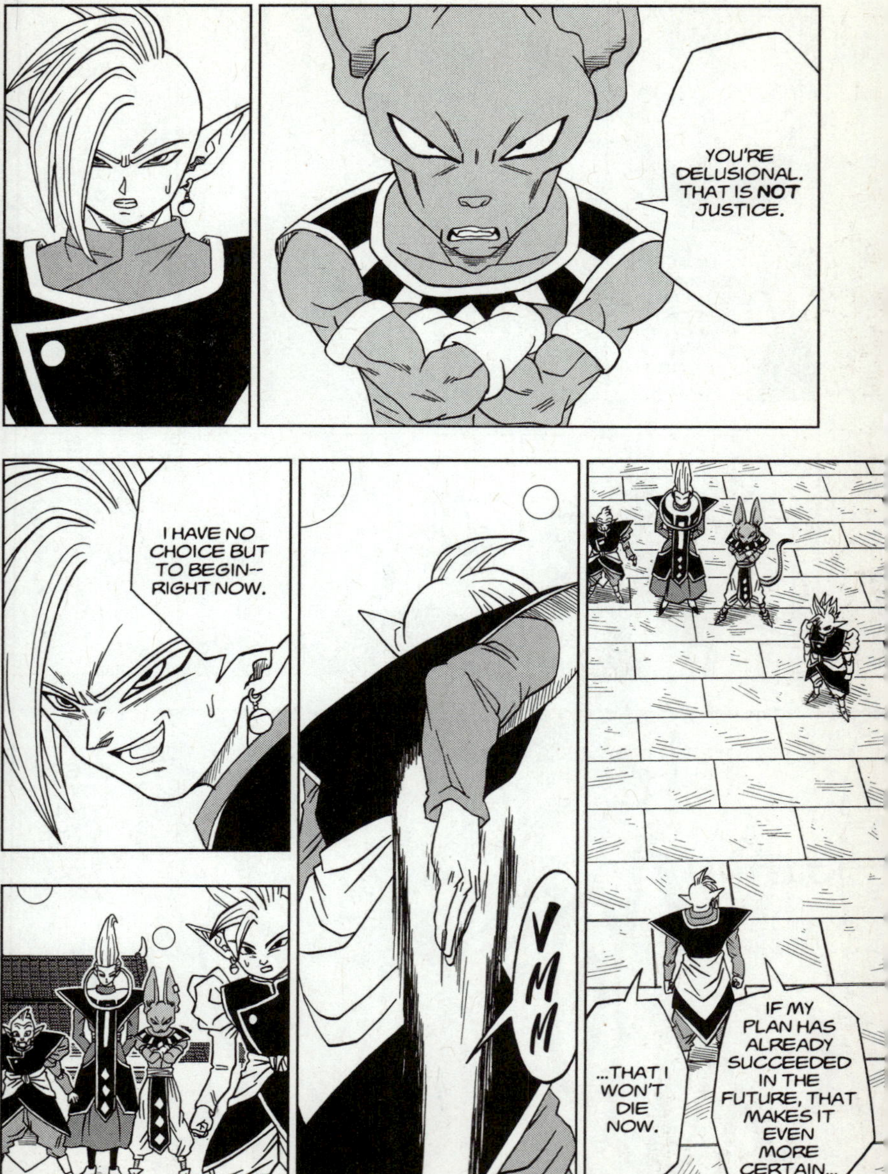
YOU'RE DELUSIONAL. THAT IS **NOT** JUSTICE.
IF MY PLAN HAS ALREADY SUCCEEDED IN THE FUTURE, THAT MAKES IT EVEN MORE CERTAIN...
...THAT I WON'T DIE NOW.
VMM
I HAVE NO CHOICE BUT TO BEGIN-- RIGHT NOW.

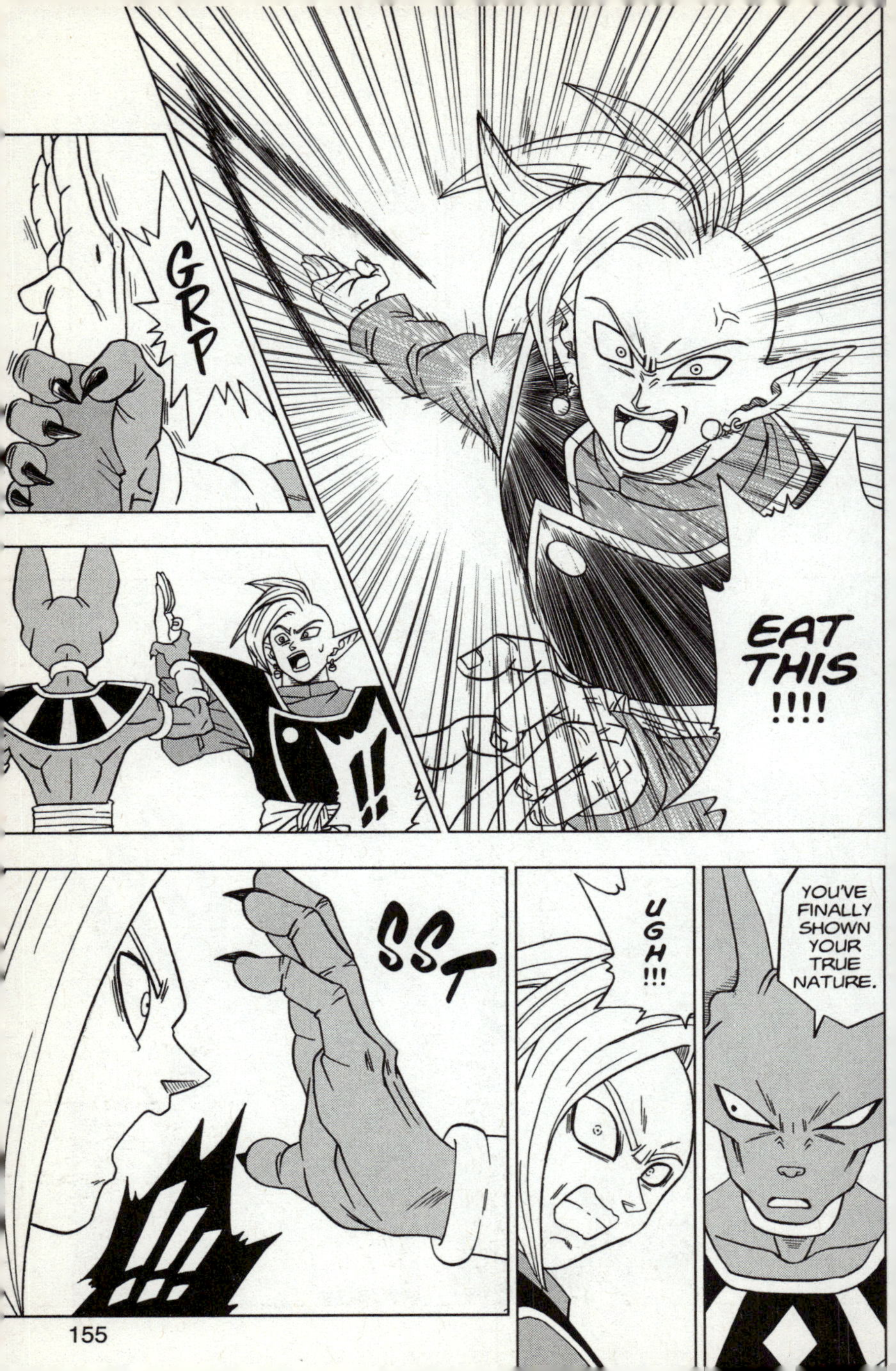
EAT THIS!!!!
GRP
!!
YOU'VE FINALLY SHOWN YOUR TRUE NATURE.
UGH!!!
SST
!!!

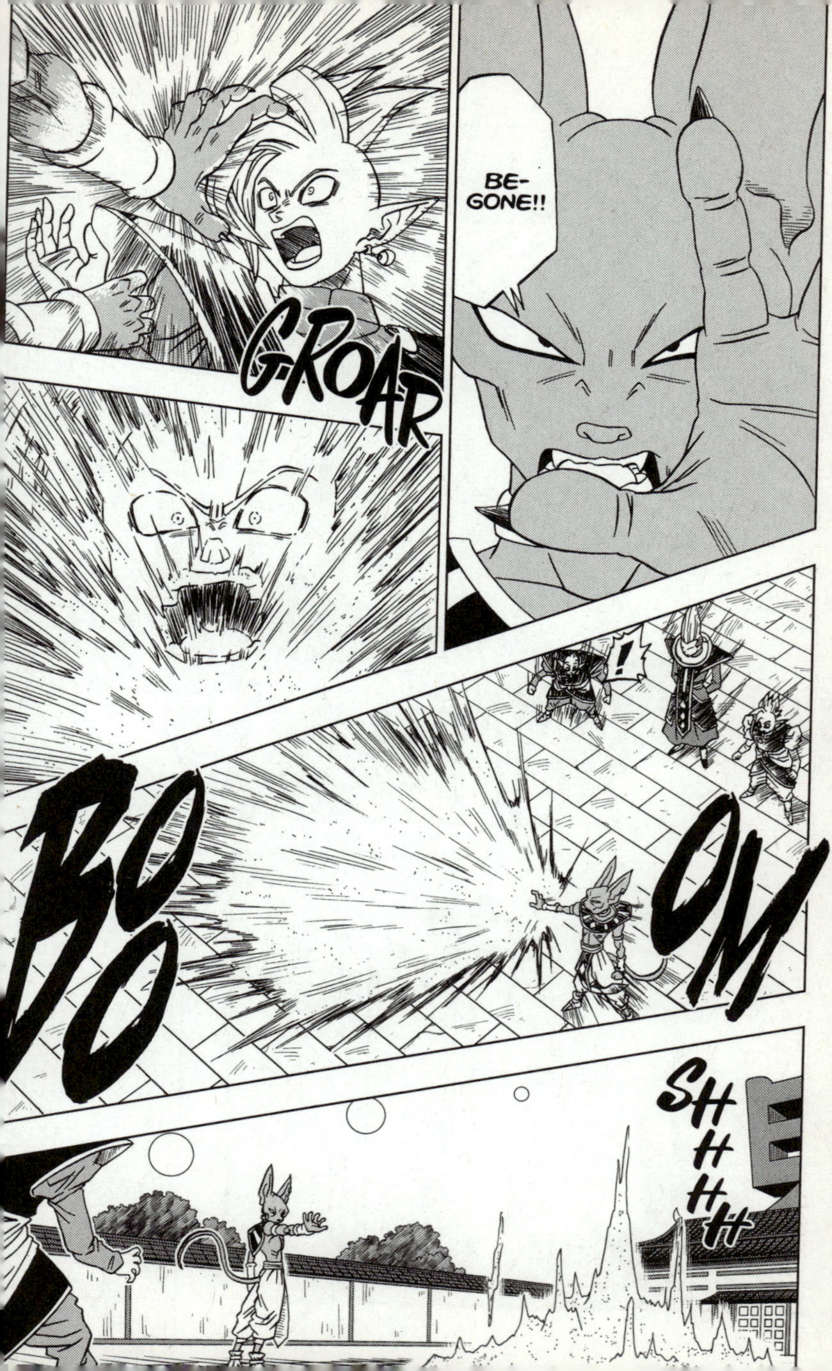
BE-
GONE!!
G-ROAR
!
BOOOM
SHHHHH

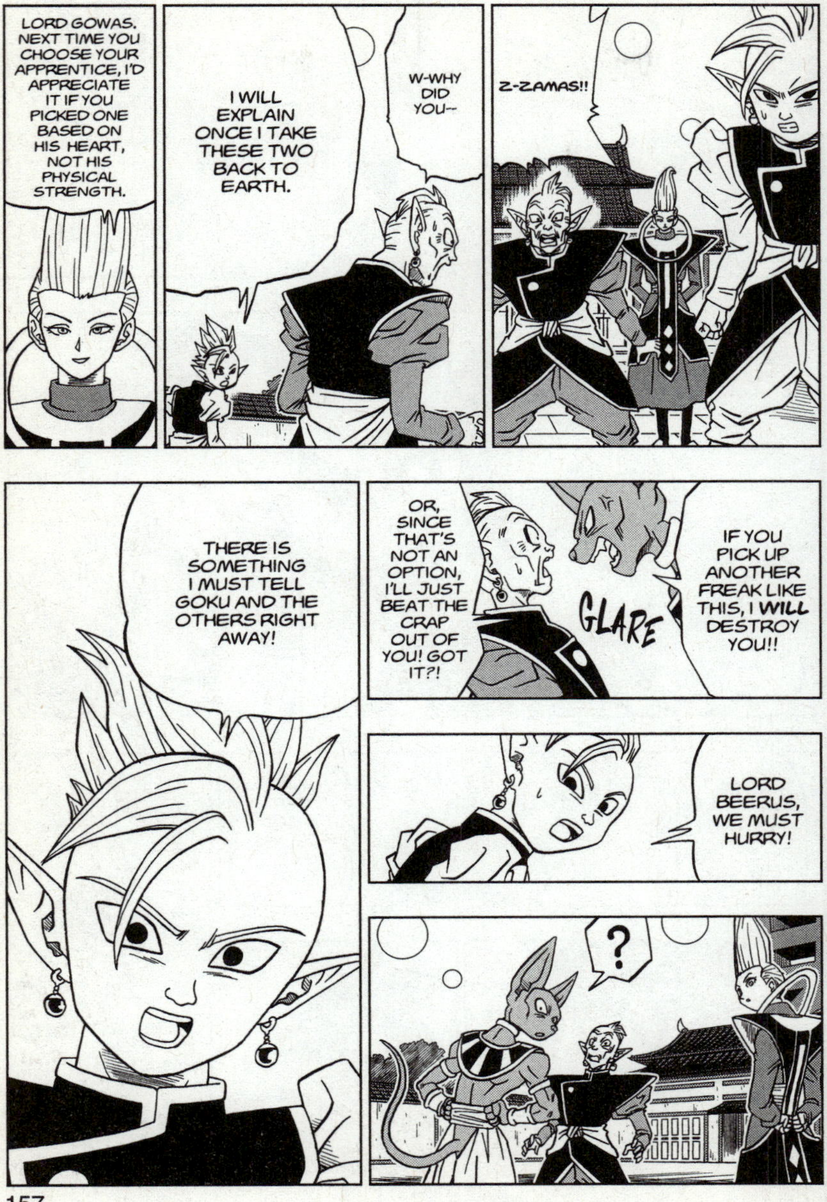
Z-ZAMAS!!
W-WHY DID YOU--
I WILL EXPLAIN ONCE I TAKE THESE TWO BACK TO EARTH.
LORD GOWAS. NEXT TIME YOU CHOOSE YOUR APPRENTICE, I'D APPRECIATE IT IF YOU PICKED ONE BASED ON HIS HEART, NOT HIS PHYSICAL STRENGTH.
IF YOU PICK UP ANOTHER FREAK LIKE THIS, I **WILL** DESTROY YOU!!
GLARE
OR, SINCE THAT'S NOT AN OPTION, I'LL JUST BEAT THE CRAP OUT OF YOU! GOT IT?!
LORD BEERUS, WE MUST HURRY!
?
THERE IS SOMETHING I MUST TELL GOKU AND THE OTHERS RIGHT AWAY!

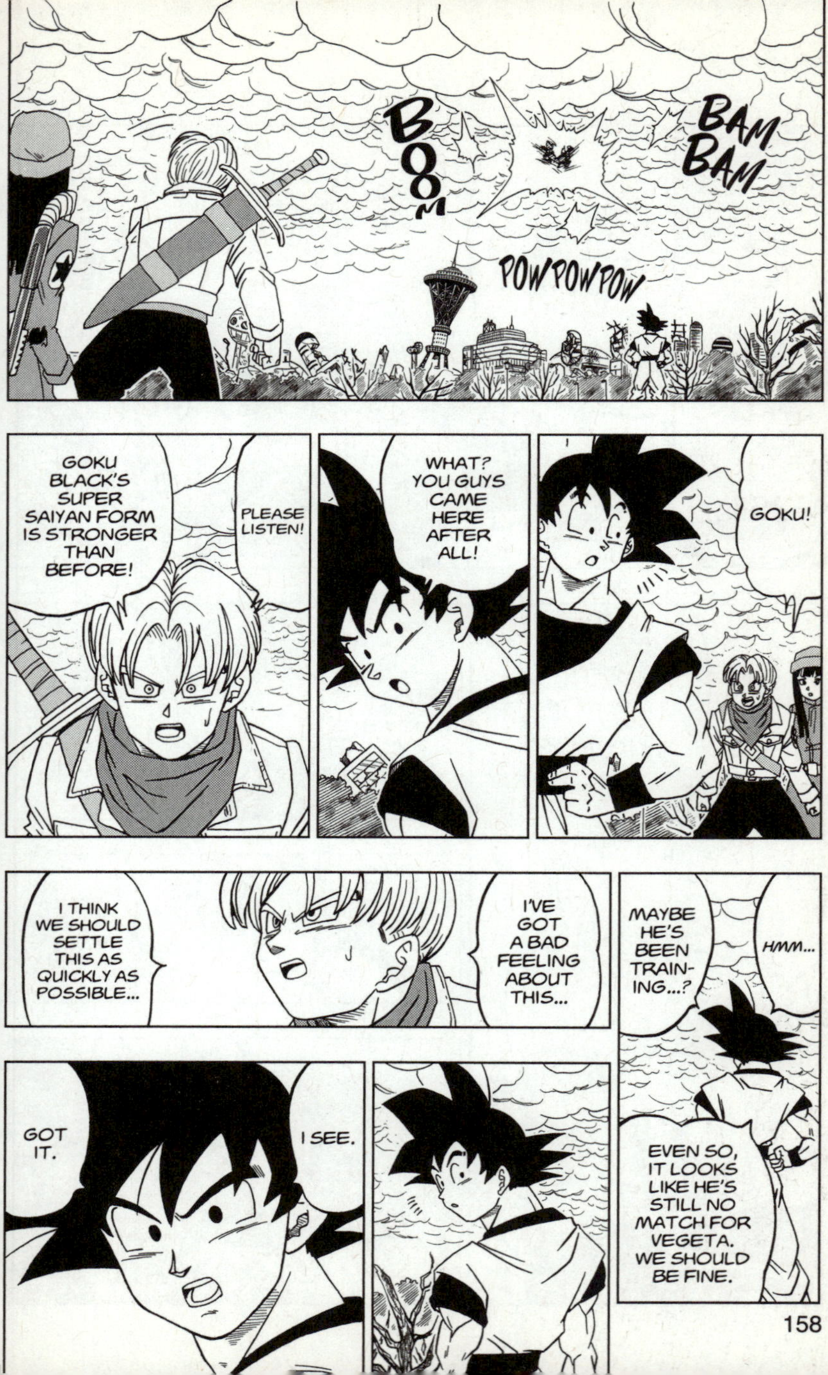
BAM BAM
BOOM
POWPOWPOW
GOKU!
WHAT? YOU GUYS CAME HERE AFTER ALL!
PLEASE LISTEN!
GOKU BLACK'S SUPER SAIYAN FORM IS STRONGER THAN BEFORE!
HMM...
MAYBE HE'S BEEN TRAIN-ING...?
EVEN SO, IT LOOKS LIKE HE'S STILL NO MATCH FOR VEGETA. WE SHOULD BE FINE.
I'VE GOT A BAD FEELING ABOUT THIS...
I THINK WE SHOULD SETTLE THIS AS QUICKLY AS POSSIBLE...
I SEE.
GOT IT.

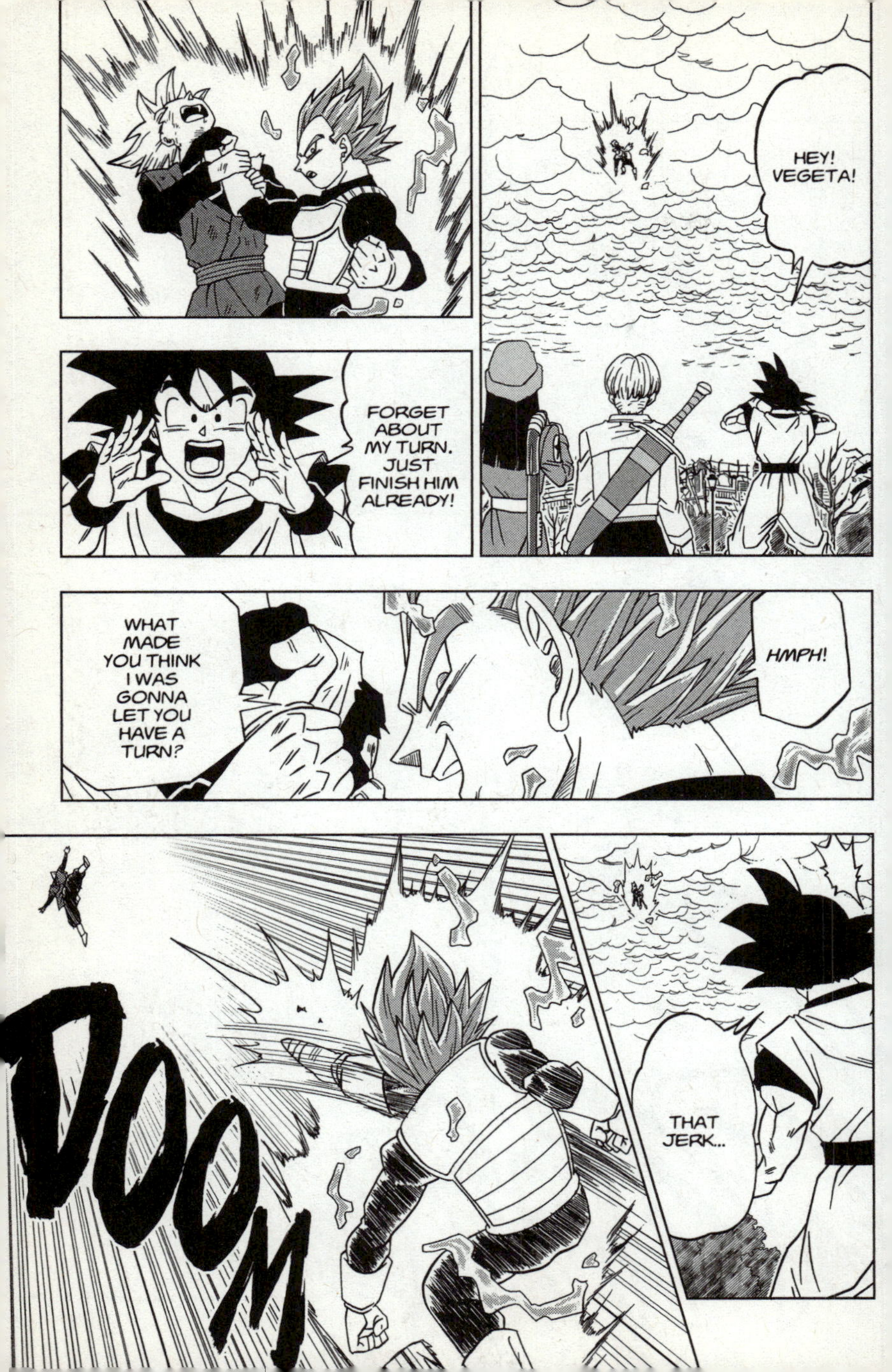
HEY! VEGETA!
FORGET ABOUT MY TURN. JUST FINISH HIM ALREADY!
HMPH!
WHAT MADE YOU THINK I WAS GONNA LET YOU HAVE A TURN?
THAT JERK...
DOOM

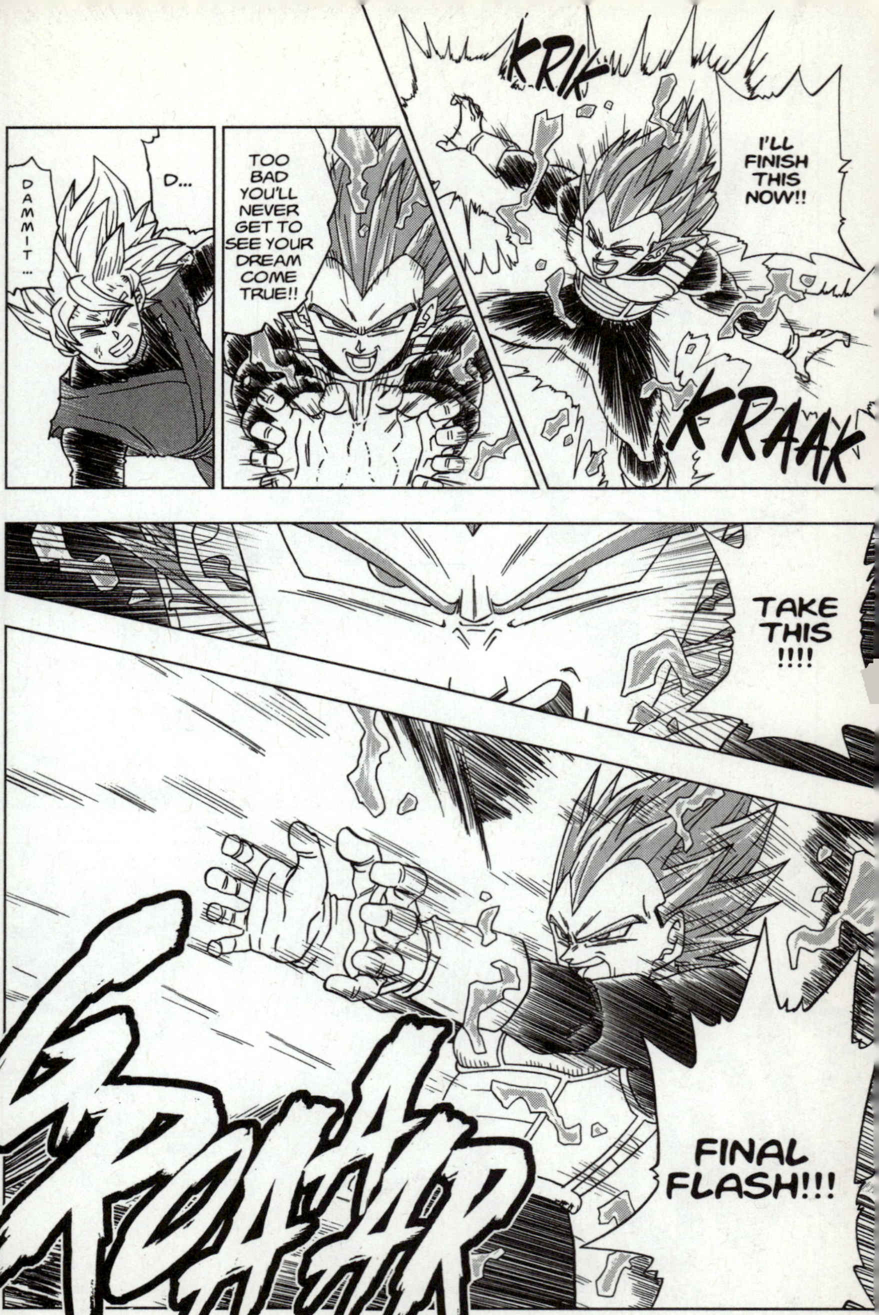

KRIK
I'LL FINISH THIS NOW!!
KRAAK
TOO BAD YOU'LL NEVER GET TO SEE YOUR DREAM COME TRUE!!
D...
DAMMIT...
TAKE THIS!!!!
FINAL FLASH!!!

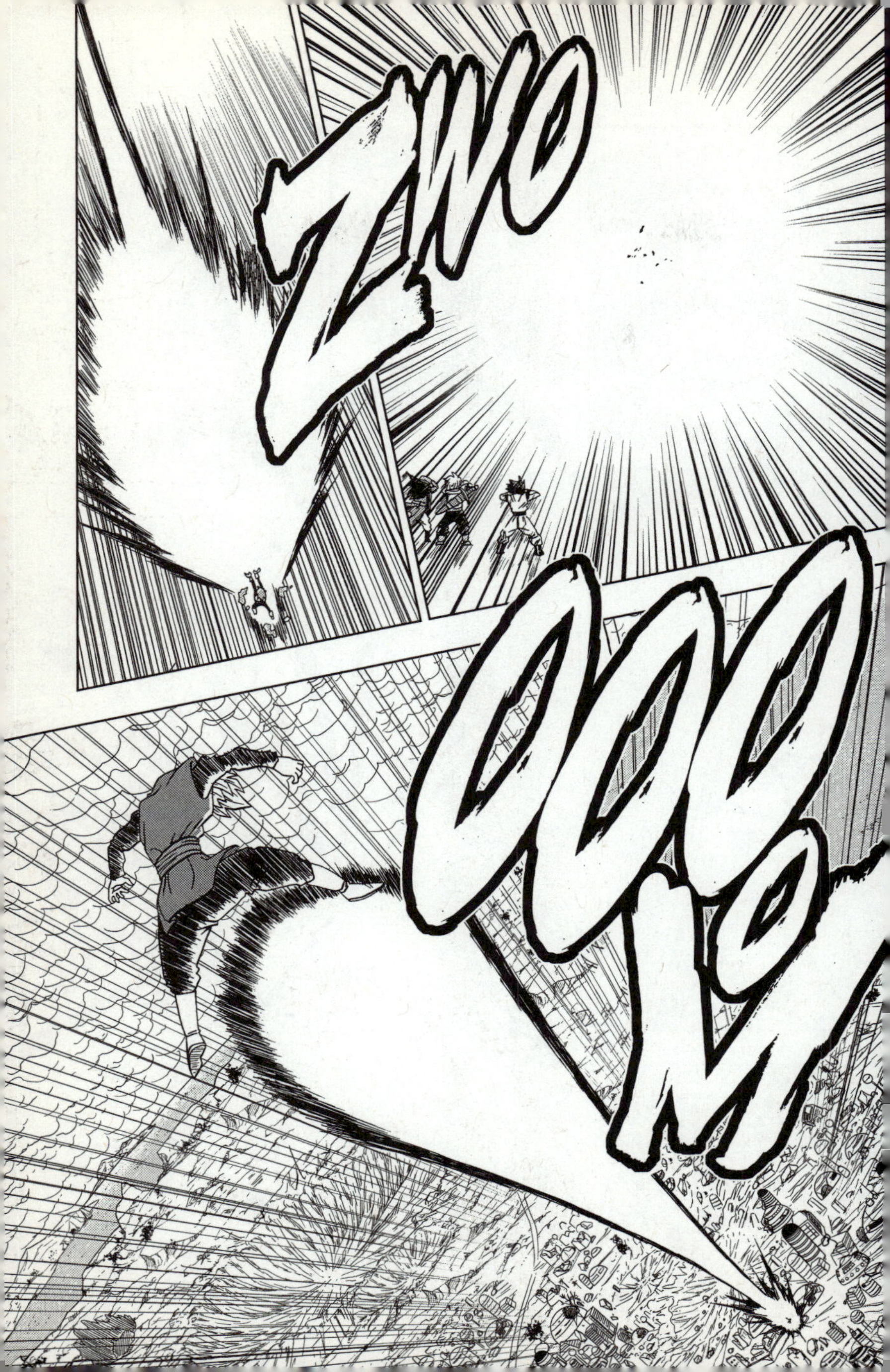
ZWO
OOOOM

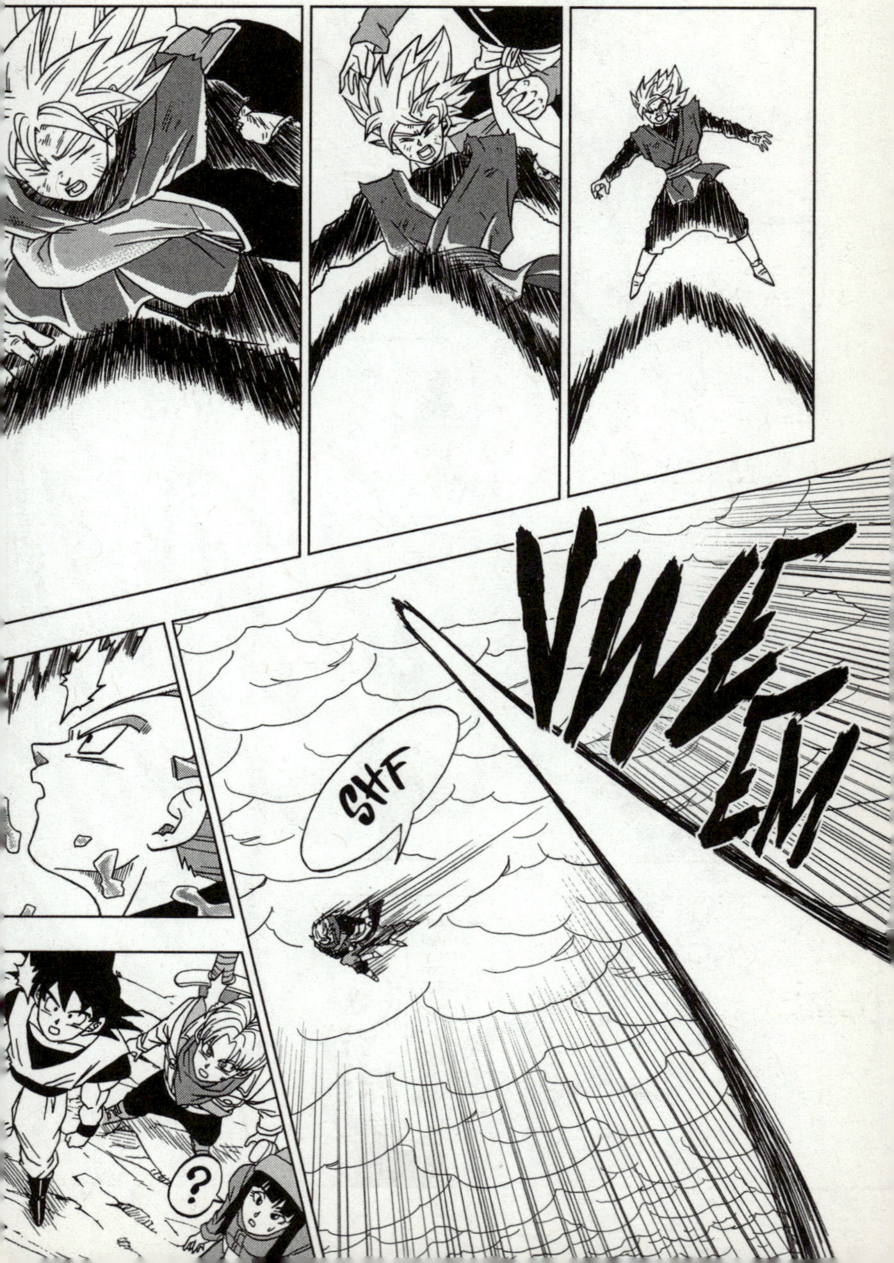

VWEEM
SHF
?

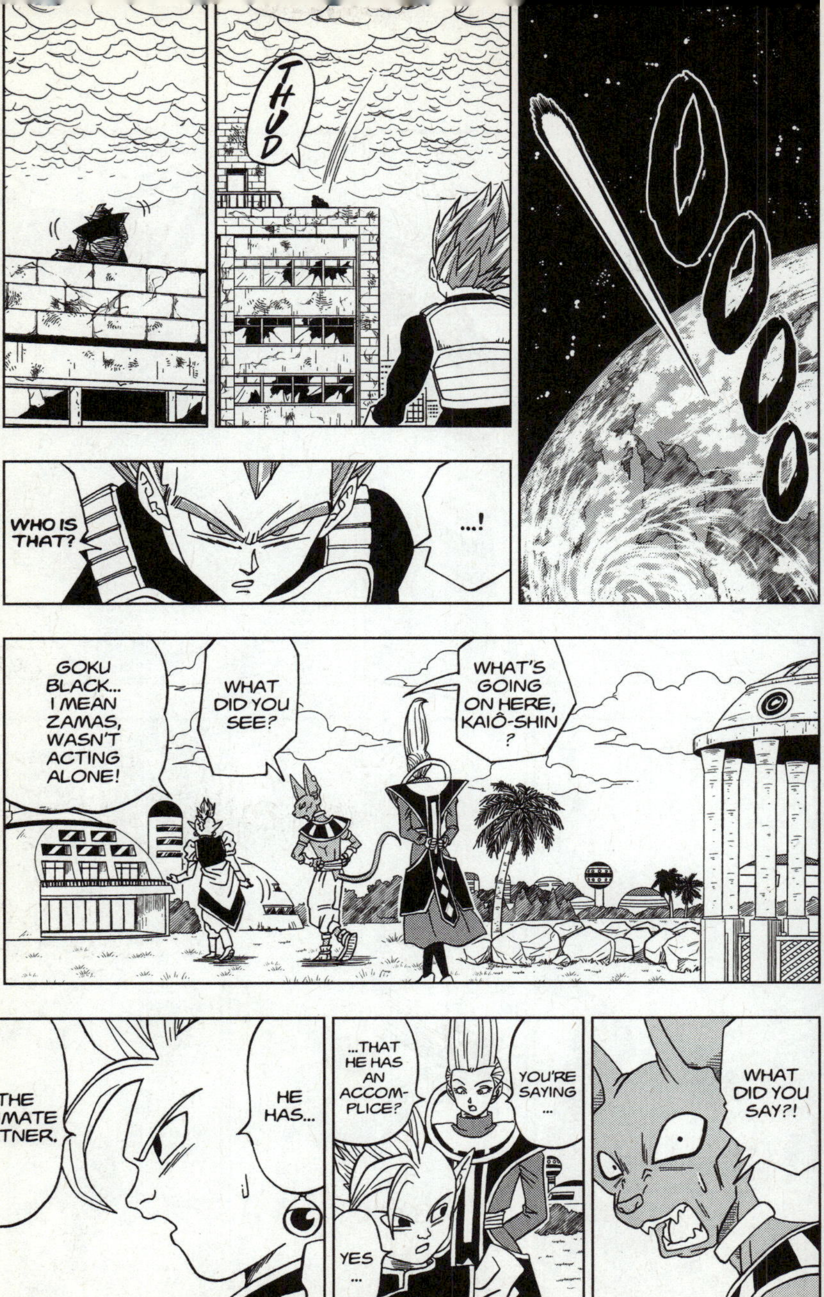
THUD
...!
WHO IS THAT?
WHAT'S GOING ON HERE, KAIÔ-SHIN?
WHAT DID YOU SEE?
GOKU BLACK... I MEAN ZAMAS, WASN'T ACTING ALONE!
WHAT DID YOU SAY?!
YOU'RE SAYING...
...THAT HE HAS AN ACCOMPLICE?
YES...
HE HAS...
...THE ULTIMATE PARTNER.

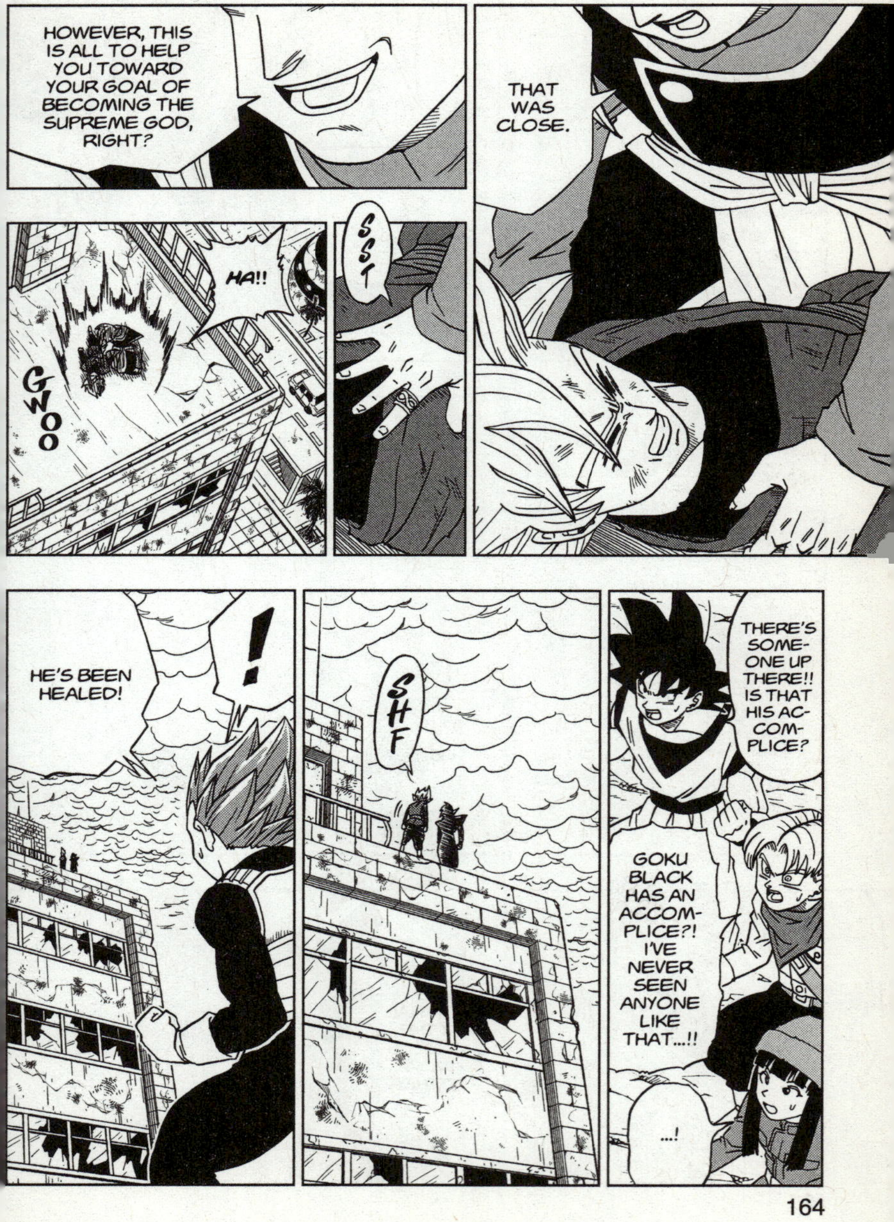
THAT WAS CLOSE.
HOWEVER, THIS IS ALL TO HELP YOU TOWARD YOUR GOAL OF BECOMING THE SUPREME GOD, RIGHT?
SST
HA!!
GWOO
THERE'S SOME-ONE UP THERE!! IS THAT HIS AC-COM-PLICE?
GOKU BLACK HAS AN ACCOM-PLICE?! I'VE NEVER SEEN ANYONE LIKE THAT...!!
...!
SHF
!
HE'S BEEN HEALED!

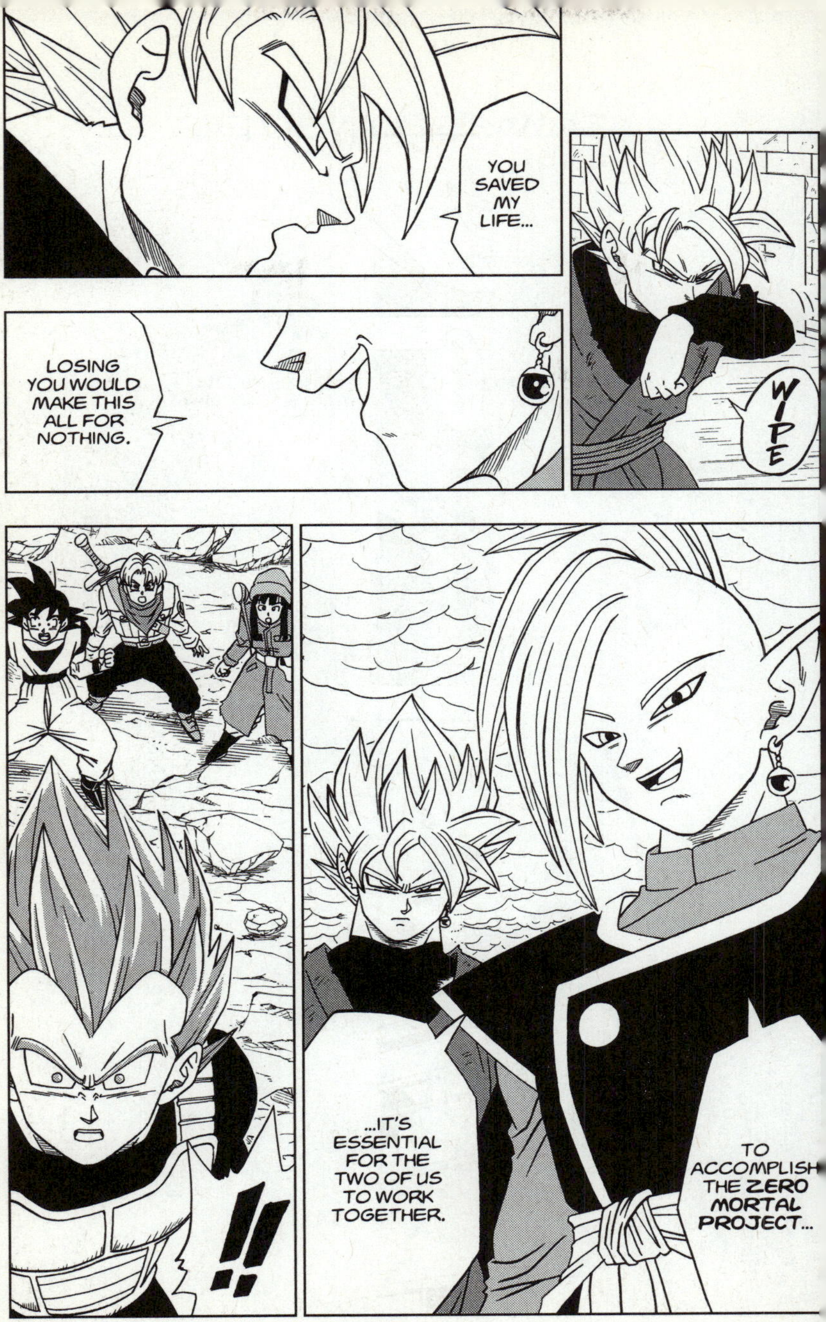
WIPE
YOU SAVED MY LIFE...
LOSING YOU WOULD MAKE THIS ALL FOR NOTHING.
TO ACCOMPLISH THE **ZERO MORTAL PROJECT**...
...IT'S ESSENTIAL FOR THE TWO OF US TO WORK TOGETHER.
!!

# ZAMAS'S PLAN SO FAR...

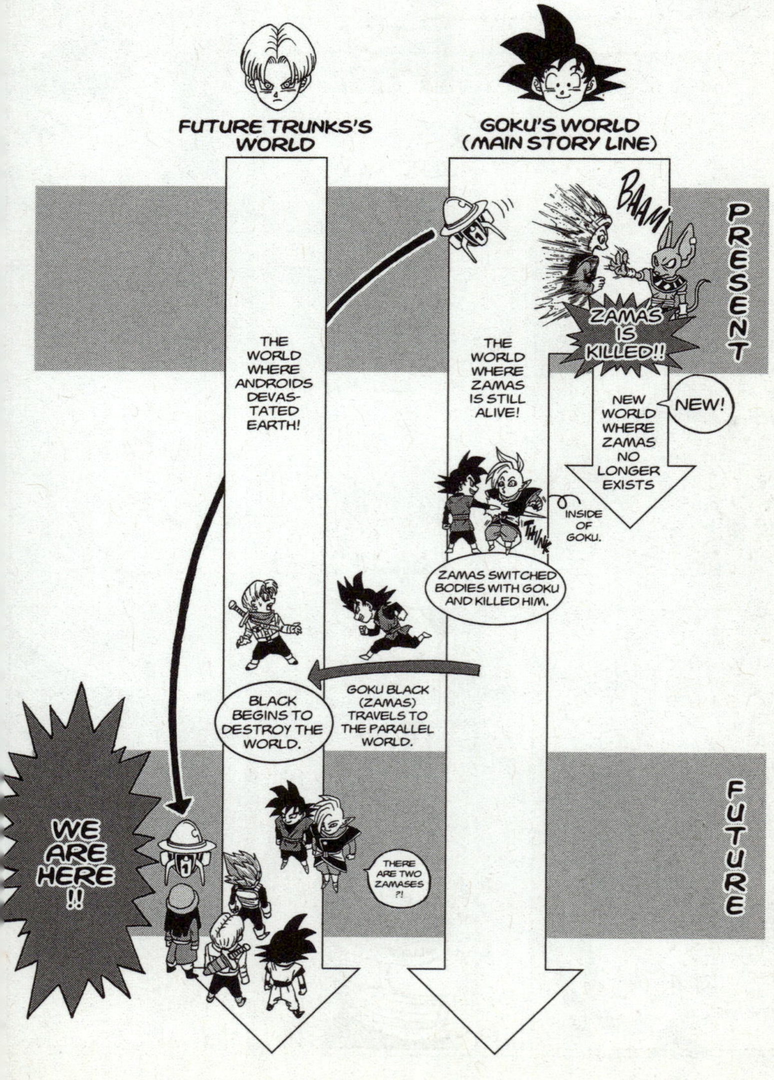

GOKU'S WORLD (MAIN STORY LINE)
FUTURE TRUNKS'S WORLD
PRESENT
BAAM
ZAMAS IS KILLED!!
THE WORLD WHERE ZAMAS IS STILL ALIVE!
NEW!
NEW WORLD WHERE ZAMAS NO LONGER EXISTS
THE WORLD WHERE ANDROIDS DEVAS-TATED EARTH!
INSIDE OF GOKU.
THUNK
ZAMAS SWITCHED BODIES WITH GOKU AND KILLED HIM.
GOKU BLACK (ZAMAS) TRAVELS TO THE PARALLEL WORLD.
BLACK BEGINS TO DESTROY THE WORLD.
FUTURE
THERE ARE TWO ZAMASES ?!
WE ARE HERE !!

# DRAGON BALL SUPER

## CHAPTER 20: THE ZERO MORTAL PROJECT

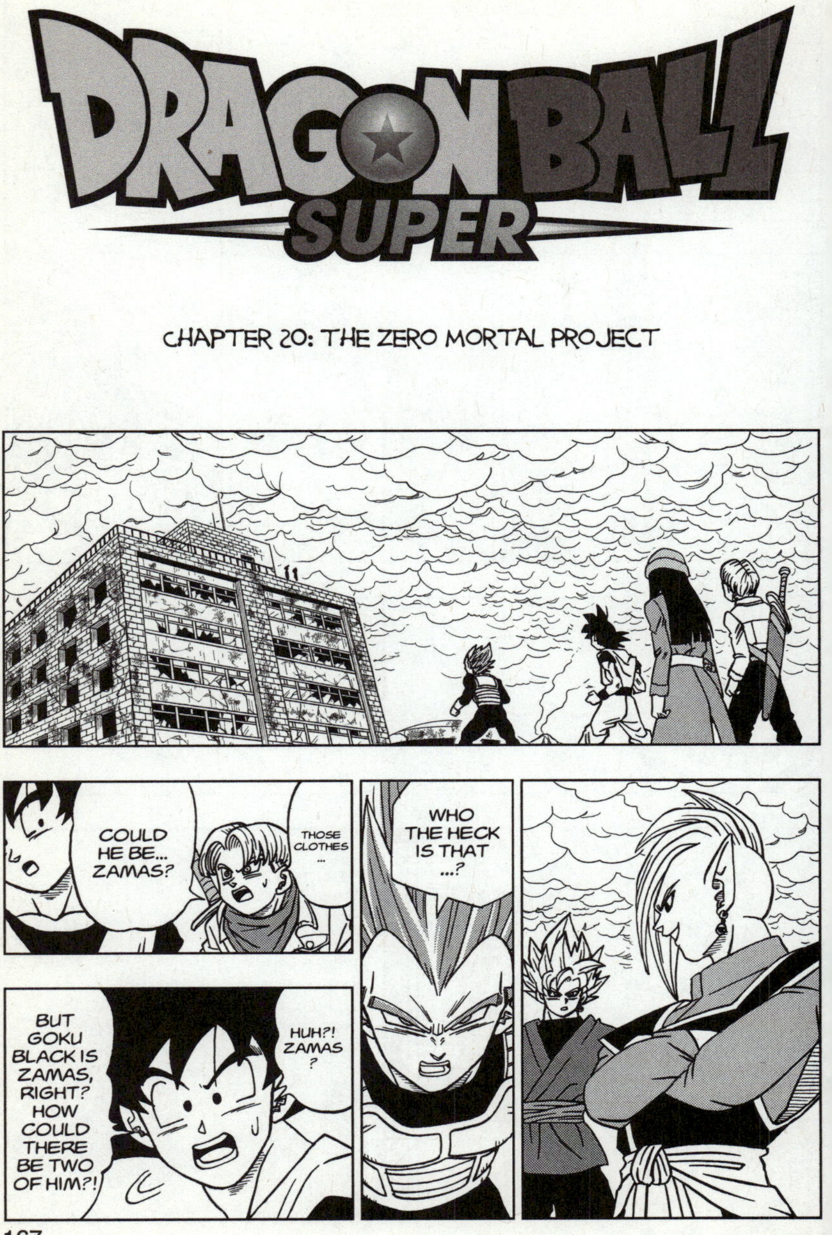

WHO THE HECK IS THAT ...?
THOSE CLOTHES ...
COULD HE BE... ZAMAS?
HUH?! ZAMAS ?
BUT GOKU BLACK IS ZAMAS, RIGHT? HOW COULD THERE BE TWO OF HIM?!

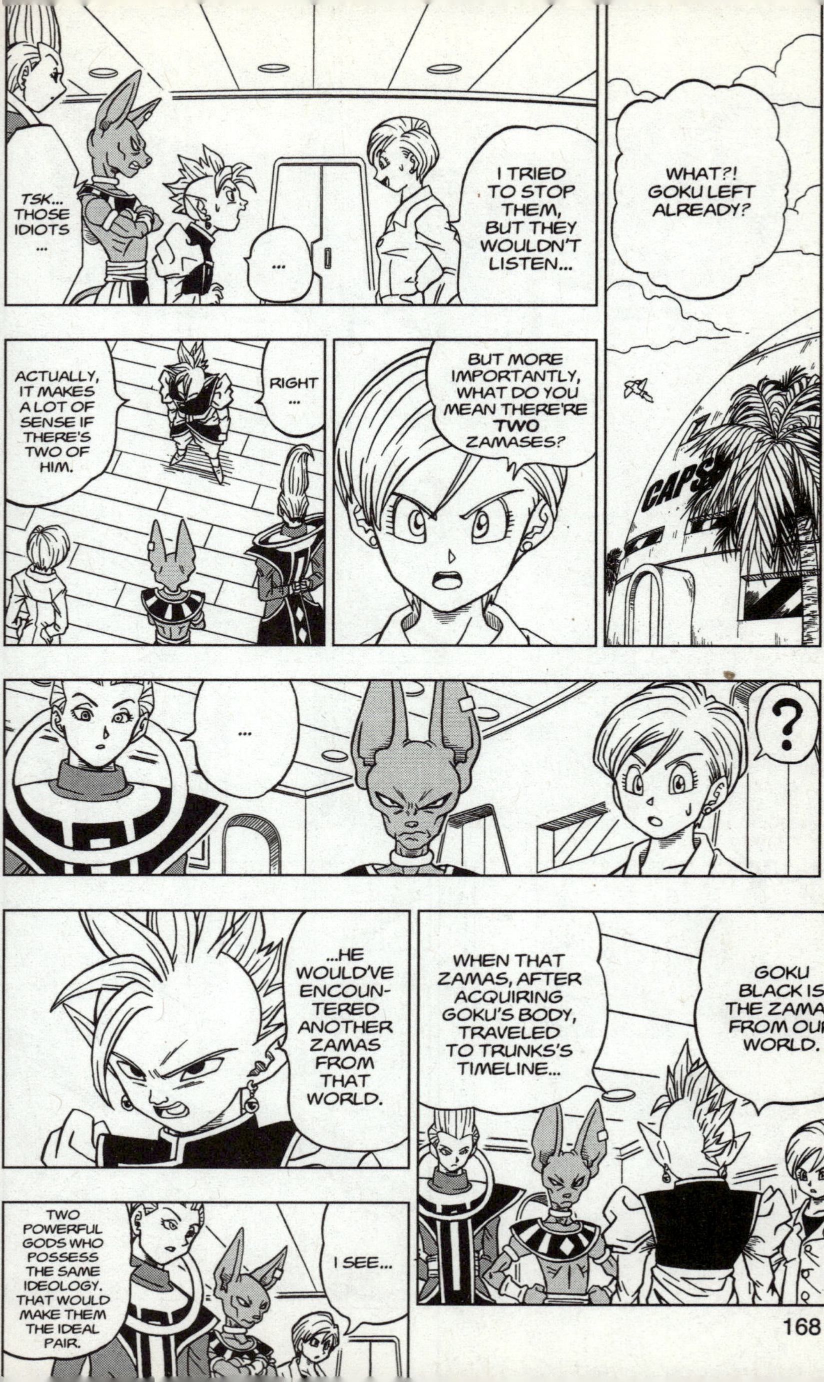

WHAT?! GOKU LEFT ALREADY?
I TRIED TO STOP THEM, BUT THEY WOULDN'T LISTEN...
...
TSK... THOSE IDIOTS ...
BUT MORE IMPORTANTLY, WHAT DO YOU MEAN THERE'RE **TWO** ZAMASES?
RIGHT ...
ACTUALLY, IT MAKES A LOT OF SENSE IF THERE'S TWO OF HIM.
?
...
GOKU BLACK IS THE ZAMAS FROM OUR WORLD.
WHEN THAT ZAMAS, AFTER ACQUIRING GOKU'S BODY, TRAVELED TO TRUNKS'S TIMELINE...
...HE WOULD'VE ENCOUN-TERED ANOTHER ZAMAS FROM THAT WORLD.
I SEE...
TWO POWERFUL GODS WHO POSSESS THE SAME IDEOLOGY. THAT WOULD MAKE THEM THE IDEAL PAIR.

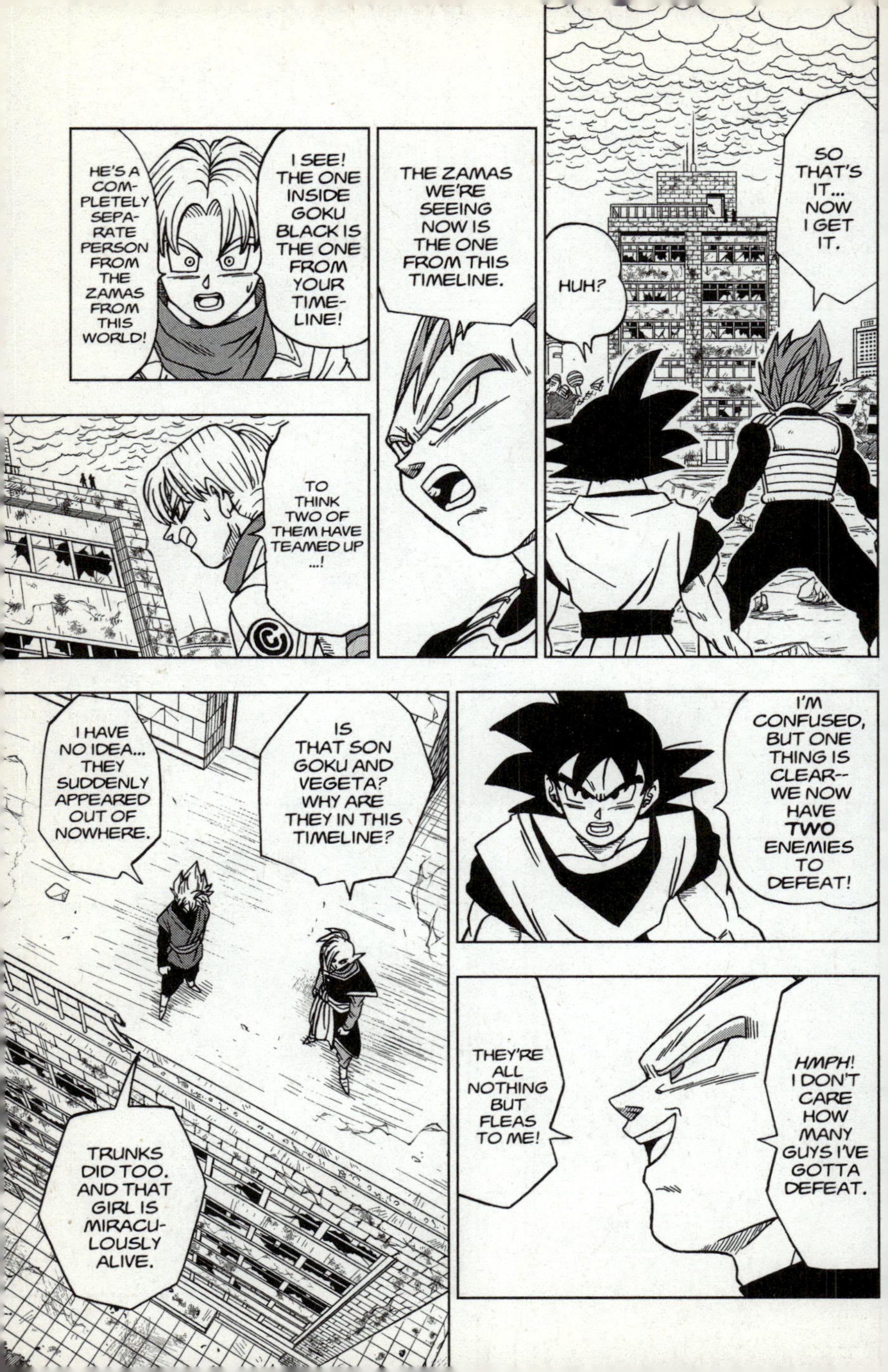
SO THAT'S IT... NOW I GET IT.
HUH?
THE ZAMAS WE'RE SEEING NOW IS THE ONE FROM THIS TIMELINE.
I SEE! THE ONE INSIDE GOKU BLACK IS THE ONE FROM YOUR TIMELINE!
HE'S A COMPLETELY SEPARATE PERSON FROM THE ZAMAS FROM THIS WORLD!
TO THINK TWO OF THEM HAVE TEAMED UP ...!
I'M CONFUSED, BUT ONE THING IS CLEAR-- WE NOW HAVE **TWO** ENEMIES TO DEFEAT!
*HMPH!* I DON'T CARE HOW MANY GUYS I'VE GOTTA DEFEAT.
THEY'RE ALL NOTHING BUT FLEAS TO ME!
IS THAT SON GOKU AND VEGETA? WHY ARE THEY IN THIS TIMELINE?
I HAVE NO IDEA... THEY SUDDENLY APPEARED OUT OF NOWHERE.
TRUNKS DID TOO. AND THAT GIRL IS MIRACULOUSLY ALIVE.

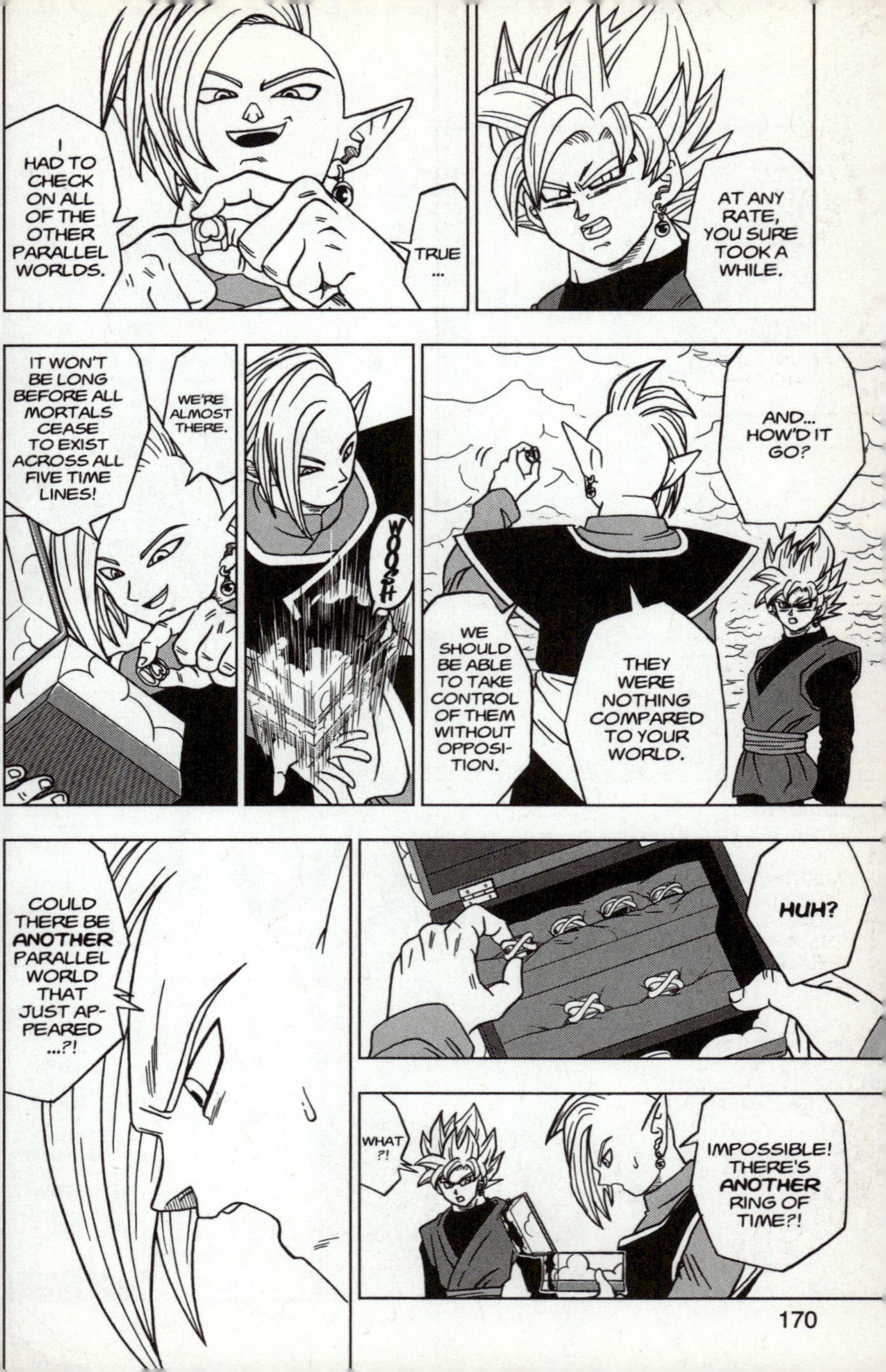
AT ANY RATE, YOU SURE TOOK A WHILE.
TRUE...
I HAD TO CHECK ON ALL OF THE OTHER PARALLEL WORLDS.
AND... HOW'D IT GO?
THEY WERE NOTHING COMPARED TO YOUR WORLD.
WE SHOULD BE ABLE TO TAKE CONTROL OF THEM WITHOUT OPPOSITION.
WOOSH
WE'RE ALMOST THERE.
IT WON'T BE LONG BEFORE ALL MORTALS CEASE TO EXIST ACROSS ALL FIVE TIME LINES!
HUH?
IMPOSSIBLE! THERE'S **ANOTHER** RING OF TIME?!
WHAT?!
COULD THERE BE **ANOTHER** PARALLEL WORLD THAT JUST APPEARED...?!

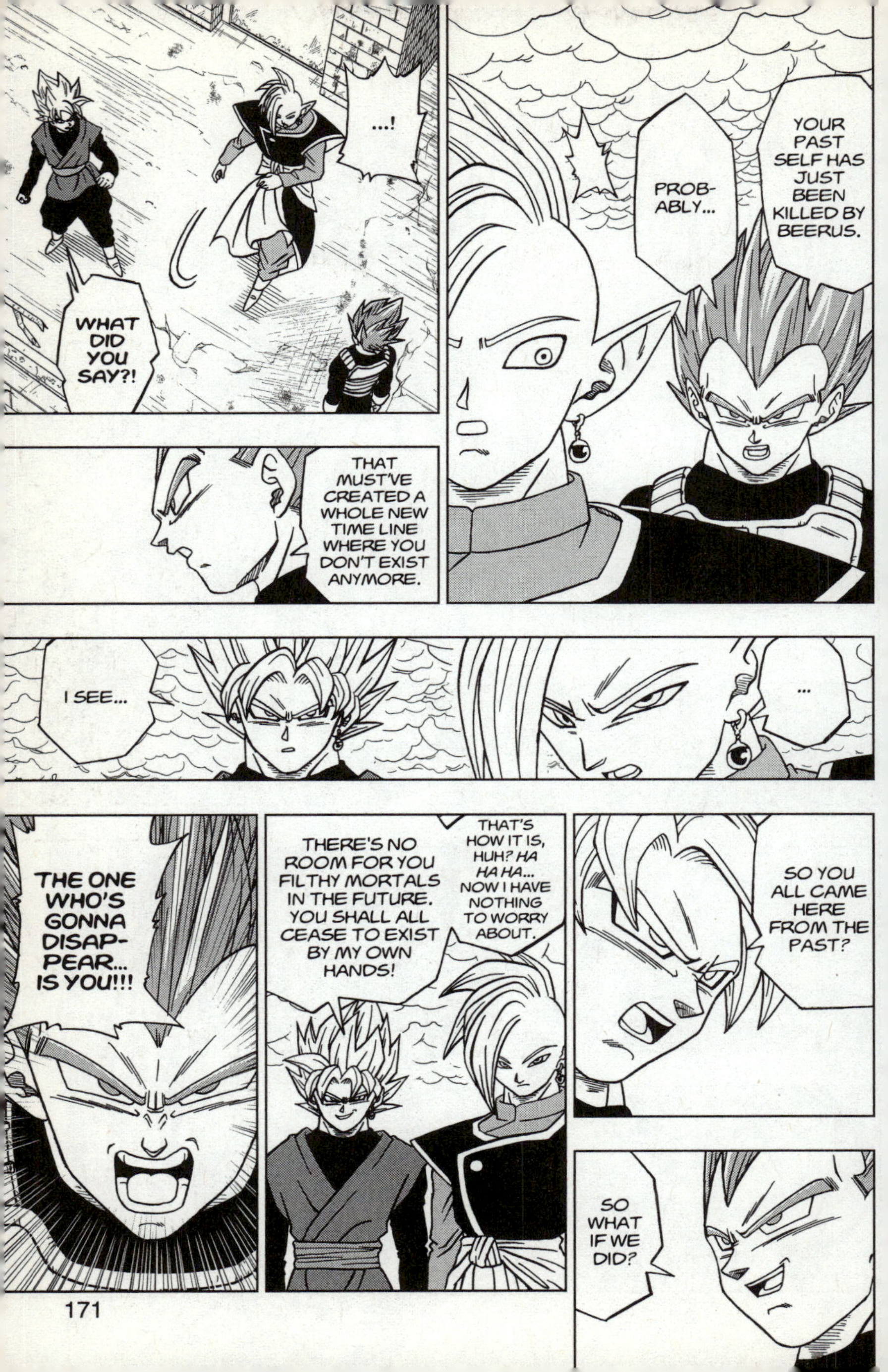
YOUR PAST SELF HAS JUST BEEN KILLED BY BEERUS.
PROB-ABLY...
...!
WHAT DID YOU SAY?!
THAT MUST'VE CREATED A WHOLE NEW TIME LINE WHERE YOU DON'T EXIST ANYMORE.
...
I SEE...
SO YOU ALL CAME HERE FROM THE PAST?
SO WHAT IF WE DID?
THAT'S HOW IT IS, HUH? *HA HA HA...* NOW I HAVE NOTHING TO WORRY ABOUT.
THERE'S NO ROOM FOR YOU FILTHY MORTALS IN THE FUTURE. YOU SHALL ALL CEASE TO EXIST BY MY OWN HANDS!
THE ONE WHO'S GONNA DISAP-PEAR... IS YOU!!!

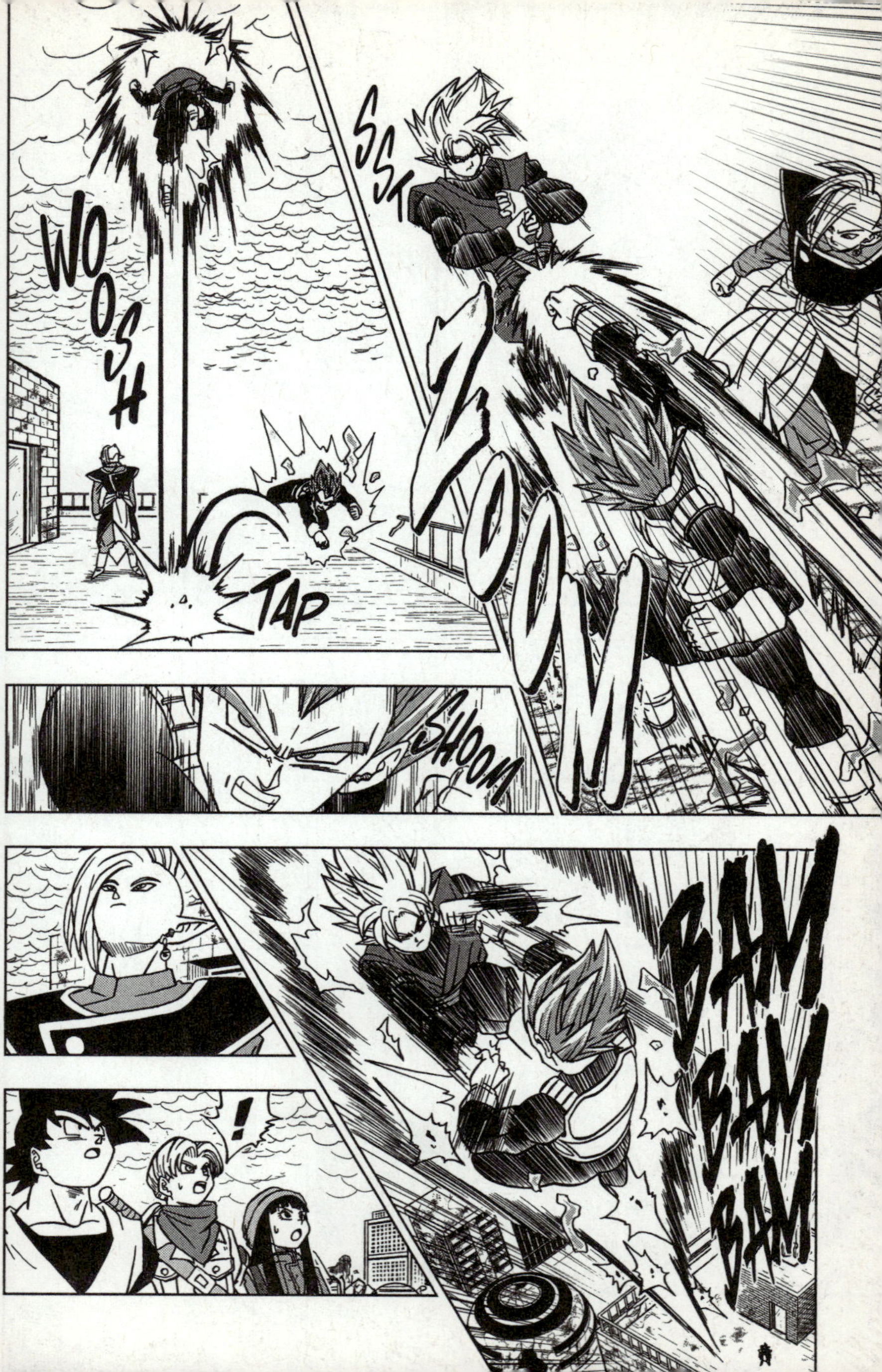
SST
ZOOOM
WOOSH
TAP
SHOOM
BAM BAM BAM
!

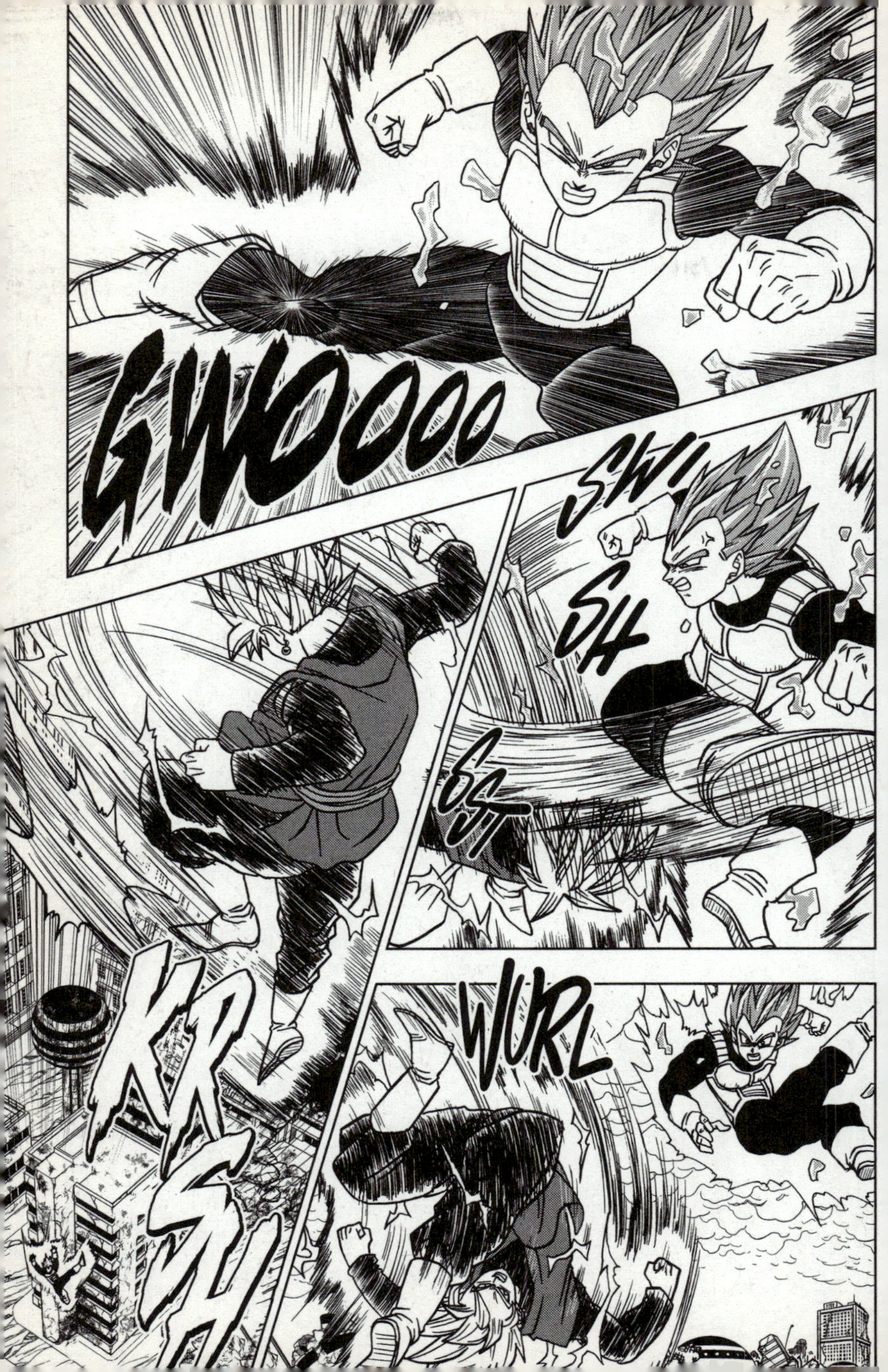
GWOOOO
SWI SH
SST
WURL
KRSH

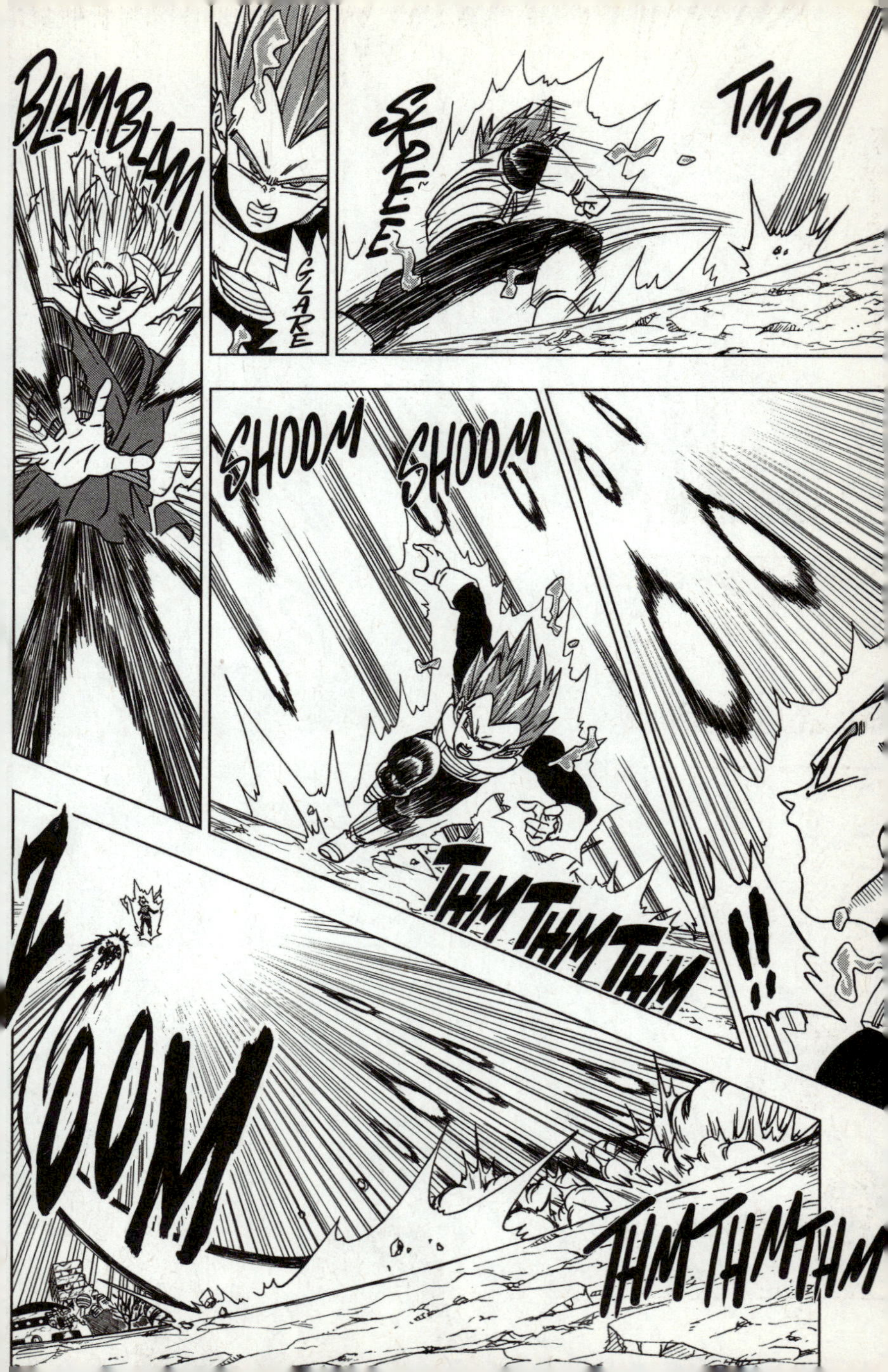

TMP
SKREEE
GLARE
!!
SHOOM
SHOOM
THM THM THM
BLAM BLAM
THM THM THM
ZOOM

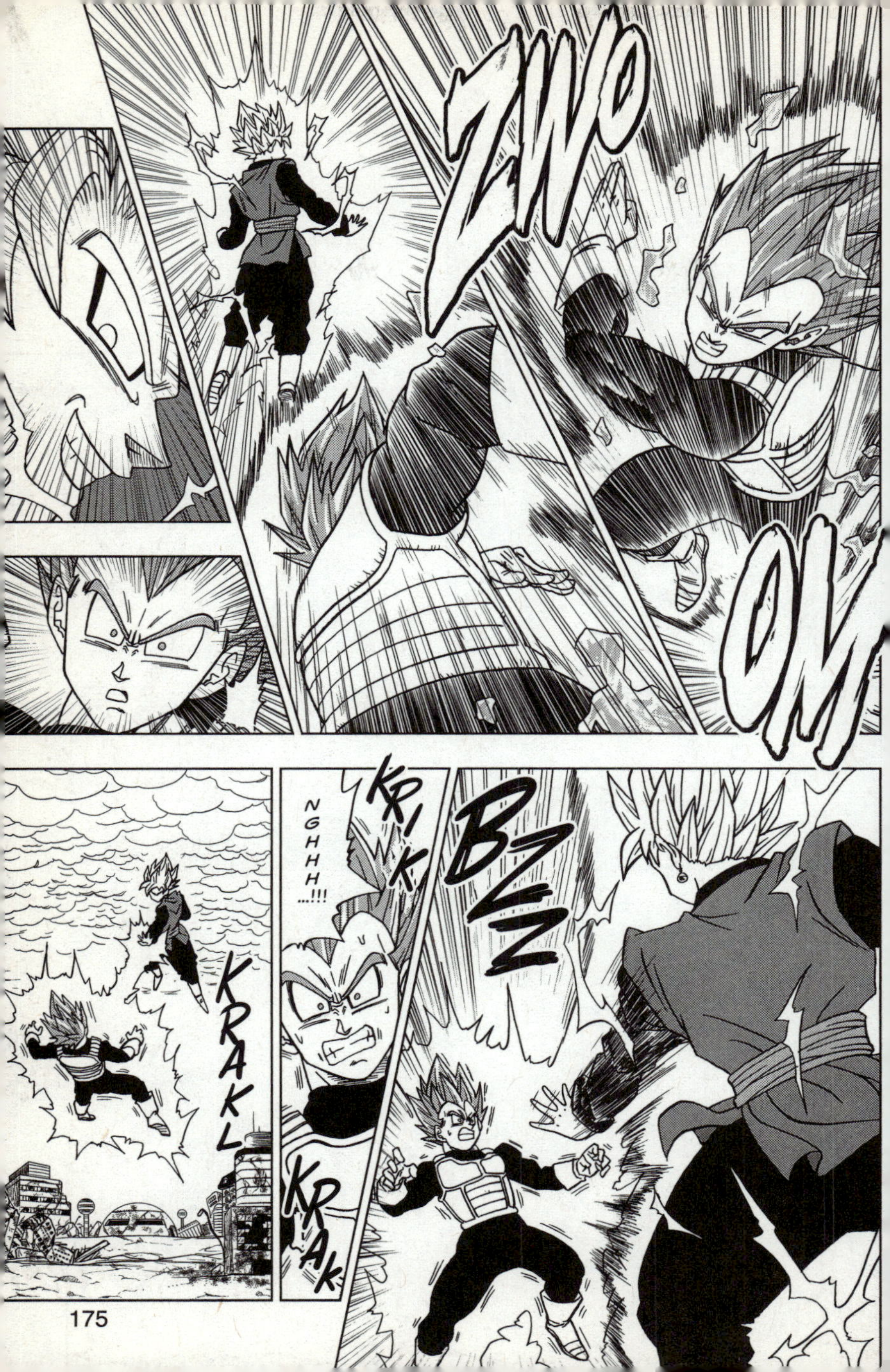
ZWO
OM
BZZ
KRIK
NGHHH.....!!!
KRAK
KRAKL

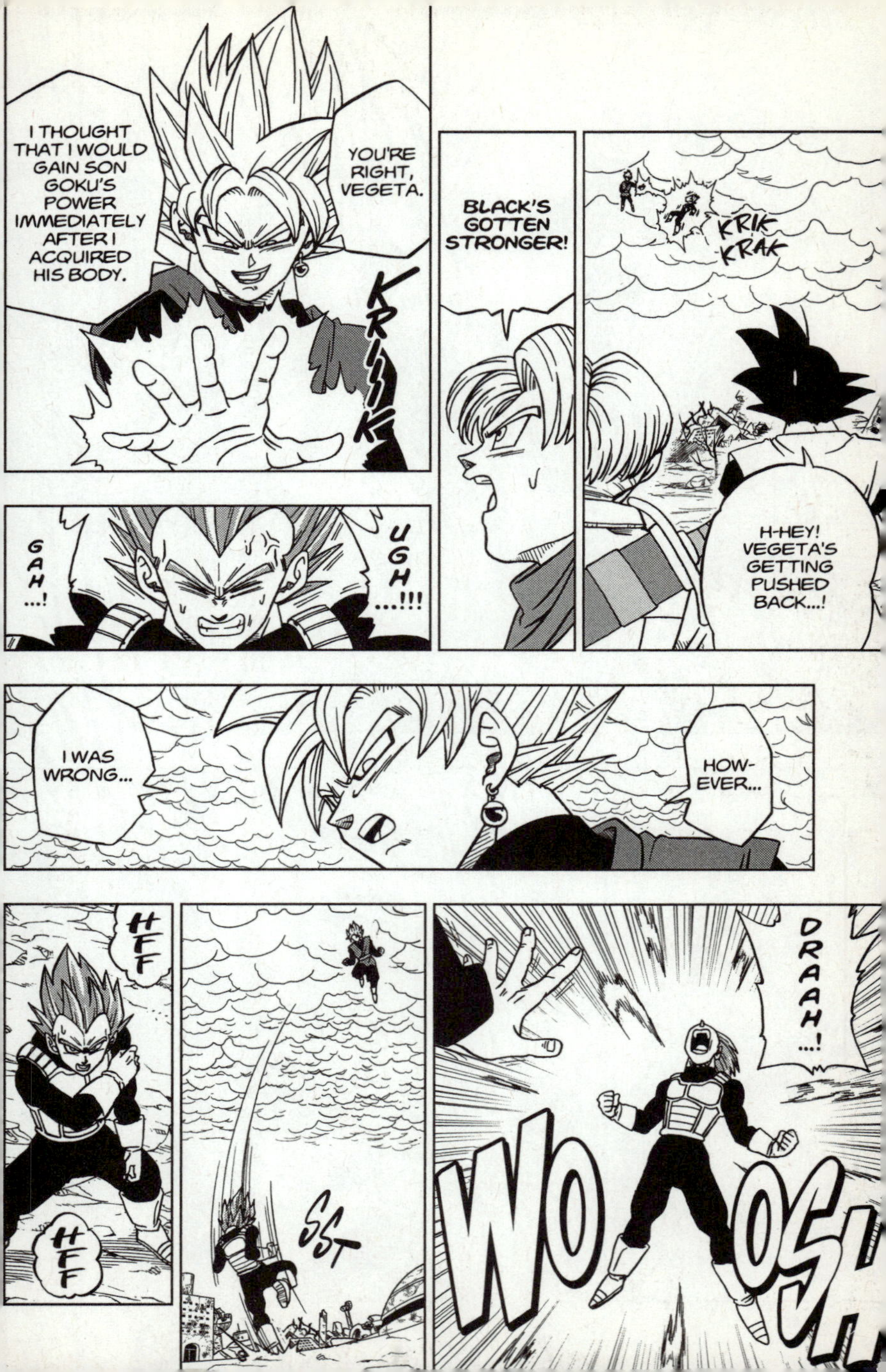
KRIK KRAK
H-HEY! VEGETA'S GETTING PUSHED BACK...!
BLACK'S GOTTEN STRONGER!
YOU'RE RIGHT, VEGETA.
I THOUGHT THAT I WOULD GAIN SON GOKU'S POWER IMMEDIATELY AFTER I ACQUIRED HIS BODY.
KRIIIK
UGH...!!!
GAH...!
HOW-EVER...
I WAS WRONG...
DRAAAH...!
WOOSH
SST
HFF
HFF

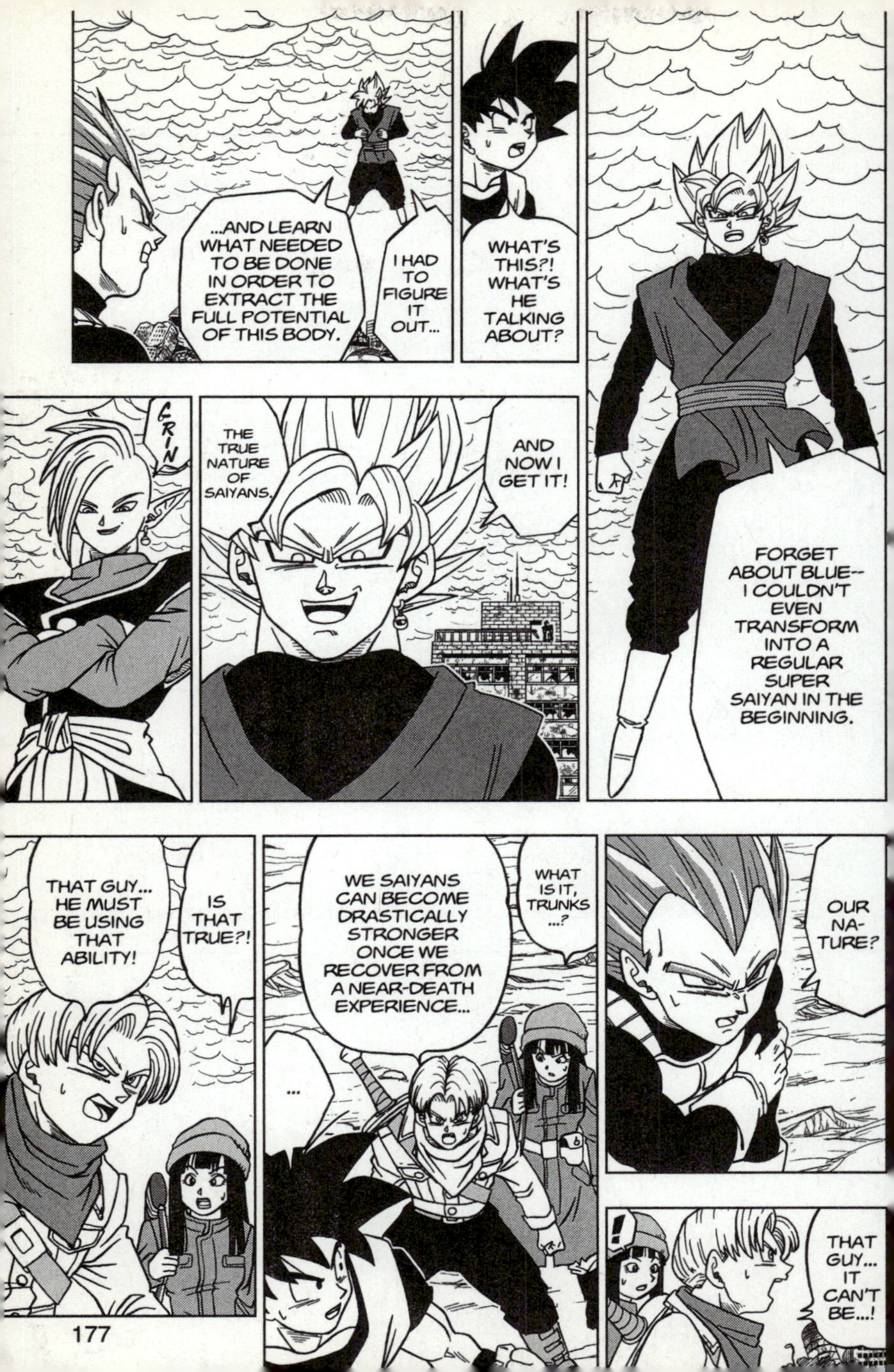
FORGET ABOUT BLUE-- I COULDN'T EVEN TRANSFORM INTO A REGULAR SUPER SAIYAN IN THE BEGINNING.
WHAT'S THIS?! WHAT'S HE TALKING ABOUT?
I HAD TO FIGURE IT OUT...
...AND LEARN WHAT NEEDED TO BE DONE IN ORDER TO EXTRACT THE FULL POTENTIAL OF THIS BODY.
AND NOW I GET IT!
THE TRUE NATURE OF SAIYANS.
GRIN
OUR NA-TURE?
THAT GUY... IT CAN'T BE...!
WHAT IS IT, TRUNKS ...?
WE SAIYANS CAN BECOME DRASTICALLY STRONGER ONCE WE RECOVER FROM A NEAR-DEATH EXPERIENCE...
...
IS THAT TRUE?!
THAT GUY... HE MUST BE USING THAT ABILITY!

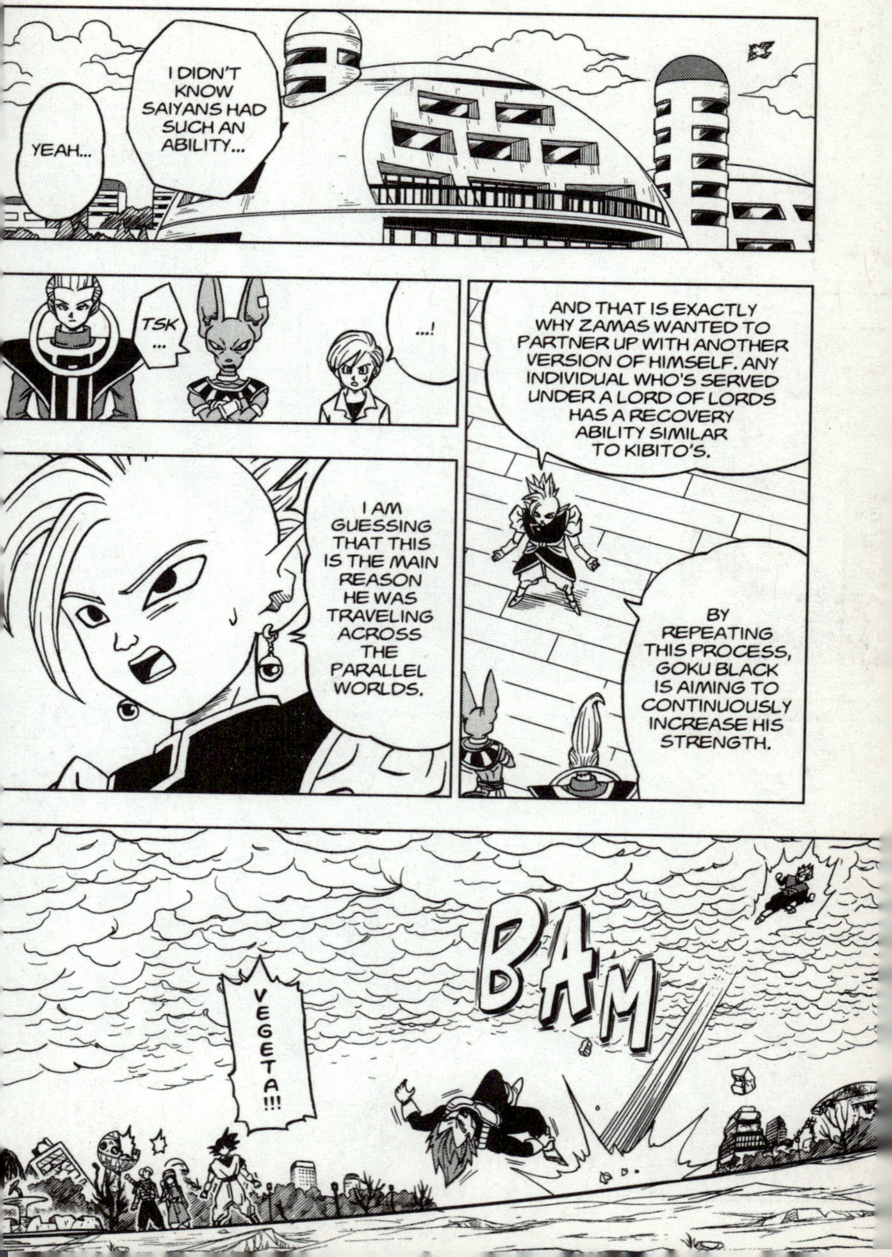
I DIDN'T KNOW SAIYANS HAD SUCH AN ABILITY...
YEAH...
AND THAT IS EXACTLY WHY ZAMAS WANTED TO PARTNER UP WITH ANOTHER VERSION OF HIMSELF. ANY INDIVIDUAL WHO'S SERVED UNDER A LORD OF LORDS HAS A RECOVERY ABILITY SIMILAR TO KIBITO'S.
BY REPEATING THIS PROCESS, GOKU BLACK IS AIMING TO CONTINUOUSLY INCREASE HIS STRENGTH.
...!
TSK ...
I AM GUESSING THAT THIS IS THE MAIN REASON HE WAS TRAVELING ACROSS THE PARALLEL WORLDS.
BAM
VEGETA!!!

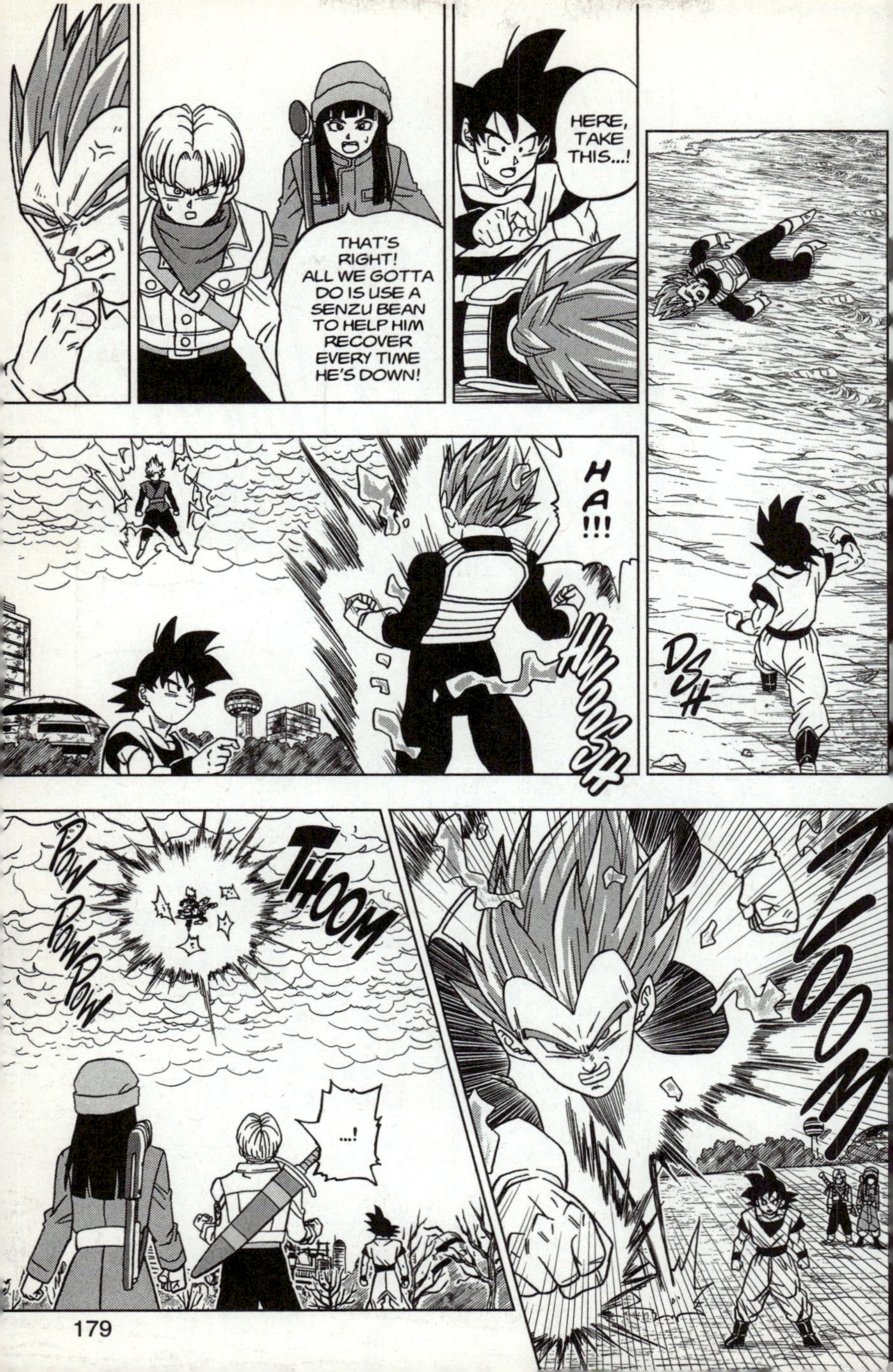
DSH
HERE, TAKE THIS...!
THAT'S RIGHT! ALL WE GOTTA DO IS USE A SENZU BEAN TO HELP HIM RECOVER EVERY TIME HE'S DOWN!
HA!!!
HWOOSH
VOOM
THOOM
POW POW POW POW
...!

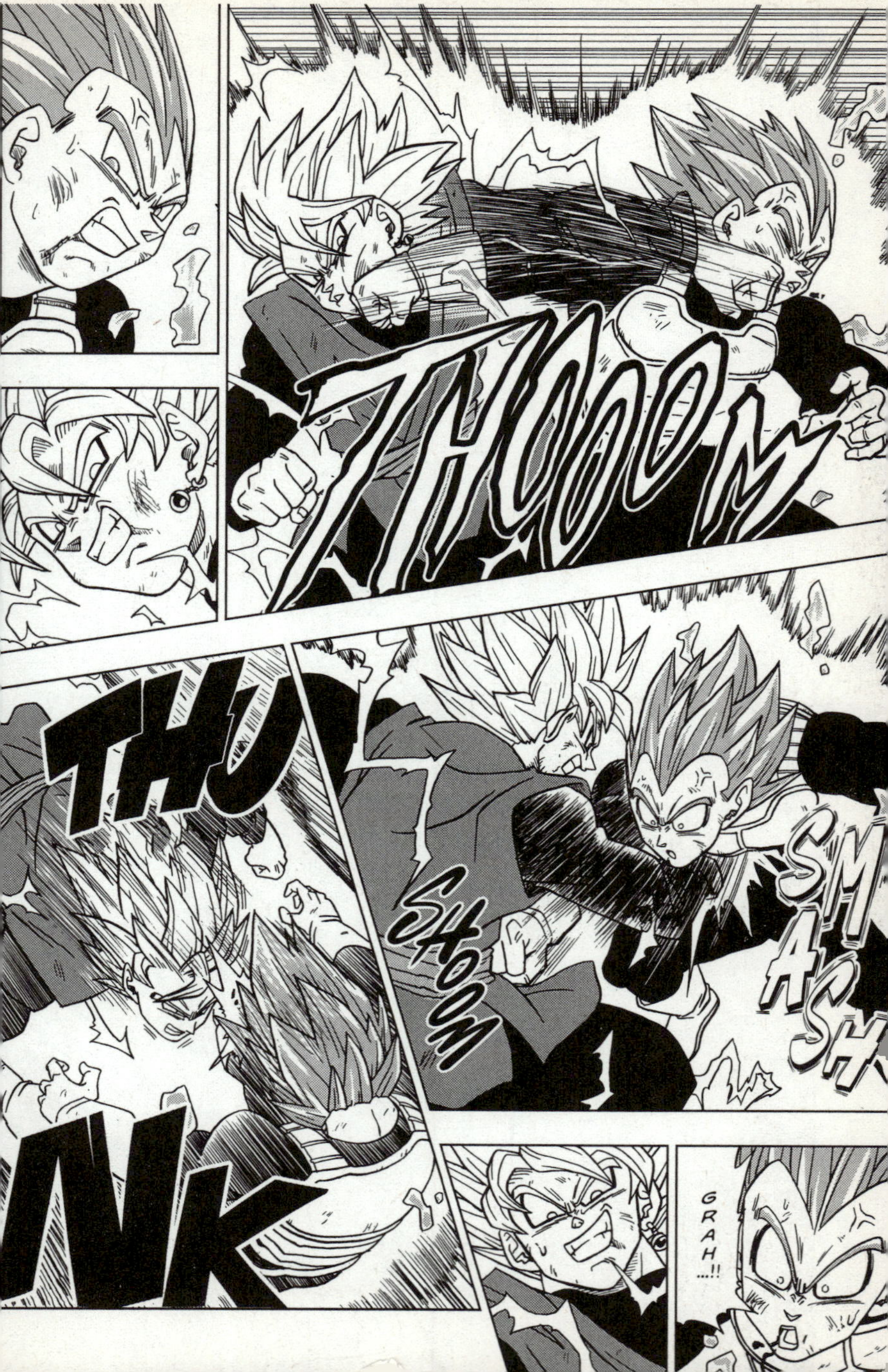
THOOOM
SMASH
SHOOM
THUNK
GRAH....!!

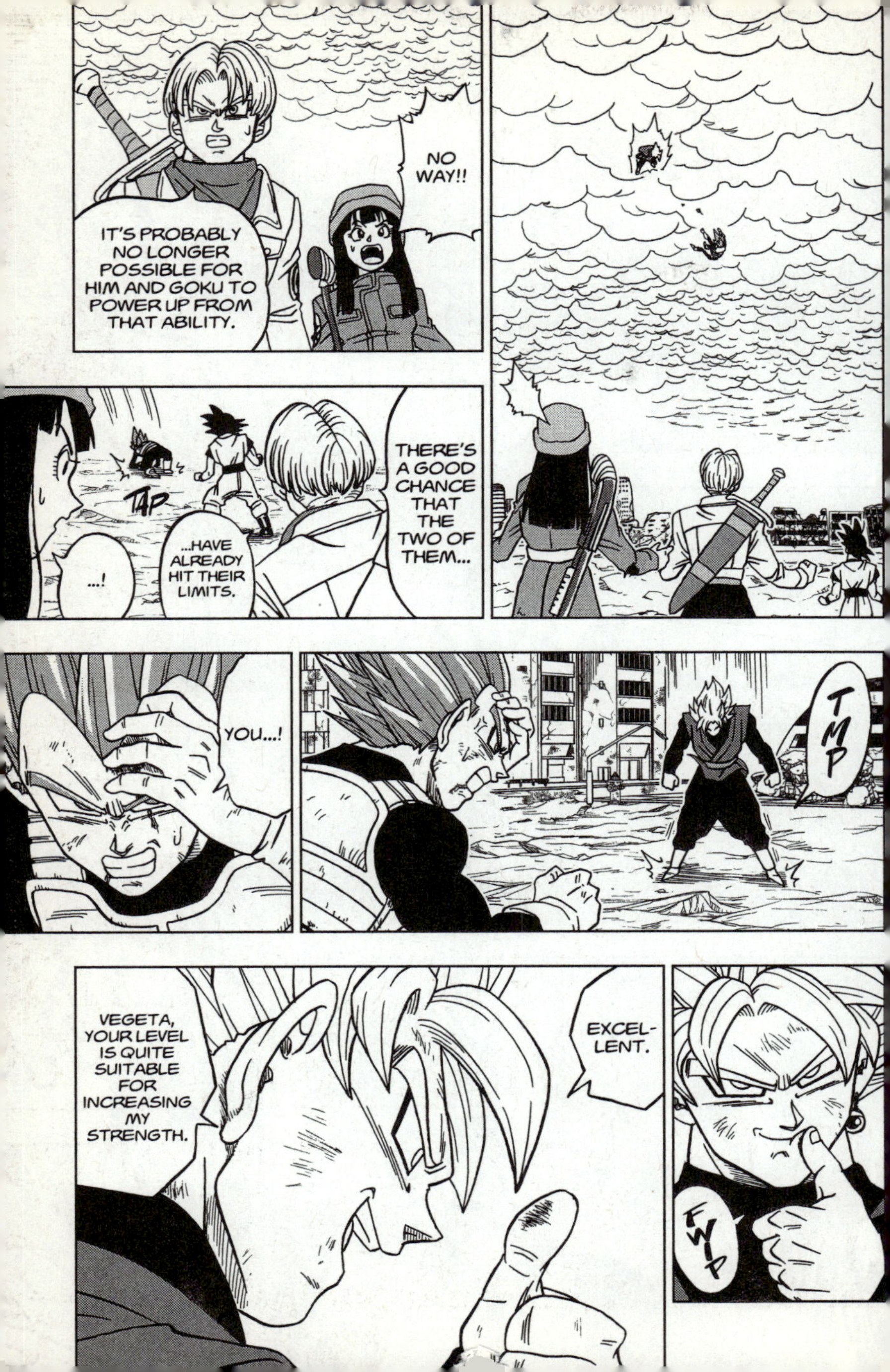
NO WAY!!
IT'S PROBABLY NO LONGER POSSIBLE FOR HIM AND GOKU TO POWER UP FROM THAT ABILITY.
THERE'S A GOOD CHANCE THAT THE TWO OF THEM...
...HAVE ALREADY HIT THEIR LIMITS.
TAP
...!
TMP
YOU...!
FWIP
EXCEL-LENT.
VEGETA, YOUR LEVEL IS QUITE SUITABLE FOR INCREASING MY STRENGTH.

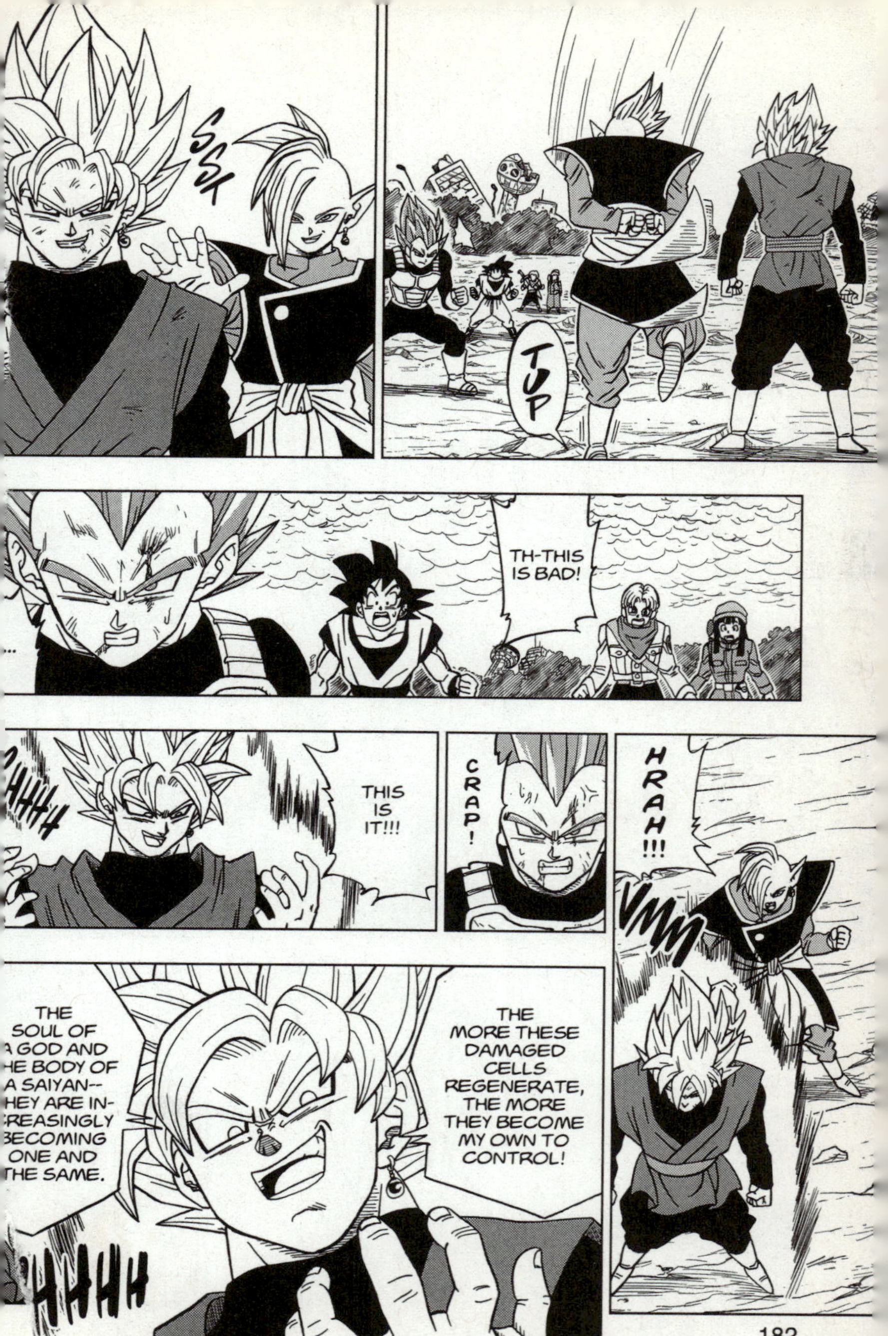
TUP
SSK
TH-THIS IS BAD!
...
HRAH!!!
VMM
CRAP!
THIS IS IT!!!
HHHH
THE MORE THESE DAMAGED CELLS REGENERATE, THE MORE THEY BECOME MY OWN TO CONTROL!
THE SOUL OF A GOD AND THE BODY OF A SAIYAN--THEY ARE IN-CREASINGLY BECOMING ONE AND THE SAME.
HHHH

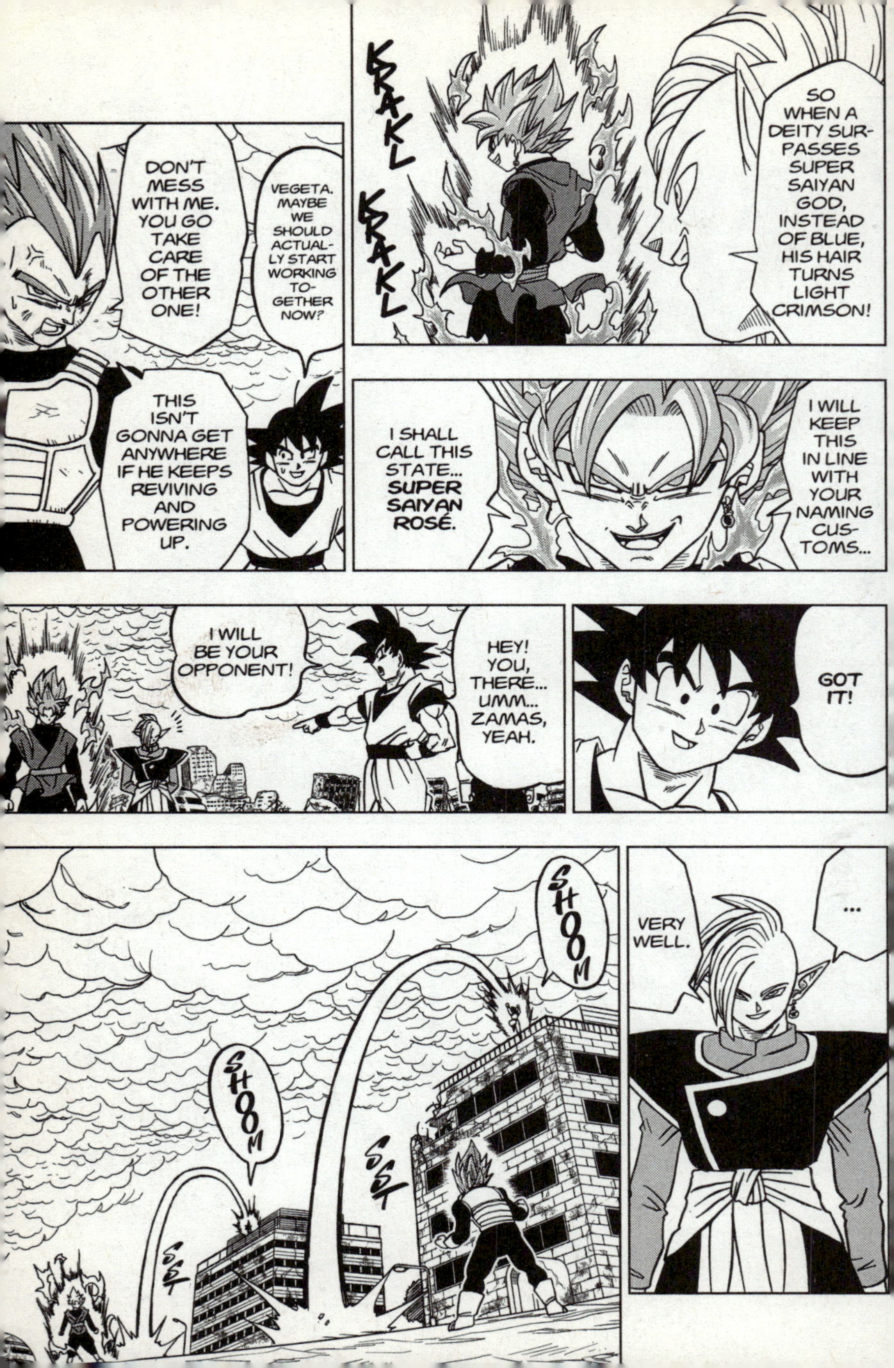

SO WHEN A DEITY SURPASSES SUPER SAIYAN GOD, INSTEAD OF BLUE, HIS HAIR TURNS LIGHT CRIMSON!
KRAKL
KRAKL
I WILL KEEP THIS IN LINE WITH YOUR NAMING CUSTOMS...
I SHALL CALL THIS STATE... **SUPER SAIYAN ROSÉ.**
VEGETA. MAYBE WE SHOULD ACTUALLY START WORKING TOGETHER NOW?
DON'T MESS WITH ME. YOU GO TAKE CARE OF THE OTHER ONE!
THIS ISN'T GONNA GET ANYWHERE IF HE KEEPS REVIVING AND POWERING UP.
GOT IT!
HEY! YOU, THERE... UMM... ZAMAS, YEAH.
I WILL BE YOUR OPPONENT!
...
VERY WELL.
SHOOM
SSK
SHOOM
SSK

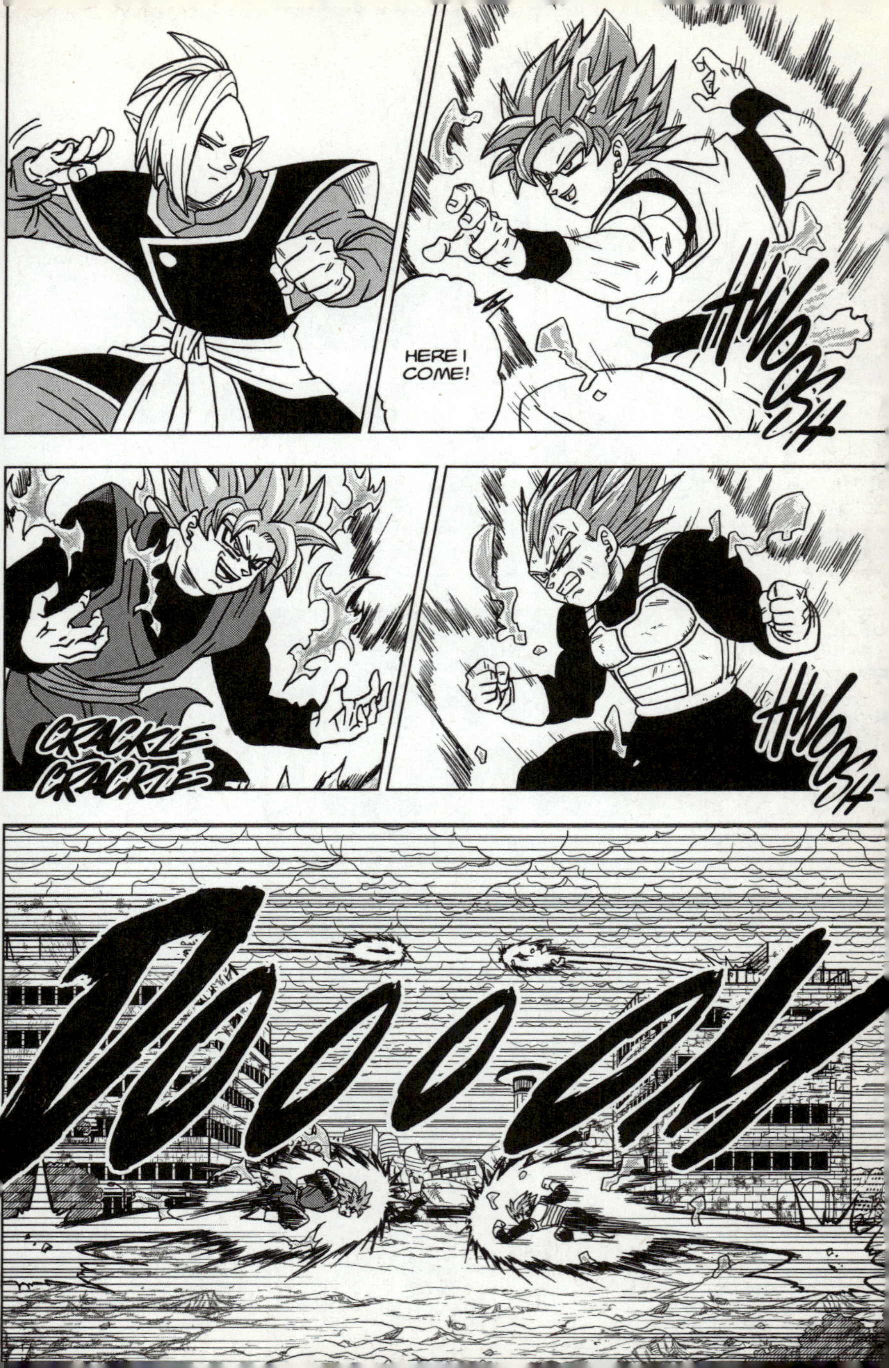
HERE I COME!
HWOOSH
HWOOSH
CRACKLE CRACKLE
ZOOOOM

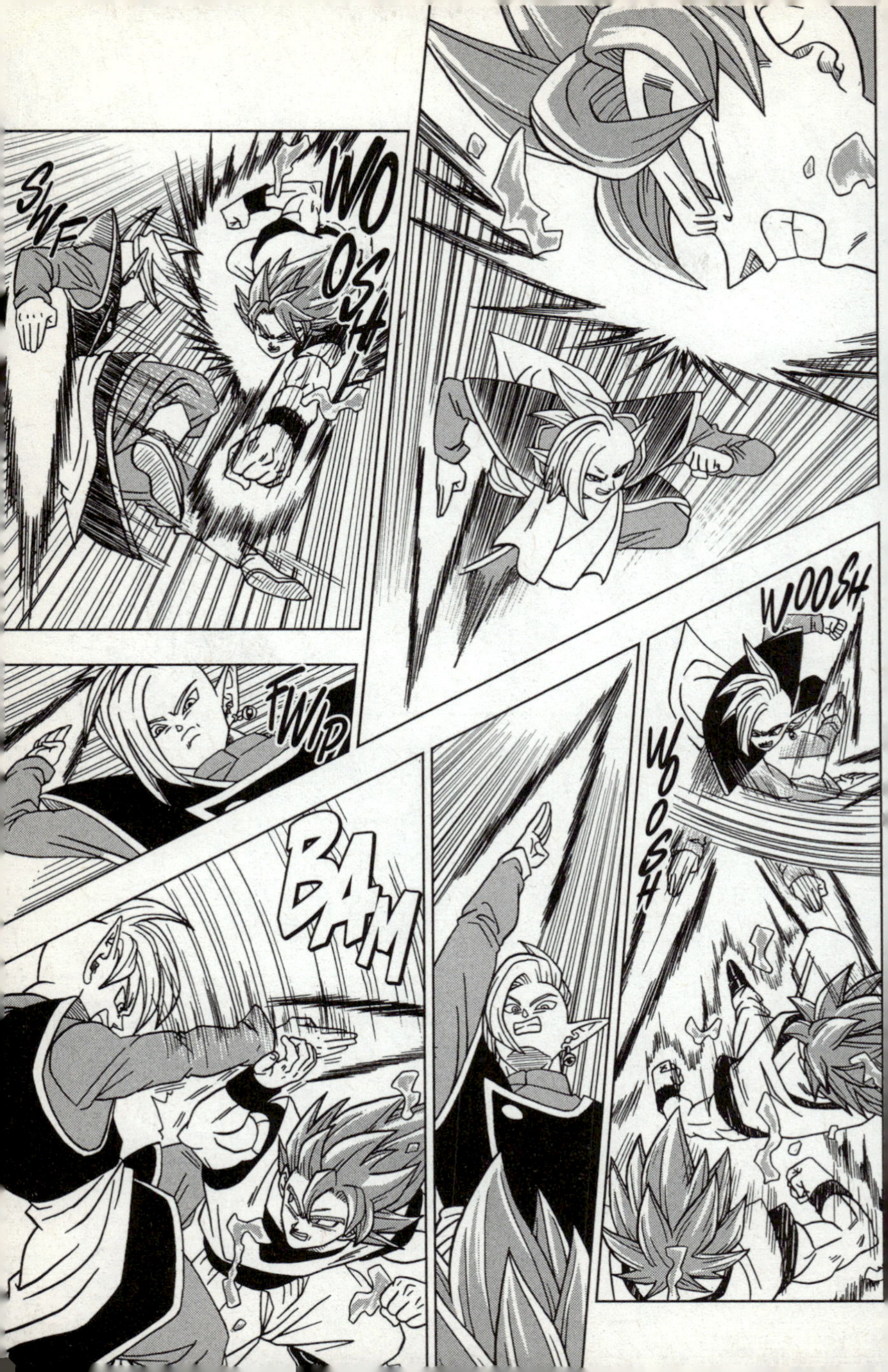
WOOSH
SWF
WOOSH
WOOSH
FWIP
BAM

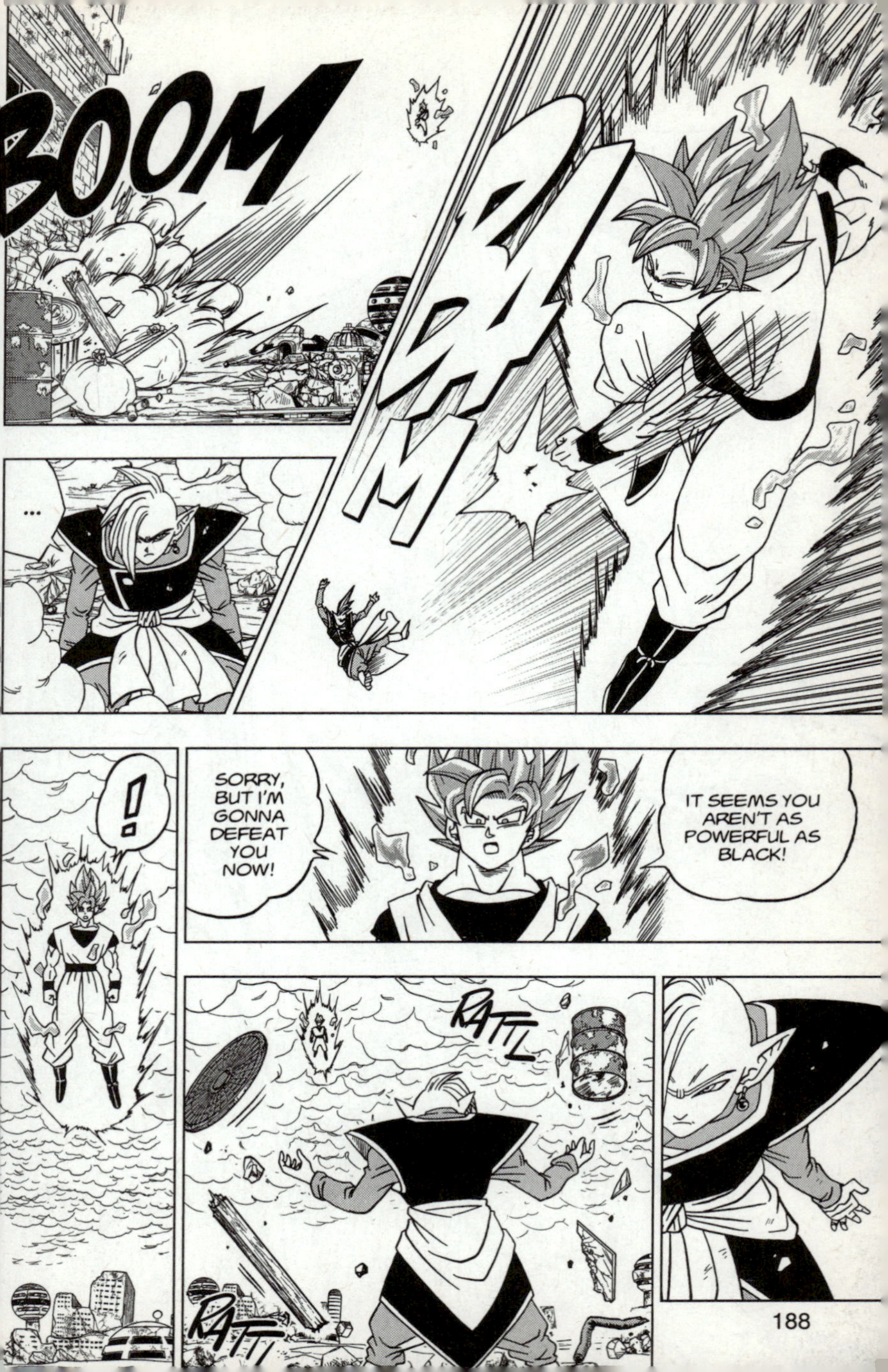
BAM
BOOM
...
IT SEEMS YOU AREN'T AS POWERFUL AS BLACK!
SORRY, BUT I'M GONNA DEFEAT YOU NOW!
RATTL
RATTL
!

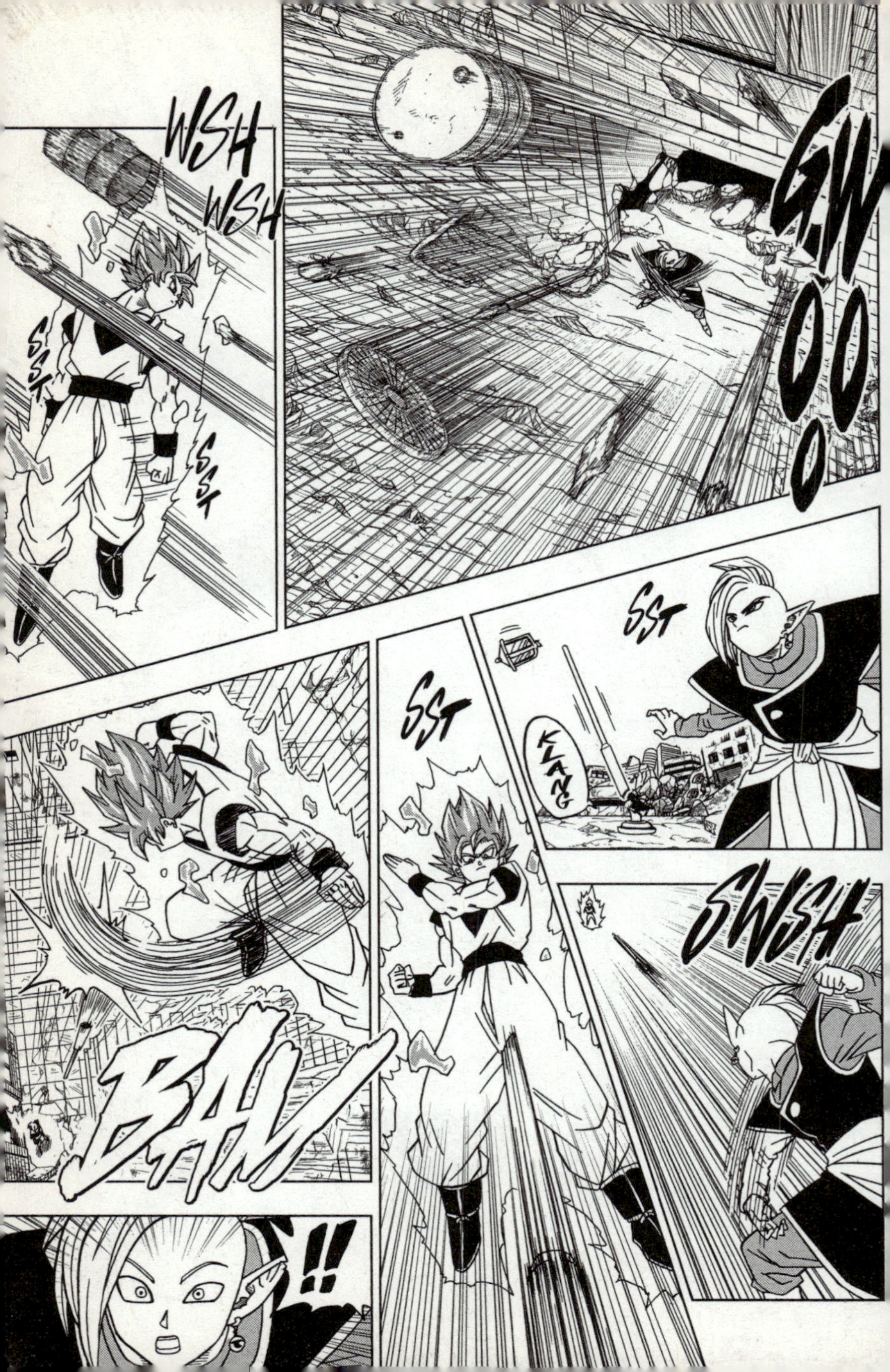
GWOOOO
WSH
WSH
SST
SSK
SST
KLANG
SWISH
SST
BAM
!!

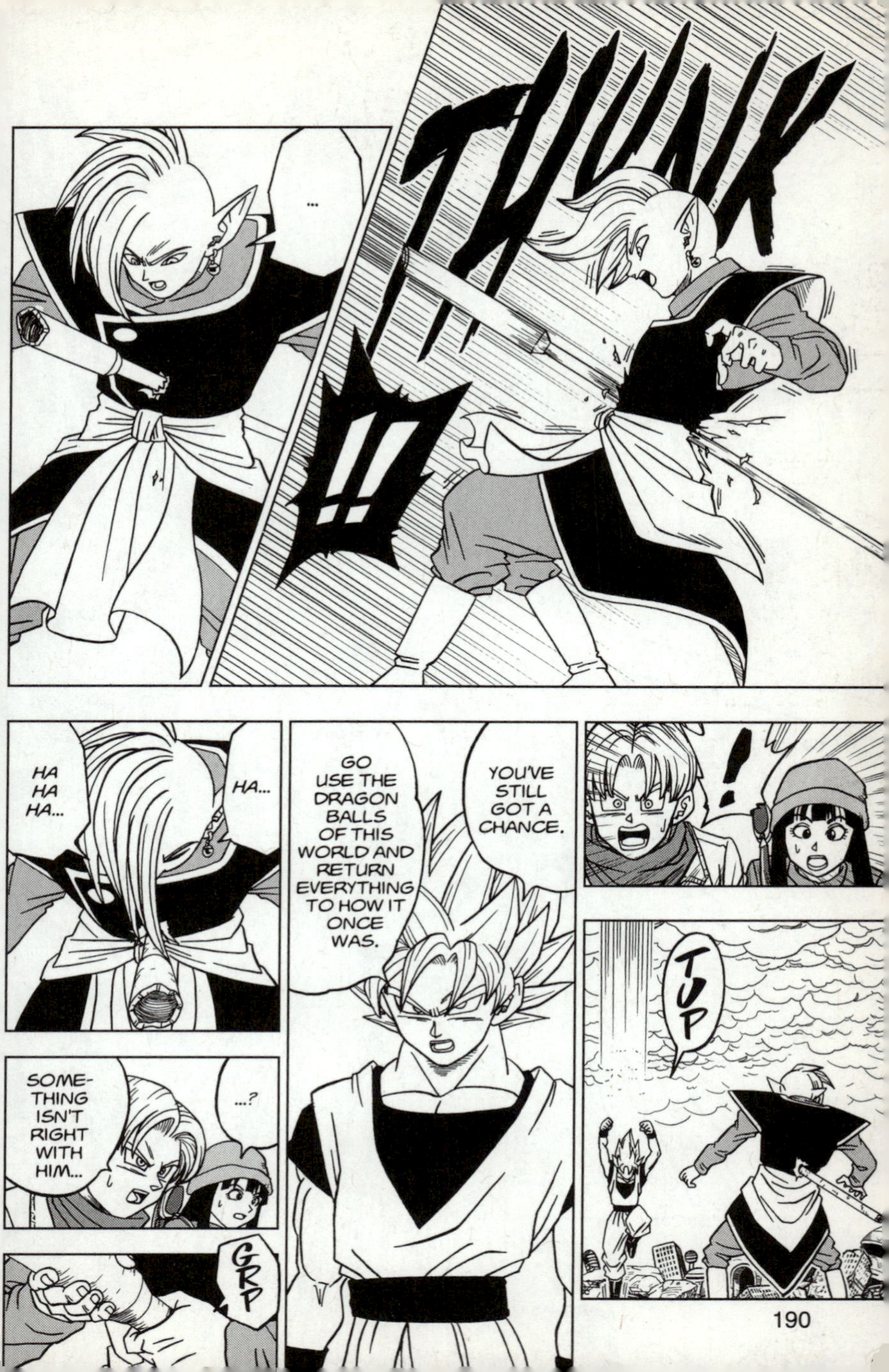
THUNK
!!
...
!
TUP
YOU'VE STILL GOT A CHANCE.
GO USE THE DRAGON BALLS OF THIS WORLD AND RETURN EVERYTHING TO HOW IT ONCE WAS.
HA...
HA HA HA...
...?
SOME-THING ISN'T RIGHT WITH HIM...
GRP

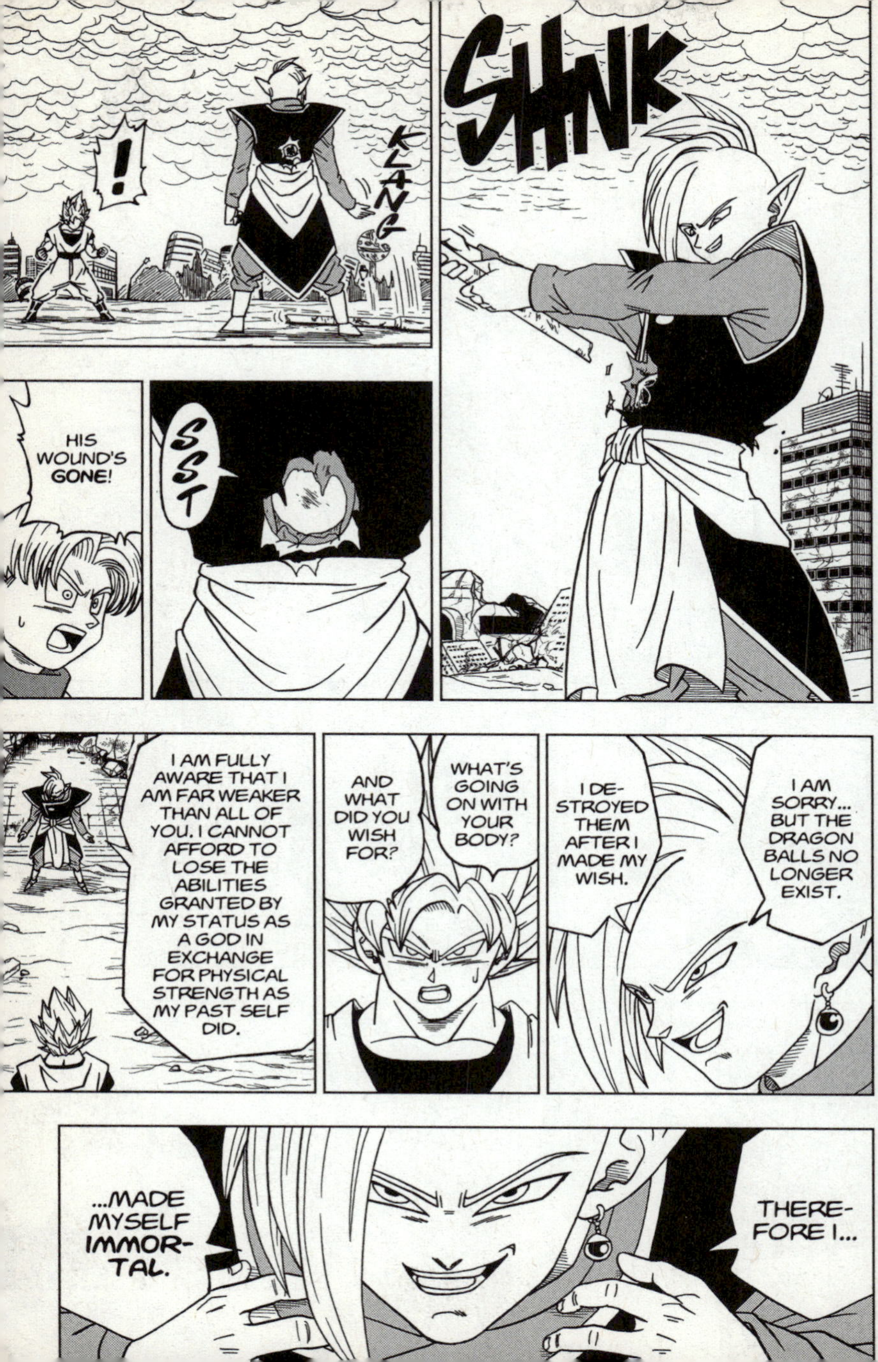
SHNK
KLANG
!
SSST
HIS WOUND'S GONE!
I AM SORRY... BUT THE DRAGON BALLS NO LONGER EXIST.
I DESTROYED THEM AFTER I MADE MY WISH.
WHAT'S GOING ON WITH YOUR BODY?
AND WHAT DID YOU WISH FOR?
I AM FULLY AWARE THAT I AM FAR WEAKER THAN ALL OF YOU. I CANNOT AFFORD TO LOSE THE ABILITIES GRANTED BY MY STATUS AS A GOD IN EXCHANGE FOR PHYSICAL STRENGTH AS MY PAST SELF DID.
THEREFORE I...
...MADE MYSELF IMMORTAL.

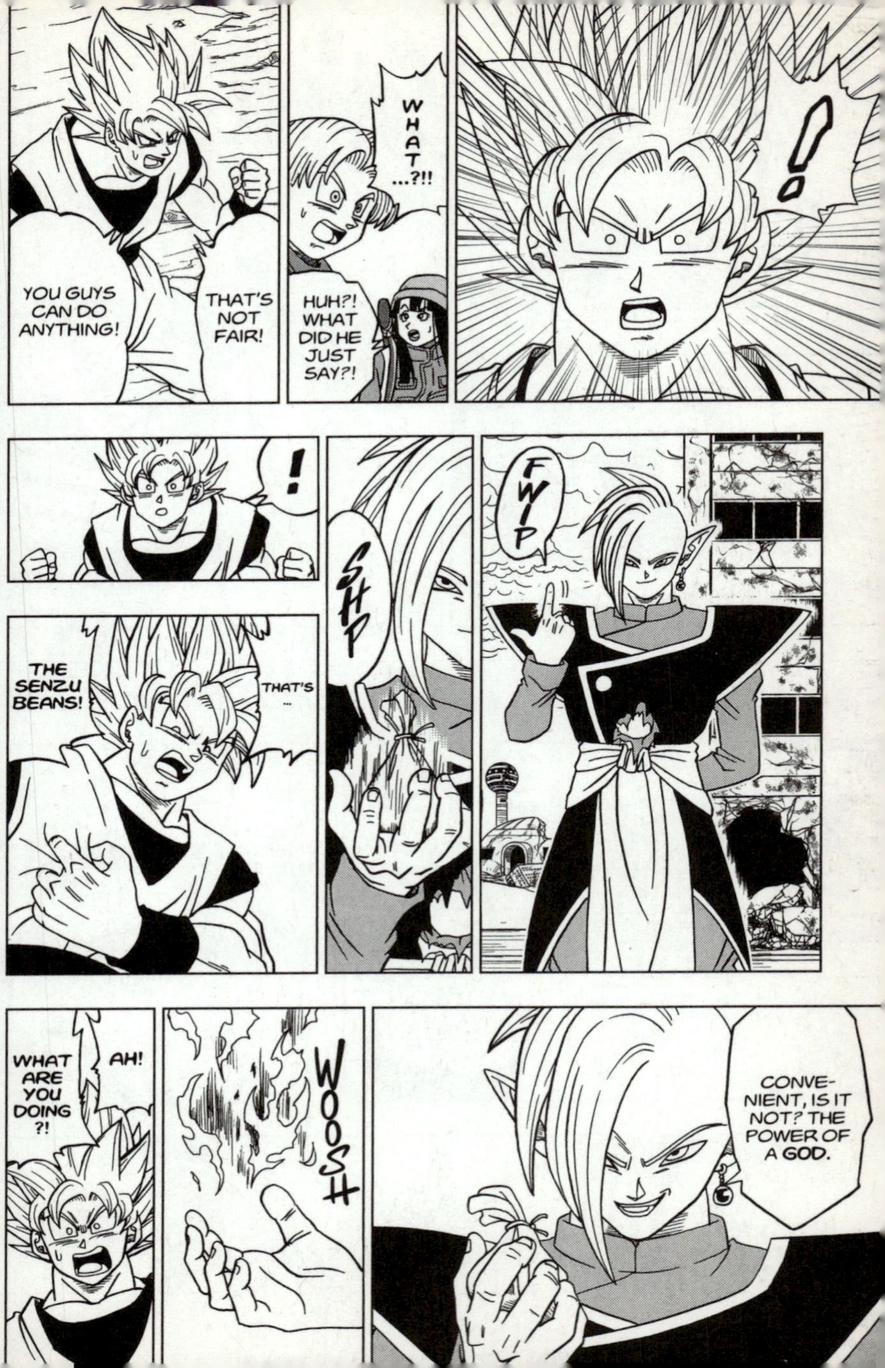
!
WHAT ...?!!
HUH?! WHAT DID HE JUST SAY?!
THAT'S NOT FAIR!
YOU GUYS CAN DO ANYTHING!
FWIP
SHP
!
THAT'S ...
THE SENZU BEANS!
CONVE-NIENT, IS IT NOT? THE POWER OF A GOD.
WOOSH
AH!
WHAT ARE YOU DOING ?!

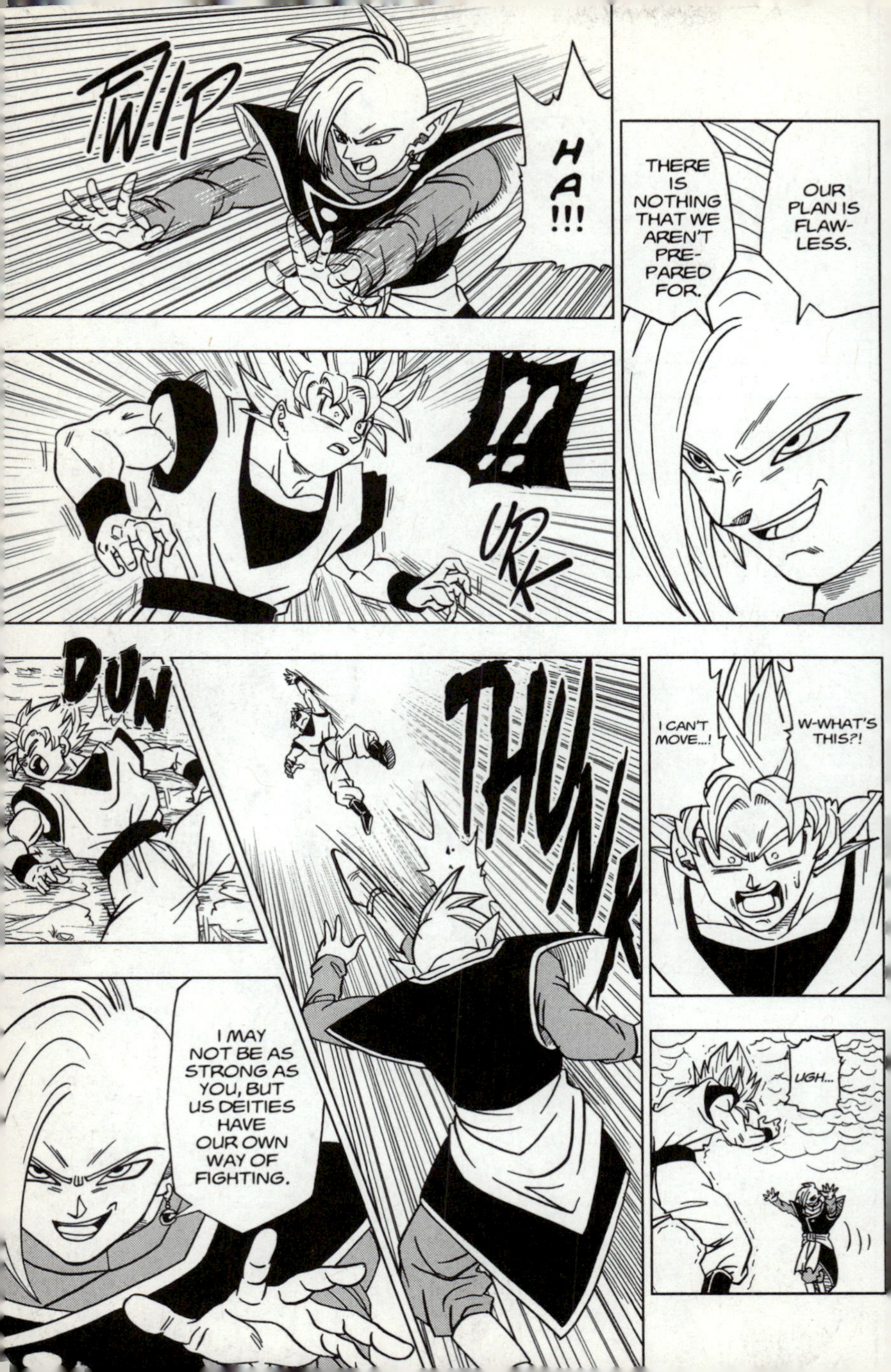
OUR PLAN IS FLAWLESS.
THERE IS NOTHING THAT WE AREN'T PREPARED FOR.
HA!!!
TWIP
!!
URK
W-WHAT'S THIS?!
I CAN'T MOVE...!
UGH...
THUNK
DUN
I MAY NOT BE AS STRONG AS YOU, BUT US DEITIES HAVE OUR OWN WAY OF FIGHTING.

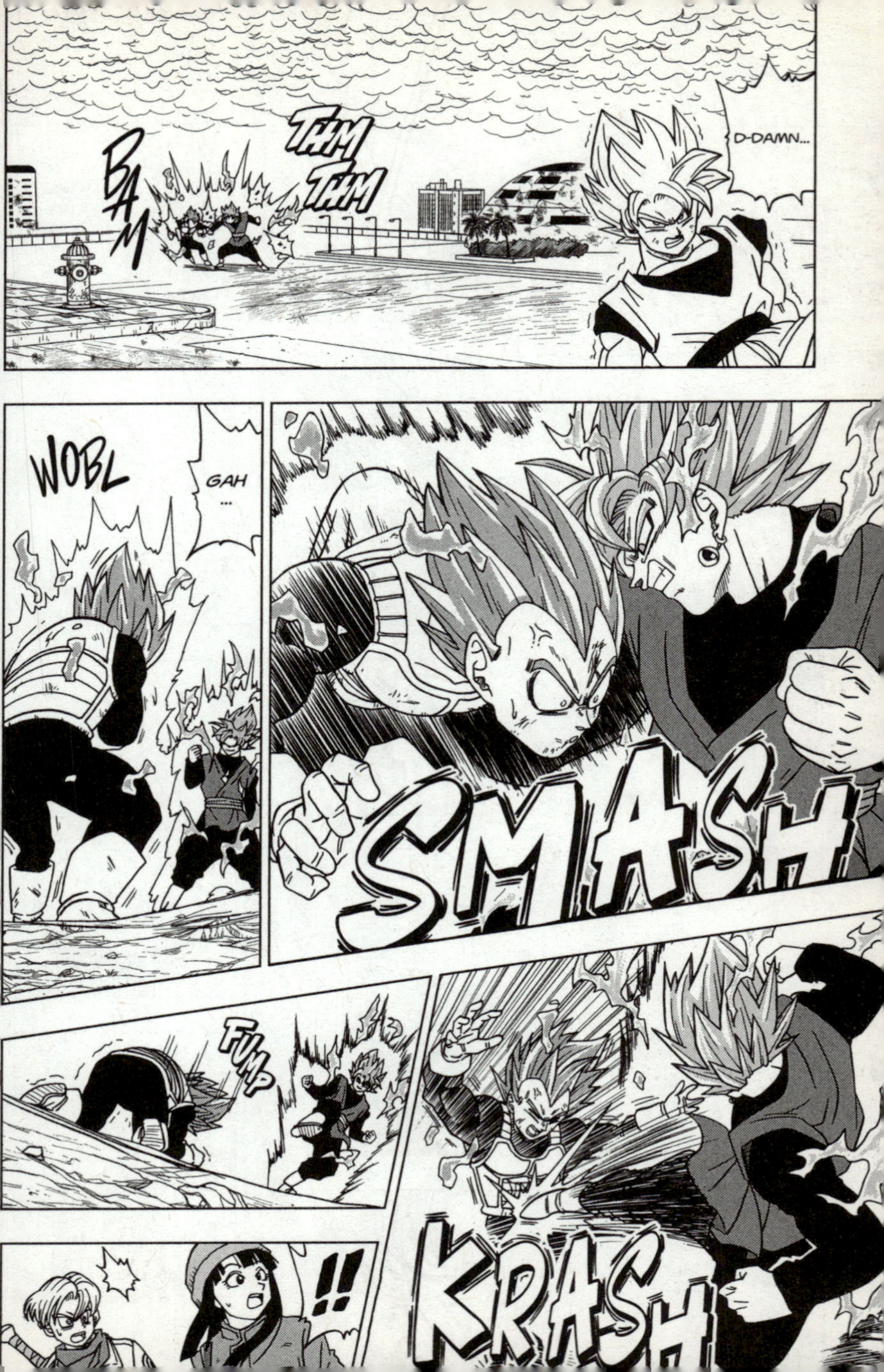
D-DAMN...
THM THM
BAM
SMASH
GAH ...
WOBL
KRASH
FUMP
!!

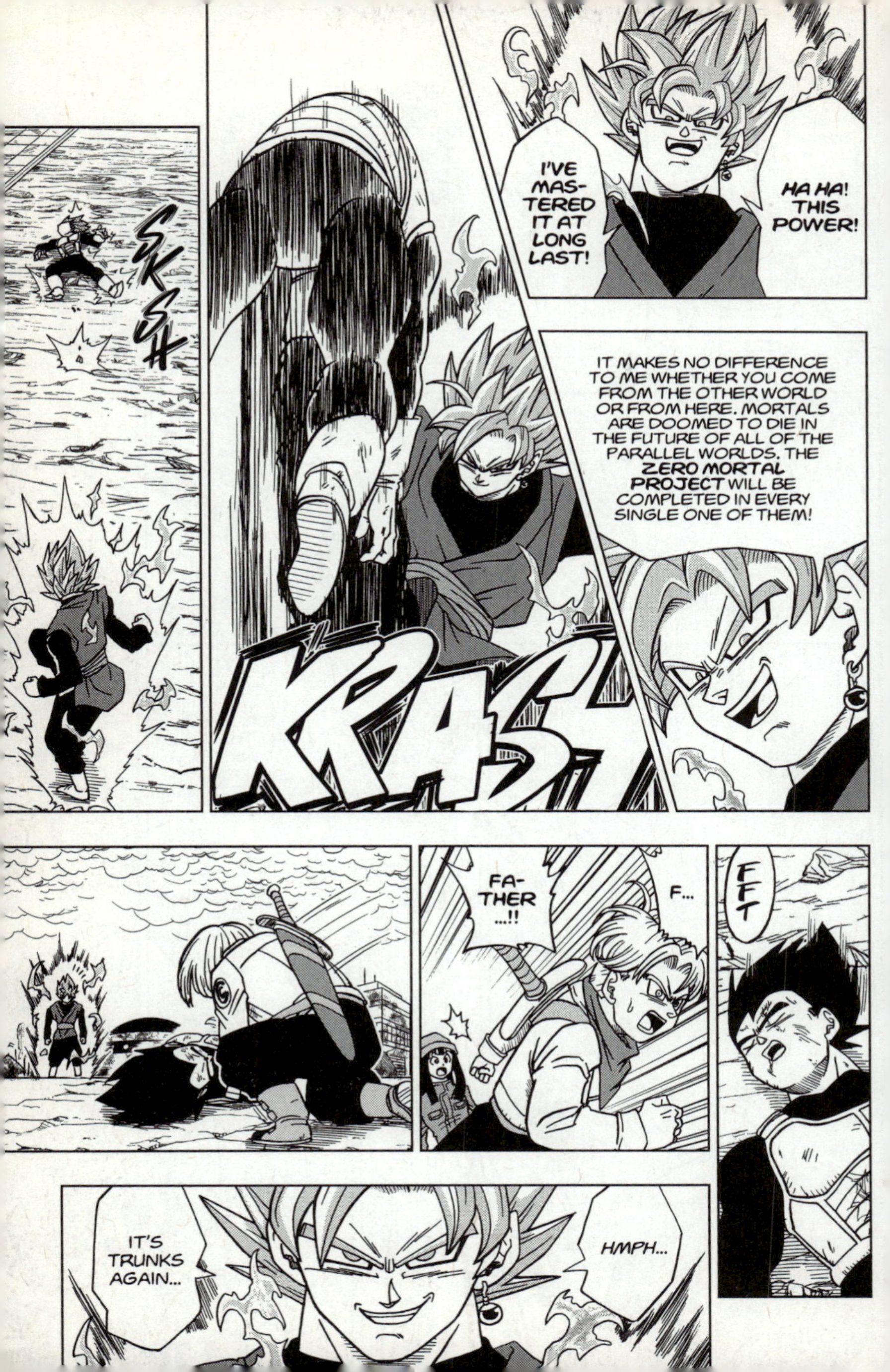
HA HA! THIS POWER!
I'VE MASTERED IT AT LONG LAST!
IT MAKES NO DIFFERENCE TO ME WHETHER YOU COME FROM THE OTHER WORLD OR FROM HERE. MORTALS ARE DOOMED TO DIE IN THE FUTURE OF ALL OF THE PARALLEL WORLDS. THE **ZERO MORTAL PROJECT** WILL BE COMPLETED IN EVERY SINGLE ONE OF THEM!
KRAS
SKSH
FFT
F...
FATHER ...!!
HMPH...
IT'S TRUNKS AGAIN...

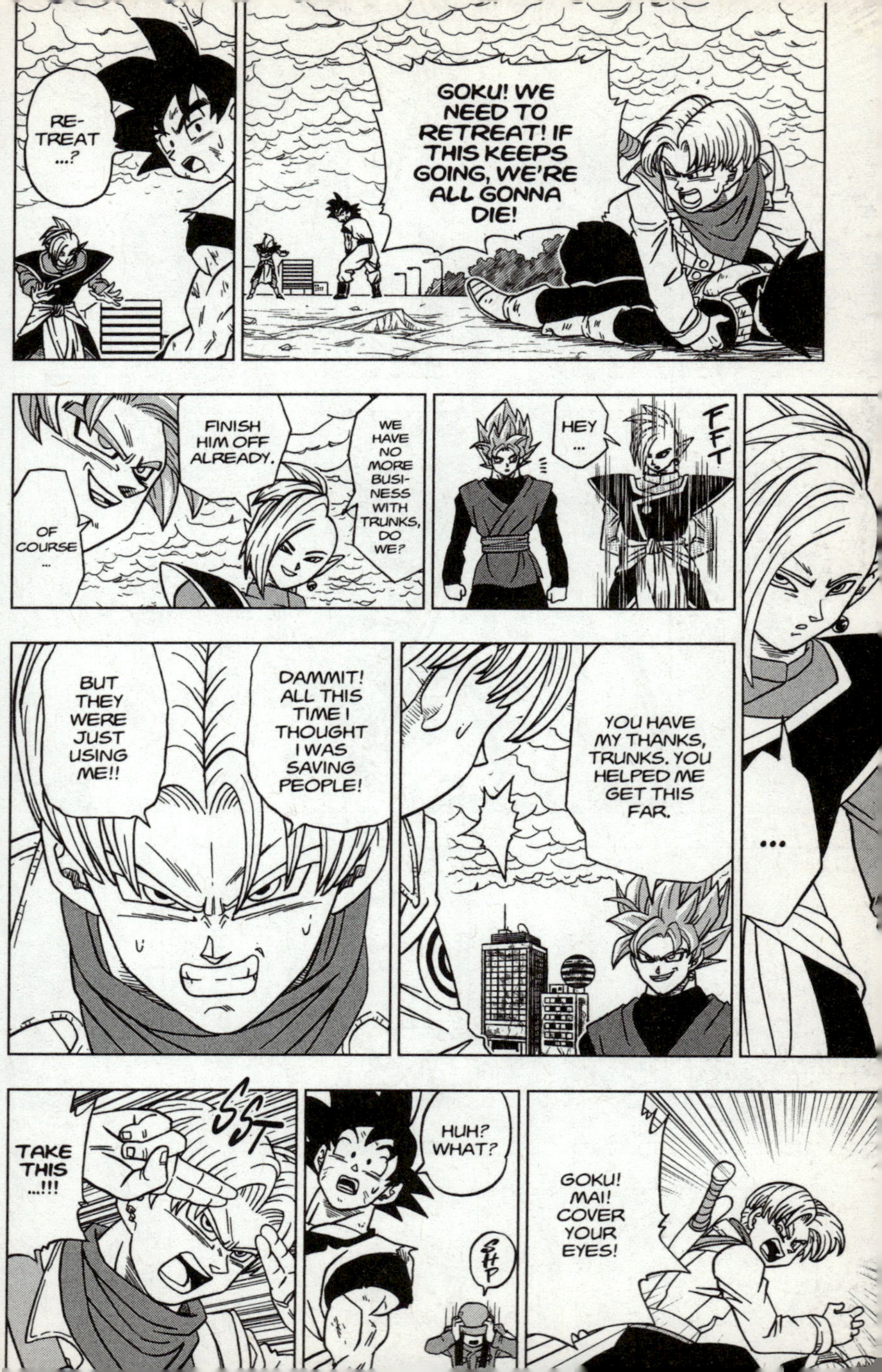
GOKU! WE NEED TO RETREAT! IF THIS KEEPS GOING, WE'RE ALL GONNA DIE!
RE-TREAT ...?
...
HEY ...
FFT
WE HAVE NO MORE BUSINESS WITH TRUNKS, DO WE?
FINISH HIM OFF ALREADY.
OF COURSE ...
YOU HAVE MY THANKS, TRUNKS. YOU HELPED ME GET THIS FAR.
DAMMIT! ALL THIS TIME I THOUGHT I WAS SAVING PEOPLE!
BUT THEY WERE JUST USING ME!!
GOKU! MAI! COVER YOUR EYES!
HUH? WHAT?
SHP
SST
TAKE THIS ...!!!

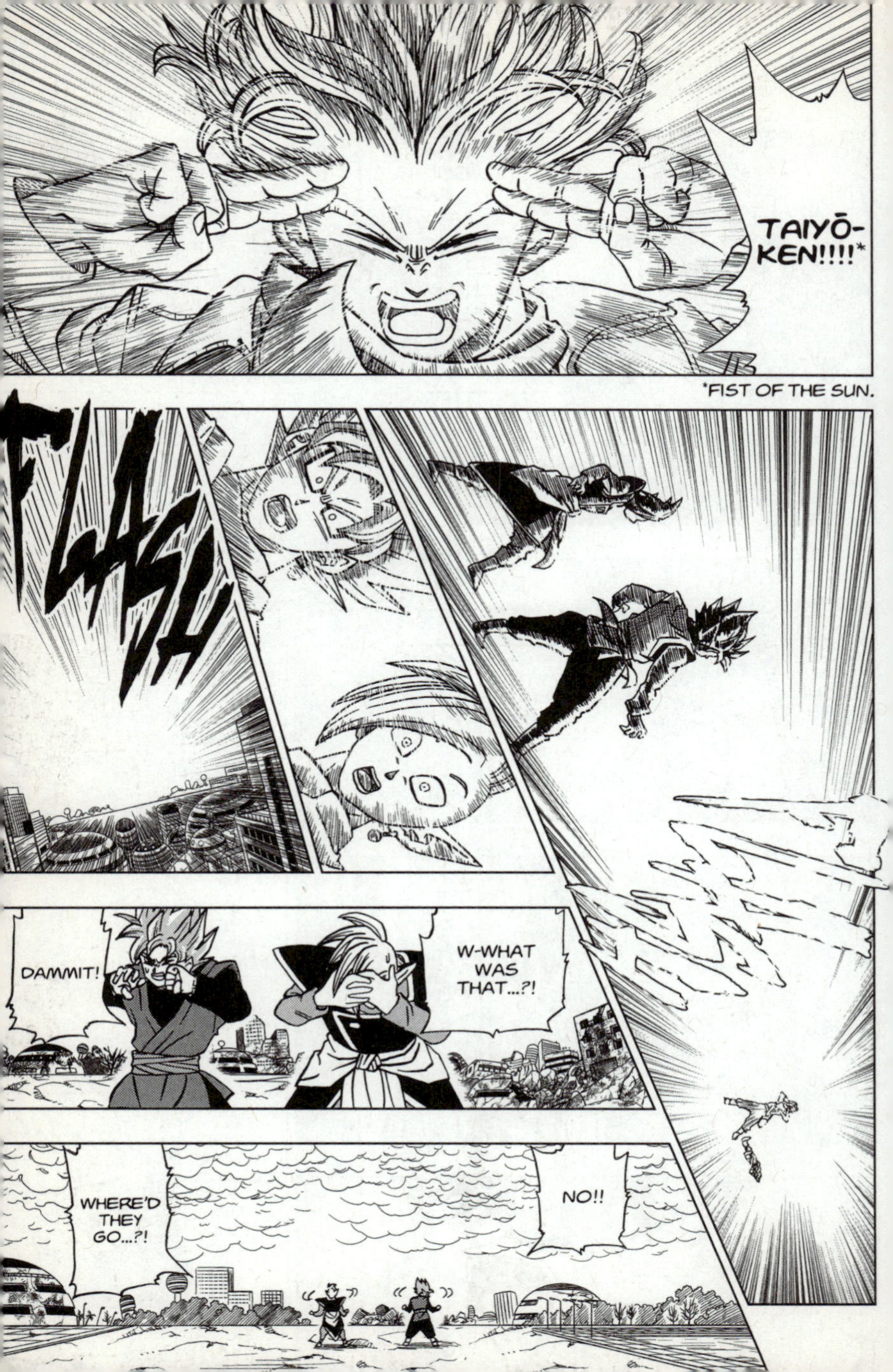
TAIYŌ-KEN!!!!*
*FIST OF THE SUN.
FLASH
W-WHAT WAS THAT...?!
DAMMIT!
NO!!
WHERE'D THEY GO...?!

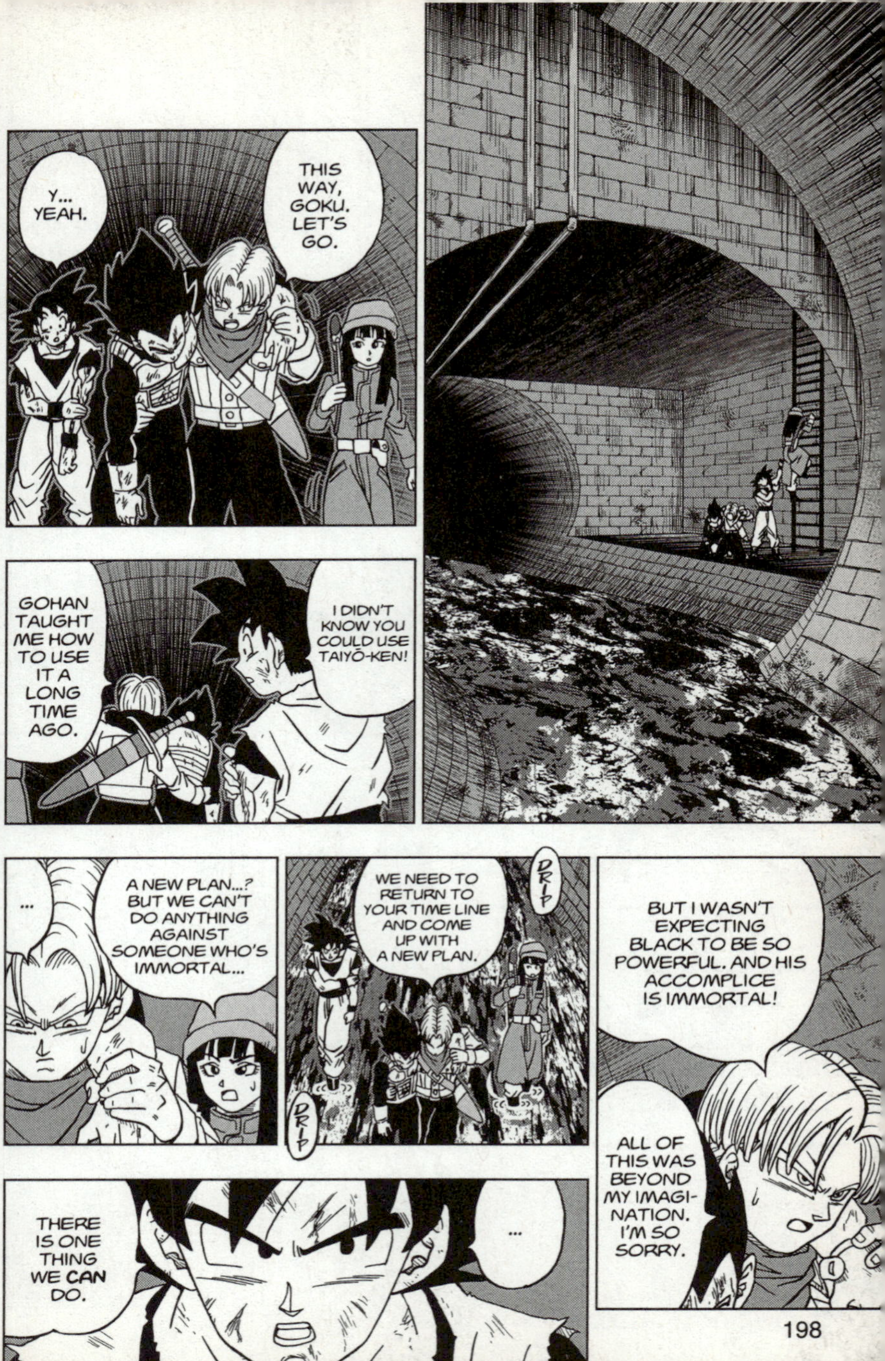

THIS WAY, GOKU. LET'S GO.
Y... YEAH.
I DIDN'T KNOW YOU COULD USE TAIYŌ-KEN!
GOHAN TAUGHT ME HOW TO USE IT A LONG TIME AGO.
BUT I WASN'T EXPECTING BLACK TO BE SO POWERFUL. AND HIS ACCOMPLICE IS IMMORTAL!
ALL OF THIS WAS BEYOND MY IMAGINATION. I'M SO SORRY.
DRIP
WE NEED TO RETURN TO YOUR TIME LINE AND COME UP WITH A NEW PLAN.
DRIP
A NEW PLAN...? BUT WE CAN'T DO ANYTHING AGAINST SOMEONE WHO'S IMMORTAL...
...
...
THERE IS ONE THING WE CAN DO.

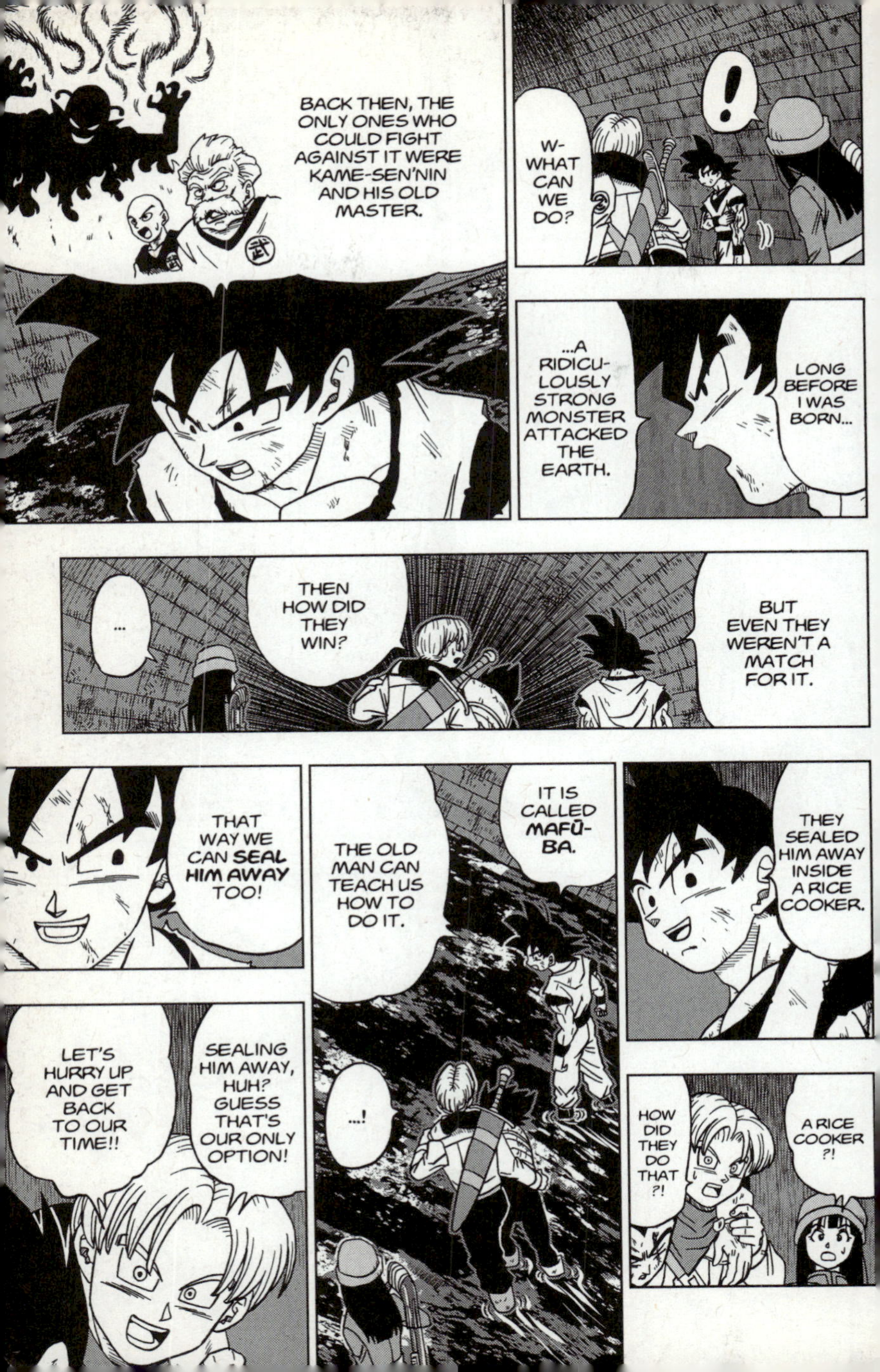
!
W-WHAT CAN WE DO?
LONG BEFORE I WAS BORN...
...A RIDICULOUSLY STRONG MONSTER ATTACKED THE EARTH.
BACK THEN, THE ONLY ONES WHO COULD FIGHT AGAINST IT WERE KAME-SEN'NIN AND HIS OLD MASTER.
BUT EVEN THEY WEREN'T A MATCH FOR IT.
THEN HOW DID THEY WIN?
...
THEY SEALED HIM AWAY INSIDE A RICE COOKER.
A RICE COOKER ?!
HOW DID THEY DO THAT ?!
IT IS CALLED **MAFŪBA.**
THE OLD MAN CAN TEACH US HOW TO DO IT.
...!
THAT WAY WE CAN **SEAL HIM AWAY** TOO!
SEALING HIM AWAY, HUH? GUESS THAT'S OUR ONLY OPTION!
LET'S HURRY UP AND GET BACK TO OUR TIME!!

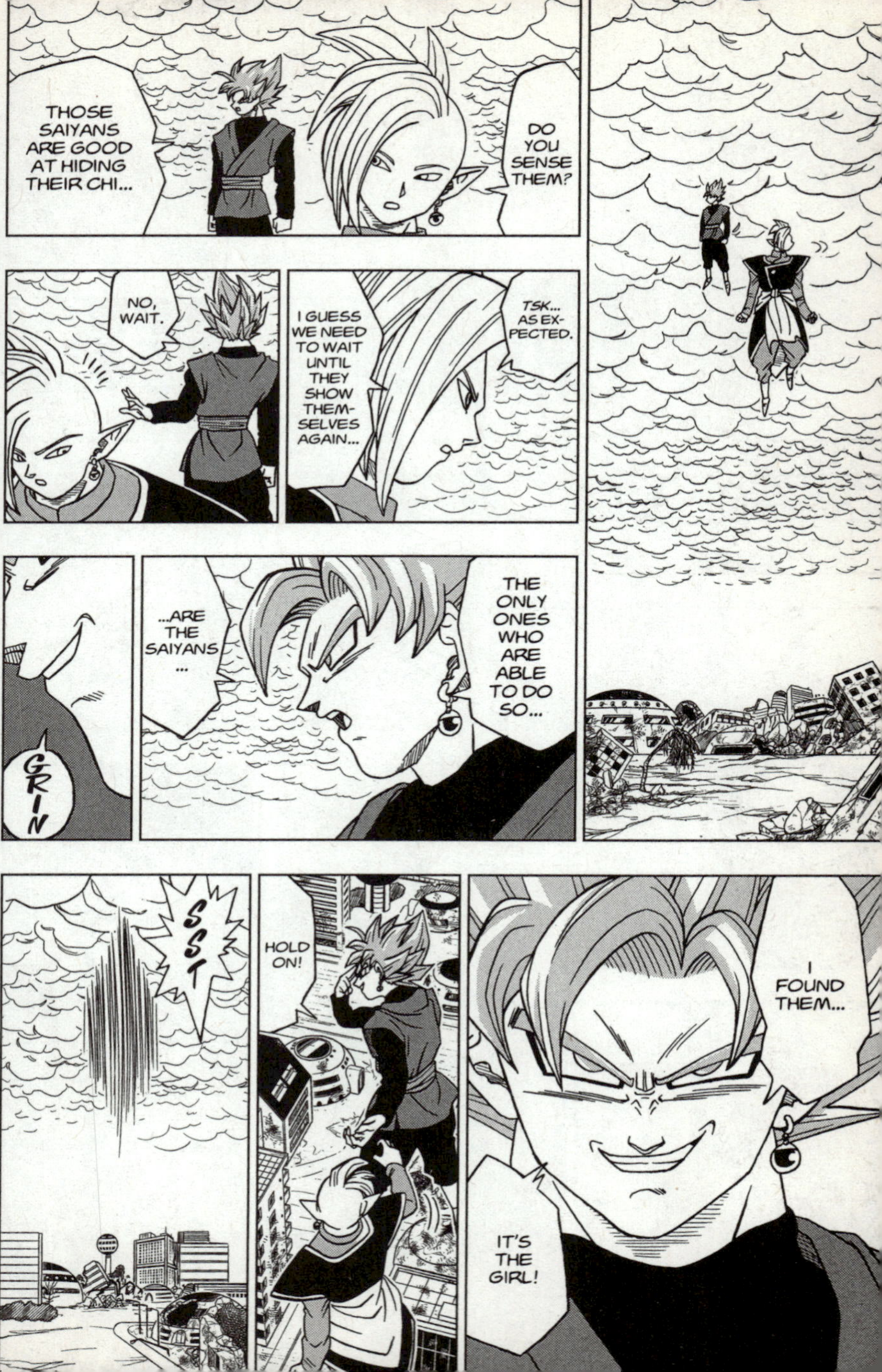
DO YOU SENSE THEM?
THOSE SAIYANS ARE GOOD AT HIDING THEIR CHI...
TSK... AS EXPECTED.
I GUESS WE NEED TO WAIT UNTIL THEY SHOW THEMSELVES AGAIN...
NO, WAIT.
THE ONLY ONES WHO ARE ABLE TO DO SO...
...ARE THE SAIYANS...
GRIN
I FOUND THEM...
IT'S THE GIRL!
HOLD ON!
SST

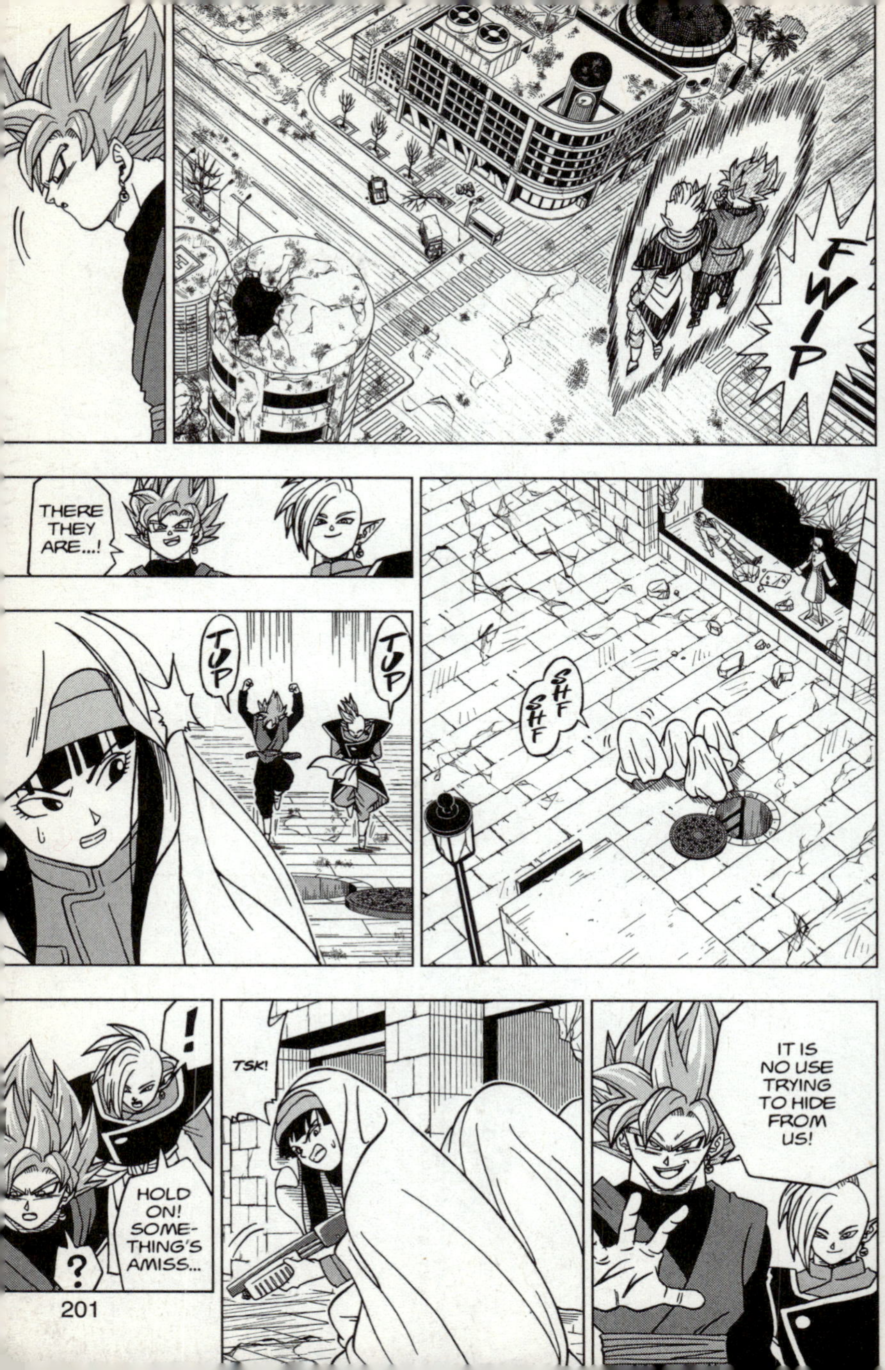
FWIP
SHF SHF
THERE THEY ARE...!
TUP
TUP
IT IS NO USE TRYING TO HIDE FROM US!
TSK!
!
HOLD ON! SOME-THING'S AMISS...
?

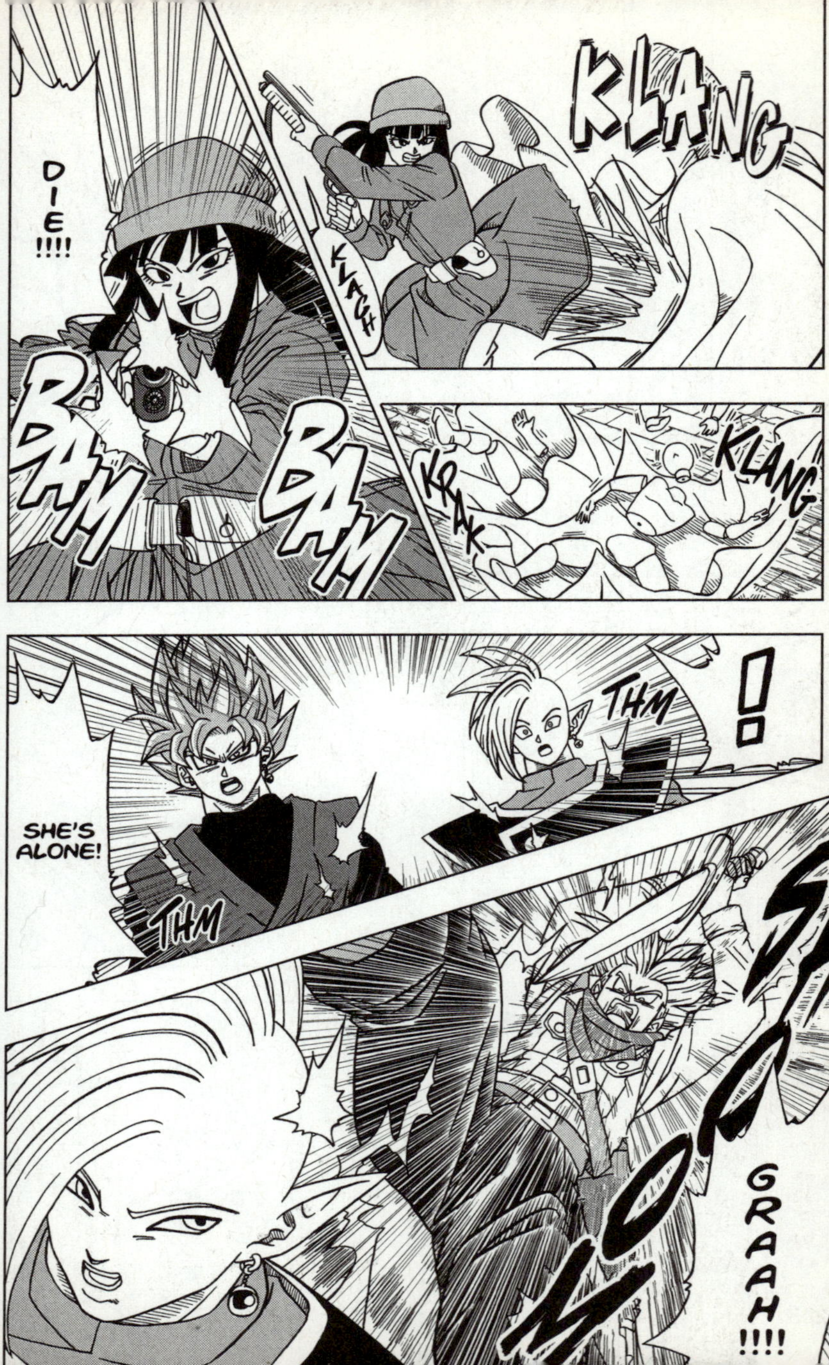
KLANG
KLACH
KLANG
KRAK
DIE!!!!
BAM
BAM
!!
THM
SHE'S ALONE!
THM
SHOOM
GRAAH!!!!

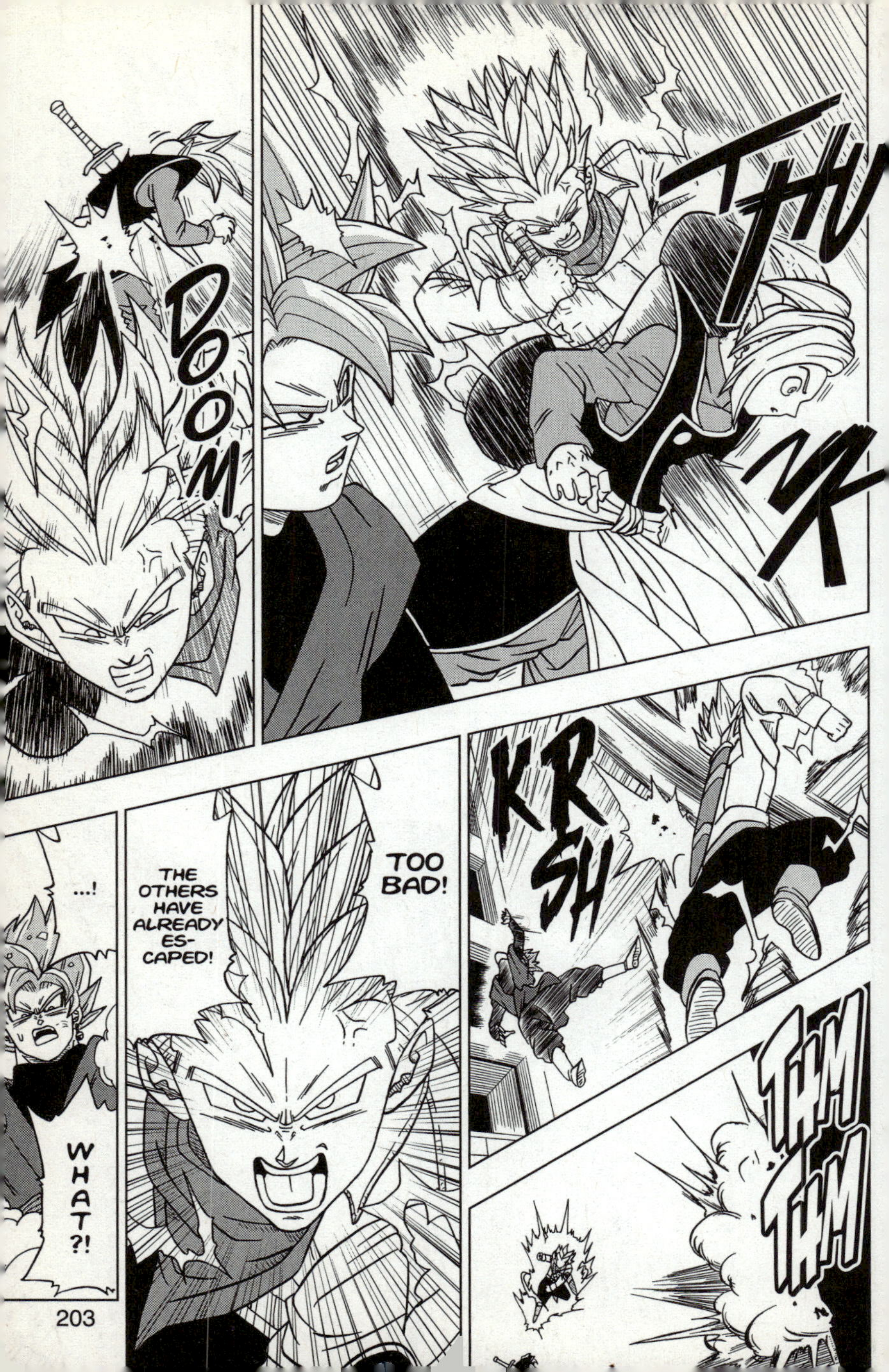
THUNK
DOOM
KRSH
THM THM
TOO BAD!
THE OTHERS HAVE ALREADY ES-CAPED!
...!
WHAT?!

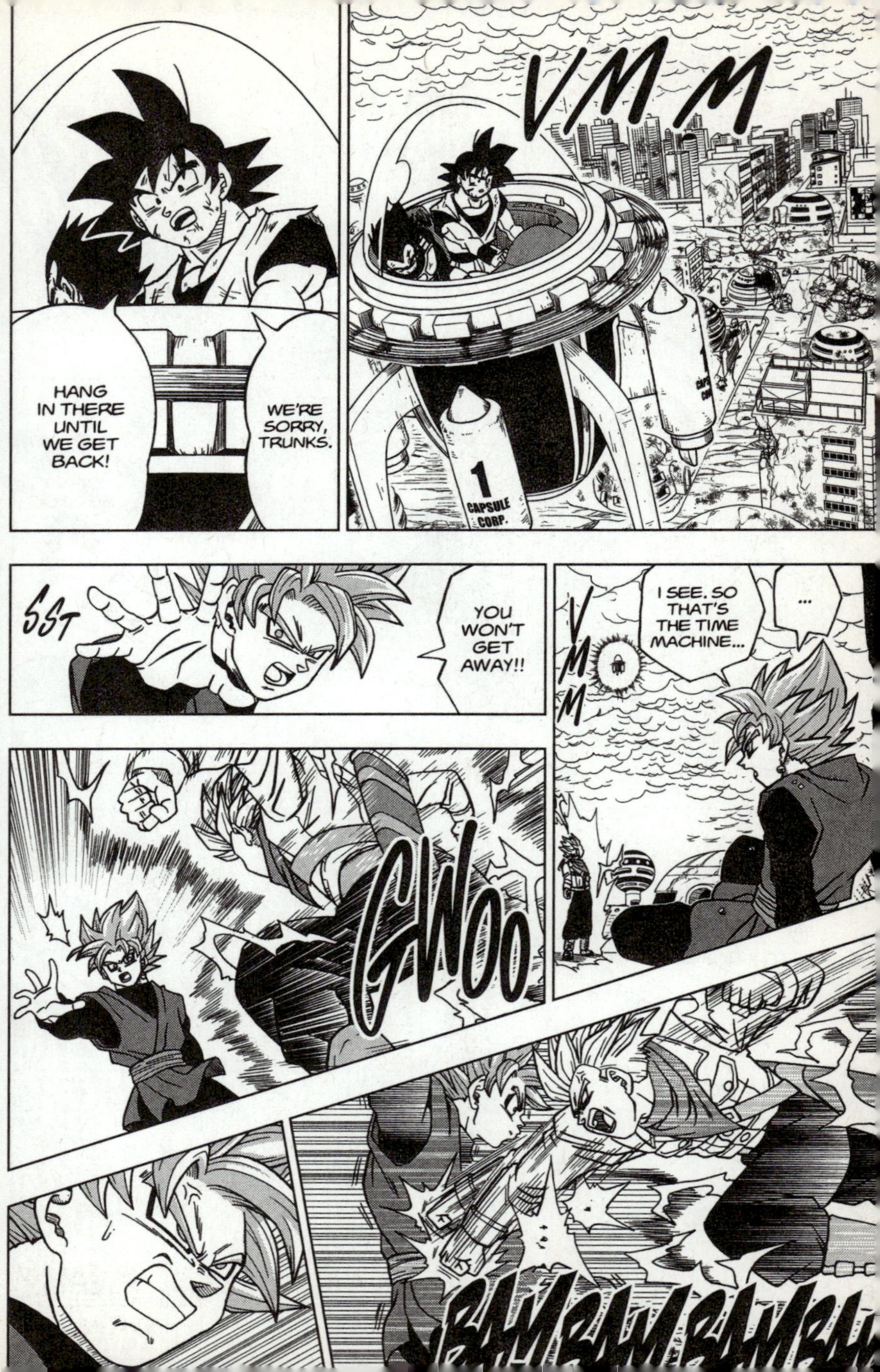
VMM
WE'RE SORRY, TRUNKS.
HANG IN THERE UNTIL WE GET BACK!
...
I SEE. SO THAT'S THE TIME MACHINE...
VMM
YOU WON'T GET AWAY!!
SST
GWOO
BAMBAMBAMBAM

DON'T GET TOO COCKY, TRUNKS.

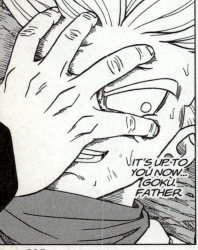

IT'S UP TO YOU NOW... GOKU, FATHER.

205

TO BE CONTINUED!

# TORIYAMA SENSEI CORRECTIONS (1)

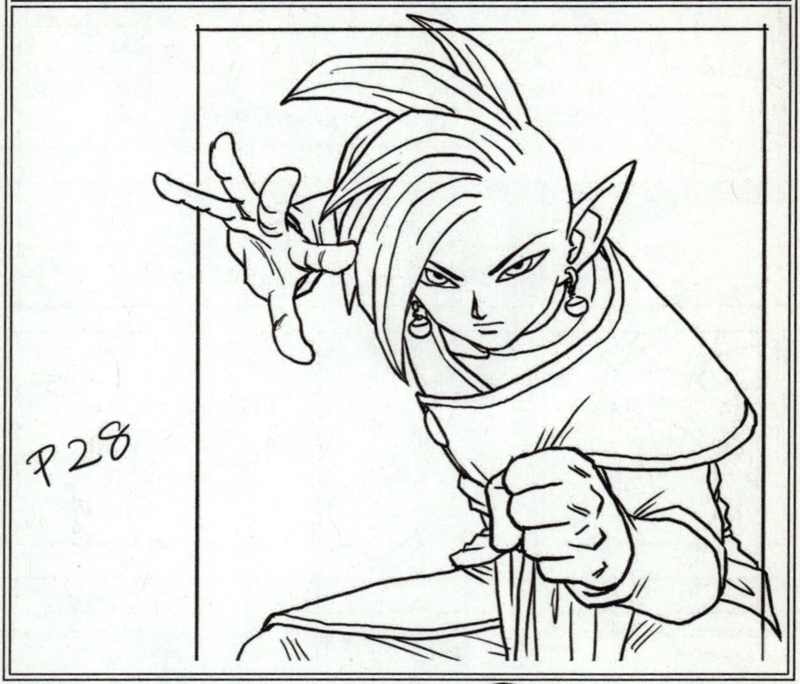
P28

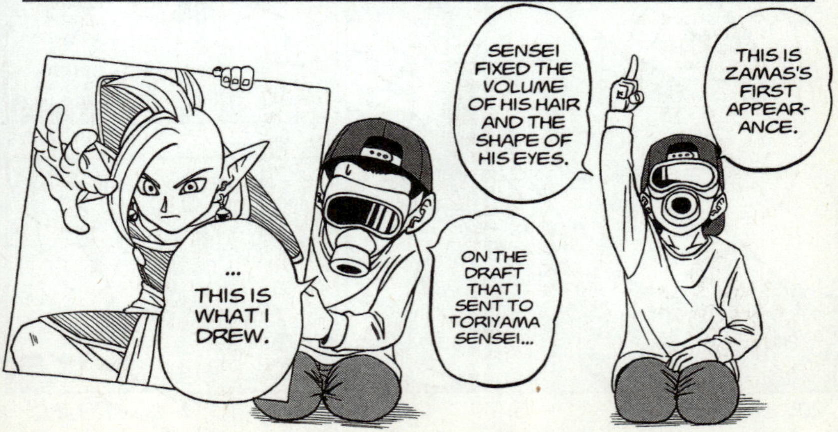
THIS IS ZAMAS'S FIRST APPEARANCE.
SENSEI FIXED THE VOLUME OF HIS HAIR AND THE SHAPE OF HIS EYES.
ON THE DRAFT THAT I SENT TO TORIYAMA SENSEI...
... THIS IS WHAT I DREW.

# TORIYAMA SENSEI CORRECTIONS (2)

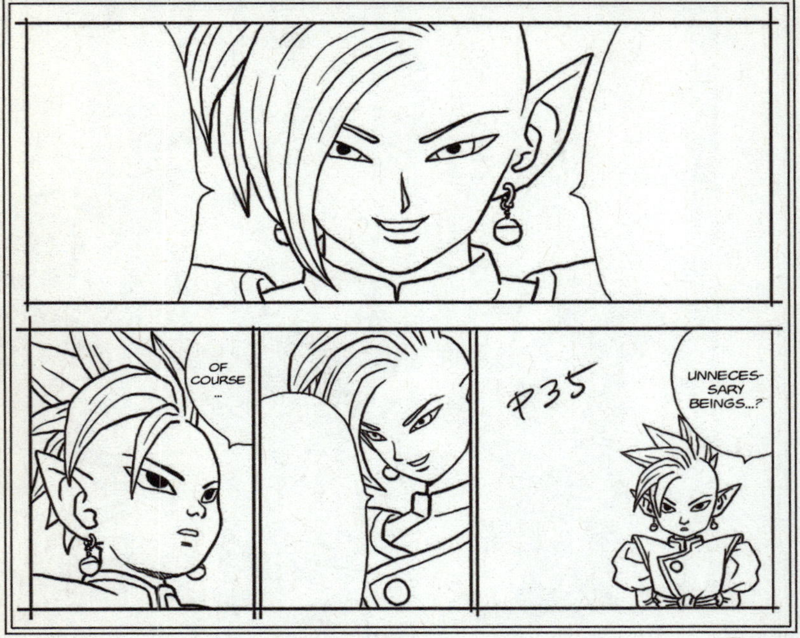

P35
UNNECES-SARY BEINGS...?
OF COURSE ...


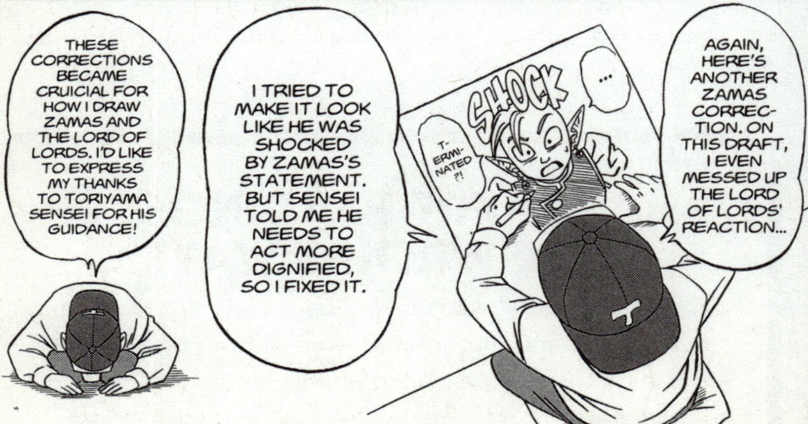

AGAIN, HERE'S ANOTHER ZAMAS CORRECTION. ON THIS DRAFT, I EVEN MESSED UP THE LORD OF LORDS' REACTION...
...
SHOCK
T-ERMINATED?!
I TRIED TO MAKE IT LOOK LIKE HE WAS SHOCKED BY ZAMAS'S STATEMENT. BUT SENSEI TOLD ME HE NEEDS TO ACT MORE DIGNIFIED, SO I FIXED IT.
THESE CORRECTIONS BECAME CRUICIAL FOR HOW I DRAW ZAMAS AND THE LORD OF LORDS. I'D LIKE TO EXPRESS MY THANKS TO TORIYAMA SENSEI FOR HIS GUIDANCE!

# YOU'RE READING
# THE WRONG WAY!

*Dragon Ball Super* reads from right to left, starting in the upper-right corner. Japanese is read from right to left, meaning that action, sound effects, and word-balloon order are completely reversed from English order.